PARLIAMENT AT WORK

A CASE-BOOK OF PARLIAMENTARY PROCEDURE

by

A. H. HANSON
Reader in Public Administration, University of Leeds

and

H. V. WISEMAN
Senior Lecturer in Government, University of Leeds

LONDON

STEVENS & SONS LIMITED

1962

Published by
Stevens & Sons Limited
of 11 New Fetter Lane
London—Law Publishers
and printed in
Great Britain
by
Staples Printers Limited
of London and Rochester

TABLE OF CONTENTS

		page
Foreword ... ...by Sir Edward Fellowes		*vii*
Preface		*ix*

1. PRIVILEGE

1. No *Prima Facie* Case	1
2. Procedural Technicalities not complied with	3
3. Cases Referred to the Select Committee of Privileges	4

2. ORDER

1. The Election of a Speaker	12
2. Points of Order	17
3. Suspensions...	32

3. THE OPENING OF A SESSION AND THE DEBATE ON THE QUEEN'S SPEECH

44

4. BUSINESS ARRANGEMENTS

1. The Business of a Session	57
2. The Business of the Week...	61

5. QUESTIONS

1. General	68
2. Questions leading to notice of raising a matter on the Adjournment when notice was not effective	69
3. Question followed by raising matter on Adjournment	72
4. Question leading to failure to obtain acceptance of "Urgency" Motion, followed by debate on a substantive motion regretting Mr. Speaker's refusal	73
5. Question leading to successful attempt to move the Adjournment under Standing Order No. 9	75
6. Question leading to judicial proceedings – the Scarcroft Affair ...	79
7. Questions on the Nationalised Industries	87

6. DEBATES ON SOME TYPICAL MOTIONS

1. Introduction	94
2. Half-Hour Adjournment Debate...	97
3. Debate on an "Urgency" Motion	99
4. Motion regretting refusal of "Urgency" Motion	104
5. Government and Opposition Motions	108
6. Private Members' Motions	115

7. LEGISLATION

page

1. Public Bills: (a) Government Bills 121
           (b) Private Members' Bills 180
2. Private Bills: The Leeds Private Bill, 1956 192

8. DELEGATED LEGISLATION

1. Statutory Instruments 203
2. Special Procedure Orders... 216

9. FINANCIAL PROCEDURE

1. Introduction 236
2. The Session 1958–59:
   (a) from the beginning of the Session to the end of the 1958–59 Financial Year (31st March, 1959) 238
   (b) from the beginning of the 1959–60 Financial Year (April 1, 1959) to the passing of the Finance and Appropriation Acts ... 248
3. Appendix:
   (a) Granting Supply "on the nod": the back-bench revolt of February–March, 1960 271
   (b) the Revolt continues: the Second Reading of the Consolidated Fund Bill, March 16, 1960 273
   (c) the Government's Response: Mr. Butler's Statement of July 26, 1960 277

10. SELECT COMMITTEES

1. The Public Accounts Committee... 279
2. The Select Committee on Estimates 292
3. The Select Committee on Statutory Instruments 302
4. The Select Committee on Nationalised Industries (Reports and Accounts) 309

11. THE HOUSE CONSIDERS ITS PROCEDURE

1. The Select Committee on Procedure, 1945–46 315
2. The Select Committee on Procedure, 1958 326

Index 343

FOREWORD

SIR EDWARD FELLOWES, K.C.B., C.M.G., M.C.

Clerk of the House of Commons

DIFFERING as it does from the usual form of textbook, I found this a fascinatingly interesting volume. The authors' intention as set out in their Preface is to provide for readers, who have a general knowledge of the development of British parliamentary institutions, concrete and fairly-detailed examples of Parliament at work. The authors have admitted the difficulty of providing 'typical' examples of the various aspects of procedure which they wished to illustrate, since in some ways the 'typical' is the 'ordinary' which raises no procedural questions. But recognising this difficulty, the authors have, I think, fairly balanced their examples. For instance, they deal at length with the Iron and Steel Nationalisation Bill which was passed under the guillotine, which can scarcely be called 'typical' of the way in which governments pass their legislation; while, on the other hand, the Finance Bill of the year which they have chosen to illustrate financial procedure is equally untypical in its peaceful passage through the House.

Nevertheless, the section on financial procedure struck me as one of the most instructive in a book which does succeed in giving a pretty comprehensive view of how the House of Commons goes about its business. Parliamentary institutions are by their very nature open to criticism. Rightly so too, for without criticism Parliaments might wither and die as easily, or more easily, than they perish as a result of such attacks. Critics who have read this book may not find their shafts blunted, but they should be more certain of their aim.

PREFACE

Our justification for the temerity of adding yet another to the enormous number of books about Parliament is that, as teachers of government, we have become aware of a gap in the existing literature.

We are not so foolish as to attempt to rival Sir Ivor Jennings' *Parliament*, or to supersede any of the very competent shorter books about the parliamentary institutions of this country. Our aim is simply to provide a case book which will illustrate the use to which the House of Commons puts its various procedures, and the ways in which it attempts to adapt ancient forms to modern needs. We believe that the concrete and fairly detailed examples of parliament at work, herein contained, are necessary if parliamentary procedure is to become, for the student, something more than a collection of curiosities, as difficult to justify as they are hard to learn.

We do not, however, claim any methodological originality. The idea came to us as a result of reading Stephen K. Bailey's and Howard D. Samuel's brilliant case-book of American Congressional procedure, entitled *Congress at Work*. Although we have not attempted to imitate it, our debt to it is considerable.

We assume that our readers have a general knowledge of the development of British parliamentary institutions. Our concern is with their *modus operandi* in the mid-twentieth century. Hence all our cases have been selected from the period since 1945.

We have not worried unduly about illustrating the *minutiae* of parliamentary procedure, and hence will not be stricken with grief when someone draws our attention to a section of *Erskine May* which we have entirely neglected. For our aim has been to illustrate what we consider to be the important things, with special emphasis on those around which controversies have revolved. Parliamentary procedure is always evolving, and the most interesting points are those where growth is – or ought to be – taking place. It is also for this reason, as well as for reasons of space, that we have concentrated on the House of Commons, and brought in the Lords only when the context required us to do so.

Our hope is that both teachers and students of government will find this work useful. But we would be very gratified if it proved to have also a wider utility. For we have not written it solely as an aid to teaching and study. We are conscious that in the modern world parliamentary institutions are faced with serious challenges, and we are by no means convinced that the future of even a parliamentary system as well established in the hearts and minds of the people as the British is automatically assured. Today, Parliament's procedures are subject to widespread criticism, parliamentarians are less highly esteemed than they used to be, and books with titles such as *The Passing of Parliament, Can Parliament Survive?* and *Parliament in Danger* appear with ominous frequency. Admittedly, Parliament is a much tougher institution than some imagine; but its survival as an effective democratic body depends on its capacity to adapt itself to rapidly-changing twentieth-century needs, and few would claim that it is at present meeting this challenge with sufficient speed and determination. If it is to do so, it needs the help of an informed public opinion, which all those who have made the study of Parliament their special concern ought to be helping to create and strengthen. What is required, above all, is knowledge of how Parliament goes about its business; for without such knowledge criticisms will be misdirected and proposals for reform dismissed with contempt by the practical politician who, inadequate as his vision of the future of parliamentary democracy may be, at least knows the limits of the possible. The task is to find out what things parliament can do well, and to enable it to do them better; not to demand that it shall undertake functions for which it is unsuited. Although the business of prescription is beyond the scope of this book, we hope that it will be facilitated by a study of the examples of parliament at work here given.

Our very best thanks are due to Sir Edward Fellowes, K.C.B., C.M.G., M.C., Clerk of the House of Commons, who read the proofs of this book at a time when heavily engaged in parliamentary duties, and did us the honour of contributing a

Foreword. We are also greatly indebted to Mr. David Pring, M.C., a Senior Clerk on Sir Edward's staff, and to some of his colleagues, for criticisms and suggestions. Without their help we should have fallen into error on many occasions. Such error as remains is in no way their responsibility; and it should not be taken that they endorse any of the opinions we have expressed.

For providing us with documentary material, we are grateful to Mr. M. F. Bond, O.B.E., Clerk of the Records, House of Lords, and Mr. Robert Crute, Town Clerk of Leeds.

Leeds 1960   A.H.H.
                                                            H.V.W.

PRIVILEGE

PRIVILEGE is the subject of our first case-study because it is fundamental to parliamentary procedure in the sense that it provides the means of protecting Parliament, and through Parliament individual Members, in the performance of the functions that our subsequent case-studies illustrate. It is an immense and complicated subject, covering eight chapters in *Erskine May* and eleven pages in Campion's *Introduction*.[1]

Here, proceedings in cases of contempt[2] are our principal concern. The aspects covered are (1) rulings by Mr. Speaker that no *prima facie* case has been made out; (2) rulings where the claim to breach of privilege is turned down on a technicality; and (3) claims which, having received *prima facie* acceptance, are referred to the Committee of Privileges.

1. No Prima Facie Case

Our first example concerns an attempt by Mr. Wigg[3] to claim that the activities of the Whips were a breach of privilege. On December 10, 1956,[4] he drew attention to a statement in the *Daily Herald*, attributed to Mr. Patrick Maitland,[5] that 'in view of the extraordinary and unexampled pressures – some of them altogether underhand – which have been used to force Tories into line, I think we did pretty well to have fifteen of our number daring to show themselves'. Mr. Wigg continued:

As that statement obviously refers to pressures on hon. Members as to how they should vote, I submit that there is a *prima facie* case of breach of Privilege.

[1] Chapter 11, pp. 62–73.   [2] *Erskine May*, pp. 133–148.
[3] Lab., Dudley.   [4] *H.C. Debates*, Vol. 562, cols. 32–34 : 225–228.
[5] Cons., Lanark.

He handed in a copy of the newspaper in question.

Mr. Speaker, after saying that he could not possibly rule on the matter without hearing Mr. Maitland (whom Mr. Wigg said he had not been able to inform), said that there appeared 'to be no *prima facie* case of breach of Privilege against the newspaper, anyhow'. Mr. Wigg replied:

The breach of Privilege, if there be any, is with the Patronage Secretary and the hon. Member for Lanark.

On December 11, Mr. Speaker gave his Ruling on whether Mr. Wigg had 'made out a *prima facie* case such as would enable me to give it priority over the Orders of the Day'. Mr. Maitland did not complain about the newspaper. Nor, Mr. Speaker went on,

in what has been said do I see any *prima facie* case of any breach of Privilege by him . . . I would remark that animadversions against the conduct of Whips are common on both sides of the House. These have never hitherto been treated as breaches of the Privilege of the whole House. As for any question of breach of Privilege by the usual channels, if that be the proper term, the only hon. Member who could complain about it with real knowledge is the hon. Member for Lanark himself.

Mr. Maitland had made the speech on the previous Friday; if he had wanted to complain about the subject on that Friday, that would have been his earliest opportunity of so doing.

Therefore, I cannot see that there is a *prima facie* case of breach of privilege against anyone such as would enable me to give the matter precedence over the Orders of the Day.

Mr. Wigg rose to point out 'one small slip' – (Hon Members: 'Oh') – 'one slight error of fact'. Mr. Maitland had not made a speech but had given a personal statement to the Press. That, said Mr. Speaker, was 'irrelevant in the matter'. Mr. Wigg persisted in arguing the point amid cries of 'Sit down' and, at one point, 'Withdraw!', and with several interventions by Mr. Speaker. 'The charge of a breach of Privilege', Mr. Wigg persisted, 'lies against the Patronage Secretary.'

Mr. Speaker remarked that he was 'quite prepared to participate in a little harmless amusement occasionally, if that be the intention of hon. Members.' He 'would point out, however, that Privilege is a very serious thing and that personally (he could) not find (himself) in the position of treating it lightly.'

Mr. Maitland closed the incident. 'I did not invite the protection of Mr. Wigg,' he said.

2. PROCEDURAL TECHNICALITIES NOT COMPLIED WITH

The strictness with which the Speaker habitually applies the procedural rules of the House to the *manner* of alleging breach of privilege is well illustrated by the exchanges which took place between him and Lieut.-Col. Lipton[6] on December 19 and 20, 1955.[7]

On the first day, Lieut.-Col. Lipton drew attention to what he considered two *prima facie* cases of breach of privilege. One of these he had already brought to Mr. Speaker's notice, in accordance with the usual practice when advance notification is possible. The other had not been similarly notified, for lack of time.

The first concerned a publication of the British Medical Association, *Homosexuality and Prostitution*, of which Lieut.-Col. Lipton had had difficulty in obtaining a copy, although parts of it had appeared in the Press on the previous Friday. Referring to a passage alleging 'the existence of practising homosexuals in Parliament', Lieut.-Col. Lipton said:

In the present state of the law, whatever our views may be of possible future legislation in the matter, any assumption of the existence of practising homosexuals in Parliament must be regarded as serious.

Mr. Speaker first explained his duty to see whether the conditions necessary to enable the complaint to get precedence over the Orders of the Day were fulfilled. One such condition was that the complaint must be made at the earliest possible moment. The publication had appeared on Wednesday and Press reports on Friday. The matter should have been raised at the beginning of business on Friday to obtain precedence. A Motion could still be tabled 'for the consideration of the House which is the final guard of its own privileges'.

Lieut.-Col. Lipton then raised his second case. An article in the *People* the previous Sunday was headed 'Vice in Parliament', and went on to say that 'the doctors who reported last week ... knew of actual cases of homosexual Members. ...' The hon. Member then handed in 'only a piece' of the paper. Mr.

---

[6] Lab., Lambeth, Brixton.
[7] *H.C. Debates*, Vol. 547, cols. 1660–1662: 1858–1862.

Speaker ruled that the matter had been raised 'at the earliest possible moment', but reserved his final Ruling.

Next day he referred to the fact that he had been given 'not the whole paper, as the rules demanded, but a cutting from it'. Nevertheless he 'was so moved by the statement . . . and felt so much sympathy with it that (he) was anxious not to give a hasty decision if there were any way round the technical objection'. He had found, however, that it was 'a clear rule of the House that if any document is made the foundation for a complaint of Privilege, the whole document must be produced. . . .' He advised the hon. Member to put down a Motion on the matter. The technicality could not be overcome by handing in a full copy.

Mr. Silverman asked whether, since the point was 'purely procedural', Mr. Speaker would see that Lieut.-Col. Lipton was 'not prejudiced in having the matter properly considered by the House'. Mr. Speaker replied that a Motion was the way out:

The House always has a distinct bias in its procedure to stick to the Orders of the Day. If, for a special reason, provision is made for them to be departed from as in the case of Standing Order No. 9 or something like that, it is hedged about with rules which must be complied with, and it is part of my duty to enforce them.

We must note that on this occasion Mr. Speaker did not decide that no *prima facie* case had been made out.[8] He had 'on a purely technical point' been compelled by the rules of the House to rule against the hon. Member.

3. CASES REFERRED TO THE COMMITTEE OF PRIVILEGES

Reference to Select Committee may follow Mr. Speaker's Ruling that a *prima facie* case has been made out, or in the absence of such Ruling, when the House so decides. The Select Committee may then recommend that no further action be taken, even though a breach of Privilege is established; it may recommend further action; and the House may decide, in either case, contrary to the recommendation.

Mr. John Junor (and other cases). On December 17, 1956,[9] Sir C. Taylor[10] drew attention to an article in the *Sunday Express*,

[8] cf. *H.C. Debates*, Vol. 547, col. 1859.   [9] *H.C. Debates*, Vol. 562, cols. 934–937.
[10] Cons., Eastbourne.

December 16. The implication was that when petrol rationing started 'politicians' would get 'prodigious supplementary allowances'. The article went on, 'if politicians are more interested in privileges for themselves than in fair shares for all, let it simply be made plain to them that the public do not propose to tolerate it'.

This, the hon. Member contended, was not a party matter. The article was not only untrue but 'a disgraceful libel against the High Court of Parliament'. Mr. Speaker, who had then heard the article for the first time, remarked:

There are cases where contempt of this House as a whole have been treated as breaches of Privilege, but, also, there have been many cases in the past where hon. Members have been subjected collectively to a certain amount of journalistic censure, and possibly abuse. . . . In the past these matters have not been considered as breaches of the Privilege of the House.

Mr. Speaker ruled 'as a procedural matter' that no *prima facie* case had been established.

Three members, however, pursued the point. Mr. Burden[11] thought the article might cause 'considerable unrest'. Mr. Paget[12] thought that the test of this kind of Privilege was 'the test of truth'. In the old days, attacks had been regarded as a breach of Privilege. The House had subsequently taken the view that the public and the newspapers were free to comment:

But have we ever gone further and said they are free to lie?

Mr. Silverman[13] thought it 'difficult to imagine a grosser or clearer libel upon the House collectively'.

Mr. Speaker: . . . I always take the view that the Privilege of the House is a very serious matter, not to be lightly invoked. For that reason I do not feel that every attack of this silly nature should be regarded by the House as a breach of Privilege. I have given my opinion on the matter, but, as I have said, that does not finish it. If it be the general sense of the House that the matter should go to the Committee of Privileges –

Hon. Members: Hear, hear.

Mr. Speaker: – and the House so decides, I shall not dissent in any way.

Mr. Butler then moved accordingly and the House agreed.

---

[11] Cons., Gillingham. [12] Lab., Northampton.
[13] Lab., Nelson and Colne.

Before pursuing this case further, we note that other matters connected with petrol rationing were subsequently raised. On December 18, Mr. Pannell[14] complained of a cartoon in the *Evening News* which showed cars in a crowded park by the Houses of Parliament. Spivs were siphoning petrol from the cars. The caption spoke of 'M.P.s giving themselves such a generous supplementary. . . .' Mr. Pannell submitted that this was 'an even more flagrant affront than the one complained of yesterday'. Mr. Speaker ruled that a *prima facie* case had been made out and the House referred the matter to the Committee of Privileges.

Two days before the first of the two foregoing cases was concluded by the House, further points of the same nature were raised. On January 22, 1956, Mr. George Wigg referred to a discussion in 'Any Questions', on December 21 last, in which the statement was made that 'the only people who are really well off under this rationing scheme are M.P.s . . . who, apparently, have as much petrol as they want to drive about their constituencies'. Mr. Wigg suggested that the expression of these views was the more serious because it occurred after the previous cases had been referred to the Committee of Privileges and the matter was *sub judice*. Moreover, the B.B.C. had had four or five weeks in which to apologise. This also was referred to the Committee.

Mr. Lagden[15] then brought up a report in the *Romford Recorder*, January 4, of a speech including a statement to the effect that the 750-miles-a-month supplementary petrol allocation which he had just received was 'outrageously high', and that the increasing privileges of the Members of the 'best club' were inimical to democracy. Mr. R. Ledger[16] supported Mr. Lagden. His allowance of 100 miles a month was 'totally inadequate'. There was also, he thought, a breach of Privilege in the statement issued by the prospective Liberal candidate to the effect that comment had been 'effectively muzzled by the recent action of the House of Commons Committee of Privileges against the editors of two national newspapers. Mr. Speaker held that a *prima facie* case had been made out in both instances; but considerable discussion developed on the Motion to refer them to the Committee.

[14] Lab., Leeds West.   [15] Cons., Hornchurch.
[16] Lab., Romford.

Sir Godfrey Nicholson[17] thought the House was 'in danger of becoming pompous and highly sensitive' and of 'taking a sledge hammer to crush a nut'. Mr. Desmond Donnelly[18] agreed. 'In this case the facts speak for themselves. What does it matter if some people say that we have too large a petrol allowance, if we do not?' He wanted Mr. Butler to 'find some procedure by which we could dispose of these cases without making too heavy weather of them, without dragging somebody to the Bar of the House of Commons to explain himself and without bringing Parliamentary Privilege, which is very important indeed, into the position where it is lightly regarded by the public'. But Mr. Shinwell[19] believed that it was 'the duty and responsibility of hon. Members to repel serious allegations about their behaviour'.

Mr. Bevan, supported by Mr. Butler, suggested that once a *prima facie* case was made out, the Leader of the House had no alternative but to 'move'. But the Motion was debatable and Members could oppose it. Mr. Silverman thought there was no precedent for the House's deciding not to submit a *prima facie* case to the Committee. Mr. Hale,[20] however, recalled that he had raised a matter concerning the Attorney-General of Northern Ireland and a *prima facie* case had been made out; but the gentleman in question had apologised and no reference was made to the Committee. 'A totally different kind of case,' retorted Mr. Silverman. Asked specifically about the constitutional position, Mr. Speaker said:

. . . there is nothing wrong, or unconstitutional, or contrary to the practice of the House in refusing a Motion that a matter be referred to the Committee of Privileges. The duty of the Chair is to see that the maximum requirements which constitute a *prima facie* case of breach of Privilege are present, and he merely says that they are in order to give the Motion priority over the Orders of the Day. That does not imply a Ruling on the part of the Chair that a breach of Privilege has been committed or that the House ought to send the matter to the Committee of Privileges. It is entirely a matter for the House to debate. For example, there are many technical breaches of Privilege, such as giving reports of our debates in the Press, which the House has been content to ignore for a large number of years, but which, if they were raised, would no doubt still be considered as technical breaches of Privilege. There may be many other such cases. . . . The duty of the Speaker is to safeguard the House from entirely frivolous invocations of the Law of Privilege. In this case, in view of what has happened in an earlier case, I took the view – as the House took upon an earlier occasion – that it was my duty so to rule. But it is by no means incumbent upon hon. Members to vote either for or against the Motion.

Mr. Speaker added, in reply to a question, that acceptance of the Motion would not prevent the Government from making a statement; the question of petrol allocation and the question of Privilege were two different things. On this, Mr. Butler said that the facts were 'almost *in toto* in the Second Report of the Committee of Privileges'; he would discuss the question of a further statement with the Minister of Transport and Civil Aviation and the Minister of Power.

The Question was put and agreed to.

We shall not follow the subsequent history of all these cases in detail. In the second, third and fourth Reports of the Committee of Privileges, 1956–57,[21] the Committee recommended no action on the statement referring to the 'muzzling of comment'.[22] The criticisms in the *Romford Recorder* and in the B.B.C. broadcast were 'directed to the rationing scheme rather than to the conduct of Members'. The remark about 'the best club in London' and the increase of 'privileges' was untrue, but not calculated to diminish the respect due to the House, or lessen its authority. It was not a 'contempt'. The Committee, however, could not take so light a view of the article in the *Sunday Express*. It recommended that the Editor, Mr. Junor, be 'severely reprimanded'.

On January 23, 1957,[23] the Leader of the House moved a Motion 'that Mr. John Junor do attend this House tomorrow at a quarter past three o'clock'. Mr. Butler suggested that 'the person affected' be given an opportunity of making submission to the House before the Report was considered. In reply to Mr. Gaitskell, he said that he must be left to move 'spontaneously' an appropriate Motion after hearing Mr. Junor. It might follow the recommendation of the Second Report of the Select Committee, but would be open to immediate debate.

[21] *H.C. Paper* 38 (1956–57); *H.C. Paper* 39 (1956–57); *H.C. Paper* 74 (1956–57).
[22] Geoffrey Marshall, Parliamentary Privilege in 1957, in *Parliamentary Affairs*, Vol. XI, No. 2, Spring, 1958.
[23] *H.C. Debates*, Vol. 563, cols. 201–216.

Mr. Shinwell pointed out that in reply to interrogation by the Select Committee Mr. Junor had said that 'if the interpretation placed on what appeared in the *Sunday Express* ... was regarded as discourteous to hon. Members, he regretted it'. Did Mr. Butler expect him 'to say something in addition'? The Committee had given a clear lead to the House by recommending that Mr. Junor be 'severely reprimanded'. What, then, was the House to discuss tomorrow? Mr. Crossman[24] urged that Mr. Junor be not asked to appear. He had been 'found guilty of a breach of privilege. ... His failure to make an overt and unconditional apology to the Committee was a very grave error. [But] who will gain most out of this sensational appearance at the Bar of the House ... the Beaverbrook Press?' If Mr. Junor did not act as expected, 'are we to arrest and imprison the man? We have the power to do so. ... [Would] we increase the dignity of Parliament and strengthen public confidence by committing Mr. Junor to the Tower because he refuses to apologise ... ?' Mr. Crossman, a member of the Committee of Privileges, went on:

I care about the privileges of the House. But I care also very much about the freedom of the Press. ... Should not we, who have been granted this tremendous privilege of free speech without fear of accusation or of being brought into court, be the last people to give the impression that we are afraid of being criticised?

Mr. Crossman reminded the House that John Wilkes had been expelled three times, but was 'now acclaimed to have been one of the founders of the freedom of democracy in this country'. It would be wiser to leave the reprimand implicit in the Select Committee's Report.

Sir Beverley Baxter[25] supported this plea. To bring Mr. Junor to the Bar was 'a rather mediaeval pantomime' (amended to 'drama' when Mr. Speaker described it as lacking in respect for the House). But Mr. Pannell thought it was 'their job to see that right is done according to our standards and not play to the gallery – even the Press Gallery'.

Mr. Butler intervened again to say that there was an 'explicit request' in the Select Committee's Report that Mr. Junor be 'severely reprimanded'. His Motion followed automatically. Mr. Junor should be heard before a further Motion was moved.

---

[24] Lab., Coventry East.   [25] Cons., Southgate.

The House then agreed to the Motion, and accordingly, on January 24, 1957, Mr. John Junor was brought to the Bar by the Serjeant-at-Arms.[26]

Mr. Speaker informed him that he had not sought to establish the truth of the facts contained in his article, and had made 'an entirely inadequate apology', but that the House was willing to hear anything that he might have to say 'in extenuation'.

Mr. John Junor: Mr. Speaker, I wish to express my sincere and unreserved apologies for any imputations or reflections which I may have cast upon the honour and integrity of the Members of this House. . . . At no time did I intend to be discourteous to Parliament. My only aim was to focus attention on what I considered to be an injustice in the allocation of petrol, namely, the petrol allowances given to political parties in the constituencies. In my judgment these allowances were a proper, and, indeed an inescapable subject of comment in a free Press. That was a view which I held then and hold now, Sir, but I do regret, deeply and sincerely, that the manner in which I expressed myself should have been such as to be a contempt of this House.

I have nothing more to say. I now leave myself in the hands of this House.

Mr. Junor was then directed to withdraw.

Mr. Butler, as Leader of the House, rose to move the Motion, 'That this House doth agree with the Committee of Privileges in their opinion that Mr. John Junor has been guilty of a serious contempt of this House, but, in view of the apology made to this House by him, this House will proceed no further in the matter'. Had the apology been couched in different terms, or had the demeanour been different, Mr. Butler said, it would have been his duty to move a different Motion. Under the circumstances, the least said the better:

The dignity of this House is maintained and sustained by a generous regard for an apology properly given.

Mr. Gaitskell supported. Sir Charles Taylor, who had raised the matter, expressed his full agreement. The House accepted the Motion without further debate and without a Division and proceeded to the Committee Stage of the Homicide Bill.

It may seem odd that we have made no reference to the 'Strauss' Case, which at the time seemed likely to open a new chapter in the history of Privilege. It involved the first reference

[26]*H.C. Debates*, Vol. 563, cols. 403–405.

ever of a Privilege question to the Judicial Committee of the Privy Council, led to two lengthy debates in the House of Commons and even produced the comment that fundamental changes and additions to *Erskine May* would be necessary. Nevertheless, it ended by adding little or nothing new to our knowledge of the subject, and in any case has been exhaustively discussed elsewhere.

'ORDER'

PRIVILEGE, although primarily concerned with the relations between the House and outsiders, also impinges on the control of the House over its own constitution and proceedings. Mr. Speaker, the representative of the House in its relations with outside bodies, also presides over its debates and enforces its rules for the preservation of Order. He is thus the link between the previous chapter and this one, and we deal first with his position.

1. The Election of a Speaker

The history of the office of Speaker, its significance in maintaining the essentials of democracy as embodied in parliamentary procedure, are too well known to need elaboration.[1]

In 1951,[2] for the first time since 1895, there was a contest for the office. The debate on October 31 illustrates the procedure of election; the nature of the negotiations to obtain agreement between Government and Opposition; the qualities and experience normally required of a Speaker; and his traditional position as the choice of neither the Crown nor the Government but of the House itself.

The newly-elected House met for the first time at 2.30 p.m. Summoned by the Gentleman Usher of the Black Rod, Members went to hear read the Commission for opening and holding the Parliament and a direction to elect a Speaker and present

---

[1] *See* Erskine May, *Parliamentary Practice*, 16th ed., pp. 247–251 and 285–287; Campion, *Introduction to the Procedure of the House of Commons*, 3rd ed., pp. 73–77 and 99–102; Jennings, *Parliament*, 2nd ed., pp. 63–73, and W. S. Livingston, The Security of Tenure of the Speaker, in *Parliamentary Affairs*, Vol. XI, No. 4.
[2] *H.C. Debates*, Vol. 493, cols. 1–24.

him next day for Royal Approbation. Without Mr. Speaker there is officially no House: accordingly the Clerk of the House stands and points to the Member who, by pre-arrangement, will move the election of a Speaker.[3] Sir Hugh O'Neil,[4] chosen spokesman, moved, 'That the right hon. William Shepherd Morrison do take the Chair of this House as Speaker'.

This was Sir Hugh's fourth experience of the election of a new Speaker. The previous candidates had occupied the Chair either as Chairman or Deputy-Chairman of Ways and Means. But, he said,

it does not always happen to be the case that a good Chairman of Committees is necessarily a good Speaker. Perhaps it is a good thing that the candidate I am proposing breaks with that custom.

This election differed from previous ones also because it came at the beginning of a new Parliament (which also happened later, in 1959). Generally, Mr. Speaker had retired during the course of a Parliament, which gave more time for consideration as to his successor than during a General Election. Sir Hugh emphasised the significance of the office; so much depended upon the election of the right man,

whether the House is an orderly assembly or a bad one, whether its proceedings are business-like and efficient or dilatory and inefficient, and whether its ancient traditions are maintained or are allowed to deteriorate.

From his speech we may extract the qualities necessary to a good Speaker. He must be absolutely impartial, divorcing all party affiliations from his mind and being the servant only of the whole House. He must 'give a fair crack of the whip to all sections of the House, without fear, favour or affection'. He must give due consideration to minorities. He must have a calm and equable temperament, not be easily flurried and possess 'a superabundance of patience'. Further, he must have a complete knowledge of the practice and procedure of the House. Sir Hugh implied that Mr. Morrison, although an unusual candidate in so far as he had never been a member of the Chairman's panel, possessed the requisite qualities. Sir Hugh added that in recent years Mr. Speaker's job had been somewhat easier. The House

---

[3] The Clerk, in fact, points to each Member who is to speak, and finally puts the Question to the House.
[4] Cons., Antrim, North.

is an infinitely more orderly assembly than it used to be. . . . It is a long time since a Member has been suspended and I do not know how long it is since Mr. Speaker had to suspend a Sitting through grave disorder arising.

Finally, after speaking of the 'most extraordinary mellowing influence' the House had 'on even the most fiery temper', he said:

Our rights, our traditions, our liberties and our ceremonials all find their qualities in the presence of Mr. Speaker. He is one of us and part of us, and his authority can only rest on the support and good-will of the House as a whole.

Sir Ralph Glyn[5] seconded.

The claims of Major James Milner were put by Mr. S. P. Viant,[6] exercising, as he said, 'the right of every Member of this Assembly'. Major Milner had become a Member of the Chairman's Panel in 1935. In 1943 he was elected Deputy-Chairman of Ways and Means, and on Mr. Speaker Fitzroy's death presided over the House. He had 'been apprenticed to the Chair' for sixteen years. He had occupied Mr. Speaker's Chair on occasion for several days and once for a fortnight during Mr. Speaker's illness. He was Chairman of the Defence Committee during the war and of two committees for revising the whole of Standing Orders for Public and Private Business. When Mr. Viant stressed the 'independence and impartiality' of his candidate, which had 'never been in doubt, or in question', there were some cries of 'Oh'. This unwonted expression of disagreement was quickly passed over, but it indicated that some Members, at least, failed to perceive in Major Milner all the qualities expected of a Speaker. Mr. Viant, however, continued:

I would say frankly that there have been times when we who are now on this side of the House thought that the right hon. and gallant Gentleman favoured the Opposition. . . . In my experience there always has been that feeling in regard to a Speaker elected from one's own side. It is perhaps the best proof of impartiality.

Mr. David Logan,[7] who seconded, emphasised that the election of a Speaker was a matter for the individual decision of the House; it would be regrettable if it became purely a party matter.

[5] Cons., Abingdon. [6] Lab., Willesden West.
[7] Lab., Liverpool, Scotland.

Mr. W. S. Morrison and Major Milner, 'in accordance with ancient custom and usage', then made brief speeches 'submitting themselves to the will of the House'. Major Milner adopted as his own the words of Mr. Speaker Onslow: 'I have loved independency and pursued it. I have kept to my original principles and upon conscience have never deviated from them to serve any party cause whatsoever.' In the Division each candidate voted for his rival.

The Prime Minister[8] threw light on the negotiations which had, on this occasion, failed to produce an agreed candidate. He had received the King's Commission to form a Government on October 26. Parliament was due to meet on October 31 and to begin the Debate on the Address on November 6. A Speaker had to be chosen on October 28, less than forty-eight hours after the appointment of a new Prime Minister. He had written to Mr. Attlee saying that two names were in mind, Mr. W. S. Morrison and Mr. Hopkin Morris. Talks through 'the usual channels' were suggested. The offer of the Deputy Chairmanship to the Labour Party was also suggested. The Prime Minister admitted that the time for consultations was short, but 'in a free, democratic assembly and in parties in which there are great elements of separate and individual opinions, it is not always possible to produce machine-like, drilled results, and it ought not to be so'.

Mr. Anthony Eden, Mr. Buchan-Hepburn (Chief Whip), Mr. Attlee, Mr. Herbert Morrison and Mr. Whiteley (Opposition Chief Whip) met on October 29. According to Mr. Churchill's account, Mr. Attlee and his friends expressed preference for Mr. W. S. Morrison over Mr. Hopkin Morris and suggested Mr. Bowles[9] as Deputy-Chairman.

Later that evening it was understood by us – but perhaps a wrong impression was gathered – that they also agreed to second Mr. W. S. Morrison. . . . At any rate the question of [Major Milner] was raised by [Mr. Eden] on the general issue of a Labour Speaker. [Mr. Eden] made it clear that if the suggestion were pursued, he did not know whether it would be acceptable to the Government Party, who had a majority. The idea was not, however, pressed at all.

Mr. Churchill had been informed of these discussions and later the understanding was confirmed by the two Chief Whips.

---

[8] Mr. Winston Churchill.   [9] Lab., Nuneaton.

He then asked Mr. W. S. Morrison to allow his name to go forward.

On October 30 the Government Chief Whip was informed that the Liaison Committee of the Labour Party[10] felt there should be a Labour Speaker and asked that Major Milner be considered. If this could not be agreed they could not second Mr. W. S. Morrison nor accept the Deputy-Chairmanship. Mr. Churchill went on to tell the House that it was then too late because he had made his proposal to submit Mr. Morrison's name.

Individuals who are Members of this House and who are chosen for this position of unique dignity are chosen by the House with the eyes of all the Parliaments of the world directed upon them. If their names are to be hawked about, not merely in the informal party discussions but between the Leaders of different parties and after quite definite indication had been given and a definite offer has been made . . . I am sure that there is a very considerable disparity between the way in which we manage our affairs and the spirit in which this Parliament has to fulfil its duties.

There had been discussions before on this matter, Mr. Churchill continued, and there was no reason for ill-feeling. Yet, so important was agreement that,

if I had been told earlier, I very likely might have taken a different course.

Mr. Attlee said he would have preferred the Division to have been taken at once after the two names had been proposed and seconded. He did not think it very useful to discuss the informal talks. There had been no opportunity to consult with anybody at the time of the meeting on October 29. Mr. Attlee's version of the talks differed only in emphasis from Mr. Churchill's:

I expressed the opinion that there was no objection whatever on our part to [Mr. W. S. Morrison]. We put forward the point that we considered that [Mr. Milner], by his long experience, was a suitable man to occupy the Chair: and we asked that his name should be considered as well. We did also mention [Sir Charles MacAndrew] because he has also occupied the Chair with distinction. . . . I did not decide on behalf of anybody. It is essentially a House of Commons matter. I took what soundings I could, but the time was rather short. We subsequently discussed the matter fully on this side. We think there is a great advantage in having someone who has already occupied the Chair and has great experience.

[10] cf. H. Morrison, *Government and Parliament* .p. 123 *et seq.*

Without impugning Mr. W. S. Morrison's qualities, the Leader of the Opposition concluded that Major Milner, who had occupied the Chair as Chairman of Ways and Means, was eminently qualified to preside over the proceedings of the House.

Mr. Eden intervened only to say that he did not understand at any time in the conversations that there was any preference expressed for Sir Charles MacAndrew. Mr. Clement Davies, Liberal leader, made a brief, unheeded plea for reconsideration and postponement until next day. On the Question, 'That the right hon. William Shepherd Morrison do take the Chair of this House as Speaker', there voted for the Ayes 318, for the Noes 251.

Mr. Speaker-elect[11] – standing on the upper step and not occupying the Chair – expressed his thanks and was congratulated by the Prime Minister, the Leader of the Opposition and the Liberal leader. Mr. Speaker-elect then put the Question, 'That this House do now adjourn,' which being carried, he 'went away without the Mace before him'.

On Tuesday, November 6, the swearing-in of Members having been completed, and various Sessional Orders agreed to, Sir Charles MacAndrew was appointed Chairman of Ways and Means and Mr. Hopkin Morris Deputy-Chairman.

We conclude with a brief reference to the election of another Speaker, Sir Harry Hylton-Foster, formerly Solicitor-General, in the newly-elected Parliament of 1959. There had been some suggestion that the Speakership might be offered to a member of the Labour Opposition. It was eventually couched in the form of the specific suggestion of Sir Frank Soskice. He was unwilling to go forward, but, in any case, the Labour Party rather resented the offer to a particular person instead of a general offer that they should put forward a name. In the event, Sir Harry was not opposed, but there were some loud ironic murmurings when his proposer and seconder made the traditional speeches to the effect that the nominee was one 'approved in consultation' with all sides of the House.

2. POINTS OF ORDER

The maintenance of Order in debate is a wider subject than

---

[11] Royal Approbation followed next day.

'points of Order', though in the raising of the latter the cry 'Order! Order!' is frequently heard. Some of the general rules of Order are discussed in connection with legislation.[12] Others are too technical for detailed treatment. *Erskine May*[13] refers to (1) rules governing the time and manner of speeches, (2) rules governing the content of speeches, (3) rules of behaviour for Members not speaking, and (4) powers of the Chair to enforce order. *Campion*[14] ranges even more widely and includes such matters as the Closure. Here we are concerned with 'points of Order' in the narrow sense, though the examples illustrate other matters of procedure also.

Erskine May[15] states: 'Although it is the duty of the Speaker to interfere in the first instance for the preservation of order when, in his judgment, the occasion demands his interference, it is also the right of any Member who conceives that a breach of order has been committed, if the Speaker refrains from interfering (either because he does not consider it necessary to do so, or because he does not perceive that a breach of order has been committed), to rise in his place, interrupting any Member who may be speaking, and direct the attention of the Chair to the matter, provided he does so at the moment the alleged breach of order occurs.' Theoretically, it is possible to distinguish between genuine points of Order and those raised for debating purposes, to waste time, or to embarrass Members on their feet. In practice, the line is difficult to draw; moreover, the Chair cannot know whether the point of Order is 'genuine' until he has heard it. Our examples, therefore, are chosen to illustrate arguments on points of Order – whether genuine or 'fraudulent'; their place both in procedure and in parliamentary tactics is thus made clear.

(a) On March 26, 1952, Mr. Speaker had occasion to define the purpose of 'points of Order'. The background to his pronouncement is important. Just after 3.30 p.m., on the Third Reading of the Consolidated Fund (No. 2) Bill, a debate began on the textile industry.[16] It was interrupted at 7 p.m. for Private Business (Ealing Corporation Bill, Second Reading) and, being exempted business, resumed just after 10 p.m.[17] Sometime after 8 a.m. on March 27, the Parliamentary Secretary to the Board of Trade began to speak. Then began a

---

12 Chap. 7.
13 *Erskine May*, pp. 444–473.
14 *Campion*, pp. 170–200, *Forms and Rules of Debate*.
15 *Erskine May*, p. 470.
16 *H.C. Debates*, Vol. 498, col. 413 *et seq.*
17 *Ibid.*, col. 533 *et seq.*

series of interruptions on 'points of Order' which continued at intervals until 1 p.m.[18]

First, it was suggested that further 'grievances' were still to be raised. Should not the Government postpone its reply? If the Parliamentary Secretary spoke could the debate continue? After an interlude in which Mrs. Braddock[19] was 'named'[20] Mr. Silverman[21] rose 'on a point of Order' to suggest an adjournment in order to draw attention to the 'serious limitation of debate'.[22] The Parliamentary Secretary's reference to 'frivolous interruptions and waste of time' led to further argument. Closure being moved, 'points of Order' were raised as to whether this was not 'an infringement of the rights of minorities': not only did other Members wish to intervene on textiles; other subjects should be raised on the Consolidated Fund Bill. When Mr. Speaker proceeded to 'collect the voices' preparatory to a Division, argument developed as to whether the 'Noes' did not, in fact, 'have it'. The Closure was carried on a Division. The Bill was then given a Third Reading. Further points of Order were then raised about the 'collection of voices'. In reminding the House that when the Closure is moved the Question must be put without debate, Mr. Speaker declared that in that context points of Order were 'debate'.[23] He then made his statement:

I really must say something about points of Order. The real function of a point of Order is to enable an hon. Member . . . to draw the attention of the Chair to a breach of decorum or order which the Chair has not perceived. (An hon. Member: 'Or an injustice'.) I have noticed a growing abuse of this custom. Hon. Members raise points of Order and, of course, the Chairman or the Speaker has no idea what an hon. Member is going to say until he delivers himself; and in too many cases it is not a point of Order at all but an attempt to score a debating point or to delay the proceedings of the House.

The remaining Orders of the Day were then read and postponed. But Mr. Speaker's homily did not prevent the raising of further points of Order. Members had not heard the Clerk read the Orders. They had not heard the Minister postpone the next Order (Army and Air Force (Annual) Bill). The Leader

[18] March 27.
[20] See below p. 34.
[22] H.C. Debates, Vol. 498, col. 732.

[19] Lab., Liverpool Exchange.
[21] Lab., Nelson and Colne.
[23] Ibid., cols. 785-786.

of the House himself raised a 'point of Order' – which was not a point of Order! – to the effect that the argument was taking time from the Adjournment Debate. It is a tribute to the House that just after 1 p.m. (having sat from 2.30 p.m. the previous day) the usual half-hour debate – on Children's Hospital Wards (Visits) – was then taken. The House began its Sitting of March 27 just over an hour later.

The problem remained. On April 30, 1952,[24] Mr. Speaker again had occasion to say:

> Points of Order are, of course, very useful to the Chair when they are points of Order, but if they are not . . . it really is abusing the Rules of the House to get in debating points.

During a debate on July 1, 1952,[25] the Prime Minister himself remarked:

> If I may make a diversion, I do not think there is any practice of the House which is more a subject of abuse than this raising of points of Order of an unreal or even fraudulent character.

On November 27, 1952,[26] Sir E. Keeling[27] asked 'whether my right hon. Friend will consider giving time to the Motion on the Order Paper condemning the practice of raising false points of Order? . . . in the last complete month in which the House sat no fewer than forty-two alleged points of Order were ruled by the Chair not to be points of Order.' We turn now to actual examples of these occasions.

(*b*) The Second Reading of the National Health Service Bill was taken on March 27, 1952.[28] The Joint Under-Secretary of State for Scotland[29] replied to the Debate. He had been speaking for a few moments when interruptions began.

Mr. Manuel:[30] On a point of Order. May I ask for your advice Mr. Deputy-Speaker, as to whether the hon. and gallant Gentleman is going to answer the points raised or whether a prepared speech is to be the sole answer to the Debate?

Mr. Deputy-Speaker:[31] The hon. Member . . . must know that that is not a point of Order. I wish hon. Members would not raise as points of Order things which they know are not points of Order.

Mr. Manuel: Further to that point of Order –

---

[24] *H.C. Debates*, Vol. 499' col. 1430.
[26] *H.C. Debates*, Vol. 508, col. 628
[28] *H.C. Debates*, Vol. 498, cols. 961-1030
[30] Lab., Ayrshire Central.
[25] *H.C. Debates*, Vol. 503, col. 275.
[27] Cons., Twickenham.
[29] Commander T. O. Galbraith.
[31] Sir Charles MacAndrew.

Mr. Deputy-Speaker: I have said that it is not a point of Order, and therefore nothing further can arise from it.

Mr. Manuel: May I ask for your Ruling?

Mr. Deputy-Speaker: I cannot have my Ruling discussed.

Mr. Manuel: Do I take it from your Ruling, Mr. Deputy-Speaker, that you are now ruling that an hon. Member cannot ask you for advice about a point of Order?

Mr. Deputy-Speaker: No. My position was that these points of Order are being abused.

Mr. Manuel: By whom?

Mr. Deputy-Speaker: By hon. Members who get up and put points of Order in order to bring in a debating point when they are not points of Order at all. I am not going to have them.

After further interventions, Mr. Aneurin Bevan[32] rose to cries of 'Order' from hon. Members. Before he could say more than, 'The Minister has given way. On a point of explanation . . .', Mr. G. H. R. Rogers[33] rose:

On a point of Order. Could you give your Ruling, Mr. Deputy-Speaker, on whether a point of explanation is a point of Order, or what it is?

Mr. Deputy-Speaker: I did not notice that the Minister had given way. As he has given way the right hon. Gentleman is entitled to ask a question.

Mr. Bevan: Hon. Members with a little experience of the House know that interventions frequently take place during speeches. I wanted to ask (Interruption). Shut up!

Mr. F. Harris:[34] On a point of Order. Is the right hon. Gentleman telling you to shut up, Mr. Deputy-Speaker?

Mr. Deputy-Speaker: I think he did, but he made a mistake because I had not spoken.

Mr. Bevan: I think I indicated the direction of my remark.

Mr. Bevan asked his question; the Minister replied; Mr. Bevan rose again.

The ensuing dialogue throws light not merely on points of Order but upon practice in relation to the *reading of speeches*.

Mr. Speaker: Order. Unless the Member who has the floor gives way it is out of order for another hon. Member to stand.

Mr. Bevan: Now, Sir, I rise to a point of Order. . . . It is customary for Ministers to be allowed to read speeches, but not to read them in such a way as to frustrate the purposes of debate. In my respectful submission the hon. and gallant Gentleman has displayed his incapacity and is now compelled to read from his brief.

[32] Lab., Ebbw Vale.
[33] Cons., Kensington North.
[34] Cons., Croydon North.

Mr. Speaker: I have not seen the hon. and gallant Gentleman reading anything yet.
Hon. Members: Oh!

The Minister continued, being interrupted on several occasions, notably by Dr. Edith Summerskill.[35]

Mr. Speaker: Order. I must repeat again the well-known rule that, unless the hon. Member who has possession of the floor gives way, it is out of order for other Members to remain standing.

Later, the reading of speeches was again raised in the form of points of Order.

Mr. Speaker: It is, of course, in general, out of order to read speeches in the House, but I have noticed Ministers frequently resort to the practice on both sides of the House. The polite euphemism used in describing a Minister's speech is that he uses 'copious notes'.
Mr. H. Davies:[36] Further to that point of Order. (Interruption.) Is there any method by which back-benchers can protect themselves from this new kind of debating introduced by hon. Members opposite?
Mr. Fernyhough:[37] Further to that point of Order. Would it not have met the general convenience of the House better if this speech had been circulated?
Mr. Speaker: I have expressed myself already on the question of reading speeches, and I have nothing to add. As to the earlier point of Order that the speech was not an answer to the debate, that must, of course, remain a matter of opinion: it is not a matter for me.

Commander Galbraith was then permitted to conclude his speech.

(*c*) Our next example illustrates both 'genuine' and 'fraudulent' points of Order. It also throws light on the rules regarding *quotations from documents*. On March 31, 1952,[38] just before 10 p.m., debate began on a Prayer to annul two Statutory Instruments dealing with Iron and Steel Prices. Just before midnight (Prayers being then totally exempted business, Mr. Speaker having no option to put the Question at 11.30 p.m. as he was given in 1956), the Minister of Supply[39] rose to reply. He referred to a letter from Mr. Hardie, Chairman of the Iron and Steel Corporation (appointed by the previous Labour Government). The letter had set out certain arguments against

---

[35] Lab., Fulham West.   [36] Lab., Leek.
[37] Lab., Jarrow.   [38] *H.C. Debates*, Vol. 498, cols. 1309–1370.
[39] Mr. Duncan Sandys.

price increases. In response to inquiries as to the contents of the
letter, the Minister purported to explain. He was met with cries
of 'Read the letter'.

Mr. Ivor Owen Thomas:[40] On a point of Order. The Minister is purporting to relate the argument to what he says is contained in the
letter of January 24. Is it not essential, to enable the House to
determine whether the Minister is arguing correctly or drawing
right conclusions, that the letter should be read?
Mr. Speaker: As I understand the right hon. Gentleman, he could
not read one letter without reading the whole lot of them. Therefore,
that is not a point of Order.
Mr. Thomas: On a point of Order. The Minister has just stated that
he wishes to convey a certain meaning to the House about the conclusions drawn from the letter of January 24. I suggest to you that
there is the duty on the Minister, to enable the House to see if he is
drawing correct conclusions or not, to read the letter.
Mr. Speaker: That is a point of debate and not a point of Order.
Mr. Fernyhough:[41] On a point of Order. Would it not be for the
general convenience of the House if the right hon. Gentleman read
the particular letter in question – (Hon. Members: 'No'.) – So far
as the other letters are concerned he can have them put in tomorrow's *Hansard*.
Mr. Speaker: That is not a point of Order; it is not, in fact, a point
for me at all. It seems to me that the right hon. Gentleman's argument, if I followed him carefully, was that it would be misleading to
read one without the other.

Mr. Speaker thus regarded the above exchanges as not raising
points of Order at all. The ensuing exchanges, however, involved important and genuine points of Order.

Mr. G. R. Mitchison:[42] On a point of Order. When a single letter or a
series of letters of a public nature are referred to by a Minister in
this way, and when the question arises whether the Minister's summary of them is correct and complete, surely he is bound to lay them
on the Table?
Mr. Speaker: If the correspondence is summarised, it is not necessary
to lay it on the Table.
Mr. Mitchison: With great respect, Mr. Speaker, in the present case
surely the matter has gone beyond the summary. The point before
the House is whether what I may term the Minister's version of this
letter is correct and complete. Surely when that point arises the
Minister is bound to lay the letter on the Table.
Mr. Speaker: I think the rule is that, generally, if the Minister quotes
from a document it ought to be laid. [The Minister has been] heard

[40] Lab., The Wrekin.   [41] Lab., Jarrow.
[42] Lab., Kettering.

to summarise and give the effect of the correspondence. . . . Besides, I am not quite clear . . . how far the old rule refers to correspondence between a nationalised board and a Ministry. . . .

Sir Lynn Ungoed-Thomas:[43] Would you, Mr. Speaker, give your Ruling in this entirely new situation. . . ?

Mr. Speaker: I would have to give consideration . . . to think it over.

Mr. Mitchison: I must excuse my insistence, but surely the basis of the rule is the public character of the correspondence. . . . If the question depends on quotation surely the mere act of verbal quotation, the uttering of a few words, cannot make all the difference? . . .

Mr. Speaker: The rule in this House is analogous to the rule in courts of law. . . . A Minister who summarises correspondence, but does not actually quote from it, is not bound to lay it on the Table. . . .

Mr. Mitchison: Further to that point of Order. With respect, Sir, this is not a question of summarising correspondence. We have been given the Minister's version, letter by letter, of a whole series of letters. . . . [This] cannot be a substitute for the letter itself. . . .

Mr. Speaker: I am bound to say I differ in my judgment of what has transpired, and I say that with great respect to the hon. and learned Gentleman. I have heard nothing said by the Minister beyond a summary of the correspondence and I am within the recollection of the House.

Further exchanges tended to lapse into less genuine points of Order, mainly attempting to prove that the Minister had actually 'quoted'. The argument continued until 1 a.m., and despite the firm decision by Mr. Speaker, Mr. Ede,[44] on behalf of the Opposition, concluded by pressing again for publication. There was no further comment and no subsequent action.

(*d*) Our next example illustrates further the nature of points of Order and also raises the question of *references to speeches made outside the House.* The occasion was a debate in Committee of Supply,[45] July 1, 1952. The Civil Estimates 1951–52, Class 11, Vote 1, Foreign Service, gave rise to debate on United Nations Policy in the Far East (Korea). It was preceded by a Statement by Mr. Selwyn Lloyd, Minister of State, on a visit to the Far East, and followed (after a Prayer to annul a Statutory Instrument on Births, Marriages and Deaths (Registration Fees)), by an Adjournment Debate on Truce Talks in Korea. The House was much concerned this day with Far Eastern matters.

Mr. Philip Noel-Baker[46] opened for the Opposition. At 4.42 p.m. the Prime Minister[47] rose to reply. He referred to a speech

---

[43] Lab., Leicester North-East.   [44] Lab., South Shields.
[45] 17th Allotted Day: *H.C. Debates*, Vol. 503, cols. 255–380.
[46] Lab., Derby South.   [47] Mr. Winston Churchill.

made by Mr. Acheson in Westminster Hall a few days earlier.
Mr. S. Silverman rose to a point of Order.[48]

The Prime Minister has made reference to a speech that was made
outside here – (Hon. Members: 'No.') – He referred to a speech
made in Westminster Hall. We all understood that the speech was
made at a private meeting, and it was repeatedly said to be off the
record. It is very difficult if the Prime Minister refers to it and nobody
else is able to refer to any other part of it. Ought it not to be excluded?

Mr. Deputy-Speaker: That is not a point of Order for me.

Prime Minister: May I say that –

Mr. John Paton:[49] On a point of Order. I wish to ask a related point
of Order but not exactly the same one. I wish to ask . . . if it will be
in order for Members on this side of the House, now that the Prime
Minister has introduced this matter of a private meeting, to continue the discussion about what Mr. Acheson said?

Prime Minister: . . . the whole report is already published by the U.S.

Mr. Deputy-Speaker: No point of Order arises, and I am not going
to answer a hypothetical point of Order.

Mr. Silverman rose –

Prime Minister: The hon. Gentleman is so busy finding fault that he
is not able to keep himself abreast of the facts.

Mr. Silverman rose –

Prime Minister: I do not propose to give way because I was going to
read out –

Mr. Silverman rose –

Mr. Deputy-Speaker: If the hon. Gentleman really thinks he has a
point of Order I will hear it.

Mr. Silverman: If I had not thought that it was a point of Order, I
should not have attempted to raise it. . . . The right hon. Gentleman
has now referred to a document that we have all heard about. . . .
There are many of us who do not accept it as a full record. . . . Will
we . . . be in order in referring to those parts of Mr. Dean Acheson's
speech . . . that do not appear in the report . . . ?

Mr. Deputy-Speaker: I can only judge on a point of Order when it
arises. There has been no point of Order at the moment.

At this juncture Mr. Churchill made his reference to 'fraudulent'
points of Order.

Mr. Silverman: On a point of Order. I do not know, Mr. Deputy-
Speaker, whether you share the right hon. Gentleman's contempt
for the procedure of this House or his readiness to abuse his position
in order to offer insults –

Mr. Deputy-Speaker: Order. I would ask for the point of Order to
be put in a more temperate way.

[48] Cols. 273–277.   [49] Lab., Norwich North.

Mr. Silverman: I am exceedingly grateful to you . . . for reminding hon. Members that points of Order, or other things, might be put in a temperate way. I would ask whether the word 'fraudulent' with reference to other Members of the House and their conduct in putting points of Order is, in your view, in order, and whether the suggestion that you permit fraudulent points of Order is not a quite unjustifiable attack upon the Chair.

Mr. Deputy-Speaker: I am in absolute agreement with the first comment. The points of Order raised at the moment can clearly be described as fraudulent in my opinion.

Mr. Bevan (returning for a moment to Mr. Acheson's speech): On a point of Order. I should like to have your guidance . . . in this matter. A very large number of Members of Parliament of all parties attended the meeting at Westminster Hall. We were given to understand that the whole thing was off the record and that it was entirely private and could not be repeated. I understand that a certain report has been made purporting to be a report of what occurred at that meeting. All of it, however, has not been reported and, as no shorthand notes were taken by any official persons at that meeting, so far as I know, are we, therefore, in a position to put any interpretation and to give any report we like about what we think happened at that meeting?

Mr. Deputy-Speaker: I cannot, of course, judge on what was said and what happened at the meeting, but these matters certainly do not arise as points of Order.

Mr. Bevan: May I respectfully submit that this is an extremely serious matter . . . if interpretations not supported by objective fact can be made purporting to be what the spokesman for foreign affairs in America said. . . . Are we free to do it? If so, then we must all take the consequences.

Mr. Deputy-Speaker: If a matter is serious, it does not necessarily mean that it is a point of Order.

Mr. Silverman then reverted to the use by the Prime Minister of the word 'fraudulent'.

Mr. Deputy-Speaker: I do not think that the Prime Minister accused anyone of doing anything fraudulent – (Interruption) – I should be grateful if I could have the courtesy of the House to allow me to finish my sentence. The Prime Minister does not refer to any hon. Member as being fraudulent. He referred to the raising of fraudulent points of Order. In my experience that has been happening frequently of recent years.

Mr. Silverman: It is, of course, perfectly true that the right hon. Gentleman has not the guts to say what he had to say about any individual by name, but he used the phrase about the fraudulent raising of points of Order in a context which could only be related to the point of Order which had just been raised –

Mr. Deputy-Speaker: The word 'fraudulent' was not used in that context at all. The word 'fraudulent', as I understood it, was used against points of Order which hon. Members raise when the Minister . . . refuses to give way, and think that the only way they can get their word is by raising a point of Order. It happens time and time again, and, in my opinion, they are fraudulent points of Order. I hope they will be stopped.

(e) On November 25, 1952,[50] the Second Reading of the Iron and Steel Debate was taken. Interrupted at 7 p.m. for an 'urgency Motion' it was resumed just before 10 p.m. Just after midnight the House was 'counted out', at the instigation of Col. Wigg,[51] who, having discovered that less than forty Conservatives were in the House, warned his Labour colleagues to stay away. Proceedings on the following day, when the House had to deal with the resulting situation, throw light not merely on points of Order, but on *the way in which the time-table of the House is arranged, the relation of Government time to Private Members' business, the duty of the Whips to 'keep a House', the power available to the Government to utilise the time of the House and to the Opposition, relying on its right to table a censure motion, to get its revenge.*

On November 26,[52] after Questions, the Leader of the Opposition rose to ask for Mr. Speaker's Ruling on the position of business following on failure to give the Iron and Steel Bill a Second Reading as originally arranged. Notice of Motion for Second Reading had appeared on the Order Paper for the day. Quoting *Erskine May*, Mr. Attlee asked whether this had been done because 'it is essential that proceedings . . . be resumed'. There was nothing 'essential' about the Bill; it was a 'mere matter of convenience for the Government', whose remissness alone had caused the 'count out'.

Mr. Speaker: . . . I have looked through a great number of precedents on this matter this morning, and there does appear to be a common practice to place this notice upon the Paper when there has been an unexpected interruption of Business, either by a count or by a suspension for grave disorder, or some other cause, and frequently the House has gone on to consider the business of the day that has been put down by means of this Motion. I am bound to say, on looking at them all, that the Bills or Motions which have been thus continued in this way have all been in the non-contentious class, rather like, though not entirely parallel to, the business taken after 10 o'clock.

[50] *H.C. Debates*, Vol. 508, col. 384 *et seq.*   [51] Lab., Dudley.
[52] *H.C. Debates*, Vol. 508, cols. 455–462.

Mr. Speaker then referred to the Government of Ireland Bill, 1912, when the House was adjourned for grave disorder. On that occasion Mr. Speaker Lowther had expressed doubt concerning the attempt to resume debate next day.

I adopt that as the proper course to be taken here. As to what is or what is not essential business, I have no means of judging; that is a matter entirely for the House and not for the Chair, and it could only be decided after debate.

This first round ended with Mr. H. Crookshank's[53] announcement that he would not move the Motion on the Order Paper, but that on the following day the Government would proceed both with the Second Reading and the Money Resolution of the Iron and Steel Bill *and* with the business already announced for that day. This was to be taken up later, but Mr. Herbert Morrison first raised a different point:

My submission to you, Sir, is that what happened last night was that the House was counted out, and that therefore there was no order of the House for the resumption of the Iron and Steel Debate. I submit, therefore, that, in effect, the first day of the Iron and Steel debate has not taken place, because in any case it was not a complete day, and nor can it be so regarded, because there was no order of the House for the resumption of the debate. I submit, that, in the circumstances, the Iron and Steel debate officially has yet to commence and that two days ought to be available. Secondly, I submit that, in the circumstances, what I have said is in fact upheld by *Erskine May*, on p. 316, where it is stated that if a quorum is not present 'the immediate adjournment of the House takes place', and that it is assumed, as in fact was the case, that there was no day appointed for the second day's debate. The usual procedure is for Mr. Speaker to say 'Debate to be resumed' and someone on the Government Front Bench then says, 'Today or tomorrow'. That did not take place on this occasion. I therefore submit that this Debate did not take place.

Mr. Morrison then returned to the point about 'essential business', which, he submitted, 'should be decided, not by the House, but by the Chair, because a Government majority would naturally wish to vote it in their favour'. Finally, he observed that if the Iron and Steel Bill were taken next day, in addition to that day's original business (Emergency Powers), the Government would be 'treating the House very roughly'.

[53] Lord Privy Seal.

There followed a somewhat complicated discussion, during the course of which the Speaker ruled as follows:

As to the point of the essential character of the Bill, I think that is a matter for the House and must remain so. The Speaker or Chair cannot assess whether a Bill is essential or not. . . . As to the second day's debate, I heard it announced on Thursday last that there would be two days of debate on this Bill, and I do not think that there is anything in the Standing Orders or in the practice of the House which renders nugatory the debate we had yesterday. . . . As to the future conduct of the business that is a matter for the Government and the usual channels to discuss.

After a further protest by Mr. Ede against the proposed arrangement of the following day's business, the House proceeded to the Orders of the Day.

On November 27 Mr. Attlee asked if it was intended to take the Iron and Steel Bill, a Motion dealing with Statutory Instruments, and the Defence Regulations all on that day – there also being a Motion to exempt the business from S.O. No. 1.[54] Mr. Crookshank's affirmative reply provoked cries of 'Shame'.

Mr. Attlee: . . . there is no precedent for trying to make the House of Commons take two days business in one solely due to the incompetence of the Leader of the House and the Chief Whip. . . . Mr. Asquith did not try . . . although that was due to the Conservative Party shouting down the Liberals – I think throwing a book at the present Prime Minister.
The Prime Minister: That has nothing to do with the particular case.
Mr. Attlee: It was another instance of the disorderly habits of the Conservative Party. . . . It is the duty of the Government to keep a House . . .
Mr. Crookshank: Whether or not there is a precedent . . . the Government desire to get this business, and the Defence Regulations must be passed by the House this week.
Mr. Attlee: There is Monday. There is no special urgency for the business put down on Monday. I understand it is not urgent or necessary business.
Mr. Crookshank: But the Defence Regulations must be got through this week – (Hon. Members: 'Why?') – In order that they may become effective. That really is the case and that is why I repeat that statement.
Mr. Attlee: . . . it is quite unnecessary for the Government to have put down two Bills, one of which the Government supporters care for so little that they cannot even stay.

[54] 'Ten o'clock rule.'

Mr. Crookshank: There were quite other reasons. The presence of only four Socialists is one of them.

Mr. Attlee: That is the first time a Leader of the House has tried to excuse his failure to keep a House by trying to suggest that other Members were not present. In view of the treatment meted out to the House by the Government, I shall be obliged to put a Motion of Censure on the Order Paper.

On a point of Order, Mr. Simmons[55] inquired about the effect of the suspension of the ten o'clock rule that day on Private Members' Business, due next day (Friday). Mr. Speaker replied that if the House finished its business in time there was no reason why the Private Member's Bill should not be taken. Mr. Crookshank said that there was plenty of time to cope with Government Business long before there was any question of Friday's business. After a further ('fraudulent') point of Order, Mr. Bing[56] asked the Leader of the House if he would not be a little more frank.

If the right hon. Gentleman proposes to put down so much business as to compel a matter that deals with the Press [the Private Member's Bill] to be cut out, does he not consider that the more honest course would be to put down a Motion to suspend Private Members' time tomorrow and thus give hon. Members who have some knowledge of the matter an opportunity of discussing the motives which have led some hon. Members opposite to decide to prolong the debate to such a stage that matters relating to their friends of the Press cannot be discussed?

Mr. Crookshank: There is really no need to anticipate any of these things occurring. There is no necessity for this debate to go on until 11 o'clock tomorrow morning . . .

After some further brief exchanges, the following dialogue took place between Mr. Bevan and the Speaker:

With all respect, Mr. Speaker, this is a rather serious matter. I am sure you would like to reconsider what you said . . . that in your view there was no reason why the business could not all be carried through and still leave tomorrow's Sitting intact, which really means that what Mr. Speaker is saying is that the House of Commons should carry in one day's Sitting what was intended for two days.

Mr. Speaker: I cannot have that said – (Hon. Members: 'Hear, hear'.) Order. I am not accusing the right hon. Gentleman of anything. The Standing Orders normally provide that the Sitting of the House should stop at 10 o'clock, and business is then interrupted.

[55] Lab., Brierley Hill.   [56] Lab., Hornchurch.

What we have on the Order Paper is a Motion to exempt certain business, and the business of the Regulations is exempted business. What I mean is that there may be an equal time at night when normally we should not be doing business at all.

Mr. Bevan: With all respect, the House of Commons in its conduct of business can easily be put in a very great difficulty. The informality of the House can only be maintained if we have certain definite rules and understandings; and the Chair, towards the early hours of the morning, will find itself put in a very great difficulty in maintaining the order of the House if there is a grave sense of injustice on this side.

Mr. Speaker: The Chair is frequently placed in a position of great difficulty, but I shall endeavour to surmount any difficulty to the best of my ability.

Mr. Silverman then argued that, since the business of the day (Prayers) was normally 'exempted business', the normal time of interruption was not ten o'clock. Therefore, they were, in fact, being asked to do two days' work in one, if the Iron and Steel Bill were taken. Mr. Speaker replied:

I did state that this was exempted business; I was quite aware of that, but what I was trying to express was that by sitting late we can do work which would normally take two normal days . . . these points of Order, although they are very interesting, are not really points for me at all. The House must protect itself in these matters.

The House then proceeded to the Orders of the Day. Just before ten o'clock it divided on the Second Reading of the Iron and Steel Bill. The Money Resolution was not debated, though the Opposition divided the House. At 10.33 p.m. debate began on a Motion for 'an humble Address' for the continuance of the Emergency Laws (Miscellaneous Provisions) Act, 1947, for a further period of one year. This continued, with Divisions at 3.5 a.m., 6.25 a.m., and 7.55 a.m., until just after 8 a.m. There was further brief debate on the Committee Stage of the New Valuation Lists (Postponement) Bill. The House then took three further brief items and at 8.43 a.m. the usual half-hour Adjournment Debate took place. The House rose just after 9 a.m. The Government had thus fulfilled its aim to 'take two days' business in one', to compensate for the 'count out', and this without the feared exclusion of Mr. Simmons's Press Council Bill.[57]

[57] On the Friday Sitting this was 'talked out', the House adjourning at 4 p.m., after a Closure Motion had been defeated.

An additional stage in these prolonged proceedings came on December 8,[58] when Mr. Chuter Ede[59] moved a Motion of 'no confidence' in the Chairman of Ways and Means, for having accepted on three occasions motions for the *Closure*, thus having 'improperly curtailed debate' on the Expiring Laws Continuance Bill. Mr. Ede also referred in his Motion to an incident on December 31 when, he asserted, the Chairman had 'previously allowed great latitude to the Prime Minister in permitting him to intervene on a point of Order' but had declined to allow the Deputy-Leader of the Opposition to rise to a point of Order. After some debate the Motion was, by leave, withdrawn. The Opposition, however, was clearly perturbed by what it regarded as an 'infringement of the rights of the minority' and made plain that it attached considerable blame to the Leader of the House. These incidents may fairly be regarded as having arisen out of the original failure to 'keep a House' on November 25.

But the real dénouement had been played out on December 4,[60] when Mr. Attlee moved his censure Motion on the Government for 'dealing with the Business of the House incompetently, unfairly, and in defiance of the best principles of Parliamentary democracy and the national interest'. The five-and-a-half-hours' debate was the occasion of much hard hitting and the making of party points; it also covered the difficulties of the House when the Government majority is a very narrow one. But it cannot be summarised here. Instead, we turn to occasions when disagreement resulted in a rather more severe application by Mr. Speaker of his powers to maintain order.

3. SUSPENSIONS

Despite Sir Hugh O'Neil's reference, in moving the election of Mr. W. S. Morrison as Speaker in 1951, to the 'more orderly' behaviour of the House – and running off with the Mace now seems to have ceased to be a pastime even for the more exuberant Members – the 1951 Parliament, with parties evenly divided, with Labour in Opposition for the first time since 1945, and with a new Speaker, did provide some instances of uproarious conduct and saw the suspension of Members, which Sir Hugh had tended to regard as a thing of the past. We turn,

[58] *H.C. Debates*, Vol. 509, cols. 43–105.   [59] Lab., South Shields.
[60] *H.C. Debates*, Vol. 508, cols. 1783–1892.

however, to the 1955 Parliament for an outstanding example of the suspension of a Sitting.[61]

(a) *The Suspension of a Member*. The suspension of Mr. Sydney Silverman on November 27, 1951, is our first example of action under S.O. No. 22. The Committee Stage of the Home Guard Bill[62] was taken in Committee of the Whole House. It was a controversial Measure; the Opposition was not well disposed towards the Secretary of State for War, Mr. Antony Head; a large number of Amendments were tabled, many inevitably not selected by the Chairman under his powers; the ten o'clock rule had been suspended, and the Government hoped to get the Committee Stage through at one Sitting, concluding the Report and Third Reading stages next day.

Debate began on Clause 1 at 3.45 p.m. From the beginning the Opposition purported to fear the use of the Home Guard for 'strike-breaking'. At about 10.45 p.m. Mr. Shinwell[63] unsuccessfully tried to move to 'report progress', a first attempt to obtain more time for debate. Just after midnight the Closure was successfully moved and a Division on the Amendment under discussion taken. After a very short debate on a further Amendment, Mr. Head spoke. As he sat down, several Members rose but the Closure was at once moved.[63]

Among the Members who rose when the Closure was moved (above) was Mr. Silverman.[64]

On a point of Order. I think I am right in saying that I and some of my hon. Friends were on our feet to continue the debate long before the Motion was moved. Therefore, with the greatest respect, I say that it is not within your competence – (Hon. Members: 'Order, order'.) – to accept the Motion – (interruptions) while a

[61] The disciplinary powers of the Chair, the offences and the appropriate methods of dealing with them are discussed by *Erskine May* under six headings [pp. 467 *et seq.*]. (*Campion* deals briefly with the maintenance of order on pp. 198–200.) We are concerned primarily in this section with (4) 'grossly disorderly conduct', and in the next section with (5) 'gross disorder'. It is possible for a Member to be guilty of (6) 'obstruction of the business of the House otherwise than by disorderly conduct', e.g., by 'misusing the forms of the House', but 'comparatively little use has been made by the Chair of the power of naming a Member' for such misuse. The procedures used to enforce order are described by Erskine May [pp. 470–473].

[62] *H.C. Debates*, Vol. 494, cols. 1126–1475.   [63] Lab., Easington.

[64] To indicate the atmosphere of the debate it may be mentioned that subsequently Mr. Shinwell tried unsuccessfully to move to report progress three times more; the Closure was moved again, and after twenty hours Mr. Crookshank, at 10 a.m. (28 Nov.) offered further time at the next Sitting – actually the same afternoon.

[65] *H.C. Debates*, Vol. 494, col. 1305.

Member is on his feet prepared to continue the debate, or in the act of continuing it.

The Deputy-Chairman (Mr. Hopkin Morris): That is not a point of Order. I have accepted the Motion.

Mr. Adams[66] : On a point of Order. The Secretary of State has just made some further important –

The Deputy-Chairman: That is not a point of Order. I have accepted the Motion. It cannot be debated.

Mr. Silverman: On a point of Order.

Hon. Members: Sit down.

The Deputy-Chairman: I am on my feet. Once I have accepted the Motion it is accepted. It is my decision. There is a proper method of challenging it, if the hon. Gentleman wishes to do so.

Mr. Silverman: I do challenge it.

The Deputy-Chairman: That must be done by a Motion.

Mr. Silverman: I am not prepared to accept that Ruling.

Hon. Members: Withdraw.

Mr. Silverman: No, I am not going to.

The Deputy-Chairman: If the hon. Gentleman persists in defying my Ruling I must ask him to withdraw from the House.

Mr. Silverman: I am not going to withdraw. I was on my feet before the Motion was moved, and I claim the right of every Member —

Hon. Members: Withdraw.

Mr. Silverman: I am not going to withdraw.

The Deputy-Chairman: In that case I must report the hon. Member to Mr. Speaker.

Mr. Silverman: I am on my feet to continue the debate.

The Deputy-Chairman: Order, order. If the hon. Gentleman refuses to obey my Ruling I must send for Mr. Speaker.

Whereupon the Deputy-Chairman left the Chair to report the circumstances to the House.

The Deputy-Chairman: I have, Sir, to report Mr. Sydney Silverman for disregarding the authority of the Chair.

Mr. Speaker: Then I name Mr. Sydney Silverman for persistently disregarding the authority of the Chair.

Mr. Silverman rose –

The Minister of Health: [67] I beg to move –

Mr. Shinwell rose –

Mr. Speaker: Order, order.

Mr. Silverman: On a point of Order.

Mr. Speaker: No questions of order can arise. Mr. Crookshank.

Mr. Silverman rose –

Mr. Speaker: No debate or amendment is allowed on this Question.

Mr. Crookshank: I beg to move, 'That Mr. Sydney Silverman be suspended from the House'.

Question put.

The House proceeded to a Division.

---

[66] Lab., Hammersmith South.   [67] Mr. Crookshank.

During the Division Mr. T. Driberg,[69] seated and covered, raised a point of Order. As discussion on this continued, Mr. Silverman intervened to say that it was a little late to raise a point of Order, but he welcomed the opportunity to do so.

There was no gross disorderly conduct of any kind. There was no disrespect to the Deputy-Chairman. There was no circumstance that justified the use of Standing Order 22 instead of Standing Order 21 and the Deputy-Chairman was hopelessly in the wrong in accepting a Motion for the Closure at a moment when several hon. Members were on their feet with a most important point.

Mr. Speaker: So far as I am concerned, in the circumstances reported to me I had no other course open to me, under the Standing Orders, than to do what I did.

Mr. Silverman: With very great respect, I beg to differ from that. No matter what had been reported to you, there is nothing in the Standing Orders of this House or our time-honoured procedure to justify the Chair even refusing to listen to a point of Order at any time when it is properly raised.

The House divided: Ayes 194; Noes 147.

Mr. Speaker then directed Mr. Silverman to withdraw from the House (1.15 a.m.).[70]

Mr. Shinwell immediately rose to say that he had risen to address a question to the Leader of the House; he was under the impression that before the Leader moved the customary Motion an appeal might be made, e.g., on the grounds that the hon. Members alleged to have committed an offence desired to express regret. Was there any precedent for refusing such question? Might not 'this contretemps, this little trouble' have been avoided had the Leader, after an apology, agreed not to put the Motion? Mr. Speaker must, under the Rules of Order, put the Motion - but need it have been made?

Mr. Speaker repeated that under the Standing Order his action was 'automatic' and could not be 'interrupted'. In his view things had got beyond the stage suggested by Mr. Shinwell when the matter was reported to him. Mr. Driberg again raised the point of the refusal to hear Mr. Silverman on a point

---

[69] Lab., Maldon.

[70] S.O. 21 empowers the Chair to order a Member to withdraw 'during the remainder of that day's Sitting'. S.O. 22 involves suspension (the Question being put only by Mr. Speaker) 'until the fifth day . . . on which the House shall sit after the day on which he was suspended' (a second offence involves twenty days suspension).

of Order. Mr. Speaker repeated that since Mr. Silverman's conduct was the subject of the Motion, it would not have been in order. Mr. John Wheatley[71] sought to argue that Mr. Silverman had risen before the Motion was put and could have been heard. Mr. Speaker did not agree, but declined to argue the matter then. Mr. Shinwell asked him to give the matter consideration and advise the House at an early stage. Mr. Speaker was willing, but,

at the moment I tell the House that what I have done I have done with a desire to serve its best interests.

The epilogue to these events was played out after Question Time on November 29.[72] Mr. Speaker made a personal statement:

. . . Standing Order 22 provides that the Chairman shall forthwith suspend the proceedings of the Committee and report the circumstances . . . to the House, because it is for the House, with the Speaker or his Deputy in the Chair, to pass judgment. . . . When the Chairman makes his report to the House, through the Speaker, it is the duty of whoever is leading the House at the time to move, at once, the suspension of the hon. Member.

By practice and usage, this Motion must follow immediately upon the naming of the hon. Member by the Speaker. The House and the Speaker are entitled to assume that before matters have reached this stage the resources of the Committee and its Chairman for maintaining order have been exhausted. The time for withdrawals and apologies is, for the moment, over.

Up to 1882 it was the practice, when a Member was named in these circumstances, that he should be heard in his plea in his own defence before the House decided what course of action it should adopt. It was precisely because this practice led to obstruction and disorder that what are now Standing Orders Nos. 22–24 were passed. For the last 70 years since the modern summary procedure was introduced, the practice has been as I have described . . . it is now a long time since a similar case occurred. May I express the hope that it will be a long time before such a case happens again?

(b) *The Suspension of a Sitting.* In recent years suspension of a Sitting under S.O. No. 24 has been rare. The 'Suez Crisis', however, provided one such occasion in 1956. The events and the controversy they aroused, culminating in the Prime Minister's resignation, cannot be described here. But some background of parliamentary activity must be sketched in.

---

[71] Lab., Edinburgh East.   [72] *H.C. Debates*, Vol. 494, cols. 1731–1738.

On Friday, July 27, 1956,[73] the Prime Minister announced the unilateral decision of the Egyptian Government to expropriate the Suez Canal. On behalf of the Opposition, Mr. Gaitskell deplored 'this high-handed and totally unjustifiable step'. On Monday, July 30,[74] Sir Anthony Eden made a further statement: discussions were going on, particularly with the French Government, and he did not think it appropriate at that stage – Mr. Gaitskell having agreed – to debate the issue. An attempt next day[75] by Mr. Emrys Hughes[76] to raise the matter by Question led merely to reference to the forthcoming discussion in the House. Further questions on August 1[77] again terminated with Mr. Speaker's reminder of next day's debate.

On August 2 at 12.21 p.m., the Prime Minister opened a debate[78], formally on a Motion, 'That the House do now adjourn'. (It is worth while recalling that the famous 'Narvik' debate which led to the downfall of the Chamberlain Government in 1940 took place on a similar 'colourless' Motion.) He made a comparatively brief statement but was unable to reveal anything of importance about the talks which were in progress. Mr. Gaitskell made the Opposition viewpoint clear. He objected to the nationalisation of the Canal in the form it had taken and thought 'we were right to react sharply to this move'.[79] The 'extraordinary degree of agreement', as Mr. Denis Healey[80] called it, was perhaps not shared by many Opposition back benchers, notably Mr. Warbey;[81] it certainly disappeared later. The debate ended at 6.30 p.m. with an understanding that the House might be recalled before the end of the Recess should the occasion demand it.

The House was, in fact, recalled on September 12.[82] The Prime Minister opened a debate on the Suez situation. He outlined the steps taken since the House last met. As soon as Mr. Gaitskell replied, it was clear that the 'agreement' of August 2 no longer existed. The Opposition clearly suspected the Government of intending to use force. Major Tufton

---

[73] *H.C. Debates*, Vol. 557, cols. 777–780.   [74] *Ibid.*, cols. 918–921.
[75] *Ibid.*, col. 1151.   [76] Lab., South Ayrshire.
[77] *H.C. Debates*, Vol. 557, cols. 1365–1368.
[78] *Ibid.*, 557, cols. 1602–1675; 1681–1721.
[79] This attitude is important to note: Mr. Gaitskell's later – alleged – departure from it, as the Government took further action, was one of the main causes of bitterness on the Government side in later debates.
[80] Lab., Leeds East.   [81] Lab., Broxtowe.
[82] *H.C. Debates*, Vol. 558, cols. 2–150; 161–316.

Beamish,[83] in particular, made the most of what he considered to be a change of Opposition attitude between August 2 and September 12. The debate was adjourned at 10 p.m. and resumed at 2,37 p.m. next day, on a Government Motion to approve the Prime Minister's statement of policy, moved by the Foreign Secretary, Mr. Selwyn Lloyd. The Opposition was clearly worried that force might be used without any reference to the Security Council. Just before 10 p.m. they divided the House on an Amendment deploring the refusal of the Government to 'invoke the authority of the United Nations'. This was defeated by 321 votes to 251, and the Government Motion carried by 319 votes to 248.

On the third day of this specially-summoned meeting of Parliament there was a debate on Cyprus and the House adjourned until October 23. Though some questions were then asked, it was not until October 30–31 that further debate took place on the Middle East situation. By then, Israeli forces had advanced against Egypt and the Prime Minister began with a survey of the military situation. The Government had felt unable to await the outcome of the Security Council debate and had taken action 'to protect the Canal and separate the combatants'. Sir Anthony Eden repeated his statement of the previous day that 'British and French forces will intervene in whatever strength may be necessary to secure compliance'. Mr. Gaitskell roundly condemned this 'reckless and foolish decision'. Acrimonious debate continued until 10 p.m. Before it could be resumed on the following day, events occurred, including the actual use of force against Egypt, which – as we now proceed to describe – created such bitter argument that the Sitting had to be suspended. This was on November 1, 1956.[84]

The Minister of Defence[85] stated that on the previous night attacks had been made on Egyptian airfields. (Hon. Members: 'Shame!') Giving some details, he went on to provide the latest information about operations on the Israeli–Egyptian front. Following upon the previous day's acrimonious argument whether there had been 'a declaration of war', whether 'a state of war' existed, and what was the difference between 'war' and 'armed conflict', this announcement inevitably raised the temperature of the House at once.

---

[83] Cons., Lewes.   [84] *H.C. Debates*, Vol. 558, cols. 1619–1752.
[85] Mr. Anthony Head.

Mr. Gaitskell's first intervention began with the assertion that millions of British people were profoundly shocked and ashamed. (An hon. Member: 'Fascists.') He declared that the action was neither in self-defence nor in collective defence, but in clear defiance of the United Nations Charter. He asked for an assurance that any decisions reached by a two-thirds majority of the Assembly would be instantly accepted and that, pending such decision, no further military action would be taken.

Mr. Head replied that the action taken, restricted entirely to military targets, had as its sole purpose the inducement of the Egyptian Government to accede to certain requirements relating to the Suez Canal put forward by the British Government. (An hon. Member: 'What about U.N.O.?') Mr. Shinwell rose to speak but was forestalled by Mr. S. Silverman, who asked for guidance,

in what appears to be a completely unprecedented situation. The action was taken against a country with whom apparently we were in friendly relations. There has been no declaration of war, no breaking off of diplomatic relations. . . . Is there anything that the House of Commons can do at this moment to make certain that those who have taken an oath of allegiance to Her Majesty are not required by that oath to commit murder all over the world?
Mr. Speaker: . . . it is really a question for the House to decide. There stands on the Order Paper a Motion of Censure against the Government because of their conduct of these affairs. My answer . . . is that the House should get on with that Motion of Censure as quickly as possible.

Mr. Gaitskell pressed for an answer to his questions.

Mr. Head: The question of future policy does not rest with me, and it is not for me to give any undertaking in that respect.
Hon. Members: Answer!

Mr. Shinwell demanded to know the precise purpose of the attack – to occupy the airfields, to prevent their use by Egypt, to land troops? Mr. Head persisted that the particular action in question was 'employing the sanction which we stated if our requirement was not met'. Mr. Bevan intervened on a point of Order:

May I appeal to you, as Speaker of this House, to clarify the constitutional position? As I understand, the matter of peace and war is a matter of the Royal Prerogative and in that respect Her Majesty's

Ministers are responsible for advising Her Majesty and they are also responsible to this House.

Now, Mr. Speaker, traditionally in the past you have been the spokesman for Members of this House in order to ascertain the intentions of the Executive and even of the Crown and to see that the Crown is responsible to this House. On one famous occasion your predecessor rebuked the Sovereign who came to this House. Therefore, Sir, I ask you now, as Speaker of the House of Commons, to ascertain the legal position so that we may be informed about it.

Mr. Speaker: I am willing, so far as my limited powers and abilities extend, to discharge any duty which the House lays upon me. It is my duty to do so. If the House were to pass a resolution, I would act upon it if I could, but I am not the authority on constitutional law. I do my best, within the restricted rules of Order of this House, to interpret the law of Parliament but these wider matters are surely for Ministers and the House as a whole, and not for me.

Mr. Silverman sought to ascertain the position of any prisoners taken by the Egyptians if there were no state of war. Mr. Speaker replied:

I really must refuse to extend the sphere in which I have to operate. I find my task quite arduous enough without giving opinions on these abstract questions, many of them hypothetical, of constitutional law.

Mr. Gaitskell then asked the Government whether a declaration of war on Egypt had been made. From this point the atmosphere became more and more tense – particularly as it appeared doubtful whether all the points to which Members sought an answer could properly be raised on the Censure Motion – and the scene is best described exactly as recorded in *Hansard*. The official report, even without the background of excitement and indignation, is fully adequate to explain the climax of suspension. Mr. Gaitskell's question appeared to spark off the ultimate explosion.

Hon. Members: Answer!
Mr. Speaker: Order, order.
Hon. Members: Answer!
Mrs. L. Jeger[86] rose –
Mr. Speaker: Order, order. I said just now that I was unwilling to extend my powers over an area over which I was not responsible, but I am responsible, as far as I can be, for securing that this House conducts its debates properly – (Interruption) – Order. Also, I am jealous for the reputation of the House – (Interruption) – It would be a very bad thing if we were to enter upon the very serious debate

[86] Lab., Holborn and St. Pancras.

which lies in front of us in an atmosphere of noisy interruption. I do hope that we can conduct ourselves, as this House always does on grave matters, with a proper sense of what is due to Parliament and to the House of Commons.

Hon. Members: Let the Government answer.

Mr. Gaitskell: We all appreciate, Mr. Speaker, the difficult position in which you find yourself. It is out of no disrespect to you that we must, and are determined, to press this matter. . . . It really is essential that the Government should give us a reply on this vital issue – of whether or not a declaration of war has been made or is to be made in the very near future. I appeal to the Prime Minister, if he has any control over the situation left at all, to make a statement.

The Prime Minister:[87] The right hon. Gentleman and his colleagues have put down a Motion of Censure –

Hon. Members: Answer the question.

The Prime Minister: – which they are perfectly entitled to do, and the Government speakers will deal with all aspects of the situation in reply to what they say.

Mr. Bevan: That is not the answer to the question. . . . Under the orders of the Government, British airmen, soldiers and sailors have been sent into action. If they are captured and no declaration of war has been made, what protection have they under international law?

Hon. Members: Answer!

The Prime Minister: The action which has been taken, as I explained yesterday, in accordance with the statement we made – (Interruption) – No further declaration has been made going beyond that.

Mr. Bevan: In my respectful submission, that is not the answer to the question which was put . . . an extremely serious one. We on this side of the House are desirous that the Government should have all the instruments of authority that a Government should have, and that nothing should be said, here or elsewhere, that would deny the Government the exercise of these instruments. However, they can only be exercised if the Government act in accordance with the sentiments and aspirations of the British people – (an hon. Member: 'With existing law') – with existing law. As we understand, at present British soldiers, sailors and airmen have been sent into action without the normal protection available to them. We want to know what protection they have should they fall into the hands of those against whom they are conducting hostile actions. Can we have an answer to that question, which has nothing –

Captain Pilkington[88] rose –

Mr. Bevan: I am on a point of Order.

Mr. Speaker: Order, order. I cannot have two Members on their feet at the same time. Would it not be possible for all these matters to be brought out in the course of the debate?

Hon. Members: No!

[87] Sir Anthony Eden.   [88] Cons., Poole.

Mr. Speaker: As I read the Motion it is in the widest possible terms. All these matters could be raised.

Hon. Members: No!

Mr. Bevan: They do not come within the Motion at all.

Mr. Speaker: I think that the Motion –

Hon. Members: No!

Mr. Gaitskell rose –

Mr. Speaker: Order. The Motion is a general one.

Hon. Members: No!

Mr. Speaker: If the House will not listen to me –

Hon. Members: No!

Mr. Speaker: – I will suspend the Sitting. (Interruption.) I have to inform the House that if it will not listen to me, I shall suspend the Sitting. (*Hon. Members:* 'Hear, hear.') That appears to some hon. Members to be a desirable course. I am certainly not going to have the Chair put in the position of not being heard in this House of Commons. The Sitting is suspended for half an hour.

Grave disorder having arisen in the House, Mr. Speaker, *pursuant to Standing Order No. 24 (Power of Mr. Speaker to adjourn House or suspend Sitting), suspended the Sitting of the House for half an hour.*

When the House reassembled at 4.27 p.m. Mr. Speaker said:

I would just like to say a word to the House. I understand and sympathise with the fact that on the issue which is about to be discussed opinions in the House are sharply divided and that hon. Members on both sides of the House feel a considerable degree of tension and excitement. With all that I sympathise. I am too old a Member of this House not to have endured the same feelings myself, but at the same time I am now by your leave elected to a position in which I have certain duties to discharge, and I hope that the remainder of this debate will proceed in a manner which is creditable to the House. That is my concern.

I would say – and I am the judge of what is relevant – that a large amount at least of what has been asked hitherto would be relevant to the debate, and I should never rule it out of order on the grounds of irrelevancy. I understand that there are points of elucidation still in the Minister's statement which it is desired to elucidate and that I certainly would allow; but I have to say to the House quite frankly that my sense of responsibility is so great that if disorder of this kind persists – I am sure that it will not now – I shall have no option but to adjourn the House.[89]

The half-hour suspension and Mr. Speaker's words did have a somewhat calming effect on the House. But Mr. Gaitskell again pressed his question relating to a declaration of war and the protection, if any, enjoyed by British Armed Forces. Sir Anthony Eden again asked to be allowed to answer in his forth-

[89] *H.C. Debates,* Vol. 558, cols. 1623–1626.

coming speech. (Hon. Members: 'No.') Mr. Gaitskell expressed
surprise and disappointment; he thought it would be far more
convenient to the House if there were an opportunity – (Hon.
Members: 'No.') – to put supplementary questions. The Prime
Minister again demurred, in view of the 'complicated legal
position in connection with the Geneva Convention'. There had
been no notice of Mr. Gaitskell's question – (Hon. Members:
'Oh.') – He agreed, however, in reply to a further question,
that he would certainly 'give way' in the course of his speech in
order to allow questions to be put. Mr. Gaitskell expressed
himself satisfied with this.

Further questions on matters of detail connected with the
military operations were asked by Mr. Callaghan[90] and Mr.
Strachey[91] and, at one moment, it appeared that tension might
again develop. Mr. Jay[92] asked whether, since there had been
no actual declaration of war, these operations did not 'amount
to an act of organised murder by the British Government'.
Several hon. Members rose.

Mr. Speaker: Order. I think that these questions have had a good
run. I cannot compel answers from Ministers. It is not my place to
do so. I am concerned only with the House. I will ask Mr. James
Griffiths to move the Opposition Motion.

But there were still two relatively minor points to clear up. Mrs.
Braddock asked whether Members whose firms were supplying
materials to Egypt would *declare their interest?* Mr. Speaker was
content to remind Mrs. Braddock that such questions must be
raised immediately after a Division. Finally, a Private Notice
Question, concerning the position of British civilians in Cairo,
too late for that day, was postponed.

At 4.41 p.m. Mr. James Griffiths[93] moved the Opposition
Censure Motion, deploring the use of armed force against
Egypt. The debate made clear that the House, like the country,
was fiercely and irreconcilably divided on the issue. Inevitably
the Motion was lost by 324 votes to 255 and a Government
Amendment carried by 323 votes to 255.

---

[90] Lab., Cardiff South-East.
[92] Lab., Battersea North.
[91] Lab., Dundee West.
[93] Lab., Llanelly.

3

THE OPENING OF A SESSION AND THE
DEBATE ON THE QUEEN'S SPEECH

THE Fourth Session of the Forty-First Parliament of the United Kingdom of Great Britain and Northern Ireland opened on October 28, 1958, in the seventh year of the reign of Her Majesty Queen Elizabeth II. It was the first occasion that the ceremonial opening of a parliamentary session had been televised.

The House of Commons met at 11 a.m., with the Speaker in the Chair. After Prayers, Black Rod came with the summons to the Commons to attend Her Majesty in the House of Lords. 'The House went, and, having returned, the Sitting was suspended until half past two in the afternoon.'

The first items of business were the Sessional Orders, couched in traditional phraseology. Members 'returned for two or more places' were ordered 'to make their Election for which of the places they will serve'; Peers of the Realm were formally denied the right to a parliamentary vote; persons guilty of corrupt practices or of tampering with witnesses or giving false evidence before the House or its Committees were threatened with proceedings 'of the utmost severity'; the Metropolitan Police were ordered to keep 'the passages through the streets leading to this House . . . free and open'; the Speaker was ordered to provide for the printing of Votes and Proceedings; and a Committee of Privileges was ordered to be appointed.

There followed the 'first reading' of the famous Bill 'for the more effective preventing of Clandestine Outlawries', and Orders for the printing of the Journal of the House.

Having thus asserted its right to give prior consideration to matters other than those referred to it by the Crown, the House turned its attention to the Queen's Speech.

Using time-honoured language, Mr. Speaker said:

I have to acquaint the House that this House has this day attended
Her Majesty in the House of Peers, and Her Majesty was pleased
to make a Most Gracious Speech from the Throne to both Houses
of Parliament, of which I have, for greater accuracy, obtained a
copy, which is as follows . . .

He then read the Speech, which dealt with the following main
topics: (1) Colonial development and welfare; (2) Malta and
Cyprus; (3) the pacification of the Middle East; (4) negotiations
for the suspension of nuclear tests and for disarmament; (5) the
maintenance of the strength of sterling and of a high and stable
level of employment; (6) assistance to small farmers and to the
fishing industry; (7) a new World Conference on the Law of the
Sea; (8) the social services, with special reference to National
Insurance and Education; (9) the increase in crime; (10) land
acquisition, home ownership and building regulations; (11)
economic controls. Legislation was promised for the assistance
of small farmers, for the protection and control of deer in
Scotland, for 'placing the National Insurance Scheme on a
sound financial basis and enabling a larger section of My People
to build up pension rights related to their earnings', for the
reform of the law relating to mental illness, for the conversion
of the Catering Wages Boards into Wages Councils, for improving 'the basis of compensation for compulsory acquisition
of land', for giving 'further encouragement to home ownership',
for providing for the 'future management of the New Towns',
for establishing 'a modern code for the general regulation of
building in Scotland', and for 'the continuance, for a temporary
period and in a restricted form, of certain economic controls
deriving from war-time emergency powers.'

The Debate on the Address was opened at 2.41 p.m. by Mr.
Peter Thomas,[1] who moved 'That an humble address be presented to Her Majesty as follows:

Most Gracious Sovereign, We, Your Majesty's most dutiful and
loyal subjects, the Commons of the United Kingdom of Great
Britain and Northern Ireland, in Parliament assembled, beg leave
to offer our humble thanks for the Gracious Speech which Your
Majesty has addressed to both Houses of Parliament'.

As is usual on these occasions, his speech was non-controversial,

[1] Cons., Conway.

felicitously phrased, and partly devoted to the praise of his constituency. As is also usual, he attempted to show that certain of the proposals contained in the Gracious Speech touched beneficially on the interests of his constituents. Thus,

There are parts of my constituency which join an area which has suffered for many years for a high percentage of unemployment. There are indigenous reasons for this, which makes it a particularly stubborn problem. I mention this because we in Wales have personal knowledge of the sadness of unemployment and the expression in the Gracious Speech of the Government's determination to ensure a stable level of employment is particularly welcomed.

The motion was seconded in similar style by Mr. David Price.[2] After dwelling a little on the characteristics of his constituency, he said:

Residentially, we are becoming increasingly a dormitory for Southampton, which creates, in what were once quiet Hampshire villages, particular problems both for the older residents and for the local authorities. That is why we welcome especially the reference in the Gracious Speech to improving the basis of compensation for the compulsory acquisition of land. Most of the victims of compulsory purchase orders in the Eastleigh division are small proprietors, who can ill afford anything less than the full market value.

After demonstrating that various other proposals contained in the Speech were advantageous to his constituents, Mr. Price concluded with a few general remarks about the cultural aspects of industrialism, the occasion for which was the suggestion that hon. Members might feel that the inhabitants of Eastleigh were 'too obsessed with the science and the craft of manufacture'.

Even after Mr. Gaitskell had risen to state the case of the Opposition, these traditional preliminaries had not been brought to an end, for the Leader of the Opposition, as was expected of him, devoted the first few paragraphs of his speech to congratulating the two Government back-benchers who had moved and seconded the Address. He then got down to the business of opposition by saying – presumably with the purpose of dispelling any illusions that the televising of the Opening Ceremony might have created – that the greater part of the Speech was

---

[2] Cons., Eastleigh.

a rather unimpressive statement of stale platitudes and a dull catalogue of mostly minor legislation which nobody in their senses could possibly associate with Her Majesty the Queen.

On matters of foreign policy, to which he first turned, he said that, although there was to be a whole day devoted to foreign affairs during the Debate on the Address, events in the Middle East were of such 'immense importance' that they merited some immediate attention from him. He then criticised the Government's policy towards the Arab states and expressed his deep regret at 'the failure of Her Majesty's Government to follow up the offer of Archbishop Makarios that he was prepared, rather surprisingly . . . to throw over Enosis'.

Turning to the 'home front', Mr. Gaitskell welcomed the 'non-controversial' legislation proposed, and particularly the decision to give statutory implementation to the recommendations of the Royal Commission on Mental Illness. He was also glad that reference had been made to the increase in crime, which was such an important subject that the Opposition had suggested

that Friday might be set aside for a debate upon it in a constructive spirit, so that all hon. Members who wish to do so may make their contributions to the solution of that difficult but extremely important problem.

Of all the other measures proposed by the Speech he was critical, and he was especially censorious of the Government's alleged lack of concern with the expansion of production, which he considered to be 'the central issue facing the country'.

He was followed by the Prime Minister, who, after making complimentary remarks about the mover and seconder of the Address, informed the House that the 'usual arrangements' were being made 'for the debate on the Address and for private Members' time'.

No doubt [he said] the House may hope to hear from you, Mr. Speaker, about the former, and the Leader of the House will propose a Motion about the latter tomorrow.

He began his defence of the Government's proposals by saying that the 'Gracious Speech foreshadowed a very full programme of work'.

There is no tailing off, no diminution of energies, no weariness of office, no unseemly scuttle from power and responsibility. As far as one great category of domestic affairs is concerned, one category of home affairs, there is a sentence in the Gracious Speech which exactly describes the Government's purpose: we will continue our efforts 'to secure a just balance between the expanding demands of the modern State and the freedom and status of the individual'.

Although Mr. Macmillan spoke for over an hour and a half, he said comparatively little about the proposed legislation, except by way of general answers to Mr. Gaitskell's general criticisms of it. He dealt at somewhat greater length, and much more specifically, with the Government's economic policy, the main aim of which, he held, was to maintain what the Gracious Speech had termed 'a high and stable level of employment'.

Most of the remainder – and by far the greater part – of the Prime Minister's speech was occupied with foreign affairs. Concluding, he said:

... this Parliament opened today opens, in my view, in an atmosphere of confidence and hope. The Government will continue to deal with all these problems at home and overseas in a reasonable and balanced way, with energy but without panic, with moderation but with resolution. In this task we believe that we can count on the support of both Parliament and the nation.

The rest of the day's debate was occupied by back-benchers, who took advantage of the opportunities which this occasion annually affords them to talk, with comparatively few inhibitions arising from the Rules of Order, on the subjects in which they were particularly interested. Mr. Lipton[3] chose house-purchase, superannuation, West Indian immigration, the betting laws, the Wolfenden Report on Prostitution and Homosexuality, arrangements for the Lord Mayor's Show, subliminal advertising, and damage caused by cattle to the public highways. Many other contributors were equally diffuse, or versatile, and dealt with subjects ranging from 'the application of advanced science to the needs of mankind' to the improvement of rural bus services. Others – wisely, one might have thought – confined themselves to one or two subjects of which they felt that they had special knowledge. Mr. Rankin,[4] for instance, dealt exclusively with the affairs of Scotland, and Mr. Allaun[5] with nuclear disarmament. Some showed an anxiety to introduce as many points as possible which would be of special

[3] Lab., Brixton.   [4] Lab., Glasgow, Govan.
[5] Lab., Salford East.

interest to their constituents. The order of these contributions depended on the order in which the various Members 'caught the Speaker's eye', and although many Members were polite enough to refer to their predecessors' views, few made much serious attempt to 'follow on', for that would have involved, in the majority of cases, the sacrifice of prepared speeches.

When it reassembled at 2.30 on the following day, October 29, a New Writ was moved for East Aberdeenshire, consequent upon the former Member's elevation to the House of Peers, and six new Bills were presented and 'read' for the first time. A motion on the 'Business of the House', presented by Mr. R. A. Butler, the Leader, provided for the order of precedence of Government and Private Members' business, and for the holding of the ballots for 'unofficial Members' Bills' and 'unofficial Members' Notices of Motion'.

On the resumption of the Debate on the Address, the Speaker made the following statement, informing Members of the arrangements to which the Party Whips had agreed 'behind his chair':

Before we proceed with the debate before us, it might be for the convenience of the House if I say a few words about what I understand the future course of the debate is to be. I understand that it is desired that today's debate should be of a general nature. Tomorrow, Thursday, it is desired to deal with foreign and colonial affairs, and on Friday with the subject of the increase of crime.

Of course, on all these days the Question proposed from the Chair will be the general Question on the Address. The debate is to be continued on Monday and Tuesday. At the moment there is only one Amendment on the Order Paper, but I have no doubt there will be more; but I had better defer anything I have to say about these Amendments until I have seen them.

After a point of Order from Mrs. Braddock[6] about the allocation of tickets for the opening of Parliament had been amicably dealt with, Mr. James Griffiths[7] opened up for the Labour front bench with a forty-minute speech covering the whole field of domestic policy. He was followed, for the Government, by the Minister of Pensions and National Insurance,[8] who devoted nearly the whole of an equally long speech, rather frequently interrupted, to an exposition of the Government's superannuation scheme. Mr. Grimond[9] then made a general

[6] Lab., Liverpool Exchange.
[7] Lab., Llanelly.
[8] Mr. John Boyd-Carpenter.
[9] Lib., Orkney and Shetland.

criticism, from the Liberal point of view, of the content of the Gracious Speech. The remainder of the day's debate, during which 'constituency points' were well in evidence, was as diffuse as the previous day's. On its adjournment, at ten o'clock, Mr. R. E. Prentice[10] moved a 'prayer'[11] for the annulment of the National Insurance (Industrial Injuries) (Prescribed Diseases) Amendment Regulations, 1958.[12] After just over an hour's debate, the Question was put, negatived without a Division, and the House accordingly adjourned at 11.8 p.m.

The first business on the following day was the nomination of the Committee of Selection, the membership of which had, of course, already been agreed upon privately. The day being a Thursday,[13] Mr. Gaitskell then asked the Leader of the House to state the business for the next week, which Mr. Butler accordingly did. He agreed with a suggestion from Mr. Gaitskell for a debate before Christmas on the Government's White Paper on Pensions, in view of the fact that the Pensions Bill would not be introduced 'for some time'. In response to Mr. Butler's request that the Speaker 'might be good enough to indicate to the House which Amendment or Amendments' to the Gracious Speech he proposed to call and the days on which they would be taken, the Speaker announced that he proposed to select for discussion 'that standing in the name of the right hon. Gentleman, the Leader of the Opposition', which ran:

but noting with concern that the policies of Your Majesty's Government have led to a fall in industrial production, a continuing increase in unemployment and a failure to make full use of our industrial capacity, humbly regrets the omission from the Gracious Speech of any measures directed towards the expansion of production and employment while maintaining stable prices.

This, he said, was an Amendment of wide scope embracing the contents of some of the other Amendments which had been tabled. It was for the House to see how long it wished to discuss the Amendment, but if the debate went on for the two days it seemed to him that it would be 'very wide and useful'.

Mr. Silverman[14] then rose to draw the Speaker's attention to another amendment, standing in the names of some of his hon. friends and himself, which ran:

---

[10] Lab., East Ham North. [11] *See* below, pp. 203–205.
[12] S.I. 1958, No. 1068. [13] *See* 'The Business of the Week', pp. 61–67.
[14] Lab., Nelson and Colne.

but humbly regret that the Gracious Speech contains no proposals either for solving the most urgent problems of the cotton industry in Lancashire or for the provision of additional or alternative industries, so that Your Majesty's loyal subjects in that county may be enabled to earn their livelihood by their labour and thus make their contribution to the well-being of the nation.

In view of the possibility that this 'urgent' subject might not be given sufficient attention in the debate on Mr. Gaitskell's amendment, Mr. Silverman asked the Speaker to consider 'this aspect of the matter before finally deciding whether the Amendment ought to be called or not'. The Speaker replied that it had 'occurred' to him that the subject was an important one, but he thought that it 'was really included in the wider terms of the Leader of the Opposition's Amendment' and that 'it was not at all likely that the condition of the cotton industry would escape attention in a debate on the economic situation of the country'.

After dealing formally with the gift of a Speaker's Chair to the Parliament of Ghana, giving a 'first reading' to a Bill to amend the Factories Acts of 1937 and 1948, and agreeing to a proposal, supported, in brief speeches, by the three party leaders, to erect a monument to Viscount Trenchard, the House resumed the Debate on the Address. As arranged, this third day of the debate was devoted to foreign affairs. The discussion that followed, which was opened by the Foreign Secretary, Mr. Selwyn Lloyd, for the Government, and by Mr. Aneurin Bevan[15], for the Opposition, covered a wide field and engaged the attention of the foreign affairs 'experts' on both sides of the House, but was of no particular interest to students of parliamentary procedure. The House then appointed a Committee of Privileges, a Select Committee on Statutory Instruments and a Select Committee on Nationalised Industries (Reports and Accounts). On the Adjournment Motion, Mr. John Stonehouse[16] raised the subject of the White Highlands in Kenya. The Under-Secretary of State for the Colonies replied, and the House rose at 10.32 p.m.

On the following day, Friday, October 31, the House met at 11 a.m., and having 'read' for the first time the Building (Scotland) Bill, resumed the Debate on the Address. As

---

arranged, the theme of the day's debate was provided by the following sentences in the Gracious Speech:

My Government view with gravity the increase in crime. In the light of the most up-to-date knowledge and research they will seek to improve the penal system and to make methods of dealing with offenders more effective.

The opening speaker, Mr. Gordon Walker,[17] adopted the serious, non-party manner which was to characterise most of the remainder of the day's proceedings. Only at one point in his speech did he make a little party propaganda, when he praised the Home Secretary 'on standing up so well to his supporters when, at the Blackpool Conference, they were baying for blood and wanting the return of the gallows and whip'. Such rank-and-file opinion, he averred, was 'a natural handicap for a Conservative Home Secretary, from which a Labour Home Secretary would be exempt'.

When the debate had been in progress for just over fifty minutes, the Secretary of State for the Home Department and Lord Privy Seal[18] intervened. After saying that 'nobody could take any possible exception to the tone in which the right hon. Gentleman for Smethwick introduced this subject', and thanking the two other previous speakers for their contributions, he proceeded to give the House an analysis of recent criminal statistics, a critical review of existing methods of dealing with the criminal, and an outline of the Government's attitude. 'I hope,' he said during the course of his concluding remarks,

that these indications of how we intend in future to deal with adults and young offenders, together with the determination to spend, by degrees, some more of the nation's money in this sphere of action, will show the House that the Government mean business. I shall be only too glad to listen to the whole of this debate and take note of any constructive ideas. My hon. Friend the Member for Gravesend gave several good examples, including his references to the possible use of marriage guidance and psychiatric treatment. I shall be very glad to listen to hon. Members' constructive ideas. That is the object of this debate. It will enable me, when I come forward later with ideas, to be all the better advised by the House.

Back-bench contributors to the debate could be broadly divided into (a) 'experts', i.e., those with some special knowledge and experience of crime and its treatment, such as Miss

---

[17] Lab., Smethwick.   [18] Mr. R. A. Butler.

Joan Vickers, [19]a social welfare worker, and Col. Richard H. Glyn,[20] a magistrate; (*b*) Members, such as Mr. Godfrey Lagden,[21] in whose constituencies certain criminal tendencies seemed to be much in evidence; and (*c*) Members who, while claiming neither expertise nor a 'constituency' interest, had general ideas about the treatment of crime which they wished to try out on the House and the Home Office.

Winding up for the Opposition, Mr. Anthony Greenwood[22] covered the whole field of the debate, with plenty of references to the remarks of previous speakers. He was followed by the Joint Under-Secretary of State for the Home Department,[23] who congratulated the Opposition 'on having chosen this subject' and said that his right hon. Friend the Home Secretary was 'grateful for the interest which had been shown, very often deep and expert interest, by so many hon. Members in all quarters of the House'. After promising consideration for the various proposals that Members had made, Mr. Renton concluded by saying:

There are many other points to which I should have attempted to reply. I assure hon. Members that all they have said will be more carefully considered. To the extent that this is necessary, I will write to those to whom I have not been able to reply today.

The debate was then adjourned, and the House itself, after setting up a Select Committee on Procedure and 'concurring' with a Lords' resolution on the referring of Consolidation Bills to a Joint Committee of both Houses, adjourned at four o'clock.

On Monday, November 3, it reassembled at 2.30, formally read for the third time the Manchester Corporation Bill, and then devoted the usual hour to Questions. The resumed debate on the Address, which began at 3.37, was on the Opposition's Amendment.[24] This debate, of course, was entirely different in character from that on the increase in crime. The Opposition had selected its front for attack in the light of an approaching election, being clearly of the opinion that the Government's economic policy was the issue on which this contest would most likely be won or lost. Labour's economic 'big guns' were therefore brought fully into action. The 'shadow Chancellor of

[19] Cons., Plymouth, Devonport.
[20] Cons., Dorset North.
[21] Cons., Hornchurch.
[22] Lab., Rossendale.
[23] Mr. David Renton.
[24] *See* above, p. 50.

the Exchequer', Mr. Harold Wilson,[25] moved the Amendment, and on the second day it was supported by Mr. Alfred Robens[26] and the Leader of the Opposition, Mr. Gaitskell.[27] For the Government, the burden of the day was sustained by the Chancellor of the Exchequer, Mr. Derick Heathcoat Amory, the Minister of Labour and National Service, Mr. Iain Macleod, the President of the Board of Trade, Sir David Eccles, and the Home Secretary and Leader of the House, Mr. R. A. Butler.

From the standpoint of the student of parliamentary procedure, it is of some interest to discover how far, in this two days' debate, the point about the Lancashire textile industry, on which Mr. Silverman had been refused a separate Amendment, was given an adequate airing, as the Speaker had virtually promised it would be.

Neither Mr. Wilson nor Mr. Heathcoat Amory, who followed him, made any mention of it, being almost exclusively concerned with what is sometimes known as 'over-all' economic strategy. Nor did the first back-bench speaker, Mr. Frederick Lee,[28] say much about it, apart from asking the Chancellor to come and see how people were suffering in the 'Lancashire cotton area' and in Wales and Scotland 'as a result of the change of Government policy from that followed by the Labour Government'. Several more speeches followed, most of them general but one dealing with the economic situation in Northern Ireland, before Mr. Silverman caught the Speaker's eye at 6.45 p.m. Most of his speech, which lasted until 7.14 p.m., was devoted to Lancashire's plight, and the Government back-bencher who followed him, Mr. Fort,[29] occupied another ten minutes or so with this subject, offering mildly phrased and rather vague criticisms of the Government's policy towards the cotton industry. Miss Margaret Herbison[30] then shifted the field of battle to Scotland, while Mr. Douglas Marshall,[31] after certain general remarks, chose to draw attention to the special needs of Cornwall. Mr. H. Boardman[32] returned to Lancashire, very naturally combining his remarks about the textile industry with a general criticism of the Government's employment policy (8.10–8.24 p.m.). For the next contributor, the Speaker chose

[25] Lab., Lancashire, Huyton.
[27] Lab., Leeds South.
[29] Cons., Clitheroe.
[31] Cons., Bodmin.

[26] Lab., Blyth.
[28] Lab., Newton.
[30] Lab., Lanarkshire North.
[32] Lab., Leigh.

Mr. G. R. Howard,[33] who talked mainly about the Icelandic fisheries dispute. Dr. J. Dickson Mabon[34] found it 'rather difficult to follow' the hon. Member, as he wanted to talk about unemployment in Scotland, which he did for sixteen minutes. Mr. Williams,[35] as befitted the Member for Sunderland South, talked about shipbuilding, and Mr. Thomas Fraser,[36] after some general criticism of the Government, returned to the woes of Scotland in a speech which lasted thirty-three minutes. Winding up the debate on the first day, Mr. Macleod announced that when it was resumed the President of the Board of Trade would deal 'in some detail' with the Amendment on the Cotton Industry.

On the following day, the President[37] was the first speaker, and gave to the cotton industry rather more than one-third of a forty-minute speech, in which, according to Mr. Robens, he was at his 'scintillating best'. Mr. Robens himself made only an incidental reference to cotton, on which he said that Mr. Silverman had expressed the Labour Party's feelings 'perfectly well'. In the remainder of the debate, the subject occupied (1) just over half of a seventeen-minute speech by Sir John Barlow,[38] (2) a few sentences in a speech by Mr. Douglas Glover,[39] (3) a sentence or two in Mr. Gaitskell's winding-up speech, and (4) a paragraph in Mr. Butler's winding-up speech. In all, cotton claimed the attention of the House for just over an hour in a debate which lasted nine hours and forty minutes. Even though this was a small proportion of the total time, Mr. Silverman and his Lancashire colleagues could hardly complain of unfair treatment – nor did they do so. Several Lancashire members succeeded in catching the Speaker's eye, and the President of the Board of Trade dealt fairly fully with their complaints. Obviously, in a debate covering the whole field of economic policy, there was no possibility of dealing with the Lancashire cotton industry in a coherent way, for speeches about it, as we have seen, were mixed up with speeches about quite different subjects. This tends to be characteristic of the Debate on the Address, except when the Opposition puts down for discussion some clearly defined and limited theme, such as

[33] Cons., St. Ives.
[35] Cons.
[37] Sir David Eccles.
[39] Cons., Ormskirk.

[34] Lab., Greenock.
[36] Lab., Hamilton.
[38] Cons., Middleton and Prestwich.

the increase in crime. Mr. Silverman and his colleagues were anxious that Lancashire should be given this advantage, but so, no doubt, were Members from constituencies in other areas, such as Scotland, Wales and the Tyneside, suffering from a higher-than-average rate of unemployment. It was clearly one of the Speaker's objects to give the greatest possible opportunity for making 'area' and 'constituency' points, which back-benchers are nearly always anxious to do whenever a suitable subject is under discussion, and it cannot be said that either Lancashire or the other areas with special problems failed to get a fair crack of the whip, within the context of a two-day debate covering a very wide field.

At the end of the first day of the economic policy debate (November 3), the House appointed its 'Kitchen' Committee. At the end of the second day (November 4) it divided (255–324) on the Amendment, after which it resolved that the humble Address should be presented to Her Majesty 'by Privy Councillors or Members of Her Majesty's Household'. The House then formally established the two Committees of the Whole House, Supply and Ways and Means, to deal with financial matters, and discussed 'the Trial of William Jordan' on the half-hour Adjournment Motion.

The following day (November 5) it received a report from the Vice-Chamberlain of the Household of the following Answer by Her Majesty to the Address:

I have received with great satisfaction the loyal and dutiful expression of your thanks for the Speech with which I opened the present Session of Parliament.

Proceedings in connection with the Gracious Speech were thus concluded.

4

BUSINESS ARRANGEMENTS

1. THE BUSINESS OF A SESSION

WEDNESDAY, November 7, 1956, was the occasion of the second day's debate on the Queen's Speech. The House met at 2.30 p.m., and after Prayers, one private notice Question, three ministerial statements (on the Situation in the Middle East, Oil Supplies, and Hungary), and the formal first readings of four Bills, the Lord Privy Seal[1] moved a resolution on the Business of the House for the remainder of the Session.

This gave Government Business precedence at every sitting except as otherwise provided. Private Members' Bills (described as Public Bills other than Government Bills) were to have precedence over Government Business on ten Fridays, distributed between December 7 and June 28. 'Unofficial Members' Notices of Motion and unofficial Members' Bills' were to have precedence 'in that order' on another ten Fridays, distributed between November 30 and May 31. The other clauses of the resolution dealt with notices of motion, ballots for notices of motion, and the order of business on Private Members' Bills.

This Motion [commented Mr. Butler] is somewhat long, but it is simple in form. It carries out the recommendations of the Select Committee of 1946 to the effect that twenty days should be reserved for private Members' business. Ten Fridays will be for Bills and ten for Motions, and of the ten days for Bills, six will be reserved for Second Readings, and four for the later stages which will have priority. Thus we are attempting to preserve, according to tradition, the business of private Members.[2]

Under more normal circumstances this resolution would have provoked little discussion. On this occasion, however, the House

[1] Mr. Butler.   [2] *H.C. Debates*, Vol. 560, cols. 119–120.

could not be allowed to forget that a very important Private Member's Bill had been passed the previous session and rejected by the Lords – the Death Penalty Abolition Bill, promoted by Mr. Sidney Silverman.[3] Mr. Silverman, therefore, had a reasonable case for being given a special allocation of time for its reintroduction, and asked for this by moving an amendment, adding to the last paragraph of the resolution, which in effect restricted the right of bringing in Bills to successful balloters, the following words:

unless such . . . Bill shall be concerned with legislation having for its principal object the abolition of the death penalty.

Mr. Silverman began by saying that, in normal circumstances, the principle embodied in the Leader of the House's resolution 'would be absolutely right and unchallengable'.

The purpose of it is to ensure that no private Member of Parliament shall jump the queue. Since the House is giving its consent to a ballot system, in which each of us who wishes to share in it has an equal place and an equal right, it would be very wrong to allow any private Member, in anticipation of that machinery, to get some kind of priority on the Order Paper or some lien on Parliamentary time in advance of the lottery which is to take place.

The Bill with which his amendment was concerned, however, was 'no longer really private Members' legislation at all', for two reasons, viz., (1) that the House had already decided in favour of it, on a free vote, and (2) that the policy contained in it 'ought now, according to the Government's declaration, to be Government policy'.

Elaborating the latter point, Mr. Silverman said that, in a debate preceding the Second Reading of his Bill, Mr. Butler had stated

that the House must make up its mind very responsibly indeed just because the Government expected to base their policy on what the House of Commons has decided.

The House of Commons decided [he continued] and I think I am entitled to say that the Government cannot honour the pledge which they then gave without making the principle of that Bill their own policy. Consequently, the principle of the Measure goes right outside the run of Private Members' Bills.

If the Government preferred not to take over the measure

[3] Lab., Nelson and Colne.

themselves, but to give private Members 'the responsibility of seeing it through the House of Commons again', he would have no objection;

but they must not now seek to go back to the position that obtained twelve months ago, and in those circumstances to treat the Death Penalty (Abolition) Bill as if it were *de novo*, a new Private Member's Bill, liable to take its place with other Private Members' Bills in the Ballot. That would be a total repudiation of every pledge which the Government gave on that occasion.

What the Government was in fact trying to do was something completely alien to its constitutional function – to act as a 'kind of arbiter' between the Commons and the Lords.[4] The duty of the Government was to the House of Commons, and if there was a conflict of opinion between the two Houses,

the Government must at least provide the House of Commons with the necessary time so that the House . . . can decide for itself whether it wishes to avail itself of its rights under the Parliament Act or not.

It was the purpose of the Amendment to enable the Government thus to do its duty.

Mr. Silverman was seconded by Mr. Montgomery Hyde[5] and supported by Mr. Wedgwood Benn[6] and Mr. Hector Hughes.[7]

Mr. Butler declined to accept the Amendment, on the grounds that the House ought to 'adhere to the traditional handling of Private Members' business'. If the Amendment were passed, he said,

we should not be able to keep faith with other Private Members who might have other Bills relating to other subjects which we should have to treat in a similar way.

The Government, moreover, were introducing their own Homicide Bill, 'which represented the greatest maximum measure of consent'. He advised Members to 'read and examine' this when it was published the following morning. Taking his stand on the letter of the law, he then said:

That does not affect the order in relation to Private Members' Bills; it does not affect the operation of a Private Member's Bill, namely the Death Penalty (Abolition) Bill, which may be brought in under Ballot; and it does not affect the operation of the Parliament Act, because there is nothing in the bringing forward of a Government

[4] *i.e.*, by introducing its own Homicide Bill (*see* below).   [5] Cons., Belfast.
[6] Lab., Bristol South-East.   [7] Lab., Aberdeen North.

Bill which affects the operation of the Parliament Act in relation to a Private Member's Bill relating to the death penalty.

To Mr. Silverman's interjections, 'What about the time?' and 'If it gets a place in the ballot', Mr. Butler's replies were lengthy and evasive. Challenged again by Mr. Hughes, he produced the following:

It is not wrong for a Government to put forward a constructive line on these matters, particularly when many prominent leaders of the Government, including the Home Secretary, myself and others, spoke against the abolition of the death penalty. This is still a free country, and it is quite possible for the Government to put forward a constructive view. As has been stated by the Prime Minister, there is a possibility, and indeed I think the likelihood, of a Bill being put forward by a private Member for the abolition of the death penalty. It will be extremely intriguing to see what the final position of the House of Commons is.

He then made it clear, amid interruption, that, whereas there would be a free vote on any Private Member's Bill that might be introduced, there would be no free vote on the Government's Homicide Bill. What would happen if there was no Private Member's Bill he refused to surmise. At this point a new Member, Mr. D. Howell,[8] rather understandably asked for the Speaker's guidance.

Suppose the Government [he said] passed their Bill through on Second Reading and that my hon. Friend the Member for Nelson and Colne,[9] or another of my hon. Friends, is successful in the Ballot and a Death Penalty (Abolition) Bill passes its Second Reading on a free vote, we shall then have before us two Second Readings of contradictory principles. What will then be the position of the House of Commons?

The Speaker replied:

That is a hypothetical situation about which I cannot give an answer today. I have not seen the Government Bill and know nothing about its contents.

Mr. Butler, refusing to be drawn further, said finally:

Nothing I have said today has prejudged the final issue. All I have said is that we cannot make an exception for a particular Private Member's Bill in moving this Motion to reserve twenty days for Private Members' business. That is what I have said. The rest will depend on the result of the Bill and the opinion of the House of

[8] Lab., Birmingham, All Saints.   [9] Mr. Silverman.

Commons. We are all ruled by the opinion of the House of Commons. I am only asking hon. Members now to decide the simple issue whether we can make an exception for one Bill.

Mr. Silverman, while continuing to express his dissatisfaction, then withdrew his Amendment because he 'did not think it would be right to divide the House on an issue which in principle went beyond the merits of the broad question it was discussing'; and the Resolution was put and agreed to. Thus ended a peculiarly complicated discussion on an announcement of the session's business.

2. THE BUSINESS OF THE WEEK

On Thursdays, immediately after Questions and in response to a request from the Opposition, the Leader of the House normally announces the Business for the coming week. This has been preceded, of course, by consultations through the 'usual channels', but the Opposition often uses the occasion to make further representations, and private Members regard it as an opportunity to demand of the Government time for debates on subjects near to their hearts.

On November 15, 1956, the Leader, Mr. Butler, announced the business for the following week thus:

Monday, 19 *November* – Second Reading of the Air Corporations Bill.
Committee stage of the necessary Money Resolution, which it is hoped to obtain by 7.30 p.m.
Committee stage of the Ways and Means Resolution relating to Customs Duties (Dumping and Subsidies).
Consideration of Motions to approve the Registration of Restrictive Trading Agreements Order; and of the Draft Census of Distribution (1958) (Restriction of Disclosure) Order.
Tuesday, 20 *November* – Consideration of Motions for Addresses to continue in force for a further year certain Emergency Legislation and Regulations. The Motions are already on the Order Paper.
Committee and remaining stages of the Expiring Laws Continuance Bill.
Consideration of the Double Taxation Relief (Austria) Order.
Wednesday, 21 *November, and Thursday*, 22 *November* – Second Reading of the Rent Bill.
Committee stage of the necessary Money Resolution.
At the end of business on Thursday we shall also ask the House to take the Report stage of the Ways and Means Resolution relating to Customs Duties, so that the Bill may be brought in.
Friday, 23 *November* – Committee and remaining stages of the Air Corporations Bill; and of the Agriculture (Silo Subsidies) Bill.

To a request from Mr. J. Griffiths[10] for 'consultations, through the usual channels, to provide, in the week after next, adequate time' for discussing the Prayers that the Opposition had tabled against the Statutory Instruments giving effect to increased prescription charges under the National Health Service, Mr. Butler replied:

I anticipated that there might be such a request. I will deal with it in the usual way.

He then declined to give an assurance to a Scottish Member, Mr. T. Fraser,[11] that the part of the Rent Bill applying solely to Scotland should be sent to the Scottish Grand Committee. This had been done with the Teachers (Superannuation) Bill, but such a 'surgical operation' was 'much more difficult in the case of the Rent Bill'. He would, however, discuss it with his right hon. Friend, the Secretary of State for Scotland.

In answer to Mr. Nabarro's[12] request for an 'early debate' on the common-market proposals, he said he 'thought' that that debate would take place in the week after next.

Mr. Harold Wilson[13] then referred to a subject, the Suez War, which was incomparably the greatest *casus belli* between Government and Opposition at that time, by asking:

In view of . . . concern . . . about the economic effects of recent international events, will the Lord Privy Seal say whether he expects the Chancellor of the Exchequer will be able to make a statement on that subject early next week, following the failure of both Ministers to give any information whatever in last Monday's debate?

Mr. Butler replied that he thought the statements already made were 'not only adequate but comprehensive'.

Mr. Robens[14] followed by asking if any arrangements had been made for a statement to the House on the 'present situation in the Middle East'. Mr. Butler agreed that such a statement would be advantageous, and hoped to be able to arrange for one to be made 'in the earlier part of next week'.

Mr. Mitchison[15] reverted to the Scottish part of the Rent Bill, drawing from the Lord Privy Seal a repetition of his assurance that he would discuss the matter with the Secretary of State for Scotland.

[10] Lab., Llanelly.
[12] Cons., Kidderminster.
[14] Lab., Blyth.

[11] Lab., Lanarkshire, Hamilton.
[13] Lab., Lancashire, Huyton.
[15] Lab., Northamptonshire, Kettering.

In reply to Mr. N. Pannell,[16] he said he could give no definite date for the discussion of the Gold Coast Independence Bill, but would inform his hon. Friend 'as soon as he was aware of it'.

Another reference, by Mr. M. Stewart,[17] to the Scottish part of the Rent Bill, produced only a slightly facetious reply.

Mr. Bellenger[18] then raised a rather important point about announcements of the House's business.

With reference to the notice which the right hon. Gentleman gave to . . . [Mr. Nabarro] about business not for next week but for the week afterwards, may I ask the right hon. Gentleman to be very careful about departing from the custom which, as his predecessor often told us, was to give notice on an occasion such as this only of the business for the next week. What the right hon. Gentleman may have done, under the fourteen-day rule, is to prevent any discussion on the air of the subject to which the hon. Member . . . referred in his impromptu question.

Mr. Butler thought that there was 'some substance' in this point, but chose to extract minor party advantage from it by saying:

The trouble is that the Government is so far seeing that we look a long way ahead.

He nevertheless thought that, 'under the circumstances', he had better make 'no prognostication at all' about the occasion for discussing the Australian Trade Agreement, on which he was questioned by another Member.

The Business of the House concluded with the raising, for party purposes, of what was an obviously bogus point of Order. (This, as we have noted, is frequently done, treated with considerable tolerance, and not necessarily to the discredit of the perpetrator.) Mr. Lewis[19] asked thus for 'guidance' from the Speaker:

As you know, it is a rule of the House that before hon. Members vote on a matter from which they may have direct financial or pecuniary advantage they should declare their interest. As, next week, we are to have the Rents Bill before us, and many hon. Members opposite are directors of property companies – in one case of forty companies – and will directly benefit, will you tell the House what action those hon. Members should take? Should they abstain or declare their interest before the Second Reading of the Bill?

[16] Cons., Liverpool, Kirkdale.
[17] Lab., Fulham.
[18] Lab., Northamptonshire, Bassetlaw.
[19] Lab., West Ham North.

To this piece of sniping the Speaker replied:

I have frequently stated the rule. The interest to disallow a vote must be direct and peculiar to the person himself and not shared with other members of Her Majesty's subjects in a similar position, nor must it be a matter of State policy. The rule has been clear for a hundred years. It is for hon. Members to obey the rules as they stand.

On being asked by Mr. Hamilton[20] whether it was not anomalous 'that hon. Members of the House of Commons could vote where they had an interest, but that a councillor in a local authority who lived in a council house was not allowed to vote', the Speaker declined to involve himself in 'municipal matters'.

The week's business does not, of course, invariably follow the Government's plan. An accepted 'urgency adjournment' motion, for instance, can alter the projected pattern of a day's debating. Rather more frequently, the main business of the day may begin later than was intended, because the Government finds it necessary to occupy time after Questions with a statement on a matter of current public importance. Such a statement cannot give rise to a debate (unless it becomes the subject of an accepted 'urgency' motion) but it can, if sufficiently controversial, produce extended questioning.

This happened on the Thursday of the following week (November 24), when Mr. Butler made a statement on the Situation in the Middle East, which, with the many Questions to which it gave rise, occupied more than half an hour of the House's time. This statement was preceded by the normal 'Business of the House' announcement that the Leader makes on a Thursday, and this announcement, in its turn, was preceded by what Mr. Gaitskell described as an 'uproar' over a Question about 'Suez'. Thus not only was the planned business of the House delayed, but the 'Business of the House' announcement itself, on this occasion, uncomfortably sandwiched between two heated exchanges on substantially the same subject. As is almost inevitable in such circumstances, the matter which was most occupying Members' minds tended to 'spill over' into 'Business of the House'.

Mr. Gaitskell took the opportunity to say that the Opposition was 'by no means satisfied' with the answers that the Leader had just given and to ask 'whether he was aware' that it was

[20] Lab., Fife West.

likely to want to debate the international situation the following week. Mr. Lewis again gave one of his characteristic 'political' twists to procedural and business matters by asking:

On business, will the right hon. Gentleman, sometime next week, categorically deny that the Prime Minister was informed on 16 October by the French Prime Minister of the intended Israeli attack on Egypt?

Mr. Wedgwood Benn took the opportunity, on an alleged point of Order, to ask for the Speaker's 'guidance' on the situation that had developed at Question Time, when the Lord Privy Seal had preceded each of his answers with the words 'I have been asked to reply' and had then answered on behalf of the Prime Minister or Foreign Secretary, without specifically associating himself with the answer's content. According to Mr. Wedgwood Benn, this raised the 'question of Cabinet responsibility' – but his real object in ventilating the matter, one may reasonably surmise, was not to protect the honour of the British Constitution, but to widen any possible split in the Conservatives' ministerial ranks. At any rate, the Speaker said that he did not think that any point of Order had been raised, and carefully explained the custom of the House in respect of the transference of Questions from one Minister to another. After Mr. Butler had assured the House that his words represented the views of 'a collective and united Government', several Members rose, presumably to continue the attack. The Speaker, however, by calling for Order and saying that it seemed to him that the House had 'passed from business altogether', brought the discussion to a close.

In all this excitement, other matters on Business of the House might easily have been overlooked; but three Members were pertinacious enough to ask the Leader about items of business which had nothing to do with 'Suez'. Mr. Fraser raised once more the matter of the Scottish Grand Committee and the Rent Act, to be informed that discussions were still continuing and that the decision would be conveyed 'through the usual channels'. Mr. Gower[21] asked whether machinery existed through which a Bill for the flooding of part of a valley in North Wales could be discussed by a Welsh Grand Committee, and received a promise that this 'technical point' would be looked

---

[21] Cons., Barry, Glamorganshire.

into. Mr. Silverman asked why the Committee Stage of the Homicide Bill had been so long delayed, and whether there would be a free vote on Part II of the Bill, and received a reply which he could hardly have regarded as in any way satisfactory.

On the following Thursday, Business of the House was again sandwiched between Questions about and a Statement on the Suez affair. Mr. Butler announced that on Wednesday, December 5, and Thursday, December 6, there would be a debate on the Situation in the Middle East, whereupon Mr. Gaitskell asked him if it was the Government's intention that the House should debate any of the motions on the Order Paper (including one signed by 130 Conservative members congratulating the Foreign Secretary on 'his efforts to secure international control of the Suez Canal' and deploring the attitudes expressed both by the United Nations and the United States Government) or if the Government had 'in mind a motion of their own', or were waiting for the Opposition to table one. Mr. Butler replied:

We had better await the statement to be made by . . . the Foreign Secretary and after that we can have discussions on the nature of the debate. I think it is unlikely to take place on one of the Motions to which the right hon. Gentleman has referred. I think that it is likely to take place on one of the two other alternatives which he posed.

Mr. Pitman[22] then asked if time could be found for a 'quite different kind of Motion', which had been placed on the Order Paper by himself and Mr. Usborne. This ran as follows:

That this House urges Her Majesty's Government to initiate discussions as soon as possible in the United Nations, so that the United Nations should acquire, by purchase or on long lease or by other means, the sovereignty of the Sinai peninsula, with control over the islands of Tiran and Sanafir in the Gulf of Aqaba, as an assembly point and first base for a permanent United Nations World Constabulary, and so that the Charter may be suitably revised for setting up an Authority of the United Nations for carrying out the responsibilities and exercising the powers relative to such an acquisition.

Mr. Butler regretted that the Government could not find time 'for all these Motions', although he 'realised' that Mr. Pitman's motion was 'actuated by the highest ideals'.

Later, Mr. Daines[23] asked for an assurance

that on the main debate on Suez we shall have a clear statement of the Government's case at the beginning of the debate and not

[22] Cons., Bath.   [23] Lab., East Ham North.

statements reserved for the end of the debate so that they are not freely debatable, such as we had on the last occasion when the President of the Board of Trade was involved.

To this, and to a further Question on similar lines from Mr. Bevan,[24] the Lord Privy Seal replied that it would be well to 'wait for the Foreign Secretary's statement and for other developments', and that things would 'work out in such a way' that 'ample material' would be available 'to indicate the line of the Government well before the debate'.

Other points raised in 'Business of the House' were the Scottish Clauses of the Rent Bill (which Mr. Butler announced would not be referred to the Scottish Grand Committee), the Second Reading of the Ghana Independence Bill (for which he could not give an 'actual date'), a Motion on the Order Paper about the health, safety and welfare of railway workers (which he said he would 'look into'), and the time-tabling of the Committee Stage of the Homicide Bill. In dealing with the last, in response to an objection from Mr. Silverman, the Lord Privy Seal chose to re-state a general principle relating to the arrangement of Government business.

I was not aware that Tuesday was inconvenient to the hon. Member and some of his hon. Friends, [said Mr. Butler]. I must say that when it is a case of Government business there is no absolute duty upon me to indulge in consultations with other than the Opposition, but it is my duty, as Leader of the House, to pay attention to any representations that are made to me. I think it will be very difficult now to change this business, but if the hon. Member would like to see me and explain his difficulties I shall, of course, be glad to see him.

Apart from the tendency, already noted, for 'Suez' to crop up everywhere, the examples we have quoted are fairly typical of the kind of exchange that takes place under 'Business of the House'. But not always does comparative peace prevail on these occasions. Only if the Opposition feels that the Government is 'playing fair' will it allow the time-table to go through without vigorous protest. If, on the other hand, it is convinced that the Government is attempting unreasonably to avoid or curtail debate on a matter of importance, it will be prepared to make the 'Business' discussion a noisy one. Examples of such an occasion are included in our chapter on Legislation, where the 'time-tabling' wrangles that arose in connection with the Labour Government's Iron and Steel Bill are described.

[24] Lab., Ebbw Vale.

QUESTIONS

1. GENERAL

OUR selection of Questions has been made primarily with a view to linking them with subsequent action in the House. Such action includes (1) giving notice of intention to raise the matter 'on the Adjournment', (2) attempting to invoke the 'urgency' procedure under S.O. No. 9, (3) eliciting facts which lead to legal action, as in the Scarcroft case, and (4) eliciting a Ruling from Mr. Speaker, as in the case of Questions on the nationalised industries.

The general significance of 'Question Time', 'the grand inquest of the nation', is well known; it is a distinctive feature of procedure in the British House of Commons not adequately paralleled even in legislatures where the separation of powers does not exclude Ministers. Procedure is analysed in *Erskine May*.[1] What might be called the 'pre-natal' control of Questions by Mr. Speaker and the Clerks at the Table is not our concern here; nor is it possible to illustrate every aspect of the rules of Order governing the form and content of Questions, nor the lengthy list of 'inadmissible Questions'. Some problems arising out of supplementary Questions are, however, illustrated; they are often a prelude to 'subsequent action'.

One matter of terminology deserves mention: Parliamentary Questions must not be confused with the 'Question' which is before the House (and to which an 'answer', i.e. a 'decision', may be given by a Division). During 'Questions', Mr. Speaker is frequently heard to say that there is 'no Question before the House'. The significance of this distinction becomes clear from our examples.

Our choice of Questions for particular purposes means that the occasions selected are not necessarily representative of

---

[1] *Erskine May*, pp. 353–365.

'Question Time', the general character of which is hardly suitable for the 'case-study' type of illustration and can best by gathered from a more-or-less random perusal of *Hansard's* recording of the House's proceedings between 2.30 and 3.30 p.m. on Mondays, Tuesdays, Wednesdays and Thursdays. It should be noted, in particular, that, while most of the Questions we have dealt with concern matters of considerable public importance, the bulk of those asked daily are about detailed and sometimes trivial matters of ministerial responsibility. It sometimes happens, of course, that an innocent-sounding question about a matter initially appearing to be of minor interest produces a major parliamentary 'row', but in the nature of things this is not typical.

The fullest and most authoritative treatment of the whole subject of Parliamentary Questions will be in a forthcoming book by Mr. D. N. Chester. For the procedures with which we are specially concerned in this chapter, see *Campion*, pp. 146–154, 133–137 and 154–157; *Jennings*, pp. 99–121.

2. Questions Leading to Notice of Raising a Matter on the Adjournment when Notice was not Effective

On April 24, 1958,[2] 'Question Time' was devoted to economic and financial business. The Ministers principally involved in answering a total of forty-six Questions were the President of the Board of Trade and the Chancellor of the Exchequer (for whom, however, the Paymaster-General and the Financial Secretary to the Treasury answered).

It was on Questions dealing with Protective Helmets and Footwear that some discontent with Answers appeared. Nineteen Questions on this topic appeared on the Order Paper. The Financial Secretary (Mr. J. E. S. Simon) began by saying:

With permission, I will answer these questions together.[3]

Mr. Silverman[4] immediately rose 'on a point of Order' to ask whether it was not an abuse of the practice whereby several Questions might be answered together that the Minister should purport to answer all the Questions on the Order Paper?

Mr. Speaker: I think that depends very much on the Questions. . . . The matter lies in the hands of hon. Members who put down

---

[2] *H.C. Debates*, Vol. 586, cols. 1129–1158.   [3] *Ibid.*, col. 1144.
[4] Lab., Nelson and Colne.

Questions. If they all put down the same Question, it would be a waste of the time of the House for the Minister to give separate answers.

Mr. Woodburn:[5] Further to that point of order. Has the Prime Minister been advised that all the Questions are being wiped off the Paper before he comes?

Mr. Speaker: I do not know about that. It is nothing to do with me.

Sir G. Nicholson:[6] I have never known what the sin of simony is – is it this?

Although Mr. Mason[7] pressed the point about answering *en bloc* and wished to know if the House could demand separate answers, Mr. Speaker was firm that this would be a waste of time. Mr. Simon 'thought it would be for the convenience of the House if I answered these Questions in this way'. He then gave a short Answer. Immediately the nature of the difficulty appeared.

Mr. Ainsley:[8] On a point of Order. In view of the Financial Secretary's statement that he was answering my Question, Question No. 53 . . . will he . . . note that it asks two specific Questions. . . . [He] has not so far replied to my Question.

Mr. Speaker: That is not a point of order but a supplementary Question.[9]

Members on both sides of the House were concerned with the effect of purchase tax on protective clothing and, for a time, matters of substance were raised by supplementary Questions. Should men in hazardous jobs have to pay tax on goods 'which are used solely for the protection of life and limb?' Had there been prior consultation with the Inspectorate of Mines and Factories? If the object of the tax was not revenue – it would yield a mere £100,000 – what was its purpose? Was the Minister not aware that there was a very strong feeling that all protective clothing should be free of tax? Was he aware of the strong prejudice in favour of cloth caps and would not this tax hinder the acceptance of protective helmets and boots? These matters were covered in nine supplementary Questions.

At one point several hon. Members rose.[10]

Mr. Speaker: We really cannot anticipate the debate on the Finance Bill. This is really becoming a debate; there is no Question before the House.

[5] Lab., Clackmannan.
[6] Cons., Farnham.
[7] Lab., Barnsley.
[8] Lab., Durham North-West.
[9] *H.C. Debates,* Vol. 586, col. 1145.
[10] *Ibid.,* col. 1147.

Mr. Harold Davies:[11] Whilst appreciating the difficulty that you have, Mr. Speaker, in dealing with this method of answering Parliamentary Questions. . . . am I not entitled to put a supplementary Question and not be fobbed off by this kind of omnibus answer?

Mr. Speaker: This is the kind of point which can be discussed at length in the proper way on the Finance Bill. It is an abuse of Question Time to carry it on too far. I have allowed a large number of Questions, and most of the main considerations have, I think, been put.

Mr. Jay:[12] Further to the point of Order. If a Minister takes refuge in answering all the Questions together, is it not unfair that my hon. Friends should not be allowed to ask supplementary Questions?

Mr. Speaker: If a large number of Questions of the same import are on the Order Paper, that is not a matter which the Minister can control. If the matter can be discussed in a proper way by the House, with a Question before the House and a Division if necessary, that is the proper way to deal with the matter.

Mr. H. Wilson:[13] Is it not a fact that this tax is being levied now and that if we have to wait for the Committee stage of the Finance Bill we have to wait some time and the tax will be continuing all the time. Furthermore, since it has become clear to the House that upon another provision of the Bill strong pressure is being put upon the Chancellor of the Exchequer, is it not right that we should put supplementary Questions?

Mr. Speaker: I do not think that any impartial observer of the proceedings this afternoon would deny that a great deal of pressure has been put upon the Financial Secretary to the Treasury. I have allowed far more Questions than I normally do, but I realise that there is very great feeling. My object is to see that when the House discusses a matter it does so on a Question on which it can decide, if necessary, by a Division. That is not possible at Question Time. There are other Questions on the Order Paper which are, no doubt, of great importance to other hon. Members. It is my duty to the House to try to press on and give them an opportunity.

Mr. Mason[14] pointed out that, although seventeen Questions had been put down by Opposition Members, they had been allowed only five supplementaries.

Are we not to have the right to ask supplementary Questions?[15]

Mr. Speaker: There is no such right. It is a matter of discretion and judgment in each case, and no doubt, when it is a question of discretion, there is always a difference of opinion. Discretion is a matter of opinion. There is no such right. The fact that all these Questions have been put on the Order Paper and that hon. Members have not asked supplementary Questions about them does not

11 Lab., Leek.   12 Lab., Battersea South.
13 Lab., Huyton.   14 Lab., Barnsley.
15 *H.C. Debates*, Vol. 586, col. 1149.

destroy their force or effect. I will ask the hon. Member for New-castle-under-Lyne to ask Question No. 23.

It was at this point that the question of raising the matter on the Adjournment arose.

Sir T. Moore:[16] Further to that point of Order. In view of the obvious interest in this matter being further discussed at a later date, *I beg to give notice that I will raise it on the Adjournment.*[17]

But there was an obstacle to this, apart from the question of the hon. Member's luck in the ballot or his subject being selected by Mr. Speaker.

Mr. Speaker: The hon. Member's notice is invalid. *I think it might require legislation and, if so, it could not be raised on the Adjournment* [our italics]. I hope that the House will allow us to proceed. I am trying to save the time of the House in the interests of other hon. Members who have Questions on the Order Paper, but, of course, my purpose can be defeated if hon. Members rise to points of Order, and I hope that they will not do so.

Mr. Shinwell made a further attempt, without success, to obtain an assurance of reconsideration. Then, in response to Mr. Speaker's question, 'Are there any further points of order?', Mr. Silverman again raised the effect on supplementary Questions of the Minister's decision to answer all his Questions together. After a brief reply, the Speaker announced that he could not 'hear any more on this matter'.[18]

3. QUESTION FOLLOWED BY RAISING MATTER ON ADJOURNMENT

This Question concerned the B.B.C. programme, 'Your Life in their Hands'.

Sir I. Clark Hutchinson[19] asked the Postmaster-General

whether he was aware that, many doctors believe that [this programme] would have a bad effect upon viewers; and if he would use his powers under Section 15 (4) of the Licence and Agreement to instruct the British Broadcasting Corporation to refrain from showing this type of programme.

Mr. Marples: I am aware that opinions differ about the merits of these programmes, but I see no reason to interfere with the independence of the B.B.C. in making programmes.

---

[16] Cons., Ayr.   [17] *H.C. Debates*, Vol. 586, col. 1149. Our italics.
[18] He had already dealt with it at some length on an earlier occasion. *See* 568/583–5, April 4, 1957.   [19] Cons., Edinburgh South.

Sir I. Clark Hutchinson: Does not my right hon. Friend think that this is rather a morbid type of programme? Will he consult representatives of medical opinion and consider this again?

Mr. Marples: I must emphasise that the B.B.C. is responsible for the programme and not the Postmaster-General. As to consulting medical opinion . . . the B.B.C. consulted the Royal College of Surgeons, the Royal College of Physicians and the College of General Practitioners. After the programme, these Colleges said that they appreciated the programme.

Mr. Ness Edwards:[20] Will the Postmaster-General give an undertaking that he will do nothing to stop the B.B.C. proceeding with educational programmes of this sort?

Mr. Marples: As I say, the B.B.C. is independent in its choice of programmes.

Mr. H. Morrison:[21] Is the right hon. Gentleman aware that I saw this programme last night? It dealt with an operation on the heart, and I thought that it was done very carefully and respectfully; it was educational, and was conducted in co-operation with the local hospital authorities. May I ask the Postmaster-General not to be unduly influenced by his hon. Friends?

Mr. Marples: I assure the right hon. Gentleman that I shall endeavour to be impartial.

Sir H. Linstead:[22] Does my right hon. Friend agree that the reaction from the public, as received by the B.B.C., has been almost entirely favourable to this programme?

Mr. Marples: As far as I understand, there had been, up to 20 February, very little reaction in the form of letters. There were twenty-five letters approving and encouraging the programme, six suggesting additions to the service, and, I think, seven suggesting that the programme is unsuitable. The Post Office has received no letters.

Sir I. Clark Hutchinson: In view of that Answer, I will endeavour to raise this matter in the course of the Adjournment debate tomorrow.[23]

The sequel to this is described below (pp. 97-99).

4. QUESTION LEADING TO FAILURE TO OBTAIN ACCEPTANCE OF 'URGENCY' MOTION, FOLLOWED BY DEBATE ON A SUBSTANTIVE MOTION REGRETTING MR. SPEAKER'S REFUSAL

On July 22, 1957,[24] in reply to a *Private Notice Question* from Mr. Grimond,[25] the Secretary of State for Foreign Affairs (Mr. Selwyn Lloyd) made a statement on the disturbances in

---

[20] Lab., Caerphilly.　　　[21] Lab., Lewisham South.　　　[22] Cons., Putney.

[23] Usually there is no appropriate adjournment opportunity available. The Member then simply gives notice of his intention to 'raise the matter on the adjournment'. He may then enter for the ballot. Or he may give notice to raise the matter on some other forthcoming occasion, *e.g.*, an announced debate, the Consolidated Fund Bill, or a Supply day.

[24] *H.C. Debates*, Vol. 574, cols. 32–40.　　　[25] Lib., Orkney and Shetland.

Central Oman. A series of supplementary Questions followed. Mr. Lloyd refused an assurance that no British forces would be engaged in support of the Sultan of Muscat and Oman until the House had been informed in advance.

Mr. Wedgwood Benn[26] then sought to move the Adjournment under S.O. No. 9 to draw attention to 'a definite matter of urgent public importance' – the decision of the Government 'to offer British military assistance to the Sultan'. Mr. Speaker refused leave: there were no British troops in Muscat and he knew of no fact which entitled him to regard the matter as urgent.

Mr. Wedgwood Benn: Mr. Speaker, may I submit very briefly the grounds on which I ask leave to move this Motion? First, it is a definite request by the Sultan to Her Majesty's Government, so that on the grounds of definiteness there may be no question. Its urgency arises, surely, on two grounds. There is, first, the Foreign Secretary's refusal to give an assurance that British troops will not be committed before the House is informed; and, secondly, that Middle East Land Forces, and also Army spokesmen in Kenya and in this country have made it perfectly clear that military action is contemplated. Only a year ago precautionary measures of this kind did lead, within a week, to armed conflict.

May I, further, put this? It is a well-established principle of international law that intervention by a foreign state in a country where there are civil disturbances is contrary to international law, and that it was on those grounds that the Foreign Secretary condemned Russian intervention in Hungary.

Mr. Speaker: The hon. Member has raised a large number of questions, I would remind him, which might very properly be the subject of an extensive debate, but, under the Standing Order, it has to be one definite matter, which the hon. Member has specified – the decision of her Majesty's Government to offer British military assistance to the Sultan of Muscat and Oman. What I heard the right hon. and learned Gentleman say was that the British Government had decided to respond to the request of this sovereign for help. If the hon. Gentleman says that it is against any treaty that we should do so, it is a legal matter that he should argue at the proper time. . . .

Mr. Paget:[27] On a point of Order, Mr. Speaker. Surely the point of urgency is this. The Foreign Secretary says that he has issued instructions that British troops may be deployed and committed to battle on foreign soil, not pursuant to any treaty obligations but because it is the way one likes to help a good and firm friend. Now, Mr. Speaker, surely it is impossible to say that [such] an announcement is not urgent, that it does not matter.

Mr. Speaker: It was not so specific as that. . . . Local British authori-

[26] Lab., Bristol South-East.   [27] Lab., Northampton.

ties [the Foreign Secretary said] have been given discretion within certain limits to take military action.

Hon. Members: Hear, hear.

Mr. Speaker: Order. In my view, unless we know something more about this case – (Interruption) – Order – and the limits which have been placed on that discretion, I do not think that I can call it under the Standing Order.

Mr. Speaker went on to remind the House that there were, that week, four Supply Days, and that next week there was the Appropriation Bill – all occasions of possible debate on the matter. That, in itself, was sufficient grounds to refuse the Motion.

Mr. Hale[28] rose –

Mr. Speaker: Order. I have ruled on the point of Order. If there is a new submission, I will gladly hear it.

Mr. Hale's point was that Mr. Speaker had terminated discussion when a large number of Members desired to put further Questions. The Ruling had rested upon lack of information; but Members were prevented from eliciting further information.

Mr. Speaker: The hon. Gentleman is really obliquely criticising my action in the Chair. If he wishes to criticise my action, he knows that there is one way of doing so.

When there are a large number of supplementary questions, particularly after the time for Questions, they tend to drag on to a disorderly debate . . . it should be debated when all the facts can be gone into properly.

Mr. Gaitskell had 'rather hoped' for an opportunity of putting one or two further Questions. He wished to establish that Mr. Speaker's ruling did not preclude the moving of the Adjournment next day if it seemed necessary. Mr. Speaker agreed that further information might alter the whole position. But he was not prepared to accept a further point from Mr. Wedgwood Benn that the fact that instructions had already been sent to military commanders created immediate urgency; nor Mr. Paget's point that not only had the Foreign Secretary refused assurance that British troops would not be committed 'without his coming to the House', but also assurance that he would make a statement next day. In response to Mr. Gaitskell, however, the Foreign Secretary did agree to make such statement.

The Foreign Secretary's statement on July 23 led to further exchanges, but when several Members rose to put further

[28] Lab., Oldham.

supplementary Questions[29] Mr. Speaker intimated that the matter could be pursued further in the debate which was to follow in Committee of Supply. At this point Mr. Wedgwood Benn rose to give notice that, after further consideration, he and another Member had decided to table a Motion regretting the previous day's Ruling. The debate on this Motion is described below.[30]

5. QUESTION LEADING TO SUCCESSFUL ATTEMPT TO MOVE THE ADJOURNMENT UNDER STANDING ORDER No. 9

This example does not arise out of ordinary 'Question Time', but as the result of questions on 'Business of the House'[31] March 6, 1958. On this, Mr. Fenner Brockway[32] asked the Leader of the House, who, as it happened, was also the Home Secretary, for an early opportunity to debate a Motion, supported by over 100 names, urging the Government to grant political asylum to one Joaquim Perez-Selles, then awaiting deportation to Spain. Mr. Butler refused. Mr. Callaghan[33] asked that the man be not deported until after the forthcoming debate on the Home Office Estimates. Mr. Butler felt that it would not be fair to keep the case hanging on 'if we are satisfied about the merits'. Pressed further, the Home Secretary said that there were features of the case which were not political but which involved refusal to do military service. In reply to Mr. Bevan, he said that at the request of certain Members he had examined the possibility of sending the man to France, but there was no hope. Several hon. Members rose.

Mr. Speaker: Order. We seem to be getting away from the question of Business.

Further exchanges took place between Mr. Butler and Mr. Gaitskell, the latter contrasting the attitude of Government supporters to refugees from Fascist countries with that towards those from Communist countries. The former repeated that the

[29] *H.C. Debates*, Vol. 574, cols. 230–235.
[29] *See* below, p. 104. For the general question cf. H. V. Wiseman, 'Private Members' Opportunities and S.O., No. 9', in *Parliamentary Affairs*, Summer-Autumn 1959 and W. H. Greenleaf, *Urgency Motions in the Commons*, in *Public Law*, Autumn, 1960.
[31] *H.C. Debates*, Vol. 583, col. 1338 *et seq.* The example is, therefore, not completely typical in that Mr. Speaker was persuaded into changing his mind. Frequently he will have received notice or will have anticipated a motion and will have his ruling prepared.
[32] Eton and Slough.   [33] Lab., Cardiff South-East.

man was not qualified for political asylum and there was no alternative to deportation. Again several hon. Members rose.

Mr. Speaker: Order. I must remind the House that this question arose out of the discussion of business for next week.

Mr. Dugdale:[34] On a point of Order, Sir. Would it be in order to move the Adjournment of the House on a matter of urgent and definite public importance, namely, the refusal of the Home Secretary to grant asylum in this country to a man threatened with death if he returns to Spain?

Mr. Speaker: That would not comply with the conditions of the Standing Order. This *is an operation in the ordinary course of law* [our italics]. Are there any other questions which are strictly related to business?

One further question was asked, but Mr. Paget immediately returned to Mr. Dugdale's point of Order.

Mr. Speaker: I have dealt with that point of Order. We have passed from it.

Mr. Paget: With respect, Mr. Speaker. . . . I venture to say – I am speaking from recollection – that there is a direct precedent, which you will find in *Erskine May*, for granting the Adjournment in the case of a proposal to deport an alien who claims political asylum. . . .

Mr. Speaker: This question has been at issue for a long time. There is a Motion on the Order Paper about it. It is not like a question that has suddenly arisen.

A further question on another matter of business was dealt with, but Mr. Brockway again returned to the deportation issue. The Home Secretary had announced his decision that day and Perez-Selles was in danger of being sent to Spain 'to-morrow'. He again asked that the matter be treated as one of 'urgency'.

Mr. Speaker: I cannot do so under the Rulings which exist on the interpretation of the Standing Order. This is a matter which follows in the due course of law. The decision is left with the Home Secretary. He may be accused afterwards of having done wrong, but there is no power to raise this matter on the Adjournment.

Mr. Gordon Walker:[35] With great respect, Mr. Speaker, *this is not a matter of due progress of law, but of administration* [our italics] which is under the direct responsibility of the Home Secretary. There is no court involved and no matter of law. This is a matter of Government and administration, and it is very urgent.[36]

---

[34] Lab., West Bromwich.   [35] Lab., Smethwick.
[36] On this point cf. Third Report of Select Committee of Procedure, 1946; paras. 53-56.

Mr. Speaker: I understood that it was a matter of extradition or repatriation and entirely a matter laid down by Statute.

Mr. Bevan: The whole question could never have arisen were the Home Secretary automatically obliged to repatriate this man, but it rests entirely within the clemency of the right hon. Gentleman and his administration. . . . As the facts of the case have not been unfolded to the House of Commons . . . surely it is perfectly reasonable and within the rules of order to raise this matter this way.

Mr. Speaker: I must adhere to my Ruling. I do not consider that this matter has reached a stage which justifies me –

Mr. Brockway: Tomorrow he goes!

Mr. Speaker: Order. I do not know the facts about this. [Hon. Members: 'Let us get the facts.'] The House should listen to me. I have just heard about this man being deported tomorrow. Is that so?

Hon. Members: Answer!

Mr. Butler: I am not aware which day he would be deported, Mr. Speaker. . . .

Mr. Brockway: Joaquim goes tomorrow!

Mr. Butler: . . .

Mr. Bevan: So that you, Mr. Speaker, may be able to form your judgment upon the urgency of the matter, is it not proper that the Home Secretary should inform you how urgent it is?

Mr. Speaker: I should like to know, to enable me to make up my mind, when this deportation is to take place. Can somebody tell me?

Following upon a somewhat lengthy reply by Mr. Butler which, however, provided no definite answer to Mr. Speaker's question, Mr. Bevan urged that exact information be given at once so that Mr. Speaker could reach a decision.

Mr. Speaker: I have to act on the best information I receive. [Mr. Brockway] said definitely that this man is to be deported tomorrow. Is that correct?

Mr. Brockway: According to my information, Sir, – [Hon. Members: 'Oh!'] – this boy was a stowaway on the MacAndrew Line and the boat . . . leaves tomorrow or on the 11th.

Mr. Speaker: Will the right hon. Member for West Bromwich [Mr. Dugdale] bring his Motion to me?

The right hon. Member for West Bromwich, said the Speaker, was moving that leave be given, under Standing Order No. 9,

to move the Adjournment for discussing a definite matter of urgent public importance, namely, the refusal of the Home Secretary to grant asylum to Joaquim Perez-Selles threatened with death. I think that the House is sufficiently seized of the matter. I am in the dark as to the precise facts, but I think that in the circumstances, accepting what is said by the hon. Member for Eton and Slough, I should allow this Motion. If we have a short discussion at seven o'clock, the facts can them come out and we might feel justified in providing an opportunity for the House to find out what is happening.

Hansard continues: The pleasure of the House not having been signified, Mr. Speaker called on those Members who supported the Motion to rise in their places, and not less than forty Members having accordingly risen, the Motion stood over, under Standing Order No. 9 . . . until seven o'clock this evening.

Mr. Butler added one comment 'on a point of order'. He had had no warning that the matter would be raised on 'Business'. Although he accepted Mr. Speaker's Ruling 'absolutely', he sought guidance for the future as to whether such questions might not be raised not 'on business but in a more formal manner'. He could not give the House the latest information because he had no warning.

Mr. Speaker: I think that we should pass to other business now, but in answer to the right hon. Gentleman, the Leader of the House, I would recall that this matter started with a proper question on business, whether the right hon. Gentleman would find time for a debate on the matter. In reply, the right hon. Gentleman informed the House that he could not do so and gave reasons which led to a rather prolonged debate on the merits of the matter, which came into question. I have taken the course, which is, perhaps, the best in the circumstances, but may I say that hon. Members should not use business questions for raising matters of substance. . . .

The debate which followed at 7 p.m. is described below.[37]

6. QUESTION LEADING TO JUDICIAL PROCEEDINGS – THE SCARCROFT AFFAIR

The 'scandal' that culminated in the prosecution of the Chairman and Vice-Chairman of the Yorkshire Electricity Board for contravening Defence Regulation 56A was exposed as a result of the industry and persistence of a Conservative back-bencher, Mr. Donald Kaberry.[38]

It was on December 4, 1950, that he first suggested to the House of Commons that there might be something worth looking into. 'Written Answers' for that day contains the following item:

Mr. Kaberry asked the Minister of Fuel and Power what was the amount of the licence, or other permit granted for the extension of

[37] pp. 99–104.
[38] North Leeds.

the Yorkshire Electricity Board's headquarters at Scarcroft, near Leeds; what was the date of such licence; and what was the amount which had actually been spent or the value of work done to date. *Mr. P. Noel-Baker:* Two authorisations under Defence Regulation 56A for the extension of the Yorkshire Electricity Board headquarters at Scarcroft have been issued; the first was issued in January, 1949, the second in September, 1949. The amounts sanctioned were £7,250 and £3,200. I am informed that these sums have been spent and that the work is now complete.[39]

On February 10, 1951, Mr. Kaberry asked precisely the same Question about certain Y.E.B. premises at Bramhope, near Leeds. The Minister, in another Written Answer, replied that in this case no licence had been issued but that he was 'inquiring whether any work had been done there which should have been authorised' and that he would write to the hon. Member.

It subsequently transpired that, during the period between the first and second of these Questions, Mr. Kaberry was encountering certain procedural difficulties, which compelled him temporarily to abandon the parliamentary Question as a means of extracting information, and to 'pursue the matter by letter'. (See his Adjournment Debate speech, referred to below.) Presumably these difficulties were the result of the restrictions imposed on Questions relating to the 'day-to-day' administration of nationalised industries. As a result of his persistence – and with the help of Mr. Noel-Baker, who, during his period of office as Minister of Fuel and Power, was more than usually willing to satisfy the inquisitiveness of M.P.s – he 'was informed' that the cost of the work done by the Yorkshire Electricity Board exceeded by some £40,000 the expenditure for which it had obtained licences. Parliament received its first official intimation that this was the situation on February 26, when a ministerial answer was given to a Question from Mr. Kaberry asking what was the extent of the excess and what instructions the Minister had given or intended to give 'for the prosecution of any offenders'. The answer ran as follows:

In 1949 my predecessor approved plans for the extension in stages of the old Yorkshire Electrical Power Company's headquarters at Scarcroft so as to enable the new Yorkshire Electricity Board to concentrate their staff as far as possible. The total estimated cost of this extension was £39,250, but this did not include expenditure

[39] *H.C. Debates,* Vol. 482, Written Answers, col. 22.

later found necessary to replace the worn-out heating system in the old buildings and extend it into the new buildings, nor did it include electrical wiring and other work that was carried out by the Board's own employees and did not appear in the contractors' estimates. The omission of this work from the estimates led to its omission also from the application to the authorities. Nor was any authorisation sought for the extra expenditure arising from increased costs (£8,534), for that arising from requirements of the local authority (£2,969), for the removal and re-erection of outbuildings (£2,020) and for the resurfacing of the car park (£60).

Except for a very small amount this expenditure was necessary for the proper completion of the buildings in accordance with the plans which had been approved and, therefore, had the various items been submitted to me before the work was started on them, I have no doubt that I should have authorised them. I am satisfied, after consultation with my right hon. Friend the Minister of Works, that this is not the sort of case in which proceedings should be taken, whether they involved a private individual or a public body.[40]

Such an answer was grist to the mill for any Opposition Member, and it was not long before Mr. Kaberry had the opportunity of saying exactly what he thought of it. For on March 6 Wing-Commander Bullus[41] ,having been successful in the ballot for the Adjournment, chose 'Scarcroft' as the subject for debate. He himself made a brief opening speech raising two 'questions of principle', viz., whether the Government should build elaborate offices when so many new houses were needed, and whether there should be 'one law for the Government and its agents, and one law for the people'; and then gave the floor to his colleague.

Mr. Kaberry began by dilating on the 'splendour and comfort' in which the Y.E.B. was housing itself. He then described the answer to his Question of December 4 as 'evasive', indicated the methods by which he had pursued his subsequent inquiries, and gave the figure of £40,000 which he had received from the Minister. This, he said, he did not accept, 'excessive' as it was; for the Minister had sought 'to cover up the expenditure by suggesting that he must not inquire into the day-to-day maintenance figures'. These he asked for, suggesting that they would amount to another £40,000. The excuses offered, including the suggestion that the admitted breach of the law was only 'technical', would not hold water. Evidently there was one law

[40] *H.C. Debates*, Vol. 484, Written Answers, cols. 257–258.
[41] Cons., Wembley North.

for the ordinary man and another for the public boards. The Minister would be well advised, 'even at this late stage, to order an outside inquiry and, if necessary, to allow the Director of Public Prosecutions to decide whether there was a case for legal action'. If this was happening in one case, in how many other cases might it not be happening?

Mr. Alfred Robens, the Parliamentary Secretary to the Ministry of Fuel and Power, rose to make the Government's reply. That so accomplished a debater should have produced such a feeble effort showed either that the Government was not, even at this late stage, fully aware of the seriousness of the issue, or that, weary of office with so small and insecure a majority, it was rapidly losing its political grip.

Clearly [he said in conclusion] the administrative machinery of the Board was not efficient. I ought to say that my right hon. Friend, the Minister of Fuel and Power, has been assured by the Board that they are taking steps to see that this technical breach cannot possibly occur again; and I hope that the House will recognise the facts and that this explanation will suffice.[42]

But it did not suffice, by any means. The Opposition officially took the matter up with the Leader of the House, Mr. Chuter Ede, who announced, during the course of his 'Business of the House' statement on March 15, that on the following Monday there would be a 'debate on the Motion to be tabled by the Opposition dealing with the Yorkshire Electricity Board and Building Regulations until 7 p.m.'[43]. Before this debate could take place, however, the Attorney-General had intervened. On the day before the debate was scheduled, 'the following Questions stood upon the Order Paper':

Sir W. Smithers[44]: To ask the Attorney-General when, in view of the fact that £40,000 was spent in excess of licences in fitting up Scarcroft Lodge for headquarters of the Yorkshire Electricity Board, he proposed to institute legal proceedings against those concerned.
Mr. Kaberry: To ask the Attorney-General whether his attention has been called to the admitted contravention of building regulations, Defence Regulations 56A, by the Yorkshire Electricity Board to an amount of at least £42,000; and what action he intends to take.

The Attorney-General, Sir Hartley Shawcross, 'asked per-

---

[42] *H.C. Debates*, Vol. 485, cols. 397–406.
[43] *H.C. Debates*, Vol. 485, col. 1773.
[44] Cons., Orpington.

mission of the Speaker and the House to reply', and replied as follows:

These allegations . . . were brought to my notice by the reports of the debate on the adjournment on March 6, and I immediately directed that inquiries should be conducted into the matter by the Director of Public Prosecutions with a view to the possibility of legal proceedings being taken. The inquiries which I have set on foot are now proceeding and their result will be reported to me in due course.

Mr. Bowles[45] asked whether this announcement would make any difference to the 'week's business' (i.e., to the 'Scarcroft' debate) in view of the fact that the matter now appeared to be *sub judice*; and Mr. Eden asked for 'guidance' on the subject. The Attorney-General replied that, although it was not 'technically' *sub judice*, 'in a practical way' it was sufficiently so to inhibit complete freedom of discussion. Mr. Eden then announced that 'he had consulted his friends' and 'did not want to discuss the matter tomorrow'.[46] Later, Mr. Eden stated that his party had chosen for debate (on an Adjournment Motion after the Third Reading of the Consolidated Fund Bill) the subject of the Anglo-Egyptian Financial Agreement instead of the 'subject previously announced'.[47]

Even though the Conservative back-benchers who had raised this issue had thus achieved a considerable triumph, they did not let the matter rest; for the weaknesses and ambiguities of Mr. Robens' reply to the Adjournment debate gave them an opportunity too good to miss. On March 20 Mr. Bossom[48] asked the Minister of Works whether, in view of the fact that he was 'not prosecuting the Yorkshire Electricity Board', he would in future 'treat all other firms or individuals who transgress in the same way with the same leniency'; to which Mr. Stokes replied (a) that he was not responsible for the application of the Defence Regulations to an Electricity Authority; (b) that he was not responsible for deciding whether legal proceedings should be taken; and (c) that 'as regards work which is to be licensed under the Regulation' he took 'full account of the particular circumstances in which an apparent breach of the Regulations had occurred when considering whether he should report the case to the Director of Public Prosecutions'. He then

[45] Lab., Nuneaton.
[47] *Ibid.*, col. 2106.
[46] *H.C. Debates*, Vol. 485, cols. 2103–2106.
[48] Cons., Maidstone, Kent.

avoided the inevitable awkward Supplementaries by taking refuge in the *quasi sub judice* situation of the *affaire* Scarcroft. He again took similar refuge when asked by Mr. Kaberry to state the advice he had given to the Minister of Fuel and Power, the facts on which it was based, the inquiries he had pursued, and the reports he had called for. Mr. Kaberry then quoted Mr. Robens to the effect that the Minister of Fuel and Power regarded the Minister of Works as 'expert in these matters', and asked: 'Upon what evidence does the right hon. Gentleman work in giving expert information?' The best that the Minister could do with this very fast ball was to say that he 'suspected that his right hon. Friend was being misquoted', but that it was impossible to explain the situation without 'prejudicing' what was 'now under consideration'. 'The matter is quite simple and perfectly clear,' he concluded, 'and truth will out in the end.'[49]

There, so far as the House was concerned, the matter rested until June 4, when Mr. Kaberry criticised the Attorney-General for his lack of expedition and asked him how much longer the investigation would take and whether he would introduce 'expert accountants and others' into it. The Attorney-General replied that he was satisfied both with the expedition and with the qualifications of the personnel employed, and that 'he was informed' that the inquiry would be completed in about three weeks.[50]

The Parliament of 1950–51 had its last news of 'Scarcroft' – music, no doubt, to Conservative ears – on July 23, when, in reply to a Question from Wing-Commander Bullus,[51] the Attorney-General stated that the inquiry had revealed a *prima facie* case of infringement of the Regulations and that he had given instructions for the pursuit of criminal proceedings against those responsible.

Although in every way this is most unfortunate [commented the Wing-Commander], hon. Members who know the circumstances will applaud the decision of the Attorney-General.[52]

The prosecution took place at the Leeds Assizes. The Board and its Vice-Chairman were fined, and its Chairman was sent to prison for six months. This, however, did not end par-

---

[49] *H.C. Debates*, Vol. 485, cols. 2285–2287.
[50] *H.C. Debates*, Vol. 488, Written Answers, cols. 59–60; N.B.—*not* 50–60, as incorrectly stated in the Index to *Hansard*.
[51] Cons., Wembley North.　　　　　　[52] *H.C. Debates*, Vol. 491, col. 27.

liamentary interest in the affair, particularly as the Lord Chief Justice, who conducted the trial, had chosen to describe the 'information' given in Mr. Noel-Baker's answer of December 5, 1950, as a 'downright lie'. Even though the Conservatives had now come into office, and the roles of Government and Opposition were consequently reversed, neither side could disregard what appeared to be aspersions cast from the Bench on ministerial or Civil Service integrity.

On November 26 Sir Waldron Smithers asked Mr. Geoffrey Lloyd, the new Minister of Fuel and Power, whether 'in view of the criticisms made by the Lord Chief Justice at the Leeds Assizes concerning the inaccuracy of an answer to a Parliamentary Question, he would make a statement and say what action he proposed to take'. In answer to this and to a similar query from Wing-Commander Bullus, the Minister replied:

I have carefully examined the records, and I wish to say at once that in my opinion not the slightest question arises of the right hon. Gentleman the Member for Derby South (Mr. Noel-Baker) not having exercised all the usual care in giving information to this House.

The criticised answer, Mr. Lloyd continued, was divided into three parts. No exception could be taken to the first two. The third was preceded by the phrase 'I am informed that', because the information concerned had to be obtained from the Yorkshire Electricity Board. 'The information given by the Board to the Department was incorrect and that is why the answer was incorrect.'

This elucidation, however, did not go far enough for several Members, including Mr. Bellenger,[53] who asked:

Will the right hon. Gentleman say explicitly whether the answer given in this House came from the Board itself or was suggested to the Board by an officer of his Department, as seems to be the case in viewing the evidence at the trial?

Mr. Lloyd thereupon consented to lift the curtain a little further.

What happened was that the original information was asked for by the Department. On the later instructions of an assistant secretary, the principal, whose business it was, was instructed to check the answer with the Yorkshire Electricity Board. I think it was from that that the suggestion arose somewhere during the trial that the answer had been suggested in London.

[53] Lab., Bassetlaw.

A further Question on the Order Paper, from Mr. Anthony Marlowe,[54] again took up, this time with the Prime Minister, the Lord Chief Justice's 'downright lie' statement, and asked for an inquiry into the circumstances leading to the giving of the answer thus described. The Prime Minister[55] was of the view that no further inquiries were necessary, and, on being further pressed by Mr. Marlowe, who considered that public opinion was disturbed by suggestions that the answer had been 'concocted somewhere between the Ministry and the Board', said:

I am of the opinion that the matter may rest where it is.

Further supplementaries indicate that Members on both sides were uneasy and anxious that further action should be taken; but the Prime Minister made no concession. The exchange concluded with Mr. Marlowe's saying that he would raise the matter "on another occasion".[56]

On December 3, 1951, he returned to the charge, and drew the following from the Minister of Fuel and Power:

Arising out of my statement a week ago, there is a further development of which I should inform the House. When I saw the part-time members of the Board last Wednesday they brought to my notice information which showed that the officer of the Ministry who was instructed to obtain and check the information from the Board may himself have been aware of the inaccuracy of the answer he agreed with the Board. I have instituted immediate investigations into this matter, which are not yet completed. I will certainly, if necessary, exercise my powers under Section 6 (4) of the Electricity Act, 1947.[57]

February 25, 1952, saw the end of the story, as far as the House of Commons was concerned. Then, in answer to Questions by Wing-Commander Bullus and Mr. Marlowe, the Minister announced that the investigation, which had been conducted by Sir G. Russell Vick, Q.C., was complete, and that copies of the resultant Report had been placed in the Library of the House.

[54] Cons., Hove.   [55] Mr. Winston Churchill.

[56] *H.C. Debates*, Vol. 494, col. 866 *et seq.*

[57] viz. 'Every Area Board shall afford to the Central Authority and, if the Minister so requires, to the Minister, facilities for obtaining information with respect to the property and activities of the Area Board, and furnish the Central Authority and, if he so requires, the Minister, with returns, accounts and other information with respect thereto, and afford to the Central Authority and the Minister facilities for the verification of information furnished, in such manner and at such times as the Central Authority or the Minister may require'. *H.C. Debates*, Vol. 494, cols. 2009–2011.

I think a very fair summary of his conclusion [said the Minister] is to say that the main responsibility for the incorrectness of the information . . . must rest on the senior officers of the Yorkshire Electricity Board. They had ample opportunity of correcting the form of reply which had been suggested to them by an officer of my Department as being the correct way of expressing the information he had been given at short notice over the telephone. But, although misled by this information, the Departmental officers concerned must bear some responsibility for allowing the draft reply to go forward when it should have been obvious that no satisfactory reply could at that time be given.[58]

Thus ended an episode in which the Parliamentary Question had been used with such effect as to lead, not only to the criminal prosecution of an important public body and of its two leading officials, but to an inquiry into the behaviour of certain civil servants and to the shedding of a little more light on the complex question of the extent of ministerial responsibility for the activities of 'semi-autonomous' agencies.

7. QUESTIONS ON THE NATIONALISED INDUSTRIES

On the admissibility of Questions generally, *Erskine May* says:

Questions addressed to Ministers should relate to the public affairs with which they are officially connected, to proceedings pending in Parliament, or to matters of administration for which they are responsible.[59]

Questions 'raising matters under the control of bodies or persons not responsible to the Government' are therefore held inadmissible. Among the examples of such bodies and persons, *Erskine May* quotes 'certain public corporations'.

In ordinary circumstances, the application of these rules causes little difficulty. But the fact that the post-war nationalisation statutes contain provisions empowering the Minister to give 'general directions' to the corporations, together with the amount of informal consultation that takes place between the Ministry and the Board, has created a new and as yet unsolved problem. In practice, the 'forthcomingness' of the Minister has largely depended on the way in which he has chosen to interpret the notoriously controversial distinction between matters of 'policy' and matters of 'day-to-day administration'. Some have

[58] *H.C. Debates*, Vol. 496, Written Answers, cols. 97–98.
[59] 16th ed., p. 356.

interpreted it restrictively, others liberally. Some have supplied information to the House fairly readily (using the formula 'I am informed by the Board that . . .') even while disclaiming responsibility for its accuracy or implications; others have quite evidently been afraid that readiness to give information not statutorily required of them will lead to *de facto* acceptance of responsibility. Quite often a Minister has deliberately chosen to leave the apportionment of responsibility undefined, by parrying a Question with the sentence, 'I think that we ought to leave that matter to the Board', or something equivalent.

Under these circumstances, all that the 'Table' has been able to do is to let through Questions on subjects for which the Minister appears to have statutory responsibility (e.g., capital allocations, long-term development plans, welfare, safety, training, education and matters on which general directions might have been issued), or on which he might reasonably be expected to provide the House with information; see whether the Minister is prepared to accept them; and then disallow all subsequent Questions similar to those which he has rejected as relating to 'matters for the Board'.

That readiness to take responsibility or to supply information is often a function of the Minister's individual will or caprice emerges quite clearly from the evidence given by Mr. Gordon, the Second Clerk Assistant, to the Select Committee on Nationalised Industries of 1952.[60]

This lack of clear principle has caused some frustration even to Members who do not hold that all Questions about the nationalised industries ought to be freely answered. The issue became acute in 1948, when a number of Questions about a major electricity 'shut-down' were rejected. This produced the following statement from the Speaker:

I have come to the conclusion that in the case of an entirely novel branch of administration, such as that relating to the nationalised industries, the strict application of the Rule (against repetition) might operate more harshly than either Ministers or Members generally would wish. I am, therefore, prepared to make a suggestion which I hope will recommend itself to the House, for the power of dispensing with its recognised rules belongs to the House alone and not to me.

I propose to leave the rule which excludes Questions on matters

[60] *See* H.C. 332–I, pp. 13–14.

outside Ministerial responsibility unchanged. But I am prepared, if it is generally approved, to exercise my discretion to direct the acceptance of Questions asking for a statement to be made on matters about which information has been previously refused, provided that, in my opinion, the matters are of sufficient public importance to justify this concession. 'Public importance' is one of the tests for Motions for the Adjournment of the House under Standing Order No. 8, and in my experience is not an unduly difficult test to apply.[61]

In practice, this concession seems to have made little difference, as 'public importance' is really very difficult to measure in this field of business, and as Members have increasingly resorted to the device of asking whether the Minister will issue a general direction to secure acceptance of Questions which might otherwise be inadmissible.

The matter was raised again in the First Report of the 1952 Select Committee on Nationalised Industries, which, while advocating no widening of the scope of admissibility, did recommend that the onus of deciding whether a Question similar (but not identical) to a previous one should be accepted or refused ought not to rest on the Table but on the Minister.[62]

In the autumn of 1959, the question of Questions on the nationalised industries again came to the fore, and the Leader of the House, Mr. Butler, suggested that the 'assumptions' under which the Speaker and the Table acted were open to question and would be the subject of 'consultation'.[63] On February 25, 1960, he made a statement which, while suggesting that Ministers would henceforth adopt more 'liberal attitudes', made no real concession to the demands of certain Members for fundamental change in the conventions governing these matters.

One of the many anomalies in this field is that a Member whose Question has been refused can raise the same matter, at much greater length, on the Adjournment, if he is lucky enough to secure it, or on some other occasion when the affairs of the industry concerned are being debated. When this is done, the Minister finds himself in the awkward position of having simultaneously to defend the Board (for this is usually a political necessity) and to disclaim responsibility for its actions.

For further information on this subject, see the Select Com-

[61] *H.C. Debates*, Vol. 451, cols. 1635–1643.   [62] H.C. 332-I, p. 10, para. 18.
[63] *H.C. Debates*, Vol. 612, col. 380.

mittee Report already quoted, and A. H. Hanson, *Parliamentary Questions on the Nationalised Industries* (*Public Administration*, Vol. XXIX, Spring, 1951); *Parliament and Public Ownership* (Hansard Society, London, 1961).

In the following 'case', the refusal of the Minister to accept responsibility is followed by the raising of the matter on an Adjournment Motion by the Member who put the Question.

On November 4, 1959, Mr. Francis Noel-Baker[64] asked the following Question of the Minister of Transport, Mr. Ernest Marples:

. . . what general direction he has given to the British Transport Commission regarding the proportions of carriage, wagon and locomotive building to be allocated to British Railways factories and to private firms, respectively.

Mr. Marples replied: 'None, Sir.'

Mr. Noel-Baker then produced a long and no doubt carefully prepared Supplementary:

Is not the Minister aware that in all railway towns there is very grave anxiety about the position of the railway workshops? A great deal of the work that could have been, and should have been, done in these shops has been sent to private firms, including one firm which, during this year, has got money from the taxpayer to the amount of £1½ million and which is now in process, or appears to be, of going bankrupt – the North British Locomotive Company. Will the right hon. Gentleman take the opportunity to have a very close look at the Transport Commission's policy with regard to repair and building work, and also take an early opportunity to reassure railway men that it is not the Government's intention gradually to run down the railway workshops, and, in the end, sell them off?

Mr. Marples countered this challenge with a long-familiar formula:

The construction and repair of locomotives and rolling stock is entirely a matter for the Commission, and I think that it ought to rest there. The Commission has the responsibility for control, and I do not think that I should interfere.

Mr. J. T. Price[65] then asked the Minister whether he was aware that the railway workshops, including the 'great Horwich locomotive works' in his own constituency, were to be 'relegated to doing the care and maintenance work of British Railway services', and that this was 'demoralising' the railway shopmen.

[64] Lab., Swindon.   [65] Lab., Westhoughton.

Is it not time [he added] that the Government should now take up the promise given by the right hon. Gentleman who introduced the modernisation scheme in 1954, who gave a pledge to me and to other hon. Members that the railway workshops would be given a fair share of the new work being done under that scheme?

Again the Minister refused to accept any responsibility, and this time received encouragement from one of his own side, Mr. H. R. Gower,[66] who asked him to 'agree' that in all these matters the Transport Commission had 'worked in the closest touch with the railway trade unions'. Mr. Marples then expressed his certainty that there was 'great harmony between the Commission and the trade union leaders'.

Another long Supplementary came from Mr. Ernest Popplewell:[67]

The Minister says that he has given no directive at all, but I hope that he will have another look at this matter and give some directive. Is he aware that the policy of the Commission now is to close railway workshops and to hand this type of work to private enterprise? Is he aware that some members of his area boards have deliberately said that the British Transport Commission is doing too much of its own work, and that the work should go to private enterprise? In the meantime, as many thousands of railway shop men are wondering where their jobs will be in the next week or so, will the Minister have another look at this, bearing in mind the suggestion that was put to his predecessor when we had our last debate on this industry, that these workshops should be used to meet other railway requirements?

This produced a more conciliatory answer, the Minister promising (a) 'to look at the last debate in the House', (b) to inform the Chairman of the Commission of 'these present exchanges', and (c) to discuss 'this question' with him at their next meeting.

Mr. Strauss,[68] in a further Supplementary, suggested that the issue was not simply one of commercial policy, as it had 'very wide social implications', and asked the Minister to discuss these with the Chairman of the Commission. Mr. Marples agreed to do so, but nevertheless continued to maintain that the matter was 'primarily . . . for the Commission, and not for the Minister'.

Finally, Mr. Noel-Baker gave notice that unless the House

had some other opportunity to discuss the question, he would raise it on the Adjournment at the earliest opportunity.

This opportunity occurred on November 10, 1959, when Mr. Noel-Baker secured the half-hour Adjournment Motion. After amplifying the substance of his charges against the Transport Commission and the Government, he dwelt briefly on the question of the responsibility of ministers for answering Questions about nationalised industries.

Can the Joint Parliamentary Secretary [he asked] give us some indication of what degree of responsibility he and his right hon. Friend now accept for guiding and influencing the Commission in its attitude to questions of this kind or say whether he proposes to maintain the fiction – we believe it is a fiction – that the Commission can operate entirely independently of Government policy?

Many Opposition Members, he continued, were 'beginning to be apprehensive about the relationship between many national-ised boards and the general public'. That was why they were pressing 'for a clearer acknowledgement of Ministerial respon-sibility for the working of these nationalised boards'. Some of the nationalised industries now appeared to be 'not more accountable to the general public, but less accountable than some private firms'.

The Parliamentary Secretary to the Ministry of Transport,[69] in his reply, justified in the following way the Minister's refusal to issue 'a direction to the Commission to turn more of their building and repair work to their own workshops and less to private enterprise':

In our view this is entirely a matter for the Commission, for it is a commercial undertaking engaged in a competitive enterprise, and we do not propose to interfere with its commercial judgment in the matter.

At the same time he appeared to suggest that, even if the matter had been one legitimately calling for Government intervention, a direction would not have been the method used for this purpose. A direction, he said,

is a kind of sledgehammer kept in some dark cupboard in Berkeley Square which can be used, if the occasion arises, on the Commission. Fortunately, only on one occasion since 1947 has it been necessary for this sledgehammer to be brought out. It was used in April, 1952,

[69] Mr. John Hay.

according to my information, to instruct the Commission not to proceed with a fares increase; and it was used a second time in August of that year to tell the Commission to disregard the previous direction. The point is that a direction of this kind, which we have been asked to use in connection with the railway workshops, is a very strong weapon.

These two passages, juxtaposed, typify the confusion in which ministerial spokesmen almost inevitably become involved when dealing with matters of this kind. In this particular instance, confusion was made worse confounded by Mr. Noel-Baker's admission, in an interruption of the Parliamentary Secretary's speech, that he had asked the Minister to issue a direction solely for the purpose of getting his original Question 'past the Table' and that the actual issue of a direction 'was not the intention behind it'. To this, Mr. Hay replied:

I was so recently on the back benches myself that I can remember that that is the drill one must adopt in these cases.

However, with or without animadversions on the use of directions, Mr. Hay's case would have been logically complete and constitutionally 'correct' if he had simply explained why the Minister considered that the degree and manner of utilisation of railway workshops was a 'matter for the Commission'. But such a dusty answer would hardly have satisfied either Mr. Noel-Baker or the House. The Parliamentary Secretary therefore followed the usual pattern of ministerial replies on these occasions by attempting to justify the policy of the Commission, thereby contriving to suggest that the real reason for the inappropriateness of a general direction was not so much the Commission's need for autonomy in matters of commercial policy as the Minister's satisfaction with the policy that it was actually pursuing.

I do not think [he concluded] that there is any need for apprehension, still less for uncertainty, about the future. I am sure that there is plenty of work ahead for a rather more healthy and more economic system of railway workshops, and it will be the Government's policy to support and help the British Transport Commission in any way we can to achieve that end.

Identification of Government policy with the 'commercial judgment' of the Transport Commission could hardly have been carried further.

6

DEBATES ON MOTIONS

1. INTRODUCTION

IN the procedure of the House of Commons, the word 'motion' has a technical meaning. No debate can take place except on consideration of a Motion, even though it be of a purely formal kind, such as 'That this House do now adjourn', or 'That Mr. Speaker do now leave the chair'. As *Erskine May* says:

Every matter is determined in both Houses upon questions put from the Chair upon a motion made by a Member, and resolved in the affirmative or negative, as the case may be. The proceedings between the rising of a Member to move a Motion and the ascertainment by the Chair of the decision of the House constitute a debate, and this process affords an opportunity for, and usually involves, discussion, although a decision may be reached without discussion. The essential stages in obtaining a decision of the House are (1) the moving and (usually) seconding of a Motion; (2) the proposing of a question by the Chair; and (3) the putting of the question and collection of voices by the Chair. These three stages are connected together by the question, which must, according to long-established practice, repeat the terms of the Motion, and which must be so framed as to be capable of expressing a decision of the House.[1]

In this chapter, however, we shall be concerned with the 'motion' in its less technical and more ordinary sense. We include: (1) a typical 'Half-hour Adjournment' Debate, (2) a debate on an 'urgency' Motion previously accepted by Mr. Speaker under S.O. No. 9, (3) a debate on a Motion regretting the refusal of Mr. Speaker to accept an urgency Motion, (4) debates on Government and Opposition Motions, and (5) debates on Private Members' Motions. In the first three cases

[1] 16th ed., p. 396.

these debates follow on the Questions described in the previous chapter. In the last two the circumstances of origin are rather different.

Members frequently give 'notice', when dissatisfied with answers to Questions, that they intend to raise the matter 'on the Adjournment'. Provided such notice is not ruled out by Mr. Speaker (cf. p. 72) for some reason, e.g., that legislation would be involved, there are three possible opportunities for giving effect to such notice, though there is no difference in kind between (2) and (3), viz., (1) the 'holiday' adjournments, used to raise 'grievances' by Private Members;[2] (2) occasions when the business on the Order Paper is completed before the hour of interruption: the Government then moves the Adjournment, but a Private Member who has been fortunate in the ballot may introduce his subject, which is debated until the hour of interruption, after which follows the normal half-hour Adjournment Debate; (3) the 'half-hour adjournment' itself, secured, on Mondays, Wednesdays and Fridays, by the Member fortunate in the ballot, and on Tuesdays and Thursdays by the Member selected by Mr. Speaker. (For changes in procedure in 1960, cf. p. 339.)

It is clear that giving 'notice' during Question Time may not, in fact, be followed up by further discussion. We are able, however, to illustrate the procedure by an occasion when the 'follow-up' was possible. It arose out of Questions on Medical Programmes on Television.[3]

Before proceeding to this debate, however, we refer to the Adjournment Debate on November 12, 1958,[4] which revealed some interesting points about the Rules affecting such debates.

As Mr. Rupert Speir[5] rose to introduce his subject, Mr. Wigg[6] raised a point of Order. The notice behind Mr. Speaker's chair, like the memoranda circulated in the Votes and Proceedings on the previous Friday, stated the subject for Friday,

---

[2] For example, on the Summer Adjournment (August 2, 1957) the following subjects were raised: Western European Union; Convicted Soldiers (Appeals); Ministry of Supply (Export Arms Controls) – this raised by Mr. Ellis Smith, Lab., Stoke-on-Trent South, who had failed the previous day to obtain Mr. Speaker's acceptance of an urgency Motion; Israel (Oil Marketing Interests); John Morley Kelly (Conviction); Motor Industry (Overseas Investment).

[3] *See* above, pp. 72–73.   [4] *H.C. Debates*, Vol. 595, cols. 527–538; 579–582.

[5] Cons., Hexham.   [6] Lab., Dudley.

November 12, as being 'Violence in Cyprus'. Was Mr. Speir 'playing the game' by altering his subject to 'Transport (Rural Areas)'? Mr. Wigg asked that Mr. Speaker should

reconsider the procedures which are outlined and which have been laid down by yourself and your predecessors in relation to the kind of action taken by the hon. Member for Hexham in quite irresponsibly, and without due notice, changing the subject.

He emphasised that there was no Standing Order, only Mr. Speaker's 'diktat' of March 25, 1955.

Mr. Speaker, in reply, quoted the ruling of his predecessor, Mr. Clifton Brown, to the effect that 'the Adjournment is given to an hon. Member as an individual'. It was for the convenience of the House that a list of subjects was put up but the Member might change his mind. But he hoped that Members would do their best not to change their minds.

This Ruling was immediately followed by a spate of 'points of Order'. Eventually, Mr. Delargy[7] got in the point that the subject of the Adjournment might be altered because of the absence of the Minister. Mr. Speaker replied that this was 'only an instance of where the subject might be changed'. This did not satisfy Mr. Wigg, who pressed his accusation that Mr. Speir was abusing the rules of the House.

Mr. Short[8] followed this up by arguing that the principle that the Adjournment belonged to the man and not to the subject had been modified by the fact that certain subjects were selected on certain nights of the week, and Mr. Wigg intervened again to ask Mr. Speaker to give the matter further consideration – 'not tonight'. This Mr. Speaker agreed to do. Mr. Speir rose. Again Mr. Wigg rose to cries of 'Oh!' – which led him to complain that, owing to the 'hullabaloo', he was not being allowed to put his point. Mr. Speir rose again. Mr. Donnelly[9] intervened with what Mr. Speaker described as 'a series of comments'. Undeterred, he continued. His point was that Mr. Speir would not have had 'an audience like this in ordinary circumstances'. The subject of Cyprus had been the attraction. Mr. Speaker replied that all hon. Members had their own ideas of what was important.

A constituency case about a poor widow may be just as important

[7] Lab., Thurrock.   [8] Lab., Newcastle-upon-Tyne Central.
[9] Lab., Pembroke.

as any of these larger topics. On the Adjournment is one of the few opportunities that an hon. Member has of raising such matters. This is the sort of case to which I naturally give preference. The hon. Member for Hexham is entitled to go on with his speech. . . .

Entitled, but not allowed! A succession of 'points of Order' prevented Mr. Speir from saying more than five sentences, by the end of which the time available for the Adjournment Motion had expired. Mr. Speir had decided not to speak on Cyprus. Other hon. Members had decided that he should not speak on anything else.

Next day, in reply to Mr. Hale,[10] Mr. Speaker informed the House that, on consideration, Members could change their subject. If Members desired it to be otherwise, the Select Committee on Procedure, as Mr. Hale himself suggested, might consider the matter. He told Mr. Speir that it would not be in order for him to move the Adjournment of the House at that moment 'so that it might have the pleasure of hearing at least one' of his speeches!

2. HALF-HOUR ADJOURNMENT DEBATE

We turn now from the Adjournment Debate 'which never was' to one which did occur. On Thursday, February 27, 1958,[11] although Sir I. Clark Hutchinson was not himself successful in obtaining an opportunity to raise the matter to which he had referred to at Question Time on the previous day (pp. 72–73), it was raised on the Adjournment by Dr. Edith Summerskill.[12]

Dr. Summerskill began by saying that the series of films, 'Your Life in their Hands', was, in the opinion of many responsible people, causing distress to the sick and planting the seeds of fear and apprehension in many other people.

The matter had been brought to the attention of the B.B.C., whose defence was that viewers had a healthy interest in disease which it was legitimate to satisfy. Dr. Summerskill thought only a public health worker had a 'healthy' interest in disease; a lay person had only a 'morbid' interest which the films fostered. She went on to emphasise the fact that half the hospital beds were filled with patients suffering from some nervous disease; one-third of all prescriptions were to allay some nervous

<hr>

[10] Lab., Oldham.
[11] *H.C. Debates*, Vol. 583, cols. 688–700.
[12] Lab., Warrington.

symptom. The films were fit only for 'intelligent, well-balanced men and women who take an interest in medical and surgical techniques'. But T.V. was viewed by a vast number of emotionally unstable people. The Minister had given the impression at Question Time that people were quite undisturbed, but there had already been many protests against this type of programme. The Minister had also said he had no power to intervene, but surely 'advice could go from this House?'

Sir Ian Clark Hutchinson[13] said that despite the fact that most Members apparently felt nothing was wrong with the programme he still had grave doubts. Many doctors were seriously worried about its effect.

The Assistant Postmaster-General[14] replied for the Minister. He began by referring to the oft-expressed wish of the House,

to leave the B.B.C. as untrammelled as possible from interference in or supervision over the subjects or treatment of broadcast programmes. [This freedom] except so far as the ordinary decencies and accepted habits of our society demand self-restraint . . . must be complete, or it is a mockery, a sham freedom. Taste is the arbiter of the limits beyond which it must not trespass.

Dr. Summerskill: What about licence?

Mr. Thompson: Having said that, I acknowledge tonight, as I have acknowledged before, that this honourable House is the forum for debates of opinion and of fact. The right hon. Lady is right to bring here her misgivings and her prejudices.

. . . These are controversial programmes . . . although I part very widely from the description of [them] which [Dr. Summerskill] used, as I part a very long way from her in the disdain, amounting to contempt, which she expressed in her opinion of the viewers and the general public in their capacity either to discriminate in this or, having made a discriminatory choice, to behave like adult citizens when they have done so. . . . There are two schools of medical opinion about [these programmes], leaving aside the opinion of the general public.

Mr. Thompson quoted the opinions of various bodies and authorities in support of B.B.C. policy. He admitted that the B.B.C. had not consulted the British Medical Association, but did not feel called upon to express an opinion on that. He felt the programmes would do more good than harm.

Mr. Wedgwood Benn[15] intervened briefly to say that,

[13] Cons., Edinburgh West.   [14] Mr. Kenneth Thompson.
[15] Lab., Bristol South-East.

although Dr. Summerskill had spoken from the Front Bench, her views did not represent Labour policy.

The House adjourned at seven minutes past eleven (certain 'exempted business' having lasted until 10.37 p.m.).

3. DEBATE ON AN 'URGENCY' MOTION

On March 6, 1958,[16] Mr. Speaker accepted 'an urgency' Motion under S.O. No. 9 on the issue of the deportation of Joachim Perez-Selles. This was debated at 7 p.m. on the same day.[17] The debate illustrates the House of Commons at its best – dealing with non-party issues involving the liberty of the subject; it also shows that an accepted 'urgency' motion, arising from Questions can be effective in securing modification of administration decisions. (Adjournment Motions under S.O. No. 9 may, of course, be raised without previous Questions should the circumstances justify this.)

Mr. John Dugdale[18] opened. The Home Secretary had appeared to disclaim responsibility for the fact that Perez-Selles was to be deported; the House had been perturbed at the Minister's refusal even to postpone the order. Nor had the Minister replied to the question whether the treatment would have been the same had the man been due to go behind the Iron Curtain. Challenged by Mr. Butler and called upon by several Members to withdraw his first and third points, Mr. Dugdale persisted that the Home Secretary might have risen earlier to accept responsibility and thus relieve Mr. Speaker's doubt whether the action was administrative or judicial. He went on to ask the reason for the different treatment of one Sergeant Ponomarenko. (It was announced on October 21, 1958, that the latter had left England, having been given refuge first in Berlin and then here, after having shot another soldier in a drunken bout.) Mr. Dugdale felt, like many others, as strongly about Spanish as about Russian 'tyranny'.

Mr. Silverman[19] intervened to refer to cases of desertion by Polish seamen who were granted political asylum.

Was desertion an extraditable offence? Did we have an extradition agreement with Spain for such offences? Had Perez-Selles been before the Court? If not, under what powers

---

[16] See above, p. 78.
[18] Lab., West Bromwich.

[17] H.C. Debates, Vol. 583, cols. 1409–1468.
[19] Lab., Nelson and Colne.

was Mr. Butler acting? Why was France alone requested to receive the man? She had, indeed, on a previous occasion given him refuge; might we not have followed this example rather than the subsequent refusal by America? Mr. Dugdale asked the Government to approach other countries, particularly Mexico.

This man's freedom may depend upon the Home Secretary's action tonight, but something much more than his freedom is concerned and that is the reputation of this country as an asylum for all who flee from tyranny and injustice. That reputation depends on the Home Secretary tonight.

Mr. Fenner Brockway[20] stated the facts of the case. Perez-Selles was only 24. His opposition to Franco began as a youth. In 1950, called for military service, he stowed away on a Swedish boat which had docked in Rouen. A French court liberated him and 'the sincerity of his refusal to serve in the navy of a Fascist government' was recognised. Later, as a seaman on a Norwegian boat, he found himself back in Spain where his boat, unexpectedly, went for repairs. He was taken off and served two years' imprisonment. Taken into the Spanish Navy, he again deserted in New York. The American authorities handed him over to Spain and he was sentenced to imprisonment for two years, six months and one day – to prevent him from gaining remission. He was then placed in the naval disciplinary battalion from which he had deserted the previous October. He stowed away in the *Velazquez* of the MacAndrew Line and arrived in England. He was applying for a French visa but was picked up by the British police and had been in Brixton Prison ever since. A few days ago he had been placed on board another ship of the MacAndrew Line, believing that it was to call at a French port before reaching Spain. When he discovered it was bound for Bilbao he panicked and threatened to throw himself overboard. There was a scuffle with the police and – the Home Secretary alleged – an assault. The captain refused to take him and he was returned to Brixton.

The case I am putting to the House is – and I shall be able to give parallels later – that deserting was not on pacifist grounds or on conscientious grounds . . . It was on the ground that he was opposed to the Fascist régime, and in that sense it was a reflection of his political views.

[20] Lab., Eton and Slough.

Mr. Brockway then described two precedents for giving asylum under similar conditions and concluded by begging the Home Secretary to reconsider his attitude.

Mr. Butler explained the technicalities of deportation and the right of asylum. Its granting or refusal was not governed by any political or ideological prepossession. There was no bias in favour of nationals of Iron Curtain countries: many had been returned to Poland, Yugoslavia and Hungary. Mr. Butler gave a somewhat different background to the case. Perez-Selles was refused leave to land as a stowaway from an Egyptian ship in 1950 and from an Honduran ship in 1951. In 1952 he returned as a stowaway and 'because of his violence' was retained in prison until he could be returned on the same ship. On the next occasion, on December 28, 1957, he gave himself up to the police in Kent and was refused leave to stay on December 31. He was taken to Glasgow, returned to London while his ship was under repair, then taken to the ship referred to by Mr. Brockway, where the 'act of violence' took place. His departure was again postponed on representations from Mr. Brockway. When an attempt to obtain support for his return to France failed, the deportation order was made.

In interpreting this man's case I had to look at his application for political asylum. I do not find in his history anything remarkable except that he has refused to carry out military service in his own country. Therefore, I do not accept that there are any grounds for allowing him to remain here as a political refugee.

Mr. Gordon Walker[21] insisted that a distinction must be made between democracy and dictatorship. On this basis the analogy between Dr. Cort and Perez-Selles broke down. He also held that Mr. Butler had too lightly dismissed evidence of political opposition. To refuse to do military service in a dictatorship was a political action. He begged the Home Secretary to try other countries, especially Mexico.

Mr. John Foster,[22] from the Government back benches, urged 'some slight delay in order to find a country that will take the person concerned', while Mr. Eric Fletcher[23] made an impassioned plea for reconsideration.

Mr. W. F. Deedes[24] stressed the difficult task of the Home

[21] Lab., Smethwick.
[23] Lab., Islington East.
[22] Cons., Northwich.
[24] Cons., Ashford.

Office in cases like this. Holding that Perez-Selles' 'crime' was
not a political one, he supported the Home Secretary

Mr. Leslie Hale, provoked to intervene, as he said, by Mr.
Deedes' contribution, made an eloquent plea for reconsideration, backed up by an historical survey of political asylum in
Britain, ranging from Louis Kossuth to Louis Napoleon
Bonaparte. Turning to the facts of the present case, he referred
to Mr. Butler's letter to Mr. Brockway, which notified the failure
to obtain permission for Perez-Selles to go to France:

> What is the good of a letter on the board to an M.P. at 4 o'clock on
> the Thursday afternoon when the chap is to be deported on Monday?
> Let us face that single fact to start with. What could my hon. Friend
> have done if he had not asked for the Adjournment tonight? What
> possible step could he have taken?

Mr. Hale's peroration, it seems reasonable to judge, may
have had some influence.

> If the right hon. Gentleman tonight said, 'I remain unconvinced,
> but so clear has been the expression of views of Members . . . who
> have spoken that in the circumstances I will withdraw this order for
> a period, for a fuller investigation, until we can have the facts sifted
> and examined, and I will withdraw the order, too, in the hope that
> some other country may have the opportunity of offering to give
> asylum to this man', nobody would claim to have won a political
> victory. Everyone would say, 'Here is not merely a wise man, but
> a generous man, a man so big that he never minds altering his
> decision when he has listened to other arguments'. The right hon.
> Gentleman's stature stands as high in this House at the moment as,
> I think, it has ever done. It would stand higher in an hour and a
> quarter or so if he thought it possible to take that view.

Sir Hugh Lucas-Tooth's[25] arguments brought a large number
of interruptions, particularly from Mr. Hale whom he charged
with wanting no restrictions on immigration at all – 'a travesty
of my speech', said Mr. Hale. He was also involved in lengthy
exchanges with Mr. Brockway as to Perez-Selles' political
convictions.

Mr. Frank Beswick then made a forceful speech pleading for
delay.

At 9.15 p.m. Mr. Maurice MacMillan[26] rose from the
Government back benches to make what Mr. Brockway described as 'a very courageous speech'. He agreed with those
who said the definition of political asylum in this country was

[25] Cons., Hendon South.   [26] Cons., Halifax.

too narrow. He agreed that the debate itself would endanger
Perez-Selles' freedom and liberty and possibly his life, and said:

[If] we cannot extend our tradition of political asylum to give this
man sanctuary . . . we should grant a stay of execution which will
allow him to remain here long enough to give his friends a chance
to find him a safe place.

Three further Members, two urging reconsideration, one supporting Mr. Butler, spoke. At 9.44 p.m. the Home Secretary
rose to reply to the debate.

He still thought that the decision he had taken on the merits
of the case was right.

The circumstances of the appeal for political asylum made on
behalf of this young man are not strong enough to prevail when
contrasted with the many arguments that I have to take into account
in other cases.

As for the suggestion that the debate had prejudiced the man's
chances:

Most of the responsibility for raising this matter rests upon hon.
Members opposite.

He went on to refer to difficulties arising from 'the mixture of
public pressure and private discretion' in respect of the administration of the Aliens Branch of the Home Office, and
agreed that if the debate had made Perez-Selles a marked man,
that too must be taken into consideration. But,

As to the arguments during the debate . . . I do not think that a
case has been made.

He would not go back on his main decision against political
asylum. Those who thought it was wrong could divide the
House if they wished.

Nevertheless, 'as a result of considering the circumstances
and arguments of the debate', he thought the 'only solution'
was to give an opportunity to the friends of Mr. Perez-Selles
'to find somewhere for him to go'. But this could not go on
indefinitely; the next suitable vessel would be in a week or
fortnight.

Mr. Gordon Walker, by leave of the House, rose to offer his
thanks.

This has really been a very fine night in the history of Parliament, in the history of the Home Office, and in the right hon. Gentleman's own personal reputation and record. I can tell him that none of us will want to divide on this matter . . .

Motion, by leave, withdrawn.

4. MOTION REGRETTING REFUSAL OF 'URGENCY' MOTION

On July 29, 1957,[27] Mr. Wedgwood Benn moved a Motion regretting that Mr. Speaker had not, a week earlier,[28] agreed that the statement of the Foreign Secretary ('that the British authorities in Muscat and Oman had been given discretion, within certain limits, to take military action') constituted 'a definite matter of urgent public importance under Standing Order No. 9. The hour and a quarter's debate threw much light on the position of Mr. Speaker, on the origin and development of urgency motions and the restrictions placed upon them, on the position of back-benchers who wish to raise important issues in a wider manner than is possible at Question Time, and on the spirit in which the House approaches any criticism of its august officers.

Mr. Wedgwood Benn made it clear that he did not intend to debate the rights and wrongs of Government action in Oman (on which, indeed, he and his seconder, Mr. Paget, held different views). He went on:

This is a House of Commons matter, because I am appealing to the House of Commons to review one of the Rulings [of Mr. Speaker].

The history of Parliament, he said, was the history of the Commons entrusting to its Speaker increasing responsibility for the conduct of debates. Mr. Speaker was, first, an umpire between both sides of the House, seeing that the Government got their business and the minority its right to speak – which involved, among other things, the choice of speakers. Secondly, Mr. Speaker interpreted Standing Orders – which entailed many 'judicial decisions' (e.g., certifying a Money Bill and giving a point of Privilege priority over the Orders of the Day). Mr. Wedgwood Benn was appealing to the House against a 'judicial interpretation' of Standing Order No. 9. Just as a judge whose ruling was reversed on appeal was not thereby 'censured', so this was 'not a Motion of no confidence in the Chair' or in its present occupant. Mr. Wedgwood Benn added that he did

---

[27] *H.C. Debates*, Vol. 574, cols. 878–909.   [28] *See* above, pp. 74–76.

not intend to vote for his own Motion which, if permitted, he would withdraw so that there would be no Division.

He then dealt briefly with the history of S.O. No. 9. Over a period of seventy-five years there had been great changes in the interpretation of the Standing Order. But, he argued,

even as the Standing Order stood on Monday of last week it was your duty, Mr. Speaker, to rule that 'a definite matter of urgent public importance' had occurred.

The decision to take military action and the refusal of an opportunity for debate before further action constituted such matter. Mr. Wedgwood Benn then analysed Mr. Speaker's three Rulings on July 22.

First, you said that it was not urgent [there being no British troops in Muscat]. . . . I did not raise the matter of urgency on the ground of the presence of British troops, but on the ground that a decision had already been taken. . . . I submit that if a decision to commit troops were not urgent, then it is very questionable whether anything can possibly be urgent.

Your second Ruling was on what I might call a legal matter. . . . Legal matters cannot reduce urgency. . . . [They are] an extra strong reason why you should have ruled in my favour.

Your third argument was . . . the Supply Day argument. . . . I believe that there are two answers [to that]. The first is that if the matter were urgent under the Standing Order, then it was so urgent that it could not wait as long as next week. . . . Indeed, I suggest that if any Speaker in the future were in a restrictive frame of mind he would find in Mr. Speaker Morrison's Ruling . . . precedent enough to clamp down on any plea for urgency made by a backbencher. [Secondly] your Ruling, though technically correct, is now out of keeping with the character of modern Supply Days.

Mr. Wedgwood Benn read a list of subjects tabled on the previous weeks' Supply Days and asked:

Is it true to say that, on these matters, the question of Muscat and Oman 'could be discussed in all its aspects'. [Mr. Speaker's words]. . . . If I had gone to the Chair and asked to be called on Scottish health, and had been asked 'What line are you taking?', and if I had said, 'I am against the Government on Muscat and Oman', I should have been very surprised if I had been called . . . it would have been a graver abuse to interject a speech on Muscat and Oman into a debate on Scottish health or redundancy or old-age pensions than it would have been to seek to move the Adjournment. . . .

Mr. Wedgwood Benn suggested that the Ruling made sense

only if addressed to the leader of a great party, because he could change the business for a Supply Day.

Therefore, your Ruling that the opportunities existed is addressed only to a party and not to a Member. . . .

Standing Order No. 9, he went on, affected back-benchers. Front-benchers could decide their business whenever they chose. A Parliamentary Question was all the former got and it was often difficult to slip in a Supplementary. Otherwise there was the evening Adjournment, if a Member was lucky in the ballot.

If you take away this right, Mr. Speaker, or restrict this right you are doing damage in . . . the battle of the back-benchers to win a place in the House from the Front-Benchers. . . .

Mr. R. T. Paget[29] seconded. He did not think the Motion was derogatory to Mr. Speaker or his office.

We did not elect you to be Pope. We did not ask of you, or expect of you, infallibility. We have provided a procedure, a proper procedure, whereby particular rulings of the Chair may be challenged. That is being done in this instance.

S.O. No. 9, he thought, should be considered by the Rules Committee. Mr. Speaker should hear arguments before giving his decision. This would be 'a most useful practice, because it is very difficult for the Chair to give a Ruling without hearing argument'.

Mr. Godfrey Nicholson[30] thought they really *were* censoring Mr. Speaker.

I am concerned with this, that it derogates from the dignity of the Chair, and therefore, from the reputation and the usefulness of this House if the Ruling of the Speaker of the day is criticised or challenged. . . .

He went on to regret the tendency to argue with Mr. Speaker on any ruling.

. . . in the days of Mr. Speaker Fitzroy, when a Motion for the Adjournment . . . was moved, no argument or discussion was permitted; owing to his kindness of heart, Mr. Speaker Clifton Brown began to permit argument with him over his rulings. . . . I venture humbly to suggest . . . that the time has now come when, having given your decision, you should stand by it and should not permit argument or discussion.

[29] Lab., Northampton.   [30] Lab., Farnham.

After Mr. Austen Albu[31] and Mr. Anthony Kershaw[32] had raised rather more fundamental constitutional issues relating to the Prerogative, Mr. Donald Chapman[33] returned to the 'unduly restrictive' Rulings on S.O. No. 9. He asked for a Select Committee on the whole of the Standing Orders. If, at the end of Questions, the House was due to turn to a debate on the Adjournment, or in Committee of Supply, or on the Consolidated Fund, or on Estimates, then it seemed that an S.O. No. 9 adjournment was ruled out. Such debates, however, were always arranged between the two Front Benches.

The Home Secretary and Lord Privy Seal (Mr. Butler) emphasised that the debate had certainly not been animated by any ill-will towards Mr. Speaker personally. He reminded Mr. Wedgwood Benn that, in addition to other topics, the Foreign Office Vote had been put down for consideration and that the subject of Muscat and Oman could have been raised on it. So the Motion had been refused because 'an ordinary Parliamentary opportunity' would have occurred 'shortly or in time'. He would give no undertaking either as to an investigation of Standing Orders or as to a meeting of the Rules Committee.

Mr. Gaitskell agreed that respect for the Chair was the very essence of Parliamentary democracy, but would not go as far as Mr. Nicholson in suggesting that everyone ought, automatically and without question, to accept everything Mr. Speaker said.

Even the Front Bench has been known to argue with Mr. Speaker on Rulings he has given. . . . In my view, the present arrangement by which, if we think it right, we usually try a bit of argument with Mr. Speaker but do not put down Motions is the right way round to do it.

Mr. Hale wanted regular consideration of rules and procedure; a Motion of censure was not a sensible method of dealing with these matters. He was pessimistic on the position of backbenchers:

There is no constitutional historian who does not say that however much Mr. Speaker protects the rights of Members they are whittled away by an inevitable historical process. The Statue of Liberty is constantly eroded by the necessity for Government business to take increasing priority over the rights of Members.

After two further contributions, the Motion was, by leave, withdrawn.

[31] Lab., Edmonton.　　　　[32] Cons., Stroud.　　　　[33] Lab., Northfield.

5. GOVERNMENT AND OPPOSITION MOTIONS

From time to time, motions are proposed in the form of resolutions through which the House is called upon to express its opinion on some matter of public policy or to demand that the Government should do something or refrain from doing something. At specified times, such resolutions may be proposed by Private Members; but the more important of them are usually placed on the Order Paper by either the Government or the Opposition. Their aim is to test the feeling of the House by providing opportunity for debate. Amendments may be moved and, like the original Motions, pressed to a Division.

It is rare nowadays for the Government to move a Motion of Confidence or for the Opposition to move one of Censure, couched in general terms. Normally, the resolution to be debated defends or attacks some specific aspect of Government policy. But it is none the less a matter of confidence, in so far as a defeat for the Government – in the unlikely event of its being registered – would bring in its train a resignation or an appeal to the country.

Here are a few examples of Motions of this kind, together with their accompanying Amendments, taken from the Session 1958–59:

Motion	Amendment
Government: That this House welcomes the White Paper on Provision for Old Age (Command Paper No. 538).	*Opposition:* to leave out from 'House' to the end of the Question and to add instead thereof: 'regrets that the White Paper . . . makes no provision for raising the existing retirement pension immediately, nor for maintaining its purchasing power in future, and fails to provide a fully comprehensive system of national superannuation which will abolish poverty in old age'.
Government: That this House welcomes the proposals of Her Majesty's Government as set out in the Command Paper on Secondary Education for All.	*Opposition:* to leave out from 'House' to the end of the Question and to add instead thereof: 'while expressing the hope that the improvements in education proposed in the White Paper, Secondary Education for All . . . will be achieved, notes with regret that the financial arrangements are inadequate for this purpose; that no satisfactory provision is made for a sufficient increase in the supply of teachers; and that, owing to a doctrinaire opposition to comprehensive secondary education, the White Paper fails to remove the admitted evils of segregating children at the age of eleven'.

Opposition: That this House regrets the failure of Her Majesty's Government to protest to the Federal Government of Rhodesia and Nyasaland at their action in designating the hon. Member for Wednesbury a prohibited immigrant; and declares that the entry of a citizen of the United Kingdom into a British Protectorate should not be subject to the veto of the Federal Government of Rhodesia and Nyasaland.

Government: None.

Opposition: That this House calls upon Her Majesty's Government to implement the recommendation contained in the Seventh Annual Report of the Lord Chancellor's Advisory Committee on Legal Aid to enable free legal aid to be given where the disposable income of the applicant is over £156 but not in excess of £208 and to exclude from legal aid those persons whose disposable income is over £600 instead of £420.

Government: to leave out from 'House' to the end of the Question and to add instead thereof: 'endorses the introduction by H.M.G. of a scheme for oral legal advice; welcomes the announcement of the intention of H.M.G. to implement the provisions of Sections 21 to 23 of the Legal Aid and Advice Act, 1949, relating to legal aid in criminal courts, and the provisions of Section 5, relating to legal aid in matters not involving litigation; and recognises that it is desirable to modify the financial provisions of the Legal Aid Scheme when circumstances permit'.

It is hardly necessary to provide an illustration of this type of debate, which normally becomes a duel between Government and Opposition, providing no features of procedural interest. What calls for more special note is the practice, that has increased of recent years, of arranging debates on 'neutral' motions, proposed by the Government. In its usual form, such a Motion merely calls upon the House of Commons to 'take note' of something, frequently a Report.

In one week, towards the end of 1958, the House discussed no fewer than three Motions of this kind, viz.:

That this House takes note of the Report of the Advisory Committee on Recruiting (Command Paper No. 545) and the Government's comments thereupon (Command Paper No. 570).

That this House takes note of the Report of the Committee on Homosexual Offences and Prostitution (Command Paper No. 247).

That this House takes note of Command Paper No. 530 relating to Proposals for Constitutional Change in Northern Rhodesia.

This form of Motion is useful when it is desired to have a discussion on a subject upon which the Government has not finally formulated its policy and wishes to collect the views of Members of the House. 'Take note' Motions are not in themselves controversial, and are normally passed without a Division.

But Amendments to them are, of course, possible, and are proposed when the Opposition or any other group of Members feels sufficiently strongly about the matter under discussion. For instance, on the third of the Motions listed above there was an official Opposition Amendment which proposed to substitute the following:

declines to approve the proposals for constitutional change contained in the Command Paper No. 530, which leave the African people inadequately represented, fail to promote confidence and will worsen relations between the races throughout Central Africa.

One of the most familiar uses of the 'take note' Motion is to introduce a debate on the Annual Report and Accounts of a nationalised industry. It is appropriate in this context because the Government is not itself responsible for the Report and Accounts, and does not necessarily approve of everything that they contain. Moreover, this form of Motion may be regarded as a means of encouraging the 'constructive' and 'non-political' type of debate on the nationalised industries, which most politicians, at least in theory, now regard as desirable.

Amendments to such 'take note' Motions are sometimes tabled by the Opposition. More usually, however, the Opposition chooses not to divide the House, as in the case of the example we have selected: the Debate on the Reports and Accounts of the Airways Corporations of January 27, 1958,[34] which is presented as fairly typical of those debates on the nationalised industries (now quite frequent) in which, political passion being at a low ebb, Members vie with one another in displaying their knowledge of the industry concerned and in making what seem to them realistic proposals for its improvement.

The introductory Motion ran: 'That this House, in reviewing the progress of Civil Aviation, takes note of the Reports and Accounts of the British Overseas Airways Corporation and the British European Airways Corporation for the year ended 31st March, 1957.' This contained one unusual feature, viz., the insertion of the phrase: 'in reviewing the progress of Civil Aviation', which appears to have been included to enable the House to consider the Reports and Accounts of the two Corporations against a background of the Government's whole civil

[34] *H.C. Debates*, Vol. 581, cols. 35–103.

aviation policy and to indicate to Members that their contributions need not be narrowly confined to the manner in which the Corporations had discharged their responsibilities and to the relations between these nationalised enterprises and the Minister of Transport and Civil Aviation.

The general tone of the debate was set by the Minister, Mr. Harold Watkinson, who opened by saying, 'I sometimes think that this House spends too much time in examining affairs in the abstract rather than in the concrete, and that we might more readily convince the nation that we are not all smitten in this House with what Matthew Arnold called ". . . this strange disease of modern life, With its sick hurry, its divided aims . . ."' if we dealt with the practical facts that condition our lives and future.' His speech, which lasted from 3.31 p.m. to 4.36 p.m., and was subject to very few interruptions, was factual in content and non-controversial in manner.

From the Opposition Front Bench, Mr. G. R. Strauss[35] began by congratulating the Minister for his 'full, informative and interesting survey of the civil aviation situation in this country'. After congratulating the Corporations, which, in spite of the many difficulties 'which beset them during the year', had 'a remarkable record of achievement', he proceeded to put 'a few questions' to the Minister, about (a) the effects of the Government's 'economy' measures on the airlines, (b) the prospects of Anglo-Russian interchange air services and of the opening of new passenger facilities at London Airport; (c) the cost of sales and advertising, in respect of which, according to the Reports, there appeared to be a discrepancy between B.E.A.C. and B.O.A.C.; (d) the allegation, contained in the B.E.A.C. Report, that the services provided by independent operators had 'caused a material diversion of traffic from B.E.A. services'; and (e) the policy pursued by the Government, and its relations with the Corporations, in respect of placing orders for 'planes with the aircraft companies. He concluded by expressing certain doubts about the future of the aircraft industry, and by asking (a) 'that the requirements of civil aviation and military aviation should be decided and pronounced as quickly as possible', and (b) that there should be 'no significant cut in development and research'.

As it had been agreed through the 'usual channels' that the debate should be concluded at 7 p.m., opportunities for back

35 Lab., Vauxhall.

bench participation were restricted. Mr. Strauss resumed his seat at 5.4 p.m. and Mr. Ian Mikardo[36] rose to wind up for the Opposition at 6.7 p.m., with the result that the back-benchers had just over an hour, a few minutes of which were occupied in altercation between Mr. Rankin[37] and the Deputy Speaker (on a point of Order) about the curtailment of the debating time, which this Member, prior to leaving the Chamber, described as a 'swindle'.

Those back-benchers who succeeded in catching the Speaker's eye could be divided into two classes, which sometimes overlapped, viz., (1) those with some experience of or expertise in civil aviation and the aircraft industry, and (2) those with 'constituency' points that they wished to raise.

The first speaker, Lord Balniel,[38] was of the latter class. He admitted his ignorance, expressed his diffidence about entering the debate, and justified his intervention on the grounds that 'there are many thousands of my constituents whose well-being and livelihood depend on the health of civil aviation in this country, and, more particularly, upon the health and strength of the aircraft companies'.

Mr. A. E. Hunter,[39] who followed, admitted that he was also 'a layman in these matters' and that his interest in civil aviation had 'grown from a constituency point of view'. As Member for the constituency in which London Airport was located, he clearly felt it incumbent upon himself to make a contribution, but did not succeed in saying anything very definite, except on the problem of damage to houses by aircraft vibration.

The next speaker, Sir Arthur Vere Harvey,[40] admitted a previous interest in aircraft manufacture, dealt expertly with a number of technical matters, and criticised the Ministry for its bureaucratic handling of the industry. He also asked for the establishment of an independent 'air policy tribunal', which could 'inquire into the Corporations, independent airlines and fighting services, and into any branch of the industry, and advise the Government'. Such a body was particularly necessary 'in view of the changes in Ministerial appointments'.

The interests of Wales were voiced by Mr. Cledwyn Hughes,[41] who claimed to represent 'a growing body of opinion . . . which

---

[36] Lab., Reading.
[37] Lab., Glasgow, Govan.
[38] Cons., Hertford.
[39] Lab., Feltham.
[40] Cons., Macclesfield.
[41] Lab., Anglesey.

is resentful of the continued neglect of the Principality by
B.E.A.'

The last back-bench contributor, Mr. Farey-Jones,[42] expressed himself with vigour, mixed his metaphors (the Ministry
of Transport arranged 'gunshot weddings' while the Ministry
of Supply was acting as a 'barnacle on the keel of efficiency'),
and packed an extraordinary amount of criticism and suggestion into five minutes. He deplored 'Whitehall' dictation in
respect of the placing of contracts, expressed his lack of confidence in the wisdom of the Ministry of Supply, suggested the
creation of a 'pool' to relieve the shortage of pilots, inquired
about the prospects for 'atomic-powered flying-boats', and suggested the inauguration of a helicopter corporation to serve
'the remote parts of Wales and Scotland'.

Winding up for the Opposition, Mr. Ian Mikardo began by
drawing attention to four points which he considered to emerge
from the Reports of the two Corporations. First, the Corporations were being 'seriously and adversely affected' by the
Government's economic policies; secondly, airport planning
was deficient; thirdly, the Corporations had derived great
benefit from the advice they had received from the trade union
side of the National Joint Council; fourthly, the airline
operators, both public and private, had been badly 'let down
by the aircraft manufacturing industry'. He then dealt with
'two long-term problems of the industry arising out of its
structure', suggesting that there should be greater co-operation
between the Corporations, through joint arrangements for the
provision of common services, and that a new attempt should
be made to define the respective roles of the public and private
sectors.

In his concluding speech for the Government, the Joint
Parliamentary Secretary to the Ministry of Transport and Civil
Aviation[43] expressed the opinion that the debate had been
'excellent and constructive'. Like other speakers, he offered his
congratulations to the two Corporations. On the question of
aircraft supply, he promised that the criticisms made would be
examined and that the Minister would make a statement to the
House 'at the earliest possible moment'. He defended the impartiality of the Air Transport Advisory Council, which had

[42] Cons., Watford.   [43] Mr. Airey Neave.

not really been called in question by any speaker, but refused to be drawn on the Minister's directives to that body in respect of the licensing of private operators, which had been the subject of Opposition criticism. He justified B.O.A.C.'s advertising campaign, gave an assurance that none of the Government's proposed cuts in expenditure would 'hamper the operations of the airlines', announced that the Government was still considering the proposals of the Millbourn Committee on London Airport facilities, and gave some information about forthcoming changes in fares and freights. His attitude towards some of the more detailed points of criticism made in the debate was sympathetic. The Government was either already looking into them or would shortly be considering them. He apologised for not being 'able to answer every question', said that he had 'taken note of all these matters', and thanked Members for the interest they had shown in the problem of civil aviation and for the way they had put their points.

As no Division was asked for, the Question was put and agreed to. As arranged through the 'usual channels', the House then proceeded to discuss another nationalised industry, on the Motion 'That this House takes note of the Report and Accounts of the North of Scotland Hydro-Electric Board for 1956'.

This debate is not presented as a typical one on a nationalised industry, for there is no such thing. It does, however, illustrate some general features of such debates. One is the insufficient time allowed for the discussion of a big and important subject, with the result that a large number of miscellaneous points had to be raised and disposed of very briefly indeed. As the Front Bench speakers, who had to try to 'cover the ground', necessarily held forth at some length, contributions from the back benches were few, short, and 'bitty'. The debate, however, did allow Members to make points and offer criticisms which might have been ruled out of order at Question Time, owing to the ban on matters relating to the 'day-to-day administration' of the nationalised industries. Admittedly, this was not entirely an advantage, as Members naturally seized the opportunity to raise numerous 'constituency points' which occupied time which could have been more appropriately devoted to general policy matters. All the back-benchers who contributed were either 'experts' or 'interest representatives'. Some of them were both. It is impossible to say whether Members who came

within neither category abstained from attempts at intervention
or failed to catch the Speaker's eye.

6. PRIVATE MEMBERS' MOTIONS

From 1950 to 1960, twenty parliamentary days, all Fridays,
were set aside for Private Members' Business. Half of them were
allotted to Bills, half to Motions. Since February, 1960, the
amount of time available for Motions has been 'experimentally'
increased by four half-days.[44] Currently, therefore, such
Motions occupy a total of twelve parliamentary days. The right
to introduce Motions is subject to ballot, three Motions being
'drawn' for each allotted day.

As might be expected, these Motions deal with a wide variety
of topics, great and small. Their fates differ, largely according
to the attitude towards them adopted by the Government.
Some are passed, others rejected. Some are withdrawn, others
'talked out'. Many deal with subjects of a non-political, if not
non-controversial, kind, and hence provoke discussions in which
Members express themselves much more freely than in debates
where their party loyalties are heavily engaged.

Procedurally, few of them present features of great interest.
Rather than go through the debate on any one Motion, therefore, it will be better to provide a list of the Motions proposed
during the course of a single Session to illustrate the variety of
both their subject-matter and their fate. The Session chosen
is 1958–59.

Date	Motion	Fate
(1) Nov. 21, 1958	That this House, noting the increasing power of the advertising industry and its influence upon our national life, and the growing impact of advertising on the individual, calls upon H.M.G. to recommend the appointment of a Royal Commission to consider whether further safeguards are desirable in the public interest and, if so, what form such safeguards should take.	'Talked out', the Speaker having refused to accept the Closure on the ground that, at 4 p.m., there were still many Members wishing to speak. This ruling was challenged on Points of Order for the whole of the half-hour normally devoted to the Adjournment Motion.
(2) Dec. 5, 1958	That this House, recognising that the operation of powerful aircraft, necessary for effective defence,	Agreed to.

44 On July 26, 1960, Mr. Butler announced that the 'experiment' would be
continued during the forthcoming Session (1960–61).

Date	Motion	Fate
	presents special problems to people living near military airfields, calls upon H.M.G. to do everything possible to reduce the inevitable damage and ensure that compensation claims for damage are dealt with fairly and promptly.	
(3) Dec. 5, 1958	That, whilst this House deplores all forms of colour bar or race discrimination, it nevertheless feels that some control, similar to that exercised by every other Government in the Commonwealth, is now necessary, and urges H.M.G. to take immediate steps to restrict the immigration of all persons, irrespective of race, colour, or creed, who are unfit, idle, or criminal; and to repatriate all immigrants who are found guilty of a serious criminal offence in the United Kingdom.	Talked out.
(4) Jan. 23, 1959	That this House welcomes the increasing interest of the people of G.B. in the arts; endorses the principle that artistic policy should be free from Government control and direction; proclaims the importance of maintaining the nation's cultural heritage; commends the patronage of enlightened local authorities, charitable trusts, industry, and commerce; and, while grateful for the increase in Government support for the arts, draws attention to the inadequacy of the present scale of purchase grants to museums and galleries, and urges a substantial increase.	Agreed to.
(5) Jan. 23, 1959	That this House takes note of the Report of the Colonial Development Corporation and expresses its appreciation of the increasing role of the Corporation in economic development in the Commonwealth.	Spoken to for one minute by the mover, Mr. Leather, who was cut off by the Motion for the Adjournment at 4 p.m. He complained of the 'extraordinary conduct' of two Opposition Front Bench speakers who had intervened on a Private Members' day to prolong debate on the previous Motion.
(6) Feb. 6, 1959	That this House, having regard to the present serious fall in the demand for coal in this country, the high level of coal stocks, and the decline in coal exports, calls	Moved by Labour speaker, this Motion was subject to an Amendment by Mr. Nabarro, which proposed to substitute: 'this House, having taken ac-

Date	Motion	Fate
	upon H.M.G. to frame as a matter of urgency a policy for the fuel and power industries of this country to secure a proper balance in the use of imported and indigenous fuel and the effective co-ordination of the three nationalised fuel industries – coal, gas, and electricity – and to present proposals to the House to that end.	count of the present fall in the demand for coal in this country, the high level of coal stocks, and the decline in coal exports, endorses H.M.G.'s policy for the fuel and power industries of this country'. Closure moved and agreed to; Motion defeated; Amendment agreed to; without Divisions.
(7) Feb. 20, 1959	That this House welcomes the Report of the Royal Commission on Common Land and, subject to points of detail upon which further consultations may be deemed expedient, urges H.M.G. to give early consideration to the recommendations of the Commission and to announce its intentions thereon.	Agreed to.
(8) Feb. 20, 1959	That this House takes note of the recommendations of the Select Committee on Estimates on the police in England and Wales; welcomes the observations and further observations of the Home Secretary thereon; expresses gratitude to all ranks of the police forces for their loyal and devoted service; and expresses the hope that further consideration will be given to questions affecting recruiting and training for the several ranks in the police service and for the police cadets, the pooling of ancillary services between police and local authorities and the review of establishments.	Agreed to.
(9) Mar. 6, 1959	That this House recognises, in view of the gradually rising average age of the population, the importance of making full use of the working capacity of older persons; welcomes the encouragement which H.M.G. have already given to research into the problem of the employment of older persons; and urges H.M.G. to take further steps to promote and co-ordinate such research.	Agreed to.
(10) Mar. 14, 1959	That a Select Committee be appointed to consider Sunday ob-	Talked out. A Closure Motion, put to the vote, did not receive

Date	*Motion*	*Fate*
	servance legislation, and to make recommendations as to any alterations that are necessary in present-day conditions.	a majority sufficient under Standing Order No. 30.
(11) April 17, 1959	That this House is of the opinion that, as it is the declared policy of H.M.G. to develop in its Colonial Territories the greatest practicable measure of self-government within the Commonwealth, it is desirable for H.M.G. to evolve a positive policy for those smaller territories where difficulties might arise in regard to the achievement of complete independence within the Commonwealth.	Agreed to.
(12) April 17, 1959	That this House, deeply conscious of the human tragedy that lies behind the continuing high level of road accidents, regrets that the Road Traffic Act, 1956, has not had the impact in reducing such accidents as had been hoped and pledges support for intensified efforts to this end.	Given 12 minutes debate, cut off by 4 p.m. adjournment.
(13) May 1, 1959	That this House, bearing in mind the expansion of European and North American horticultural production and the all-round increase in producers' costs, calls upon H.M.G. to give urgent consideration to the problems of developing British horticulture in the way required in the foreseeable future, and the means whereby growers may fairly be enabled to play their full part in meeting the demand of consumers.	Agreed to.
(14) May 1, 1959	That this House, recognising the need for British industry to keep abreast of modern productive methods, and the need to ensure that our workers are not inhibited in their acceptance of automation by fears of heavy unemployment, requests H.M.G. to undertake an intensive study of the probable consequences of its introduction and to invite industry to co-operate in effecting the necessary changes with a minimum of hardship to its employees, being convinced that periodic reports to the public of the results of such study would be of material importance	Agreed to.

Date	Motion	Fate
	in obtaining maximum co-operation from all sections of the nation.	
(15) June 5, 1959	That this House calls upon the Government to give immediate additional financial assistance to the elderly by increasing the retirement pension and the present earnings limit, and by waiving their wireless and television licence fees; that 100 per cent. grant be given to local authorities for the next five years to build both modern old people's homes, for 30 to 60 people, and suitable housing schemes so that the elderly wherever possible be integrated with the rest of the community and for which will be provided home helps, meals on on wheels, and other domiciliary and social aids at nominal rates, and that Part III accommodation be removed from the curtilages of hospitals.	Moved by a Labour speaker, this Motion was subject to an Amendment by Mr. A. Kershaw, which proposed to substitute: 'noting that H.M.G. are keeping under review the rates of retirement pension and other National Insurance benefits and that the limits on what a pensioner who has retired from regular work may earn without reduction of pension were increased on April 20, 1959, welcomes the improvements being effected in the provision of accommodation and other services and amenities for those old people who require them, and is of the opinion that continuing co-operation between all the authorities and bodies concerned offers the best possible guarantee of steady continuation of the progress already achieved'. Motion withdrawn; Amendment talked out.

In this particular Session, nine Conservative Motions were debated as against six Labour ones. It should be noted, however, that only two Conservative Motions needed a whole day's (or almost a whole day's) discussion, as against four Labour ones, and that two of the Conservative Motions were debated for no more than a few minutes each.

The eight Motions (six Conservative, two Labour) to which the House agreed without a Division were all 'non-controversial' in the sense that, although provoking differences of view, they were framed in such a way as to permit all sections of opinion in the House to register support for them. It is not surprising, of course, that most of the Motions of this kind were Conservative-promoted, for when a Conservative Government is in power the Conservative back-bencher's Motion is less likely than the Labour back-bencher's to be overtly critical of Government policy. Only one Conservative-promoted Motion, the extremely controversial one (No. 3) dealing with the colour bar and race discrimination, was not accepted by the Government. Of the non-accepted Labour-promoted Motions, one (No. 1) was 'talked out', amid considerable procedural wrangling, one (No. 6) was defeated, and one (No. 15) was withdrawn. Two of these (Nos. 6 and 15) were critical of Government policy, while the third (No. 1) was highly controversial in its implications.

When the House spent the whole, or nearly the whole of the day on one Motion, there were protests from the Member whose Motion was next on the list. Such protests are quite normal, for it is always galling to a Member, anxious to take advantage of a comparatively rare opportunity to raise a favourite topic, to see debating time slipping away on matters in which he is not particularly interested and to realise that he will have, at best, only a few minutes in which to make his points and, at worst, no time at all.

7

LEGISLATION

ABOUT 50 per cent. of the time of the House of Commons, according to Sir Gilbert [Lord] Campion's Memorandum to the Select Committee on Procedure, 1945, is spent on Legislation. In this chapter we consider:

1. *Public Bills*
    (*a*) Government Bills
    (*b*) Private Members' Bills
2. *Private Bills*

1. PUBLIC BILLS: (*a*) GOVERNMENT BILLS

As our example of a Government Bill we have selected the *Iron and Steel Bill, 1948-49*, one which raised matters of fundamental difference between the parties and also involved considerable attention to a large number of details. We cover (1) a preliminary discussion as to whether the Bill was a Hybrid Bill, (2) Second Reading Debate, (3) Money Resolution in Committee of the Whole House and on Report, (4) Debate on the Guillotine Resolution, (5) the Committee Stage 'upstairs', (6) the Report Stage, (7) Third Reading, (8) the Lords' amendments and their consideration by the Commons.

(a) *Introduction to the Iron and Steel Bill.* The Labour Manifesto, 'Let us Face the Future' (1945), stated of the iron and steel industry that 'only if public ownership replaces private monopoly can [it] become efficient'.[1] It was the last industry on the list for nationalisation in the 1945-50 Parliament. Other nationalisation Measures went through with reasonable speed though with increasing difficulty, as illustrated by the Oppo-

[1] The Labour Manifesto 1945, p. 7.

sition's attitude to the Gas Bill. But the Iron and Steel Bill which eventually came before Parliament, it might be argued, was not covered by the 1945 'mandate' both because of its nature and because of the lapse of time since the General Election. Further, the Conservatives felt themselves to be 'defending a last major rampart' before the onrush of the Socialist state, as Brady puts it in an excellent account of the issues involved.[2] In addition, the debates on the Bill were clearly a prelude to the General Election of 1950. Finally, the controversy was closely interlocked with the parallel one on the Parliament Bill of 1947, which, with its retrospective clause, might be used to pass the Iron and Steel Bill over the heads of the Lords.[3]

Legislation cannot be fully understood without reference to its origin outside Parliament. The immediate origin of the proposal to nationalise iron and steel was the Labour Party programme of 1945. Its roots, however, lie deeper. As early as 1931 the Labour Party included iron and steel as a public utility which must be nationalised. In 1932 the Iron and Steel Trades Confederation presented the case for nationalisation to the Trades Union Congress, which adopted it two years later. In 1942 the Labour Party made the issue a major plank in its post-war platform. The Party regarded all attempts to impose control without ownership – such as the Import Duties Advisory Committee (1932), the Iron and Steel Federation (1934) and the Iron and Steel Control (1939), later the Iron and Steel Board (1946), as completely inadequate.

Yet the Government proceeded cautiously. On April 17, 1946, the Minister of Supply, Mr. Wilmot, merely stated that it intended to extend a large measure of public ownership to a large section of the iron and steel industry. Meanwhile the 'caretaker' Iron and Steel Board would continue to operate. In the following May[4] the Commons debated a general Motion approving the decision to transfer 'to the ownership of the nation appropriate sections of the iron and steel industry'. At the same time the Government published as a White Paper[5] a special report on the industry prepared for the Coalition Government by the Iron and Steel Federation. Much of

[2] *See* Robert A. Brady, *Crisis in Britain* (Berkeley and Los Angeles, 1950), Chap. 5.
[3] *Ibid.*, Chap. 12.
[4] May 27 and 28: *H.C. Debates*, Vol. 423, cols. 838–948: 999–1122.
[5] Cmd. 6811, 1946.

Labour's case rested on this report. Mr. Wilmot made it clear that the Iron and Steel Board was not intended to 'design the pattern of nationalisation'. But the terms of reference of the Board and its acceptance by the Iron and Steel Federation gave an opportunity to the Opposition to argue later that a sufficiently powerful instrument of control had already been created. Mr. G. R. Strauss, who succeeded Mr. Wilmot on the latter's resignation in 1947 following the withdrawal of an abortive Bill, denied this. The Board was, in fact, dissolved on the eve of the introduction of the (ultimate) Iron and Steel Bill.

In the Debate in May, 1946, the Government, although making no definite legislative proposals, expressed the view that, 'faced with the necessity of carrying out vast schemes of national planning in the industry . . . a divorce of ownership from control just would not work'.[6] The clearest indication of the shape of things to come was when the Minister outlined the 'five broad divisions of the iron and steel industry' and specified which of these divisions it was proposed, after review, to take under control. To Mr. Oliver Lyttelton, however, the Government was simply proposing 'to do something to somebody, somehow, sometime'.[7] As to the divisions, effective demarcation was impossible and they would end up with some plants owned partially by the Government and partially by private enterprise.

The process of discussion, in and out of Parliament, continued unabated between this Debate and the eventual introduction of the Iron and Steel Bill. When the Third Session of the 38th Parliament of the United Kingdom opened on Tuesday, October 21, 1947, the King's Speech contained proposals to amend the Parliament Act, 1911. Everyone knew that, in part at least, this was due to fear of House of Lords opposition to the Iron and Steel Bill, though few direct references to the latter were made in the ensuing Debate on the Address. But the Prime Minister, Mr. Atlee, did say that 'in order to avoid any doubt there might be', it was 'the intention of His Majesty's Government in the present Parliament to nationalise the relevant portions of the iron and steel industry'.[8]

The Fourth Session of the 38th Parliament opened on September 14, 1948. It was a special Session summoned to deal only with the Parliament Bill. Nevertheless, references were

[6] H. C. Debates, Vol. 423, col. 845.   [7] Ibid., col. 856.
[8] H.C. Debates, Vol. 443, cols. 32–33.

made to iron and steel during the Debate on the Address.

The King's Speech at the beginning of the Fifth Session of the 38th Parliament contained reference to the Iron and Steel Bill itself. The field was set immediately by Mr. Eden's statement that 'should we be victorious at the polls, we should consider ourselves entirely free to repeal such legislation'.[9] Details of the Bill, however, could not be discussed, since Notice of the Bill had not been tabled and debate was, therefore, precluded by the rule against 'anticipation'.[10] Mr. Speaker's warning to this effect, however, was frequently disregarded, notably by Mr. Ivor Thomas,[11] who had parted from his Party on the issue.

On the Sixth Day of the Debate, Mr. R. S. Hudson[12] moved an Amendment to the Address, regretting the Government's persistence in 'obstinately persisting in a policy of nationalisation'. Mr. Dalton, Chancellor of the Exchequer, retorted that they would 'obstinately persist' in carrying out the promises which they made to the electors.[13] It is of interest to note that as a result of the Opposition Amendment, Mr. Deputy-Speaker ruled that, though they could not 'have a Second Reading Debate in anticipation of a Bill . . . general references to nationalisation are in order'.[14]

Against this background we may turn to the Debates on the Iron and Steel Bill itself.

(b) *Iron and Steel Bill: A Hybrid Bill?* Immediately after Questions on November 15, 1948, Sir David Maxwell Fyfe[15] raised a point of Order.[16] Did the Iron and Steel Bill come within S.O. No. 36, which laid down that 'where it appears that the Standing Orders relative to private business may be applicable to the Bill, the examiners of petitions shall be ordered to examine the Bill. . . .'?

A Hybrid Bill was a public Bill which appeared, on examination, to affect private rights – not those of a whole class but 'of specific individuals or corporations as distinct from all individuals or corporations of a similar category'. Clause 11 of the Iron and Steel Bill set out to nationalise 107 individual companies specified in the Third Schedule. Further, Clause 22 empowered the Minister to recover assets transferred – 'legis-

[9] *H.C. Debates*, Vol. 457, cols. 22–23.
[10] *Ibid.*, cols. 102–103.
[11] Ind., Keighley.
[12] Cons., Southport.
[13] *H.C. Debates*, Vol. 457, col. 712.
[14] *Ibid.*, 711.
[15] Cons., Liverpool, West Derby.
[16] *H.C. Debates*, Vol. 458, cols. 47–52.

lation against a number of individual companies'. Clause 11 (3)
referred to subsidiaries of steel companies, not all concerned
with steel; the latter would not be nationalised – 'a blatant
case . . . of discrimination within a category'. Selection was left
to the Minister against whom no action lay.

> If there is not the whole of a category and a discrimination is made
> between members of the category, then . . . for 500 years it has been
> the practice of the House that those who are discriminated against
> and between whom distinctions are made should have the right to
> make their own individual defence.[17]

Sir David cited three precedents: the Railways Bill, 1921, and
the Electricity (Supply) Bills, 1926 and 1934. On them, Mr.
Speaker had ruled that a question of public policy, affecting all
the undertakers of a particular class, was involved. But on the
Canals Bill, 1905, which scheduled the undertakings of certain
canal companies only, Mr. Speaker had taken the view that
S.O. No. 36 applied. When Mr. Speaker Whitley had ruled on
the 1921 Bill, this Standing Order was not mentioned to him.
It had been invoked in 1926, but, since then (a further salient
point), the S.O. had been transferred from Private Business to
Public Business.

> It therefore becomes quite clear in my submission that this is a
> definite problem posed to you by the Standing Orders.[18]

  Mr. Speaker ruled that S.O. No. 36 must be read with S.O.
No. 224 (Private Business). S.O. No. 36 first appeared in Public
Business in 1943, but contained no new provision. *Erskine May*[19]
laid down that 'it is not the practice to refer Bills dealing with
matters of public policy, whereby private rights over large areas,
or of a whole class, are affected'. This was supported by the
Rulings of 1921, 1926 and 1934. Nor had any of the large
nationalisation Measures (coal, transport, electricity, gas) been
referred to the examiners. The Railways Bill, 1921 (which
applied to all railways of a particular class) and the Transport
Bill (which excluded certain undertakings) seemed to Mr.
Speaker 'to be very complete precedents'.[20]

  (c) *Second Reading.* At 4.4 p.m., therefore, the Minister of
Supply[21] moved the Second Reading of the Bill in a speech

[17] *Ibid.*, col. 49.
[19] *Erskine May*, p. 490.
[21] Mr. G. R. Strauss.

[18] *Ibid.*, col. 50.
[20] *H.C. Debates*, Vol. 458, col. 52.

lasting just over one and a quarter hours. Some Opposition Members, he said, had denounced the Bill 'with unbridled vehemence'; others regarded it as 'half-hearted', 'timid', 'futile' – 'Strauss's mouse'. Dr. Gallup had discovered that the majority of people were opposed; he 'has been known to be wrong'. Over the coming months the great majority of people would share the Government's view – 'not on dogma or abstract theories, but on the known facts, and the conclusions to which they inevitably lead'.

Return of the vital steel industry to unregulated private ownership was out of the question. Nor was control sufficient to deal with a vast monopoly or cartel, possessing great powers without responsibility, over the well-being of our people. The Iron and Steel Board could not exercise 'a sufficiently positive influence'. Serious clashes on major matters of policy between private and public interests were bound to arise. Those with technical and commercial 'know-how' might refuse to co-operate. Efficiency was already largely affected by Government subsidies and price controls. 'To rationalise the industry properly . . . a single owner must replace the many.' We could not afford to be as conservative and cautious as the steel industry about future output.

But coal did not provide an appropriate pattern of organisation. The Government proposed 'to preserve the entity of the companies . . . and . . . simply [to transfer] their securities . . . to a public corporation'. The Corporation would take over the major concerns in iron ore, pig iron, ingot steel and the hot rolling of steel. The Minister would be able to give directions of a general character. There would be no 'wholesale dismemberment'; where necessary subsidiaries would be taken over. There would be no sudden and drastic changes, though the Corporation would 'cut out the deadwood' among directors and management. One hundred and seven firms were scheduled for transfer, with about 150 wholly-owned subsidiaries. The Ford Motor Company was excluded, despite its blast furnace, producing well over the stipulated figure of 20,000 tons. Some of the 107 might eventually be omitted. Smaller firms excluded would operate either without licence or under licence, 'as of right', up to a datum figure. The Government would consider proposals to hive-off subsidiary activities. But attempts to circumvent Parliament's purpose would evoke further legislation.

Mr. Strauss then sought to justify the principle of compensation based on Stock Exchange quotations. 'Nearly all shareholders who have bought their shares within the last ten years or so will receive in compensation more than they paid for them'. He did not accept that 'dividend limitation' affected the arguments. Steel shares had, in fact, recently been outstripping others. May 1, 1950, or such later date within eighteen months of the passing of the Act as the Minister might decide, would be vesting day.

Mr. Churchill's interjection – 'It may well be election day' – raised a point which later was to cause fierce controversy.

The Minister briefly surveyed the probable tasks of the Corporation in its early days, and expressed the view that the workers had done well 'because they wanted to help their country and because they had confidence in the Government's proposals to nationalise the industry' – witness the continuous working week. But the relative success of the industry was not an argument against nationalisation – which was 'not a sort of rescue service for semi-bankrupt private enterprises'.

This great reform removes from the private sector of our economy to the public the industry which is the citadel of British capitalism. It transfers to Parliament and the community that power to dominate the economic life of this country which now resides with the steelmasters in Steel House.[22]

A full summary of the Minister's speech has been given to indicate the Government's case. Similar treatment is now given to Mr. Oliver Lyttelton's[23] statement of the case for the Opposition. Subsequent speeches will be referred to only briefly, unless new points are raised or something of interest relating to procedure is involved.

Mr. Lyttelton spoke for just under an hour to the usual Amendment, to leave out 'now' and insert 'upon this day six months' for Second Reading. Everything Mr. Strauss had said had 'greatly deepened his anxiety'. No plan had been indicated for running the industry, 'only a few clichés about the establishment of co-ordination machinery and the like'. If the Bill went through, the public sector of the economy would be nominally 70 or 80 per cent.

In reality, private enterprise will have ceased to exist effectively . . .

[22] *H.C. Debates*, Vol. 458, cols. 53–78.   [23] Cons., Aldershot.

a revolution, not evolution, will have taken place, and that revolution at the end of a Parliament.

The industry could not be attacked on grounds of output, capacity, adequate reward to workers or hopes for further improvement. Mr. Morrison himself had admitted that this was 'in its essence, a business matter'; the onus was on the Government to prove their case and they had failed.

The real reason is that the extremists in the Socialist party wish for more power. Even when they put out one of those yellow-backed romances from the Socialist Grub Street, they call it 'Steel is Power' and give the whole thing away . . . all hon. Gentlemen opposite are nodding their heads. I congratulate them upon their rather ingenuous candour.

Were they competent, 'with the aid of a few young gentlemen from Winchester and New College, to control from Whitehall all the various problems which press upon an industry, and which can only be solved by men of long experience and expert training?' Mr. Lyttelton guessed that 'nearly half the Cabinet are, in their heart of hearts, at the best, very lukewarm about the Bill now. . . . It is because of this division of opinion that the Bill adopts an entirely novel form of nationalisation . . . a holding company.' There would be ownership without responsibility for management. Further, the method was wrong: the firms ramified into the chemical trade, the electrical industry, the manufacture of welding equipment, structural steel, the manufacture of things like the Sydney Bridge, railway equipment including axles, tyres and wheels for rolling stock . . . even into umbrella frames and florists' wire! Mr. Lyttelton analysed the undertakings of the English Steel Corporation to illustrate his point. In many of these spheres the Government would be in competition with private firms, the latter being largely dependent for raw materials on the nationalised industries.

At the end of it all we find the taxpayer competing with concerns which are to be subsidised and helped with his own money.

As to organisation, 'the bottom end of the demarcation between private enterprise and the Government will look like the chart of a man with *delirium tremens* – no one will be able to tell which way it is going'. Finally,

The Government are bringing forward this Bill for far deeper reasons and for far longer objects than those which appear on the surface. They believe in the centralisation of power in the hands of the State and they regard this as a major move towards that end. . . . It has long been our doctrine that in a democracy power should be dispersed; that the Government should govern and supervise and not own and manage.[24]

The stage was thus set: general arguments on fundamental principle and detailed argument on the merits of the proposals in the Bill. All subsequent speeches were variants on these two main themes.

Mr. S. N. Evans[25] spoke in some detail about the restrictive and discriminatory nature of the Iron and Steel Federation's control of the industry – without responsibility for social obligations, for such things as 'whole villages being put to sleep by the technical and competitive forces of . . . new plant'. As to control, already it was 'passing into the hands of comptometer champions from Holborn Bars'.[26] On this, Viscount Hinchingbrooke[27] said that all the Bill did was 'to remove the shareholders and financiers . . . and substitute the Minister and the hierarchy of the civil service'. On reorganisation, Mr. Monslow[28] knew of works which were.

a tangled riddle of gaps, corners, adjacent shops alternately empty and overcrowded, illogical separations, unbalanced and tortuous routes and methods in the handling of materials . . . major reconstruction is imperative.[29]

But to Mr. Hugh Fraser[30] the Bill was a semi-hybrid and certain to prove sterile – as, in nature, according to Darwin, was the fate of all semi-hybrids.[31] Mr. Osbert Peake[32] foresaw that the Corporation would have 'to engage in constant day-to-day interference with the management of the 107 companies' in ways never attempted by shareholders.[33]

Mr. Churchill opened for the Opposition on the second day with an eloquent onslaught on Socialist policy in general and nationalisation in particular. The Iron and Steel industry was now to be 'exploited . . . in the sectional interests of Socialist factionaries, anxious to prolong their enjoyment of the sweets of

---

[24] H.C. Debates, Vol. 458, cols. 79–96.
[25] Lab., Wednesbury.
[26] H.C. Debates, Vol. 458, cols. 96–106.
[27] Cons., Dorset South.
[28] Lab., Barrow-in-Furness.
[29] H.C. Debates, Vol. 458, col. 145.
[30] Cons., Stafford and Stone.
[31] H.C. Debates, Vol. 458, col 148.
[32] Cons., Leeds North-West.
[33] H.C. Debates, Vol. 458, col. 156.

office, and have more patronage to distribute to their backers and friends'. As to the plan, the Government were 'picking and choosing, and doing so on no principle but the caprice of a party Minister'. The Socialists were 'the handmaids and heralders of Communism'; this was 'a plot . . . a burglar's jemmy to crack the capitalist crib'. The date for taking over was to give 'the Government the utmost span of office, and at the same time to present the nationalisation of steel as the direct issue at the General Election'. It was also to adjust the differences in the Cabinet 'between the extreme nationalisers and the more sober and responsible Ministers'. [An hon. Member: 'Who are they?'] Mr. Churchill spoke for just over an hour.[34]

Mr. Jack Jones[35] argued that the Bill was workmanlike, contained opportunities for all engaged in iron and steel and provided ample scope for 'steady, effective and profitable' development. Mr. Clement Davies[36] congratulated Mr. Jones on his 'sincerity . . . conviction and experience'. But he and the Minister had followed the ideological, not the economic argument. The Government should have instituted a full, comprehensive public inquiry such as there had been for the gas industry. But Mr. Horabin,[37] a former Liberal, wanted to know why his former leader had withdrawn the support for nationalisation expressed in his signature to 'Publicly Owned Monopolies' (1940).

Sir John Anderson[38] spoke almost entirely of compensation. Stock Exchange values, he considered, were an unsound and unfair basis.

Mr. Martin Lindsay[39] felt so strongly opposed to the Bill that he said:

It is a tradition of this House that we do not let political differences interfere with personal friendship, but I am bound to say that I shall find it very hard to follow that tradition for at least some time [with] Members who wilfully jeopardise the safety of the nation.[40]

Mr. Fairhurst[41] retorted:

Never again can we allow the people we represent to toil under a system of society which allows the things which have happened in the last 50 years.[42]

[34] *Ibid.*, cols. 215–233.   [35] Joint Parliamentary Secretary to the Ministry of Supply.
[36] Lib., Montgomery.   [37] Lab., Cornwall North.
[38] Nat., Scottish Universities.   [39] Cons., Solihull.
[40] *H.C. Debates*, Vol. 458, cols. 287–288.   [41] Lab., Oldham.
[42] *H.C. Debates*, Vol. 458, col. 292.

Mr. Selwyn Lloyd[43] wound up for the Opposition, restating the orthodox case against a 'power drunk' Government. The Chancellor of the Exchequer[44] devoted most of his winding-up speech to the question of compensation and ridiculed Sir John Anderson's 'purely artificial distinction between rights . . . and assets'. During the course of many interventions he sustained what Mr. Churchill described as a 'brilliantly able argument'.

On the Bill as a whole, Sir Stafford said that it was not a question as between uncontrolled private enterprise and national ownership, but between private or public control of a vital industry. From this point he was subjected to continuous interruption, particularly from Mr. Churchill. The debate ended as follows:

Sir Stafford Cripps: . . . this challenge having been put forward by private interests, it is essential that democracy should assert its rights, as otherwise it must acknowledge for all time that it cannot touch these citadels of power, and that it is not the electorate but the owners of industrial property who shall determine the economic policies of the country. And the ugly alternative would then be that any such change . . . must be brought about by other and more violent means – [An hon. Member: 'By gunpowder?'] – and it is because we are preventing that that Socialist democracy is the true barrier against Communism – [Interruption] – I should like hon. Gentlemen opposite – [Interruption] –

Mr. Churchill rose –

Hon. Members: Order.

Mr. Speaker: The right hon. and learned Gentleman is in possession and the right hon. Gentleman must give way.

Mr. Churchill rose –

Hon. Members: Order.

Sir Stafford Cripps: I should be interested to hear –

Mr. Churchill: You have no right to –

Hon. Members: Order.

Sir Stafford Cripps: I shall be interested to hear of any case in which Conservatism has proved a barrier to Communism in the same way that Socialist democracy has been.

On the third day, Sir Andrew Duncan[45] resumed for the Opposition. To him the Bill was completely irrelevant to efficiency; he told the story of the past, leading up to the development plan submitted by the industry in 1945. There was 'effective control' by the Iron and Steel Board and progress would continue.[46]

---

[43] Cons., Wirral.
[45] Nat., City of London.
[44] Sir Stafford Cripps.
[46] *H.C. Debates*, Vol. 458, cols. 373–387.

Mr. Ronald Mackay[47] told the story of the past 'in a different way' and showed how the bulk of the key processes in iron and steel were being brought in by the Bill. Subsequent speakers made a series of particular points, though Mr. Marples[48] returned to the general charge against the Government. One day they would 'produce a Bill to abolish original sin'.[49] He complained about long speeches from the Front-Benchers; on this Lieut-Col. Sir Cuthbert Headlam[50] agreed – but pointed out that Mr. Marples had spoken for longer than the previous speaker!

Mr. Eden[51] wound up for the Opposition. Very few speeches on either side, he said, had been made by Members in close contact with the industry. He asked a number of questions about how the Bill would work, and how it would affect the industry. 'Not one single time has the efficiency argument been used,' he said.

The decision tonight should be taken on grounds of economic efficiency, and not on the purely ideological grounds that Ministers have so far advanced.

He ended with a specific warning about the future:

Supposing that at the General Election our party receives a clear majority from the nation, would the right hon. Gentleman then accept that we have the full right not only in the strict letter of the Constitution but in its spirit also as a free democracy to repeal the legislation which the Government are tonight asking us to pass, or would he regard that as a provocative act justifying revolutionary action?[52]

The Lord President of the Council (Mr. H. Morrison), replied to the debate. Naturally, he said, the Opposition – like Conservative newspapers – asserted that the Government had made no case. 'That is common form.' Yet the Chancellor of the Exchequer had 'made a speech of such outstanding positive merit that the . . . Leader of the Opposition could not stay in his seat for five minutes on end'. Mr. Morrison then replied specifically to Mr. Eden:

. . . clearly, it would be constitutionally perfectly legitimate [to repeal the Act]. . . . We are not a party which says that, if the electors have voted for a course of policy, the House of Lords should

[47] Lab., Hull North-West.
[48] Cons., Wallasey.
[49] *H.C. Debates*, Vol. 458, col. 425.
[50] Cons., Newcastle-upon-Tyne North.
[51] Cons., Warwick and Leamington.
[52] *H.C. Debates*, Vol. 458, cols. 472–481.

throw it out. If the electorate did, unhappily, vote for a Tory majority next time, the electorate must take the consequences of what it does. But, if they claim the right to repeal, then I say – and I want the leaders of the party opposite to understand this, and another place to understand it – if they get an electoral mandate to repeal this Measure then we also have the right to carry this Measure for which we have a specific electoral mandate, and the Tory Party in this House has no right to use another place for the purpose, and the deliberate purpose, of upsetting the expressed will of the people.

He then proceeded to give detailed justification for the Bill, while ridiculing the 'preposterous suggestion' that 'specific and detailed plans should have been included'.[53]

Question put, "that 'now' stand part of the Question." Ayes 373: Noes 211.

Mr. Eden then moved 'That the Bill be committed to a Committee of the whole House'. No debate being permitted, the House divided and the Motion was lost by 366 votes to 212. The Bill thus automatically stood committed to a Standing Committee.[54] The House then proceeded to take the Money Resolution in Committee of the whole House.[55]

(d) *Money Resolution.* The King's recommendation being signified, the Committee (of the whole House) proceeded to debate the Money Resolution, which authorised payment:

(a) to fulfil the Treasury guarantee of principal and interest on stock issued by the Iron and Steel Corporation and interest on temporary borrowings by the Corporation or the publicly-owned companies under the Act.

The sum was not to exceed £350,000,000 excluding amounts outstanding in respect of stock issued or moneys temporarily borrowed to redeem stock or to repay moneys temporarily borrowed.

(b) to cover (i) subsidies on imported steel (ii) remuneration and allowances of stockholders' representatives under the Act (iii) fees and allowances to referees or boards dealing with pensions rights, compensation to officers, allowances to witnesses (iv) similar payments to the arbitration tribunal and (v) the administrative expenses of the Minister or Government Department.

(c) into the Exchequer of any sums received by a Minister of the Crown or Government Department.

Mr. Peter Roberts[56] asked the Financial Secretary for certain

---

[53] *Ibid.*, cols. 481–494.
[55] S.O. No. 84.
[54] S.O. No. 38.
[56] Cons., Sheffield, Eccleshall.

explanations, arising from the divergencies between this Money Resolution and previous Resolutions of a similar kind.

Mr. C. Williams[57] thought it wrong to insist upon a Resolution of that kind being forced through at that time of night. He asked certain questions on sub-paragraphs (iii) and (iv). This was the best opportunity of finding out if there were any plan for the boards; how many officials, of what type and with what remuneration would there be?

Mr. Gallacher[58] sought to move an Amendment to exclude vast sums of money from being paid to the former owners – 'free gifts to the barons' – but the Chairman ruled this out of order. Mr. Emrys Hughes[59] and Mr. Scollan[60] also protested at the huge sums provided for compensation for the stockholders.

Mr. David Renton[61] protested at the financial burden of the new bureaucratic pyramid' with its 'tight mass of officials'.[62] Sir John Mellor[63] wished to know if the stock would be 'dated' and took the opportunity of referring to the 'Dalton Stock of unhappy memory'. Mr. George Ward[64] wanted more details of 'the irresponsible way in which the State was prepared to spend money voted by Parliament'. He, too, was ruled out of order.

The Minister of Supply said that most of the points raised were of a general character and the Committee would not want him to deal with them in detail. He would certainly not deal with the payment of compensation, nor with how the money borrowed would be spent, nor with who would be on the Corporation or boards. Pressed on these, Mr. Strauss was protected by the obvious Ruling that the salaries of members of the boards, etc., were not covered by the Resolution; nor was the sum mentioned to cover compensation for shares, etc. Interpreting Mr. C. Williams' question as one confined to the Resolution, Mr. Strauss stated that payments under sub-paragraphs (iii) and (iv) were governed by Treasury rates – of 3 to 5 guineas a day.

On the three 'points of substance', the Minister stated (1) that the sum did not include compensation, (2) that the administrative expenses would be very small and would come before

---

[57] Cons., Torquay.
[59] Lab., South Ayrshire.
[61] Cons., Huntingdon.
[63] Cons., Sutton Coldfield.

[58] Comm., Fife West.
[60] Lab., Renfrew West.
[62] *H.C. Debates*, Vol. 458, col. 510.
[64] Cons., Worcester.

the House every year, and (3) that the stock would be dated.

The Resolution was carried by 320 votes to 190 and the House adjourned at 11.22 p.m.

When the *Money Resolution was reported to the House* at 10 p.m. on November 23, Sir John Mellor raised further questions about the stock to be issued by the Corporation and guaranteed by the Treasury, and received explanations from the Minister of Supply.

(e) *The Guillotine Motion and debate.*[65] We set out below the Guillotine Motion as printed in *Hansard:*

IRON AND STEEL BILL (ALLOCATION OF TIME)

4.3 p.m.

The Lord President of the Council (Mr. Herbert Morrison): I beg to move,

That the proceedings on the Committee stage, Report stage, and Third Reading of the Iron and Steel Bill shall be proceeded with as follows:

(1) *Committee stage*

(a) The Standing Committee to which the Bill is referred shall report the Bill to the House on or before the seventeenth day of March next.

(b) At a Sitting at which any proceedings are to be brought to a conclusion under a Resolution of the Business sub-committee as agreed to by the Standing Committee, the Chairman shall not adjourn the Committee under any order relating to the Sittings of the Committee until the proceedings have been brought to a conclusion.

(c) At a Sitting at which any proceedings are to be brought to a conclusion under such a Resolution, no Motion relating to the Sittings of the Committee, no dilatory Motion with respect to proceedings on the Bill or the adjournment of the Committee, nor Motion to postpone a Clause, shall be moved except by the Government, and the Question on any such Motion (other than a Motion relating to the Sittings of the Committee), if moved by the Government shall be put forthwith without any debate.

(d) On the conclusion of the Committee stage of the Bill the Chairman shall report the Bill to the House without Question put.

(2) *Report stage and Third Reading*

(a) Four allotted days shall be given to the Report stage (including any proceedings on the re-committal of the Bill).

(b) One allotted day shall be given to the Third Reading, and the proceedings thereon shall, if not previously brought to a conclusion, be brought to a conclusion at 9.30 p.m. on that day.

[65] November 25, 1948: *Ibid.*, cols. 1424–1544.

(*c*) Any other day than a Friday on which the Bill is put down as the first Order of the Day shall be considered an allotted day for the purposes of this order.

(*d*) Any Private Business which has been set down for consideration at 7 p.m. and any Motion for Adjournment under Standing Order No. 9 on an allotted day shall on that day, instead of being taken as provided by the Standing Orders, be taken at the conclusion of the proceedings on the Bill or under this order for that day, and any private Business or Motion for Adjournment so taken may be proceeded with, though opposed, notwithstanding any Standing Order relating to the Sittings of the House.

(*e*) On a day on which any proceedings are to be brought to a conclusion under any Resolution of the Business committee as agreed to by the House or under this order, those proceedings shall not be interrupted under the provisions of any Standing Order relating to the Sittings of the House.

(*f*) On a day on which any proceedings are to be brought to a conclusion under any Resolution of the Business committee as agreed to by the House or under this order, no dilatory Motion with respect to proceedings on the Bill or under this order, nor Motion to re-commit the Bill, shall be moved unless moved by the Government, and the question on any such Motion, if moved by the Government, shall be put forthwith without any debate.

(3) *General*

(*a*) For the purpose of bringing to a conclusion any proceedings which are to be brought to a conclusion at a time appointed by a Resolution of the Business sub-committee, as agreed to by the Standing Committee, or by a Resolution of the Business committee, as agreed to by the House, or by this order, and which have not previously been brought to a conclusion, the Chairman or Mr. Speaker shall, at the time so appointed, put forthwith the question on any Amendment or Motion already proposed from the Chair, and, in the case of a new clause which has been read a Second time, also the question that the Clause be added to the Bill, and shall next proceed to put forthwith the questions on any Amendments, new clauses or new schedules moved by the Government of which notice has been given (but no other Amendments, new clauses or new schedules), and any question necessary for the disposal of the Business to be concluded, and, in the case of Government Amendments or Government new clauses or Government new schedules, he shall put only the questions that the Amendments be made or that the clauses or schedules be added to the Bill, as the case may be.

(*b*) Nothing in this order or in a Resolution of the Business sub-committee or Business committee shall—

(i) prevent any proceedings which thereunder are to be concluded on any particular day or at any particular Sitting being concluded on an earlier day or at an earlier Sitting, or necessitate any particular day or Sitting or part of a particular day or Sitting being given to any such proceedings if those proceedings have been otherwise disposed of; or

(ii) prevent any other Business being proceeded with on a particular day, or part of a particular day, in accordance with the Standing Orders of the House, if any proceedings to be concluded on that particular day, or part of a particular day, have been disposed of.

(c) In this order the expression 'Business committee' and 'Business sub-committee' respectively mean the Committee appointed under Standing Order No. 41, and the sub-committee appointed under Standing Order No. 64 of the Standing Committee to which the Bill is referred.

I move this Motion with regret.

The debate on the above is a most important illustration of the use of the guillotine and allied procedures,[66] and also of the work of *Standing Committees*.

Mr. Morrison explained that the Committee proceedings could be spread over eleven Parliamentary weeks; thirty-five Sittings, including some afternoons, would be possible. This would be four more than for the Transport Bill. Four days for the Report stage was one more than for the Transport Bill. Another day was allocated to Third Reading. In accordance with S.O.s Nos. 41 and 64, the detailed allocation of time for the different parts of the Bill would be settled by the Business Committees. This was a fairly new procedure for Standing Committees and used for the first time in the House, as such. The Government would 'take a favourable view of the demands of the Opposition, subject to the business of the Committee being conducted in a way which is practicable, and with a view to getting some finality on the issues to be determined'.[67] Mr. Morrison thought it a sensible arrangement to impose an Allocation of Time Order from the beginning; it was more realistic than to await progress 'upstairs' on such a contentious Measure. It would also get the Bill to 'another place' in reasonable time. Further time would certainly be needed to consider Lords' Amendments.[68]

At this point Mr. Morrison referred to the 'disgraceful exhibition' in Committee on the Gas Bill – 'a competition in

[66] cf. P. A. Bromhead, 'The Guillotine in the House of Commons' in *Parliamentary Affairs*, Vol. xi, No. 4.

[67] *H.C. Debates*, Vol. 458, col. 1428.   [68] *See* below, pp. 171–180.

physical exhaustion'.[69] This Bill had taken 127 hours in Committee and occupied forty-two issues of the Standing Committee *Hansard*. He ended by saying that he would have preferred an agreed time-table but the Opposition was not willing to meet the Government.[70]

Mr. Eden moved an Amendment which had the effect of destroying the Allocation of Time Order and deploring the 'arbitrary curtailment of debate'. He distinguished firmly between precedents for the application of the Guillotine on the Floor of the House and its unprecedented application to a Standing Committee. On the Gas Bill, Mr. Eden noted that there had been 111 Government Amendments on Report, so the Committee Stage had not been wasted. The Opposition had not been prepared to discuss a time-table because they thought the Bill should have been taken on the Floor of the House.

Never until this Parliament have major Bills of the Session – and this is surely the major Bill of the Session – been sent upstairs and never until this Parliament has a Bill been guillotined in Committee upstairs.[71]

The time allowed for the Report stage would be 'quite derisory'. In support of this contention, Mr. Eden cited the Transport Bill: 37 out of 127 Clauses and 7 out of 13 Schedules were not discussed at all; on Report the Guillotine fell at Clause 38. The Government itself introduced 250 Amendments in Committee, of which 94 had not been reached when the Guillotine fell. He quoted similar figures for the Town and Country Planning Bill. In 'another place' the Government had moved 139 Amendments to the Transport Bill and 289 to the Town and Country Planning Bill, besides accepting 45 Opposition Amendments. The House of Lords had, in fact, altered the two Bills by 230 and 336 Amendments respectively.

It is important that the House should understand the fundamental change in our procedure which is brought about by sending these major Bills upstairs while getting no corresponding increase of time on Report.[72]

This argument, said Mr. Eden, applied particularly to a Bill of the nature of the Iron and Steel Bill, which 'raises all sorts of

---

[69] *H.C. Debates*, Vol. 458, col. 1431.
[70] For his useful historical survey of the Guillotine cf. *Ibid.*, cols. 1436–1438.
[71] *Ibid.*, col. 1441.   [72] *Ibid.*, col. 1447.

problems of a grave and far-reaching character that were not raised by the previous nationalisation Measures'.[73]

Mr. David Eccles[74] spoke of the work done in Standing Committee on the Coal Nationalisation Bill and suggested that equal time at least for similar Clauses was required on iron and steel.[75]

Mr. James Hudson[76] argued that if discussion were regulated there was a better chance of important Amendments being selected.

We cannot [he said] sit for hours and hours under an unregulated system and expect by that process to effect a remarkable examination of either difficult or easy Clauses of any Bill which comes before Parliament.[77]

Mr. I. J. Pitman[78] retorted that the 'only reason why we sat all night at all on the Gas Bill was that the time allotted by the Government was insufficient for the purpose of discussing the Bill'.[79] To this, Mr. Proctor[80] replied that the Government side had deliberately refrained from speaking on many occasions because they knew the tactics of the Opposition were to waste time by speaking without any limits and thus delay legislation.[81] One Member had regaled them with a story of what happened to a meeting of the Primrose League in a public house owned by a railway company.

Mr. Quintin Hogg[82] was 'sincerely convinced that in proposing [guillotine measures] the Government are murdering Parliamentary democracy'. The right to vote in the way their consciences dictated was no longer a guarantee of freedom because under Parliamentary conditions the party system normally operated in such a way that the result of every vote was a foregone conclusion. Neither was the right of free speech in the Chamber an adequate guarantee of a free democracy.

Under modern Parliamentary conditions, under our actual working Constitution, there is one sanction of freedom in this House and one sanction alone. That is the fact that the Government know that a want of reason on their part, a want of desire to give in to argument,

---

[73] Ibid., col. 1449.
[74] Cons., Chippenham.
[75] From this point several speakers were called to order for discussing the merits of the Bill rather than the Guillotine Motion.
[76] Lab., Ealing.
[77] H.C. Debates, Vol. 458, col. 1471.
[78] Cons., Bath.
[79] Ibid., col. 1472.
[80] Lab., Eccles.
[81] H.C. Debates, Vol. 458, col. 1474.
[82] Cons., Oxford.

a want of willingness to pay attention to other people's convictions and feelings, will, in fact, lead to greater difficulties in the
passage of their own business. . . . Our view of Parliamentary institutions is that discussions of this House should be real discussions and
not sham discussions. . . .[83]

Mr. Maclay[84] added that to construct sound legislation it
was not possible to estimate in advance what time was needed
for various Clauses. A possible way of expediting progress was
to use the *Closure* more frequently. Viscount Hinchingbrooke[85]
charged the Government with wishing

to curtail in time the legislative function of Parliament, and to
pitch the initiative of legislation outside Parliament altogether,
somewhere in the recesses of the Civil Service, or, perhaps worse,
in the recesses of Transport House.[86]

Mr. Frederick Lee[87] took up this challenge:

When [the people] sent this Government and its supporters here they
determined that there was a need for a fundamental change in the
whole conception of the use of this Parliament. It is utterly impossible
for any Government, functioning within the period of a five-year
life, to put into operation those fundamental changes which are so
necessary unless there is a change in conception as to the uses to
which this House must be put.[88]

Major Haughton[89] retorted that the duty to make an Act of
Parliament work rested upon the assumption that 'every line,
every word, every comma, should be studied'.[90]

After a few further speeches, Mr. Oliver Stanley[91] wound up
for the Opposition. He restated the case against using the
Guillotine 'upstairs' and 'before definite and complete evidence
of obstruction'. The Committee and Report stages 'should
mean not merely making a general case against a Bill, but
criticising, altering, and making suggestions in various details;
and that really cannot be done in the time allotted'.[92]

The Home Secretary[93] wound up the debate. No argument,
he said, had any weight save the Opposition belief that the time
allowed was insufficient. A voluntary agreement was best,
witness the Electricity Act (twenty-five days). But for months
the Opposition had been saying that what happened on the

[83] *H.C. Debates*, Vol. 458, cols. 1476–1479.
[85] Cons., Dorset South.
[87] Lab., Manchester, Hulme.
[89] Cons., Antrim.
[91] Cons., Bristol West.
[93] Mr. Chuter Ede.
[84] Cons., Montrose Boroughs.
[86] *H.C. Debates*, Vol. 458, col. 1494.
[88] *H.C. Debates*, Vol. 458, col. 1497.
[90] *H.C. Debates*, Vol. 458, col. 1498.
[92] *H.C. Debates*, Vol. 458, col. 1534.

Gas Bill was child's play to what was going to happen on this Bill.

If there is anything to learn from the history of the past few years it is that where, owing to one cause or another, excessive discussion has brought Parliament into disrepute, Parliamentary democracy has suffered its most severe defeat.[94]

The Amendment was defeated and the Motion agreed to.

(f) *Committee stage*. The Iron and Steel Bill was sent 'upstairs' to Standing Committee 'C', consisting of the usual 'nucleus' of 20 Members with 30 'added' for the specific Bill. The Committee met for 36 Sittings (one being added to the original 35), each of $2\frac{1}{2}$ hours. The debates cover 1786 columns in Volume I, Session 1948–49, of Parliamentary Debates: Commons, Standing Committees. There were, in all, 105 Divisions. The first Sitting was held on December 7, 1948, and the last on March 17, 1949. All but three were held in the morning, from 10.30 a.m. to 1.0 p.m. approximately.

The Business Sub-Committee formulated the following timetable:

Sittings	*Clauses*
First – Seventh . . .	1 – 4
Eighth and Ninth . . .	5 – 10
Tenth – Twelfth . . .	11 – 13
Thirteenth – Sixteenth . .	14 – 16
Seventeenth	17 and 18
Eighteenth – Twenty-second .	19 – 26
Twenty-third . . .	27 and 28
Twenty-fourth . . .	29 – 34
Twenty-fifth . . .	35 and 36
Twenty-sixth – Twenty-eighth	37 – 40
Twenty-ninth – Thirty-first .	41 – 58
Thirty-second – Thirty-fifth .	Postponed Clauses, new Clauses, Schedules and new Schedules and any other proceedings necessary to bring the Committee stage to a conclusion.

Later the Sub-Committee added another session for the consideration of clauses 1 – 4, thus bringing the total number of sittings to 36.

On December 7 the Minister of Supply moved that the Committee meet every Tuesday, Wednesday and Thursday

[94] *H.C. Debates*, Vol. 458, col. 1538.

(except Tuesday, January 18, 1949) at 10.30 a.m. and on such afternoons as the Committee might subsequently resolve at 4.30 p.m. He indicated that three afternoons would be needed during the later Sessions. The Guillotine would fall at 12.45 on those days on which the time-table provided that consideration of a Clause or group of Clauses must be concluded. There was immediate argument, accompanied by the copious quotation of precedent, as to whether on *other* days the Sittings might be prolonged, and whether afternoons were separate Sittings. The point of this was revealed by Viscount Hinchingbrooke's accusation that the Government wished to stifle discussion on Clause 1. They had refused to use S.O. No. 49A, which provided for the adjournment of the House to permit discussions in Standing Committee. They were now trying to prevent afternoon and evening meetings. He wished to consult 'high legal authority'. The Chairman, however, pointed out that there was no appeal from his Ruling, not even to Mr. Speaker. He wished there were!

Sir Charles MacAndrew himself, however, was clearly uncertain of the position, and the argument continued. Eventually he suggested that Mr. Strauss should, for the moment, move his Resolution without the references to afternoons and these should be reconsidered with the Business Sub-Committee. The Question was then put in that form and carried by 26 votes to 15. The discussion had lasted one and a quarter hours.

On December 9 Sir Charles MacAndrew gave his Ruling on this matter. There were, he said, only two precedents governing an Allocation of Time Order when applied to proceedings in Standing Committee: the Transport Bill and the Town and Country Planning Bill. Any afternoon Sitting must be one of the separate thirty-five Sittings. Apart from these precedents, a recent S.O. No. 63 (2) directed the Chairman to adjourn Standing Committees at 1.0 p.m.; this had applied to the Gas Bill, for which there was no Guillotine. S.O. No. 63 (1) also laid down that afternoon Sittings might not begin before 3.30 p.m. The duration of such Sittings was within the discretion of the Committee unless proceedings had to be brought to an end, in which case it was two and a quarter hours. He added that there were also plenty of precedents for the grouping of Clauses. Mr. Manningham-Buller then gave notice that on the following

Tuesday Mr. Lyttelton would move to meet at 4.30 p.m. as well as at 10.30 a.m.; its effect would be to start the Fifth Sitting at 4.30 p.m. and to provide adequate time to discuss the first four Clauses, since they could sit, if necessary, until one o'clock the following day![95]

On December 14, when Mr. Lyttelton moved his Motion, Mr. Strauss agreed to make a proposal for an extra Sitting, but warned that it would last only two and a half hours. The matter was briefly debated[96] and the eventual result was the extra day referred to earlier. Subsequently, several attempts[97] were made to meet in the afternoon, the purpose obviously being to obtain extra Sittings. They were all opposed by Mr. Strauss and defeated in Divisions on party lines.

It is convenient here to illustrate another type of procedural difficulty. One possible way of telescoping discussion is to take several Amendments together, whether or not there may later be separate Divisions on them. Frequently such procedure involves no difficulty and is readily acceptable to both sides. Problems, however, may arise, and we illustrate their nature.

On December 7, Viscount Hinchingbrooke moved an Amendment to make the Minister select members of the Corporation from 'a panel of persons named by the British Iron and Steel Federation and the Iron and Steel Trades Confederation'.[98] A little later the Chairman suggested that it might be convenient to discuss at the same time an Amendment in the name of Mr. Lyttelton to provide for 'an additional member to be selected by the Minister from persons nominated by the principal steel-using organisations'.[99] Mr. Lyttelton agreed, but, after a short speech by Mr. Geoffrey Cooper, he submitted that the latter was really discussing a further Amendment to compel the Minister to 'consult such bodies as appear to him representative of the producers and the users of iron and steel and the workers engaged in the industry'.[1]

The Chairman: I think that Amendment should also be considered.
Mr. Lloyd: I suggest that the first Amendment is rather different.
The Chairman: Are they not both relevant?
Mr. Lloyd: No, the first Amendment provides that an additional

[95] Standing Committee Report, cols. 107–110.
[96] *Ibid.*, cols. 157–170.
[97] e.g., Mr. Harold Macmillan on December 16.
[98] Standing Committee Report, col. 38.
[99] *Ibid.*, col. 42.
[1] *Ibid.*, col. 43.

member be selected from a certain class, but it is the later Amendment which deals with the general principle of the composition of
the Corporation.

The Chairman: I suggest that we take both the Amendments into
consideration.

Mr. Lloyd: I suggest that the first Amendment raises a different
point, and that it is the fifth Amendment on the page to which the
hon. Member for West Middlesbrough (Mr. Cooper) has been
speaking, namely, in page 2, line 3, at the end to insert . . .[2]

The Chairman: No, I think these two Amendments can be considered
with the Amendment moved by the noble Lord.

Mr. Shepherd: The first Amendment on page 144 relates to the
appointment of an additional member and, therefore, comes into
an entirely different category from the other Amendments.

The Chairman: Yes, but the additional member has to be selected
from a number of organisations. All these Amendments can be
divided on when they are reached, but it would be for the convenience of the Committee if they were discussed together.[3]

The Debate proceeded on these lines until the Committee
was adjourned at 1.0 p.m. On its resumption the next day, Mr.
Geoffrey Cooper at once rose to suggest that the process was
introducing 'some slight confusion'.

The Chairman: [The Amendments] are a little different, but, if the
Committee wishes, they can divide on the other two when we come
to them. We thought yesterday that it was convenient to take them
together, and I think we had better carry on with that arrangement.

Colonel J. R. H. Hutchison: I understand that we are also discussing,
along with these other two Amendments, the first one on page 161,
to insert the words 'iron ore or'.

The Chairman: No, we are discussing the first Amendment on the
paper, on Clause 1. The discussion on it was proceeding when we
adjourned yesterday.[4]

Mr. Lyttelton continued the Debate on these lines. Soon after
12 noon, when several Members rose, the Chairman remarked
that there were three pages of Amendments on Clause 1 and
the Committee had already taken up two and a half hours. He
hoped that the Committee would realise that time might run
out.

A little later Mr. Osbert Peake referred to the Chairman's
remarks and said:

I do not think that anyone can really complain if the discussion has
been somewhat discursive, because we have taken in one discussion

---

[2] *Ibid.*, cf. above, col. 43.   [3] *Ibid.*, cols. 43–44.   [4] *Ibid.*, col. 56.

three Amendments which are very different in their essential character. If I may say so, with the greatest respect to you, Sir Charles, I think that it would facilitate discussion in the future and enable you to restrict the discussion to the precise point before the Committee if Amendments were taken singly rather than grouped together, unless the subject-matter is very closely related.

The Chairman: I apologise to the Committee. I thought that the Amendments were more closely related than in fact they are. It was for the convenience of the Committee that I suggested that they should be taken together.

Mr. Peake: I agree that it was only in the course of discussion that the difference in the nature of the Amendments became apparent...[5]

The Debate then continued for some little time and Viscount Hinchingbrooke's Amendment was then negatived without a Division.

Mr. Cooper: On a point of Order, Sir Charles. You have only put one Amendment. Are you putting the other Amendment separately?

The Chairman: I shall put the other Amendments when we get to them.[6]

At this point it is convenient to illustrate the procedure whereby the Chairman may use his *powers under S.O. No. 31 or S.O. 57 (5) to select Amendments*.

Mr. Lyttelton had tabled an Amendment to insert after 'production' the words: 'including the management of works or companies used for or engaged in such production'.

The Chairman: This Amendment seems to me to be unnecessary. I do not see how one can be a producer without having knowledge of the management of the works.

Mr. Manningham-Buller: The point here is the interpretation and the legal meaning of the word production. . . . I ask leave formally to move –

The Chairman: I have not yet selected the Amendment.

Mr. Manningham-Buller: I know; I was merely indicating the reasons why I was asking you to select the Amendment . . .

Mr. Mikardo: . . . the word 'production' is used in the widest sense . . .

The Chairman: My own view is that it would be unreasonable to suggest that production means only the people who do the manual work, and I shall not select the Amendment.[7]

We now turn to substance rather than procedure. The discussions fall roughly into three groups: (1) party bickerings

[5] *Ibid.*, col. 90.
[6] There are further examples of this problem of discussing Amendments together in cols. 657–658 and 1273–1274.
[7] *Ibid.*, cols. 99–100.

which seem only remotely relevant to the real task of the Committee, namely, to tidy up the details and make more workable a Bill whose principles have already been accepted by the House; (2) detailed discussions of particular points in the Bill which are primarily intended to result in constructive alterations; (3) debates on larger matters which, although necessarily related to specific Amendments, reveal fundamental differences of principle. The last two are not always easy to separate.

A further analysis might be based upon: (1) Amendments proposed by the Minister in the light of his (and his advisers') second thoughts following upon the Second Reading Debate; (2) Opposition Amendments accepted by the Minister; (3) Opposition Amendments received favourably by the Minister and in relation to which 'assurances' may be given in regard to the Report stage or, possibly, to consideration 'in another place'; (4) Opposition Amendments of an 'exploratory nature' which appear unnecessary after 'explanations' by the Minister; (5) Opposition Amendments which are resisted and rejected as being contrary to Government policy.

We deal with the discussions in such a way as to give an outline of the whole process, and select longer extracts to illustrate the categories indicated above.

On December 7, after the procedural wrangle, the Committee began its consideration of Clause 1 (The Iron and Steel Corporation of Great Britain). An Amendment to change 'Corporation' to '(Holdings) Company' was withdrawn on the Minister's promise to look at the name again if certain changes (which, however, he would resist) were made in Clause 2. An Amendment[8] to make the minimum size of the Board six (not four) with the Chairman, which was supported by Mr. S. N. Evans,[9] was accepted by Mr. Strauss and agreed to. There followed Viscount Hinchingbrooke's Amendment,[10] which was being discussed, with two others, when the Committee adjourned at 1.0 p.m. The Minister's general reply, given the next day, was that all consultations about appointments must be informal and should not be written into the Bill. The Amendment, as we have seen, was negatived. Another, to include persons experienced in the production of iron ore, was accepted

---

[8] Mr. Lyttelton.   [9] Lab., Wednesbury.   [10] *See* above p. 143.

and agreed to. A further Amendment was not selected by the Chairman as being 'unnecessary' and when the Committee adjourned at 1.0 p.m. Mr. Lyttelton had just spoken to an Amendment to include someone with knowledge of 'applied science'.

On December 9, after further debate, this was negatived. Mr. Geoffrey Cooper's Amendment, to insert 'industrial or commercial' before 'administration' – he was accused of aiming at civil servants – was, by leave, withdrawn. Mr. Harold Macmillan's attempt to include a representative of the 'users' of iron and steel products[11] was defeated on a Division by 15 votes to 23 (the Question being 'to insert' Mr. Macmillan's words, Opposition supporters were the 'Ayes', the Government supporters the 'Noes'). Mr. Macmillan's proposal to require the Chairman and not less than six other members to give 'whole-time service' was under discussion when the Committee adjourned at 1.0 p.m.

At its next Sitting, the Committee returned to Mr. Harold Macmillan's proposal for whole-time service. The Question 'that those words be there inserted' was put and the Amendment negatived without a Division. Colonel J. R. H. Hutchison's Amendment to include one member with experience in Scotland and in Wales was defeated. Mr. Lyttelton then moved an Amendment dealing with consultation with representatives of producers and users of iron and steel and of workers engaged therein.[12] It was defeated by 27 votes to 15. An Amendment by Mr. Peake, permitting members of the Corporation to resign, was accepted by Mr. Strauss and agreed to. The Sitting was adjourned at 1.0 p.m. while Mr. Ivor Thomas was speaking to his Amendment dealing with certain conditions (e.g., absence from meetings, bankruptcy, incapacity) under which the Minister might terminate appointments. At the next Sitting[13] the Minister agreed to look at the matter again and the Amendment was, by leave, withdrawn.

The remainder of this Sitting was devoted to another Amendment in the name of Mr. Lyttelton, to fix a term of three years (with eligibility for reappointment) for members of the Corporation, one-third to retire each year (defeated, 27 : 13); an attempt by Mr. Ivor Thomas to allow the House of Commons

[11] *See* above in connection with Viscount Hinchingbrooke's Amendment.
[12] *See* below, pp. 158–159.   [13] December 15.

by resolution to permit an M.P. appointed to the Corporation to continue to be an M.P. (by leave, withdrawn); and an Amendment by Mr. Peake to insert after 'appointment' (to the Corporation by the Minister) the words 'and who has consented' (to the appointment); the words were described as 'meaningless', but the Amendment was agreed to.

Mr. Lyttelton had spoken briefly to a further Amendment which would compel members of the Corporation to disclose any interest not merely in 'the publicly owned companies' but in their associated and subsidiary companies, when the Committee was adjourned at 1.0 p.m.

The Debate was continued briefly in the afternoon Session; Mr. Strauss explained that the Amendment was unnecessary but said that he would look at it again. It was negatived. The next Amendment, in Mr. Lyttelton's name, sought further to define the conditions under which disclosure of interest must be made. Mr. Strauss described it as 'small beer'; he agreed to look at the legal consequences of accepting the proposal, which was then withdrawn.

An Amendment moved by Mr. Ivor Thomas, that the remuneration of members of the Corporation should not exceed £5,000 per annum, is noteworthy mainly because of its defeat by 36 votes to 1.

A number of Amendments dealing with pensions were then disposed of, after which the Committee turned to the Motion 'That the Clause, as amended, stand part of the Bill'.

At the next Sitting several points of Order were raised bearing upon the limitations of such debate. The Chairman, confronted with Viscount Hinchingbrooke's attempt to develop a general point about the 'great concentration of power' in the hands of the Corporation and 'elaborate and frustrating systems of controls . . .', ruled that the Debate on the Motion was a 'narrow one', to be 'confined to the Clause, as amended', and held that the noble Lord was 'going beyond the scope of the Clause', which simply set up the Iron and Steel Corporation of Great Britain.

Just before one o'clock the Question was put, 'That the Clause, as amended, stand part of the Bill', and carried on a Division. The Committee then adjourned.

On Wednesday, January 19, 1959, the Committee began its Eighth Sitting at 10.30 a.m. and considered Clause 2 (Powers of the Corporation), an Amendment to which by Mr. Lyttelton was eventually negatived by 26 votes to 11. A further Amendment sought to limit the activities of the Corporation to Great Britain.

At 12.45 p.m. the Chairman, pursuant to the Order of the House of November 25, 1948, put forthwith the Question already proposed from the Chair.

Question put, 'That those words be there inserted'.
The Committee divided: Ayes, 12; Noes, 26.
The Chairman then proceeded successively to put forthwith the Questions necessary to dispose of the Business to be concluded at this Sitting.
Question put, 'That the Clause stand part of the Bill'.
Viscount Hinchingbrooke: Two Clauses undiscussed; 42 Amendments undiscussed!
Mr. Harold Macmillan: It is a scandal.
Mr. Jennings: Absolute funk.
The Committee divided: Ayes, 26; Noes, 12.
Question put, 'That Clause 3 stand part of the Bill'.
The Committee divided: Ayes, 25; Noes, 12.
Question put, 'That Clause 4 stand part of the Bill'.
Mr. Roberts: The most important Clause in the Bill undiscussed!
The Committee divided: Ayes, 25; Noes, 12.
Mr. G. R. Strauss then moved, 'That the further consideration of the Bill be now adjourned'.
The Motion was opposed by Mr. Harold Macmillan, but, the Question being put, it was agreed to without a Division.[14]

The protests against inadequate time for discussion were carried over into the next Sitting (January 20). The Committee then turned to Clause 5, over which the first Amendment was ruled out of order as going beyond the Money Resolution. Debate then ensued on the Motion, 'That the Clause stand part . . .' (carried, 27 : 9). On Clause 6, Mr. Harold Macmillan moved an Amendment to define the membership and duties of an Iron and Steel Consumers' Council. The Debate was adjourned at 1.0 p.m., continued on the next day (January 25), and the Amendment defeated by 24 votes to 14. A Government Amendment on remuneration was then carried and it was agreed (24 votes to 14) 'That the Clause stand part . . .'

The Guillotine then fell and Clauses 7, 8, 9 and 10 (the last amended on the Motion of Mr. Strauss), were ordered to 'stand part'.

[14] Standing Committee Report, cols. 397–402.

The Debate on Clause 11 (Transfer to Corporation of securities of scheduled companies) concerned 'vesting-day', a matter further discussed on the Report stage, in the House of Lords, and then on consideration of the Lords' Amendments, and a point on which the Government had finally to accept a compromise with the House of Lords.[15]

Mr. W. Shepherd moved an Amendment to insert, for the date May 1, 1950, January 1, 1951, and it was discussed together with a further Amendment and a third which was 'consequential'. The Debate on Mr. Shepherd's Amendment lasted nearly the whole of the Sitting of January 26. That on Clause 11 (which further Amendments were proposed) continued throughout January 27, and until nearly midday on February 1, a Sitting on which the Guillotine fell and which was followed by an afternoon Sitting.

Mr. Shepherd pointed out that the Government itself had provided for a latitude of eighteen months beyond their own date of May 1, 1950. Moreover, the country should be given an opportunity of deciding upon the issue. This argument was not unnaturally productive of considerable political disagreement. Mr. Erroll repeated the argument that the earliest vesting date should be deferred until after the latest possible date of the next General Election. He also held that if the Minister selected the earliest possible date there would be insufficient time for the setting up of the Corporation. 'Hiving-off' operations would be complicated. It would be difficult to persuade senior executives to accept appointment to the Corporation before the Election. Mr. Osbert Peake hoped that the Minister would rise soon to reply so that discussion might proceed on other Clauses.

The Joint Parliamentary Secretary to the Ministry of Supply (Mr. Jack Jones) quickly became involved in exchanges with the Opposition, his allegation that enthusiasm for the Bill could be deduced from the rising production figures provoking sharp protests.

Mr. Lyttelton subsequently developed the case that the Corporation could not be ready to assume responsibility in time. Great damage would be done to steel production. He concluded that the Government's mandate did not cover a Bill introduced so late in the life of Parliament, a remark which let loose another series of 'party' exchanges.

15 *See* below, pp. 171–180.

Mr. Attewell: Will the right hon. Gentleman tell us which of the Measures which the Government have already passed, he would have left out in order to include this Measure?

Mr. Lyttelton: That is the simplest question in the world to answer. I would not have introduced any of the Government's Measures.

Mr. Tiffany: Does that include social insurance?

Mr. Lyttelton: Social insurance has nothing to do with the Amendment, but the Bill was based largely on the work of the Coalition Government.

Mr. Tiffany: My right hon. Friend the Member for Wakefield (Mr. Arthur Greenwood), yes.

Mr. Lyttelton: The hon. Member remains in profound ignorance of these questions.

Mr. Hynd rose –

Mr. Lyttleton: I will not give way because I suspect I may be called to Order if I pursue that line. . . .[16]

The Minister of Supply said that they must assume the Bill would go through in the ordinary way and that the industry should not be left in suspense and unsettlement for eighteen months after its passing. The first of January, on his assumption, would be eighteen months after the Royal Assent. Nevertheless, he added, 'certain things might happen' and, therefore, authority was sought to postpone vesting date, if necessary, for eighteen months.

Mr. Attewell then became involved in exchanges about the past record of the iron and steel industry and was twice called to order by the Chairman. Mr. Hugh Fraser, in rebutting Mr. Attewell's argument, was also pulled up. Further exchanges developed about the precise relationship between the 'promise' of nationalisation and the continued improvement in production.

Viscount Hinchingbrooke spoke with some warmth but added little to his colleagues' case. Mr. Chetwynd replied with equal warmth and as little new material. Mr. Selwyn Lloyd reiterated the Opposition viewpoint, and was supported by Mr. Jennings. Mr. S. N. Evans appeared to have reached a balanced judgment.

There had to be a date in the Bill. Having regard to the possibility of prolonged Parliamentary procedure, it was the intelligent thing to do to make it 1st May, but there is a distinct possibility that in practice the Minister will avail himself of the proviso whereby the date can be deferred until 18 months after the passing of the Act. There is therefore a degree of unreality about this morning's procedure. . . .[17]

[16] *Ibid.*, col. 522.   [17] *Ibid.*, col. 543.

But Mr. Peter Roberts argued at length for an alteration of the date in the Bill.

At 12.45 p.m. the Chairman wondered 'if we can come to a decision now?'[18] Mr. Ward spoke briefly for the Opposition and the Committee then divided on the Question, 'That the words proposed to be left out stand part of the Clause'. Ayes, 22; Noes, 11.

In the brief time left Mr. Strauss accepted an Amendment proposed by Mr. Manningham-Buller that companies wishing to postpone the vesting date might approach the Minister direct, though he would consult with the Corporations. Two consequential Amendments were also made.

Clause 11 was again considered on January 27. Mr. Lyttelton first moved an 'exploratory' Amendment designed to elicit the meaning of the Sub-section dealing with the transfer of securities of subsidiary organisations. By a series of short questions and answers, typical of the more subdued and businesslike proceedings of a Standing Committee when not arguing matters of party principles, Mr. Osbert Peake drew from the Minister of Supply explanations of certain points of detail. Mr. Strauss undertook to look at the Clause again with his advisers and to be 'quite sure that it meets the purpose we all have in mind'. The Amendment was, by leave, withdrawn.[19]

Procedure and result were similar on another Amendment dealing with the repayment of loans, though in this case the Solicitor-General was engaged in a detailed 'question-session'. Further Amendments, of a minor kind, were by leave withdrawn, after explanations.[20] (At one point during this discussion, less than fifteen Members were present and the Sitting was suspended for one minute until more arrived.)[21]

Mr. Lyttelton then moved an Amendment to insert, in page 9, line 39, after 'activity', the words 'or activities'. It was discussed with a further Amendment to permit the Minister, if certain conditions were fulfilled, to make an order that the securities of the company concerned should not vest in the Corporation. Mr. Lyttelton described it as 'the most important subject which has come before the Committee this morning'.[22] The basic significance of the Amendments was that, because it engaged in

[18] *Ibid.*, col. 545.
[19] *Ibid.*, cols. 551–557.
[20] *Ibid.*, cols. 557–576.
[21] *Ibid.*, col. 577.
[22] *Ibid.*, col. 579.

certain activities and fulfilled certain conditions, the Ford
Motor Company had been excluded from the Bill: should not
other companies for similar reasons be excluded?

The Debate ranged over the point whether the exclusion of
Ford's had been due to American representations and was
broadened to include references to a large number of other
firms which, it was argued, ought rightly to be excluded. It was
adjourned at 1.0 p.m. on January 27 and resumed on February 1, when the discussion also covered an Amendment
moved by Mr. G. Thomas[23] to bring Ford's into the Bill. On
this occasion the Debate lasted for an hour and the Amendment
was then defeated by 25 votes to 12. An Amendment by Mr.
Peake to allow disputes about whether companies had fulfilled
the conditions adequate to enable them to claim 'exclusion'
should go to arbitration was negatived without a Division.

The Motion was then made and the Question proposed,
'That the Clause, as amended, stand part of the Bill'. A Debate
ensued, although at 11.48 a.m. the Sitting had once again to
be temporarily suspended for want of a quorum. Certain further
explanations were given, and on a Division the Clause was
ordered to 'stand part' by 24 votes to 10.

On Clause 12, Mr. Manningham-Buller spoke to three
Amendments which sought to ensure that in taking over companies the Corporation would assume liabilities as well as
assets. Mr. Strauss accepted these in principle and they were
withdrawn. The Clause was then ordered to stand part of the
Bill without a Division.

On Clause 13, Mr. Selwyn Lloyd moved an Amendment
(discussed with the next on the paper) to insert certain safeguards in the sections dealing with 'disclaimer of agreements
and leases'.

Mr. Lyttelton was speaking to this Amendment when the
Guillotine fell. It was put immediately and defeated by 25 votes
to 12. Two Government Amendments were then agreed to and
the Clause, as amended, was ordered to 'stand part' after
another Division (25 : 12).

Discussion of Clause 14 (Compensation to holders of securities) was begun on an Amendment moved by Mr. Erroll, which
was negatived after a brief debate.

Mr. Peake then moved a long and detailed Amendment[24]

[23] Lab., Cardiff.   [24] *Ibid.*, cols. 655–657.

which would add to the Stock Exchange values of securities (the basis chosen by the Government) the amount by which such values fell short 'of the company's undertakings and assets at the date of transfer'. Two further Amendments of a similar nature were, after some discussion with the Chairman, left for later consideration.

Mr. Peake began to speak at 5.0 p.m. on February 1. The Debate was still in progress when the Committee adjourned at 7.0 p.m. It was resumed at 10.30 a.m. on February 2, when a major contribution was made by Mr. R. Jenkins from the Government side and replied to by Mr. Lyttelton. Amidst a welter of technical detail, a lighter moment was provided by the following exchanges. (Mr. Mitchison intervened while Mr. Lyttleton was speaking.)

Mr. Lyttelton: I did not give way to the hon. and learned Member. Perhaps it was a pity, because, in cricket parlance, the hon. and learned Member loves bowling half-volleys.
Mr. Mitchison: I was trying to make the right hon. Gentleman hit his own wicket.
Mr. Lyttelton: I remember the hon. and learned Member at school. He was a wet bob, I think.
Mr. Harold Macmillan: He was captain of the Oppidans. Do not be unjust to him.[25]

Mr. Lyttelton continued at some length and the Financial Secretary to the Treasury[26] replied. The Debate was still in progress when the Committee adjourned at 1.0 p.m. Sir John Barlow continued for the Opposition at 10.30 on February 3, and Mr. S. N. Evans followed for the Government. After other interventions, the Minister of Supply rose shortly after 12 noon. Just before 12.45 Mr. Peake began his reply. He was still speaking when the Committee adjourned at 1.0 p.m., and resumed his speech at 10.30 a.m. on February 8.

Just after 10.45 the Committee divided and the Amendment was defeated by 23 votes to 16.

This Debate lasted over seven hours. The subject was discussed again on the Report stage, in the House of Lords, and on the consideration of the Lords' Amendments. A profound difference of principle was argued at length and on the basis of detailed facts relating to the valuation of assets. Technicalities abounded but the inevitable result was confirmation of the

[25] *Ibid.*, col. 708. [26] Mr. Glenvil Hall.

Government's decision to adhere to Stock Exchange valuations.

The indefatigable Mr. Peake at once moved a further Amendment to provide for additional compensation for development carried out after the announcement by the Minister on May 26, 1946, the date selected for Stock Exchange valuation. The main argument was that Stock Exchange values would not reflect capital development because of voluntary dividend limitation. The Amendment was defeated, after a debate lasting about one and a half hours, by 24 votes to 11. Mr. Peake then briefly moved an Amendment designed to protect a particular company. Mr. Strauss agreed that the matter must be dealt with, but not in that particular way. The Amendment was, by leave, withdrawn. Mr. Peake was not done, however. He moved an Amendment designed to ensure that the shares of any private company taken over would be valued as if they had been quoted in the 'Stock Exchange Daily List', the assessment to be made by the arbitrator. The question, however, was too complicated to settle in the time available and Mr. Peake withdrew his Amendment so that the matter might be raised on the Report stage.

Three small Amendments proposed by Mr. Strauss were then agreed to and, without debate, the Clause was ordered to 'stand part'.

On Clause 15 (Valuation of Securities affected by Transfer of property from one company to another), Mr. Manningham-Buller moved an Amendment designed to elicit further explanations. He was still speaking when the Guillotine fell.

Five minor Amendments to the same Clause, proposed by Mr. Strauss, were agreed to, although the Committee divided on each.

We have now followed the record of this Standing Committee as far as its Eighteenth Sitting, on February 9. It would try the patience of the reader to pursue these discussions to the bitter end, and fortunately there is no need to do so, as most of the important features of Standing Committee procedure (together with several that are happily untypical) have already been illustrated.

The remainder of the Committee's life, like the part we have examined, was characterised by fierce party conflicts alternating with tedious – but necessary – arguments about matters of technical detail. Opposition Amendments were usually rejected on straight party votes, but occasionally accepted and sometimes withdrawn after ministerial 'assurances' or 'explanations'. (On March 9, Viscount Hinchingbrooke claimed that 'only three amendments of any substance' had been allowed to get through.[27]) New Clauses, when Opposition-proposed, met similar fates. Throughout these proceedings controversy about the use of the Guillotine continued unabated, sometimes in the form of angry exchanges between Government and Opposition spokesmen. On one occasion Mr. Macmillan was provoked into describing 'this ridiculous Guillotine' as 'an absolute farce'.[28] On another Mr. Lyttelton talked about the 'monstrous way' in which the Government had handled the Bill, and claimed that more than 150 Opposition amendments had not even been discussed.[29] A little later, when a whole series of Government Amendments was put to the vote without discussion, Mr. Jennings exclaimed, 'What a democracy!' and Mr. Macmillan, 'What a procedure!'

The proceedings concluded with thanks to Sir Charles MacAndrew, the Chairman, and with appreciation of the Opposition voiced by Mr. Strauss. In responding, Mr. Lyttelton had one last 'joust' by saying that he felt that those Members on the Government side who had not spoken throughout the thirty-six Sittings had made a greater contribution than anyone else on their side![30]

(g) *The Report Stage* occupied four days, April 27, April 28, May 2 and May 3.

At the commencement of the First Allotted Day at 3.2 p.m. the Minister of Supply introduced a New Clause (General Duty of the Corporation). This was brought up and read the First time and the Minister then moved 'That the Clause be read a Second time'.

He explained that the Clause was in substitution for Clause 3 and was to meet 'points which were put forward by the Opposition ... [and] ... arguments put forward by representative bodies who approached the Government about various points which were worrying them. ... It meets to some extent the Amendments put down on the Order Paper by the Opposition during the Committee Stage. ...'[31]

[27] *Ibid.*, col. 1454.   [28] *Ibid.*, col. 1564.
[29] *Ibid.*, col. 1771.   [30] *Ibid.*, col. 1784.
[31] *H.C. Debates*, Vol. 464, col. 187.

The major change, he explained, was a specific statement that the Corporation 'must avoid undue preference' in the supply of steel, etc.

Mr. Oliver Lyttelton, for the Opposition, considered this new Clause as a considerable improvement. . . .'[32] Although criticising the power to vary terms and conditions in the light of a 'public interest' of which the Corporation would be sole judge, he announced that the Opposition would not divide the House.

Mr. Selwyn Lloyd[33] wished to know why the Minister had added the proviso that 'the duty of the Corporation under this section shall not be enforceable by proceedings before any court or tribunal'. Mr. Peter Roberts[34] used the duty 'to promote the efficient and economical supply of the products' as a means of attacking the record of the National Coal Board. Mr. Nigel Birch[35] followed up this point.

The Minister, 'by leave of the House', then intervened, without, however, giving complete satisfaction to these or subsequent Opposition critics.

The Question (that the Clause be read a Second time) was put and agreed to.

Mr. Osbert Peake then moved an Amendment the effect of which would be to place the general duties described in the Clause not merely on the Corporation but on each of the 106 subsidiaries of the Corporation listed in the Third Schedule to the Bill. He argued that changes in Clause 2 made the Corporation virtually a holding company. 'Only as an exceptional matter and with express Ministerial consent can the Corporation enter into any direct trading operation of any sort or kind.'[36] Hence the duties 'should be laid upon those who will be in a position to carry them out'.[37]

The Minister suggested that the Amendment was 'quite illogical', and said: 'We must tell the big holding body what Parliament expects it to do, and . . . it will have to see that the various companies . . . carry out the general duties which Parliament imposes. . . .'[38]

Mr. Lyttelton was not convinced. Nobody knew what powers the Minister would possess or how they would be exercised.

[32] H.C. Debates, Vol. 464, col. 188.
[33] Cons., Wirral.
[34] Cons., Eccleshall.
[35] Cons., Flint.
[36] Ibid., col. 200.
[37] Ibid., col. 202.
[38] Ibid., cols. 202–203.

Several Members pursued the argument. The Solicitor-General[39] intervened to explain that for breach of the Clause the remedy would lie against the Corporation, but Mr. P. Roberts thought that no action would lie if the Corporation could show that it had taken every possible precaution.

At 4.47 p.m. the House divided on the Question, 'That those words be there inserted'. It was defeated by 298 votes to 146.

Mr. Lyttelton then moved a further Amendment which would have the effect of applying the prohibition against undue preference or unfair discrimination not merely to products included in the Second Schedule but to 'all the products which may be produced by the large number of companies'.[40]

Mr. Strauss thought that complaints within such categories could be made through the consumers' council. He went on:

I have discussed this Clause . . . with the organisations which represent consumers' interests. I refer particularly to the F.B.I., the National Union of Manufacturers and the Association of Chambers of Commerce. . . . They are wholly satisfied with it. That does not necessarily mean that the House need accept their views. . . . It is important that the House should know that I have gone all out to meet the reasonable suggestions and criticisms of these important bodies. . . . I should be very reluctant to re-open the matter unless there was a very good reason . . .[41]

Mr. Lyttelton persisted that the Clause might be widened to include other than Second Schedule products. (Mr. P. Roberts cited coke as an example.)

At 5.24 p.m. the House divided on the Question: 'That the words proposed to be left out stand part of the proposed Clause.' It was agreed to by 301 votes to 146.

The Clause was added to the Bill.

The House next turned to a New Clause dealing with the Appointment of Consumers' Council and Committees. This was brought up, and read the First Time at 5.30 p.m. The Minister, in moving the Second Reading, admitted that the original consumers' council Clause in the Bill was 'very sketchy . . . and deliberately so'.[42] This was deliberate, with a view to consultation with the principal consumers. Their views, those of the Opposition, of trade unions and 'of my colleagues on this side of the House' had 'practically all' been incorporated in the

[39] Sir Frank Soskice.   [40] H.C. Debates, Vol. 464, col. 225.
[41] Ibid., cols. 226–227.   [42] Ibid., col. 240.

Clause. The composition of the Council was now definite; a date was fixed for its establishment; there would be an independent Chairman; it might meet at the request of any six members without Corporation representatives, though only the full council could submit a report to the Minister.

Mr. Lyttelton claimed that the 'Government incorporated in the original Bill a ridiculous Clause which was manifestly unworkable and which was shot to pieces by the arguments of the Opposition in Standing Committee, and that they have now incorporated in this new Clause most of our suggestions'.[43]

But the Clause was 'about the best that can be done in the circumstances and ... we should not dream of dividing the House against it'.[44]

Nevertheless the Debate continued for some time. At 7.45 p.m., while the Joint Parliamentary Secretary to the Ministry of Supply (Mr. Jack Jones) was speaking, Mr. Lyttelton claimed to move 'That the Question be now put' (the closure). Mr. Speaker declined then to put that Question.

Mr. Speaker: The Minister has the right to reply.
Mr. Jones: ... I promise not to take more than two or three minutes longer. Many speeches have been made by the Opposition.
Mr. Jennings: On a point of Order. Should not the Minister curtail his remarks and allow some of these very important Amendments to be moved? Should he take so much time, when the guillotine is coming?
Mr. Jones: Hon. Gentlemen opposite are the cause of the time being taken up, in that they have asked the questions. ...

Mr. Jones spoke for another minute or so and the Question was put and agreed to. The Clause was read a Second time, and added to the Bill.

The feelings of the Opposition are explained by the fact that Mr. Lyttelton wished to move a new Clause to establish an Iron and Steel Prices Board. This was brought up, and read the First time, and Mr. Lyttelton did his 'best in the scandalously short time which' remained. After a brief reply by Mr. Strauss,

It being Eight o'clock, Mr. Speaker proceeded, pursuant to Order, to put forthwith the Question already proposed from the Chair.

The House refused a Second Reading to the Clause by 320 votes to 158.

[43] *Ibid.*, col. 243.   [44] *Ibid.*, col. 244.

At the end of the Division, Mr. Lyttelton asked for guidance as to whether 'there are any means open to us by which we can ask the Government to reconsider the time-table'.[45]

Mr. Deputy-Speaker (Major Milner): I am afraid there are no such means. It is my duty to put the Questions in accordance with the Order made by the House.

Mr. Harold Macmillan: Further to that point of Order, Mr. Deputy-Speaker. Although I quite understand that it is not within the power of the Opposition to move a dilatory Motion, would it not be within the power of the Leader of the House, in view of the circumstances – [Interruption]

Mr. Deputy-Speaker: I am sorry, but no point of Order can arise here. It is my duty to put the Questions in accordance with the Order of the House.

After further 'points of Order', Mr. Deputy-Speaker proceeded to put forthwith the Question on the Amendment moved by the Government, of which notice had been given, to that part of the Bill to be concluded at Eight o'clock at that day's Sitting.

New Clauses having been dealt with, the House turned to existing Clauses and Amendments thereto.

The Solicitor-General moved to leave out sub-sections (1) and (2) of Clause 2 (Powers of the Corporation) and to insert sections 'to formulate rather more precisely the powers which the Corporation desires to retain for itself'.[46] The Amendment was 'designed to go some length to meet the criticism which was made of the original Clause during the Committee Stage . . . to the effect that the powers of the Corporation were too wide. . . .'[47]

Question, 'That sub-sections (1) and (2) stand part of the Clause', put and negatived.

Question proposed, 'That those words be then inserted'.

At this point Mr. H. Macmillan asked Mr. Deputy-Speaker whether he wished the House to debate the Government Amendment or whether it would be convenient to discuss at the same time the Amendments to the proposed Amendment (involving 'leaving out' certain words). It was, of course, for Mr. Macmillan to decide and he proceeded to move an Amendment to the proposed (Government) Amendment. He also announced his intention of dealing with three further Amendments, all of which fell 'into a general category'.

[45] *Ibid.*, col. 293.   [46] *Ibid.*, col. 295.   [47] *Ibid.*, col. 297.

His purpose was to restrict the powers of the Corporation to companies 'engaged wholly or mainly in Second Schedule activities', i.e., to what were 'genuine iron and steel activities'. More generally, as Mr. H. Fraser subsequently put it, the Opposition wished 'to prevent any incursion into the field which the Lord President of the Council referred to as the private enterprise field'.[48] This speaker listed a large number of products and by-products which might be covered by the memoranda of association of various firms.

Mr. Strauss, intervening, claimed that the 'making of basic products' was 'so closely related to the making of auxiliary products' that it would be 'quite ridiculous' to set up a body solely concerned with the former.

Viscount Hinchingbrooke mentioned the manufacture of agricultural machinery, electrical engineering, and tool making as examples of possible Corporation activities which the Opposition were 'seeking . . . to cut out'.

Mr. Selwyn Lloyd enlarged on this list of activities[49] and other Members cited further examples.

On procedure, Mr. Peake protested that it was 'a bit thick that at the Report stage . . . we should be faced with a complete redraft of the Clause . . . when we can make only one speech on a particular Amendment. . . .'[50]

Mr. Macmillan also referred to the 'fantastically short time' available, but he exercised his 'right to reply' briefly.

At 9.30 p.m. the House divided on the Question, 'That the words proposed to be left out *stand part* of the proposed Amendment.

The House divided: Ayes, 323; Noes, 164.

Mr. Macmillan then moved a further Amendment which would have the effect of compelling the Corporation, should it wish under sub-section (3) to go beyond 'the sum of the activities which the publicly-owned companies are authorised as aforesaid to carry on' (i.e., beyond even the memoranda of association), to seek *not* the Minister's consent, but an amending Act of Parliament. Mr. Strauss explained that the Corporation might wish to acquire a company whose memorandum of association gave it powers to undertake activities not included in the memorandum of association of any other company already owned by the Corporation.

---

[48] *Ibid.*, col. 302.   [49] *Ibid.*, col. 308.   [50] *Ibid.*, col. 312.

This Amendment to the proposed Amendment was negatived without a Division.

Mr. Macmillan then spoke on two further Amendments and finally moved to delete sub-section (3) altogether.

It being Ten o'clock, Mr. Speaker proceeded, pursuant to Order, to put forthwith the Question necessary to dispose of the Amendment already proposed from the Chair:

Question put, 'That the words proposed to be left out stand part of the proposed Amendment'.

The House divided: Ayes, 329; Noes, 162.

Mr. Speaker then proceeded successively to put forthwith the Questions on the Amendment moved by the Government, of which notice had been given, to that part of the Bill to be concluded at Ten o'clock at that day's Sitting.

Debate on the Second Allotted Day began at 3.43 p.m., when Mr. Lyttelton moved an Amendment to Clause 5 with the effect of deleting from the Bill the statutory provision for the payment of iron and steel subsidies. The House divided at 5.16 p.m. and the Amendment was defeated. Proceedings on a Government Amendment (accepted) and on another Opposition Amendment (defeated) then occupied the House until 5.30 p.m., when Mr. Deputy-Speaker proceeded, under the Guillotine, to put forthwith the necessary Questions to complete the part of the Bill designated to be concluded by that time.

The House turned next to an Amendment to Clause 11 (Transfer to Corporation of Securities of Scheduled Companies) moved by Mr. Lyttelton. This was the famous 'vesting-date' Clause which was subsequently to cause so much controversy. The object of the Amendment was to postpone the vesting date from May 1, 1950, to January 1, 1951. The Debate brought out clearly the fundamental points at issue between the two Sides.

Mr. Lyttelton argued that the earliest date upon which the Bill could become an Act was July or August (1949). If the House of Lords rejected it or 'amended it in a way disagreeable to the Government', the last date might be January or February, 1950.

The business of organising and taking over such an enormous business [between that latest date and May 1st] . . . would tax the best brains in the world and would be impossible for the best commercial brains to work out in that time. I need hardly say that those considerations apply with a great deal of force to very harassed

Ministers, who have no particular knowledge, from their Ministerial experience, necessary to run such a business. . . .[51]

Further, the General Election must take place within about six weeks of May 1 at the latest and

'when . . . the party on these benches is returned to power, say, about June, they will find . . . the operation of undoing the damage . . . immensely more difficult . . . It is highly objectionable to have this transfer of securities only a month or six weeks before Parliament comes to an end under the operation of the quinquennial Act.[52]

On the other hand, if the Government were returned to power, there would be no inconvenience – indeed, greater convenience – if vesting-day were postponed.

Mr. Strauss, on the other hand, thought that there would have been

common agreement that, if Parliament decides that an industry of this importance is to be nationalised, the quicker the transfer takes place the better.[53]

On the question of practicability, he pointed out that the duties of the Corporation were wholly unlike those of the National Coal Board. The latter had assumed responsibility for running the mines of the country, but it would not be the duty of the Iron and Steel Corporation to run the various iron and steel works.

Moreover, the Bill gave power to select any later date up to eighteen months after the Royal Assent.

Mr. Mitchison thought that, if anything, the Minister was erring on the side of making the period too long rather than too short. Claiming that it was the intention of the Amendment to put the vesting date beyond the latest possible date on which the next General Election could take place, he could

see no particular reason why the efficiency of the steel industry, nationalised as it is to be, should be sacrificed to the convenience of a political party opposite in order to make it easier for them to say, 'Stop it, you have time', and who do their best to create unjustified and unjustifiable panic in the country on the strength of that cry. . . .[54]

The Government, claimed Lord Hinchingbrooke, were saying:

[51] *Ibid.*, col. 418.   [52] *Ibid.*, col. 421.
[53] *Ibid.*, col. 428.   [54] *Ibid.*, cols. 436–437.

We will scramble these eggs before we go, so that there is no chance that you will be able to get the industry organised properly according to your ideas. . . .[55]

Lieut.-Commander Braithwaite argued that as the House of Lords would have to conduct 'a conscientious and meticulous examination' of all the Clauses that the House of Commons were sending them without debate, it was quite inconceivable that the 'other place' would have finished with the Bill in two months. The House, indeed, would be 'very fortunate' if it were able to discuss the Lords' Amendments before the Christmas recess.

Mr. Jenkins envisaged a situation in which the Lords held up the Bill for as long as possible.

If that is the case the Bill will probably become an Act, after the Parliament Bill goes through, sometime towards the end of February, 1950. Therefore all the Amendment ensures is that instead of the period of nine months which we regard as reasonable, there should be a period of ten months before vesting date comes into operation. . . .[56]

Mr. Roberts put the Opposition viewpoint succinctly:

I am going into the Lobby this evening on this Amendment for one reason only, and that is that if this Amendment were passed the whole of this Bill would be negatived, because we feel quite confidently in the country that by 1951 hon. Members opposite will not have the majority which they have today. They will be swept away, probably on the very arguments around this Steel Nationalisation Bill. . . .[57]

Mr. Harold Macmillan, in winding up for the Opposition, took the opportunity once more to attack the Bill as a whole.

When the House divided, the Amendment was lost, the Question, 'That the words proposed to be left out stand part of the Clause' being carried by 305 votes to 155.

Proceedings continued, at 8.30 p.m., with a minor amendment to meet an Opposition point. Mr. Lyttelton then moved an Amendment ('We are now turning from rather higher questions to technical matters'[58]) affecting the question of repayment of loans. After explanation from the Solicitor-General the Amendment was, by leave, withdrawn.

Mr. Strauss then moved an Amendment to exclude 'a number

[55] *Ibid.*, col. 440.
[57] *Ibid.*, col. 459.
[56] *Ibid.*, col. 457.
[58] *Ibid.*, col. 475.

of smaller companies which should not come within the family over which the Corporation will preside'.[59] Though the Opposition would have preferred the exclusion of companies by name rather than by formula, the Amendment was agreed to without a Division, as were further Amendments.

On Clause 13 (Disclaimer of Agreements and Leases) – 'a lawyer's Clause', in Mr. Selwyn Lloyd's words – there was nearly an hour's debate, the Question finally being put by Mr. Deputy-Speaker under the Ten o'clock Rule.

On the Third Allotted Day at 3.30 p.m. the House began with Clause 20 (Power to acquire securities of certain additional companies). The Solicitor-General moved Amendments 'to improve the drafting and to remove some ambiguity in the Clause to which hon. Members opposite drew attention during the Committee stage'.[60] Mr. Lyttelton was 'much obliged to the Government'. The Minister of Supply moved 'one of a series of drafting Amendments which have been put down to meet the views expressed in Committee by hon. Members opposite'. Mr. Lyttelton was again 'much obliged'.

After a further drafting Amendment had been disposed of, Mr. Lyttelton moved an Amendment which sought to remove penalties for certain actions if taken to avoid the consequences of the Bill after its enactment. It was negatived without a Division. Other Amendments, of a drafting or technical character, were then disposed of without difficulty or excitement.

The foregoing illustrates the dull technical work sometimes involved in the Report stage. It also illustrates the practice whereby on matters not involving fundamental principles the Government sincerely attempts to meet the views of the Opposition, which, in its turn, shows a willingness to compromise.

There followed attempts by the Opposition to obtain Amendments which the Government was not willing to accept. One moved by Mr. Manningham-Buller attempted to protect directors from action against them if the transactions in question were entered into without their knowledge or consent. It was debated from just after 4.0 p.m. until 4.50 p.m., and was then defeated on a Division (241 to 115). An Amendment by Mr. Lyttelton to protect directors acting 'in good faith', debated until 5.26 p.m., was also defeated on a Division (262 to 122).

[59] *Ibid.*, col. 480.   [60] *Ibid.*, col. 655.

The Guillotine then fell and Amendments were accordingly made to Clauses 23, 24 and 29.

At this stage, Mr. Lyttelton moved the first of several further Amendments to Clause 29. 'We are now turning', he said, 'after seven undiscussed Clauses, to the battlements and portcullis of State monopoly'. The Debate raised, once more, fundamental issues. It was concerned with the power of the Minister to restrict and control the entry of new companies to the industry, or the continuance of old companies therein without a licence.

Beginning with some good points about monopoly, planning and allied subjects, it quickly degenerated into a rehash of the old public *v.* private enterprise arguments. At 8.40 p.m. the House divided and the Opposition Amendment was defeated by 263 votes to 128.

Mr. Lyttelton then moved a further Amendment to the effect that the period of the licence should be not less than such as was reasonable in relation to the capital expenditure involved. He admitted that some of the arguments had already been touched upon. The Solicitor-General insisted that the Minister, not the Courts, must decide the period for which the licence should run. He emphasised that the Clause applied only to new entrants. The Clause showed, thought Lieut.-Commander Braithwaite, precisely that the Government did not want new entrants.

On a Division the Amendment was rejected by 265 votes to 133.

Mr. Lyttelton next moved an Amendment to allow new entrants a 'reasonable output of 40,000 tons of steel or 100,000 tons of iron ore'. After a short debate it was rejected by 277 votes to 134. A Government Amendment was then accepted, following which an Opposition Amendment, for which Mr. Lyttelton had no time to argue, was rejected on a Division by 285 votes to 140.

It being Ten o'clock, outstanding Questions were put and Amendments made in Clause 30 under the Guillotine procedure.

On the Fourth Allotted Day, Clause 35 (General Reserve) was the subject-matter of several Amendments. Mr. Lyttelton sought in what he called 'little more than a drafting Amendment'[61] to ensure proper provision for both depreciation and

[61] *Ibid.*, col. 837.

renewal of assets. Mr. Glenvil Hall pointed out that the wording was modelled on previous nationalisation Measures and that the suggested changes were unnecessary. Mr. Lyttelton hoped that 'perhaps between now and when the Bill reaches another place the Government might consider using the same words to denote the same thing'. With these emollient phrases 'he begged to ask leave to withdraw' the Amendment.

Mr. Lyttelton's second Amendment sought to confine the Minister's directions about the management of the reserve to situations where he considered the national interest to be involved. The Solicitor-General made the obvious reply that the Minister would, of course, only give directions which were in the national interest. Mr. Ivor Thomas considered that the Government were seeking 'an unjustifiable interference with the powers of management of the Corporation'. The provision was part of a general policy for the direction of investment.[62]

The Amendment was negatived without a Division.

Another 'Lyttelton' Amendment, which provoked a debate mainly on investment policy, was defeated by 269 votes to 154.

These proceedings on Clause 35 illustrate again the sometimes somewhat detailed technical nature of discussion on the Report stage, and three possible ways of dealing with Opposition Amendments – withdrawal by leave, negativing without a Division, and rejection after a Division.

On Clause 36, moving an Amendment, Mr. Selwyn Lloyd said, somewhat plaintively, 'at long last we have reached an Amendment which I think the right hon. Gentleman will be prepared to accept. So far he has not given way on a single point, and I do not think he has given a single undertaking to look at any matter again. . . .'[63] The Minister, however, while he had 'no quarrel with the general purpose of this Amendment', suggested that it was undesirable, and it was accordingly negatived.

On Clause 38, an Amendment by Mr. Peake relating to Accounts and Audit and Statistics was met by a promise to meet the point by a manuscript Amendment to a later Clause.

After a further Opposition Amendment had been defeated on a Division, the Guillotine order again came into operation.

Clause 44 is interesting as providing an example of an Opposition Amendment which was accepted. Moved by Mr.

[62] *Ibid.*, col. 846.   [63] *Ibid.*, col. 870.

Selwyn Lloyd, it removed the statutory right of the Minister to be heard in all proceedings before the Arbitration Tribunal. The Corporation, said Mr. Lloyd, would always be there and surely the Minister would appear anyhow 'in appropriate cases'.

The Solicitor-General: We have . . . carefully re-read the arguments used during the Committee stage and have re-thought over all the considerations. Although we still think it would possibly be desirable that this power thould be retained, we are prepared to accept the Amendment.

Mr. Harold Macmillan: In this interlude of happy and agreeable position before the final Guillotine falls upon us, may I thank the right hon. and learned Gentleman for his kindness?[64]

Amendment agreed to.

After consideration of further Amendments, the House turned its attention to the Schedules to the Bill. A new Schedule was brought up and read the First time; it was then read a Second time and added to the Bill. There were several Opposition Amendments to the Second Schedule, all of which failed to make the grade, despite Mr. Manningham-Buller's hope that even at such a 'late hour' the Government would 'take a more reasonable attitude'. Government Amendments to the Third Schedule were accepted; an Opposition Amendment to the Fourth Schedule was withdrawn after explanation; a Government Amendment to the Fifth Schedule (necessary 'because of a printing error') was accepted; an Opposition Amendment to the Sixth Schedule was negatived without a Division; and a Government Amendment to the Eighth Schedule was accepted.

At this stage Opposition Amendments affecting the form of compensation to be paid (the Bill based compensation on Stock Exchange quotations for certain selected days) were taken. For this it was necessary for the House to recommit the Bill to a Committee of the whole House, financial matters being involved. Mr. Peake moved the first Amendment to substitute arbitration for the method which enabled 'the Government to acquire valuable assets on the cheap'.[65] He referred to the Minister's pledge that proper allowance would be made for expenditure incurred on approved schemes of development or rehabilitation made pending the putting into effect of the Government's

---

[64] *Ibid.*, col. 916.　　　　　[65] *Ibid.*, col. 950.

proposals. Mr. Glenvil Hall argued that, where reserves had been put to good use and new equipment had been installed, this was 'now obviously reflected in the Stock Exchange price'.[66]

Mr. Hall's argument was interrupted by the final fall of the Guillotine at 10.0 p.m. The closing scenes of the Debate are quoted in full:

The Deputy-Chairman (Mr. Bowles): The Question is –
Hon. Members: Gag! Resign! [Interruption]
The Deputy-Chairman: Hon. Members must try to behave themselves. I very much deprecate that this –
Colonel Dower: Sit down.
The Deputy-Chairman: I order the hon. and gallant Gentleman to withdraw that remark or to leave the Chamber at once.
Colonel Dower: I thought that I saw an hon. Member standing up – [Interruption]
The Deputy-Chairman: Did the hon. Gentleman withdraw that remark?
Colonel Dower: No, Mr. Bowles, I was about to say –
The Deputy-Chairman: Then the hon. and gallant Gentleman withdraws from the Chamber.
Colonel Dower: I was referring to an hon. Member –
The Deputy-Chairman: Order. I am on my feet.
Colonel Dower: There was a hon. Member –
The Deputy-Chairman: The hon. Gentleman should withdraw from the Chamber at once.
Colonel Dower: I will, but there was an hon. Member –
The Deputy-Chairman: Without another word. The hon. Gentleman will now withdraw from the Chamber, otherwise I shall report the matter to the House.
Colonel Dower: On a point of Order –
The Deputy-Chairman: There is no point of Order at all.
Colonel Dower: I want to ask –
The Deputy-Chairman: I shall now –
Colonel Dower: Very well, I shall leave the Chamber, and I am very pleased to do so.
The hon. and gallant Member thereupon withdrew.
Mr. Gallacher: On a point of Order –
The Deputy-Chairman: There can be no point of Order. I shall now put the Question.
Question put, 'That those words be there inserted'.
The Committee divided: Ayes, 158; Noes, 325.

The Deputy-Chairman of Ways and Means proceeded to put forthwith the Question necessary to dispose of the Business to be concluded at this day's Sitting.

Bill reported without Amendment (on recommittal).

[66] *Ibid.*, col. 957.

To be read the Third time upon Thursday next and to be printed. [Bill No. 119.]

(h) *The Third Reading* of the Iron and Steel Bill was taken on May 9, 1949. For just under six hours the arguments were once more deployed to the extent of 116 columns in *Hansard*. The Debate began by a typical appeal from Sir Waldron Smithers to Mr. Speaker 'to stop this country going another step down the totalitarian road'. He cited Sir Thomas More's refusal, as Speaker, to grant Henry VIII a subsidy without due Debate. In explaining that the House, not he, was master of the Guillotine, Mr. Speaker added drily: 'I have no desire to lose my head'.[67] The Joint Parliamentary Secretary to the Ministry of Supply,[68] in moving the Third Reading, mentioned that 137 hours had already been spent on the Bill.

Mr. Oliver Lyttelton moved the traditional substitution for 'now' of 'upon this day six months'. To him the Bill would leave 'unwept, unhonoured and undiscussed'. On Report, 109 of 214 Opposition Amendments were guillotined; in Committee 198 out of 480. Seven Clauses were not discussed at all at any stage; sixteen Clauses and six Schedules were not discussed in Committee; eleven were not discussed on Report. Discussion had 'been curtailed, for the first time since the Mace was removed by force from this Chamber, in order, not to promote further discussion on more urgent Measures, but because the Government consider further discussion of this Measure impertinent, inconvenient and inappropriate, or perhaps merely fatiguing'.[69]

Mr. Lyttelton went over at some length all the criticisms of the Bill which had been developed earlier. In particular, he dwelt again upon the choice of May 1, 1950, as vesting day.

The baby is bound to be born in the vestry, it is bound to be born on the way to the polling booth or on the way back, and no one in a few years' time will be anxious to claim the paternity.[70]

There followed a series of contributions, most of which were restatements of the general arguments for and against the Bill. Mr. Mort sang the praises of the industry under private enterprise. Mr. E. L. Mallalieu spoke of vested interests already plotting to ensure the defeat of the Government at the next

---

[67] *H.C. Debates*, Vol. 464, col. 1501.   [68] Mr. Jack Jones.
[69] *H.C. Debates*, Vol. 464, cols. 1507–1509.   [70] *Ibid.*, cols. 1516–1517.

election. Mr. Alfred Edwards, who had left the Labour Party on the issue of iron and steel, claimed that the Government had nowhere shown how better results were to be achieved.

Mr. S. N. Evans referred to steel and insurance as 'the citadels of twentieth-century power', and said:

No society moving towards a planned economy can afford to concede autonomy to two such giants within its ranks.[71]

Mr. Martin Lindsay repeated that there was nothing in the Bill to ensure more or better or cheaper steel. Mr. Ewart spoke of the welcome for the Bill by the steel workers. Sir Peter Bennett spoke largely of inadequate compensation, Mr. G. Thomas[72] of 'doctrinaire Tories'. Mr. Erroll foresaw stagnation. Colonel Lancaster could see no good in the Bill. Mr. Awbery attacked the Opposition's attitude to compensation and dwelt on 'the human element'. Mr. Osbert Peake, although admitting that there were 'not many new arguments' which could be advanced 'upon the general principles of the Bill',[73] nevertheless spoke for twenty-five minutes on its defects.

The Minister of Supply[74] wound up the Debate. He acknowledged the value of the many suggestions put forward by the Opposition, the T.U.C., the Federation of British Industries, the National Union of Manufacturers and the Association of British Chambers of Commerce. He was sorry that the leaders of the industry itself had not made any suggestions. He denied that the Government had prevented adequate discussion. The Opposition had been unwilling even to discuss a voluntary time-table.

At this point a series of points of Order arose as to whether such remarks were in order in a Third Reading Debate. During the latter part of his speech Mr. Strauss was interrupted five times, the last occasion being a final attempt, by Lieut.-Commander Gurney Braithwaite, to protest against the Guillotine. At 9.30 p.m. the House divided and gave the Bill a *Third Reading* by 333 votes to 203.

(i) *Consideration by the House of Commons of House of Lords' Amendments*

The Bill was given a Second Reading in the Lords on May 24, Lord Salisbury, leader of the Conservative Peers, holding that although it was an 'unnecessary Bill, a bad Bill and indeed a

---

[71] *Ibid.*, col. 1548.
[73] *Ibid.*, col. 1594.
[72] Lab., Cardiff West.
[74] Mr. G. R. Strauss.

thoroughly dangerous Bill', the principle of democracy demanded that it should not be rejected out of hand. But during the Committee stage (June 23, 28, 29, 30 and July 4), fifty-seven Amendments were made, of which only twenty-eight were either proposed or accepted by the Government. When, therefore, after the Third Reading in the Lords, the Bill came back to the House of Commons, the stage was set for another heated debate, which took place on July 25 and 26.

Before dealing with Amendments to Clause 1, the Minister of Supply referred generally to the Government's attitude. There were about sixty Amendments, twenty-eight of which it was proposed to accept; they were mostly drafting points.

> We do not, however, propose to accept any Amendment moved in another place, which, in the opinion of the Government, would make any material or significant change in the Bill as it left this House.[75]

The unacceptable Amendments were of four kinds:

> The first is concerned with fundamental principles which divide the Opposition and the Government and on which there is a gulf between us.
> . . . There is a second category which concerns itself with less important proposals which raise no question of fundamental principles but which, in the opinion of the Government, would make the task of the Corporation in running the iron and steel industry efficiently more difficult or even impossible. . . .
> . . . Again, there are Amendments which . . . would harmfully and unreasonably confine the activities of the Iron and Steel Corporation and the publicly-owned companies to the detriment of the iron and steel industry and of British industry generally. . . .
> . . . There is a final set which embody restrictive proposals, apparently inserted on the assumption that the Corporation will consist of a number of ignorant busybodies and that the Minister is an irresponsible nit-wit right outside the control of Parliament. . . .

All these, said Mr. Strauss, would be rejected.

On Clause 1, the Lords had attempted to define by law more exactly the membership of the Iron and Steel Corporation and, according to Major Legge-Bourke'[76] had 'treated this particular subject with objectiveness'.[77] But to Mr. McKay[78] it

---

[75] *H.C. Debates*, Vol. 467, cols. 1827–1828.   [76] Cons., Isle of Ely.
[77] *H.C. Debates*, Vol. 467, col. 1850.   [78] Lab., Wallsend.

was 'rather peculiar that we should get such an Amendment as this, to implement democracy, from a Chamber which is undemocratic itself'. The House divided on the first Amendment at 5.29 p.m. (defeated, 299 : 153). A second Amendment was debated until 7.10 p.m., when the Parliamentary Secretary to the Treasury[79] successfully moved 'That the Question be now put'. The *Closure* being carried, the Amendment was defeated.

The House next proceeded to discuss a new Clause proposed by the House of Lords, with several consequential Amendments; its effect was to limit the activities of the publicly-owned companies as well as of the Corporation. On the proposal that certain changes should be permitted only by resolutions of both Houses, Mr. Strauss made the point that it might be 'an undesirable development that new undertakings could be stifled by the veto of the House of Lords'.[80] A brief interchange will illustrate the possibility of heat being engendered about Lords' Amendments. Mr. Erroll[81] had spoken of 'our Amendment'.

Mr. Daines:[82] The hon. Gentleman frequently refers to 'our Amendment'. Are we to understand that the Opposition in the other place and here are the same thing?
Mr. Erroll: I am sorry if there is confusion in the mind of the hon. Gentleman.
Mr. Daines: Oh, no, there is not.
Mr. Erroll: Then I am surprised at the intervention. I should have thought that, as it is on comparatively rare occasions that Lords' Amendments are discussed, my slip of the tongue in using the word 'our' would readily be understood, but, of course the head of the hon. Member for East Ham North is pretty thick, as we all know.
Mr. Daines: Even for the Tories, that stinks.[83]

Later, Mr. Attewell[84] returned to the same point:

The Opposition made great play with what the House of Lords would do to the Bill when they received it and it was a foregone conclusion in my mind that the House of Lords would carry out the policy put forward by the Tory Opposition in this House. . . .[85]

Just before 9.30 p.m. the Chief Whip successfully moved *the Closure*; the new Clause was defeated. Certain Amendments to Clause 2 were, Mr. Speaker ruled, 'covered by the Closure'. Accordingly the House proceeded to a further Amendment

---

[79] Mr. Whiteley.
[81] Cons., Altrincham and Sale.
[83] *H.C. Debates*, Vol. 467, col. 1917.
[85] *H.C. Debates*, Vol. 467, col. 1925.

[80] *H.C. Debates*, Vol. 467, col. 1903.
[82] Lab., East Ham North.
[84] Lab., Harborough.

which would have subjected ministerial consent with reference to 'other activities of the Corporation' to annulment by resolution of the House. At 11.0 p.m., after nearly one and a half hours' debate, the Chief Whip successfully moved *the Closure*; the Amendment was defeated by 324 votes to 174.

A further three Amendments affecting the duties of the Corporation to promote the efficient and economical supply of certain products were discussed. The general point was whether such duties should be confined to 'Second Schedule activities' or to all others within the purview of the Corporation and the companies. The merits of the arguments were fully canvassed in a repetition of the Lords' Debate. At 12.45 a.m., when several hon. Members rose to speak, Mr. Deputy-Speaker wondered 'whether the House might not want to come to a decision fairly soon'.[86] After one further brief intervention, the House divided on the first two of the three Amendments, which were defeated. On the third, a Member who attempted to speak was told that the previous discussion had covered it as 'consequential'. The Amendment was negatived without a division.

An Amendment to delete 'public interest' from the considerations which might be taken into account by the Corporation when granting preferential treatment was debated until 2.15 a.m., when *the Closure* was carried and the Amendment defeated. A further Amendment sought to compel the Corporation to prepare a scheme for submission to the House showing how it would exercise its powers as 'a holding company' Dismissed as 'impracticable', debate on it was *closured* at 3.30 a.m. and the Amendment defeated. The next Amendment sought to establish a right of action in the courts if 'undue preference' were alleged. The Government opposed, and gave notice of an Amendment specifically to exclude such right. At 4.30 a.m. Mr. Deputy-Speaker enquired whether it was not possible to get a decision on the Amendment and proceed to the next, 'which is really the substance of what we are now discussing'.[87] But the Debate continued until just after 5.30 a.m., when it was *closured* and the Amendment defeated.

Mr. Lyttelton[88] then asked what were the Government's intentions about the Debate and formally moved the Adjournment of further consideration of the Lords' Amendments. The

---

[86] *Ibid.*, col. 2004.   [87] *Ibid.*, col. 2073.   [88] Cons., Aldershot.

Home Secretary[89] replied that the Government proposed that the House should sit until about noon, and continue at the next Sitting after the Business already announced for that day:

The Government intend to get these Amendments considered in time for adequate consideration of our disagreements by the members of another place.[90]

Major Tufton Beamish[91] took the opportunity of pointing out that the Minister appeared to be the only Member opposite capable of speaking in the Debates – 'a complete farce' – 'a one-man band with the dumb oxen behind him',[92] added Mr. Granville.[93] The Opposition forced a Division on the Motion to adjourn and was defeated by 261 votes to 138.

At 6.15 a.m. the Government Amendment to exclude liability before the courts was taken. *The Closure* was carried just before 6.45 and the Question, 'That those words be there inserted in the Bill' carried by 259 votes to 129.

The Lords' proposal to add a new Clause establishing an Iron and Steel Prices Board was then debated. *The Closure* was carried after two hours' debate and the new Clause defeated (247 : 104).

The Lords' Amendments to Clause 11, five taken together, were all concerned with the postponement of the vesting date, a matter to which the Opposition attached the very greatest importance.

We have been told by their spokesman in another place [said Mr. Strauss] that, whatever they may do in regard to the other Amendments that they have moved into the Bill when they are returned to them by the House, they are likely to stand by this particular Amendment. . . . The object of the Amendment is to ensure that there will be a General Election between now and the vesting date to give the electorate an opportunity of recording a verdict on this Bill . . . it is intolerable that the duly elected Government of this country, elected on a very specific mandate including the nationalisation of this industry, should be told by the other House – which is not an elected body and which has no responsibility to the electorate – that this Bill may not be carried into effect until the electorate have pronounced on it twice. . . . It would mean that it would be impossible to put this Bill into operation until fifteen months after the date of the election . . . a gap of two years between the passage of the Bill and its implementation. . . .[94]

---

[89] Mr. Chuter Ede.
[91] Cons., Lewes.
[93] Cons., Eye.

[90] *H.C. Debates*, Vol. 467, col. 2100.
[92] *H.C. Debates*, Vol. 467, cols. 2100–2102.
[94] *H.C. Debates*, Vol. 467, cols. 2156–2158.

Mr. Strauss also made it clear that if the Bill had to be presented again under the Parliament Act, it would 'contain this provision of retrospective dates which are contained in the Bill we are discussing today. . . .'[95]

Mr. Lyttelton objected to the Minister's description of the Lords' delaying action as 'fantastic'. 'That is the function of the House of Lords', he said.

Shortly before midday, the Debate on the Amendment having lasted more than three hours, *the Closure* was carried and the Amendment defeated by 285 votes to 37. The four further Amendments were then negatived without a Division. The Adjournment was then moved, and after brief protest at the way in which the Guillotine had been used (*sed quaere*, Closure?), the Question was put and carried. It was then 12.18 p.m. The House resumed at 2.30 p.m.

Debate was continued that night at 11.16 p.m. (July 26), the Ten o'clock Rule having been suspended. A Lords' Amendment on Clause 13 (acceptance of certain leases and agreements), after an admission by Mr. Osbert Peake[96] that the words which were sought to be introduced in another place were already provided in a different form in the Clause as it now stood, was negatived without a Division. On Clause 15 (compensation) the Government resisted all attempts to move away from the 'Stock Exchange basis' despite lengthy argument by Mr. Lyttelton. The Amendment was defeated shortly after 12.30 a.m. Amendments to Clauses 25 and 38 were rejected without a Division. Two Amendments to Clause 50, consequential upon earlier Amendments already rejected, were also negatived; similarly a proposal to add a new Schedule to the Bill. The *Hansard* Report[97] concludes thus:

Remaining Lords' Amendments agreed to.

Committee appointed to draw up Reasons to be assigned to the Lords for disagreeing to certain of their Amendments to the Bill: Mr. S. N. Evans, Mr. Lyttleton, Mr. Peake, Mr. G. R. Strauss and Mr. G. Thomas; three to be a Quorum.

Committee to withdraw immediately.

Reasons for disagreeing to certain of the Lords Amendments reported, and agreed to; to be communicated to the Lords.

Motion made, and Question proposed, 'That this House do now adjourn'.

---

[95] *Ibid.*, col. 2160.   [96] Cons., Leeds North-East.
[97] *H.C. Debates*, Vol. 467, col. 2444.

The Lords returned to the Iron and Steel Bill on July 28. At the instigation of Lord Salisbury, they chose to 'insist' only on two groups of their Amendments which had been rejected by the Commons: those relating to the postponement of the vesting date. The effect would have been to delay the coming into operation of the Bill until after the General Election. According to Lord Salisbury, this was necessary 'to provide the British people with a protection against harsh or ill-considered legislation as to which their views are doubtful or likely to be hostile'.

On November 16, 1949,[98] the ball returned to the House of Commons, which debated the Lords' Reasons for insisting on certain of their Amendments to which the Commons have disagreed'. The Minister of Supply[99] moved 'that this House doth insist on its disagreement with the Lords in the said Amendments' and indicated that the Government proposed to move certain Amendments 'in lieu' thereof.

When the Bill was first introduced more than a year ago, he said, 'it was then reasonable and proper to assume that the passage of this Bill through the two Houses of Parliament would be similar to the passage of the previous nationalisation Measures. . . . '

' . . We assumed, therefore, that the Bill would emerge from the Commons some time in the early summer of this year and from the House of Lords at the end of July; and that it would then, modified and amended as a result of the scrutiny of both Houses, obtain the Royal Assent before the Summer Recess. . . . When the Bill went to the Lords a series of Amendments was moved by the Opposition, most of which were rejected by this House when they came here for consideration. On the return of the Bill to the Lords, the Opposition accepted our rejections, save for two groups of Amendments. One of these made the whole Bill inoperative until 1st October, 1950, and the other made the date of transfer not before 1st July, 1951.

. . . It is contrary to all principles of democratic government that an hereditary and unrepresentative House of Lords should use its powers to prevent a Measure already approved by the electorate and passed by the Commons, and which the Government of the day considers essential to the fulfilment of its policy . . . being carried into effect until the electorate have pronounced upon it a second time. . . . As the House is aware, the Government has taken the necessary steps to lessen the opportunities of the House of Lords repeating this conduct in any future Parliament.[1]

[98] *H.C. Debates*, Vol. 469, col. 2039, *et seq.*   [99] Mr. G. R. Strauss.
[1] *H.C. Debates*, Vol. 469, cols. 2039–2044.

Mr. Strauss explained that because of this delay, May 1, 1950, was now 'unrealistic' for the transfer of assets. The Government proposed to substitute January 1, 1951, or such date within the following twelve months as the Minister might determine. (The Lords proposed July 1, 1951.) He refused to accept the Amendment whereby the Bill would not operate at all until October 1, 1950.

The Bill has been drawn on the basis that it would come into operation on the day of the Royal Assent and to introduce another operating date would make nonsense of the Bill, unless a considerable number of consequential Amendments was added, and even then the Bill would be untidy and confusing.[2]

The Government Amendment would accept October 1, 1950, as the first permitted date for the formal establishment of the Corporation, but all other provisions would operate from the date of the Royal Assent. The House of Lords might then reject the Government Amendments; if so the Parliament Act would be invoked.

Mr. Churchill said that no Member would envy Mr. Strauss his task that day.

About a fortnight ago we were informed that the Government wished to end the deadlock between the two Houses . . . by accepting in principle the House of Lords' Amendment delaying its operation until after the people had been consulted. There was no question of a bargain or a compromise. The Government asked a question and the Leader of the House of Lords [sic.], after consulting with some of his friends in both Houses, gave the answer . . . that if the Amendment the Lords were insisting upon were accepted in principle, he, Lord Salisbury, would advise the House of Lords to accept it, even though the form was slightly altered. . . . It would hardly have been in accordance with the manner in which the House of Lords discharges its constitutional duties under the Parliament Act settlement of 35 years ago for the Conservative Leader in the House of Lords to advise them to take advantage of minor differences in form and to reject what is the undoubted acceptance by the Commons of their contention. It is not for us here this afternoon to forecast what the action of the Lords will be, but in this House we shall not oppose this series of Amendments. . . . I should think it very likely that a similar course will be adopted in another place.

Mr. Churchill then made it clear that should his party be returned to power,

One of our first steps will be to expunge from the Statute Book this wanton, wasteful and partisan Measure.[3]

[2] *Ibid.*, col. 2042.   [3] *Ibid.*, cols. 2044–2045.

He then proceeded to condemn the Government's forcing through of the Parliament Act:

Why . . . should they [the Lords] be stripped of part of their functions for having used them so wisely and so well? I am glad that the House of Lords should once again have vindicated their wisdom and sagacity. . . . We take our stand on the position that it is not the function of the House of Lords to govern the people but to make sure that the people have the right to govern themselves.[4]

Mr. S. N. Evans[5] took up Mr. Churchill's remark that it was not for him to anticipate what action the Lords would take:

That seems to me to show some misunderstanding, having regard to recent developments. It seems to me that he had his card marked. . . .[6]

But he welcomed 'the compromise between the two Houses . . . in the best traditions of English parliamentary democracy'.

The Debate ranged widely, the Deputy-Speaker having to remind the House that they were 'not discussing the merits or demerits of the Iron and Steel Bill or the steel industry on this Motion'.[7] Some Labour Members deplored the need to accept a compromise. Others welcomed the Parliament Act, which would make such compromises unnecessary in the future. Others pointed the traditional contrast between the positions of Labour and Conservative Governments.

Mr. Lyttelton made 'a few valedictory remarks about this Bill'. . . .

We feel that the Government's Motion, in effect, meets all the major points which the Lords had in mind . . . the differences are merely the ordinary face-saving which we expect from the Government, and for which I do not blame them.[8]

Mr. Morrison admitted that they had been forced 'by the intolerable interference of their Lordships . . . purely because of the calendar, to alter the date in the Bill'.[9]

If their Lordships passed the Transport, Electricity, Gas, Bank of England and Coal Acts and the Cable and Wireless Act – which enjoyed the support of the Opposition – and remember that they passed them, as stated by the Leader of the Opposition in another place, because there was a mandate for them from the people . . . then I say that they had no more justification to interfere with the Iron and Steel Bill than . . . with the Coal Act.[10]

[4] *Ibid.*, cols. 2048–2049.　　[5] Lab., Wednesbury.
[6] *Ibid.*, col. 2051.　　[7] *Ibid.*, col. 2056.
[8] *Ibid.*, col. 2077.　　[9] *Ibid.*, col. 2082.
[10] *Ibid.*, col. 2084.

The Lords' Amendments were defeated and the Government Amendments incorporated in the Bill.

On November 24 the Lords gave their final consent, Lord Salisbury claiming that they had been 'successful in performing their allotted duty under the Constitution'.

(b) PRIVATE MEMBERS' BILLS

(a) *Introduction.* Private Members' Bills may be dealt with, first, under S.O. No. 35, which provides that 'a Member may after notice present a Bill without previously obtaining leave from the House . . .' It is read the First time without question put and ordered to be printed. Virtually the only chance of such a Bill's proceeding further is in the event of its being 'unopposed'. Of forty-nine Private Members' Bills enacted between 1948 and 1954, eleven were unopposed, of which only four were introduced under S.O. No. 35.[11]

Next, a Bill may be introduced under the 'Ten Minute Rule'.[12] S.O. No. 12 permits, on Tuesdays and Wednesdays, the setting down of notices of motion for leave to bring in Bills. If such a notice is opposed, a brief explanatory statement is permitted, followed by one opposing the Bill, and the question may then be put. Alternatively, the debate may be adjourned. If the Motion is approved the Bill is given its First Reading forthwith. Its subsequent fate depends on the same factors as those governing any other unballoted Bill; it is unlikely to be discussed further. Seven Bills thus introduced between 1948 and 1954 were, however, passed 'unopposed'.

'Balloted Bills' are, however, the most important, and certainly the most interesting. The details of the relevant Standing Orders, and of the procedure under the Sessional Order, are given in *Bromhead*.[13] He has also a useful account of the various obstacles which Private Members' Bills in general have to overcome.[14]

Certain general tendencies concerning the character and treatment of Private Members' Bills deserve notice. From the end of the war until the end of 1953 'not a single one of the

---

[11] *See* P. A. Bromhead: *Private Members' Bills*, pp. 17–19 and 150–155.
[12] *Ibid.*, pp. 19–20 and 155–161.
[13] *Ibid.*, pp. 20–26 and Appendix A, pp. 178–180.
[14] *Ibid.*, pp. 26–42. For Financial Resolutions, cf. *H.C. Debates*, Vol. 580, cols. 207–212, 217–218.

Private Members' Bills *enacted* [our italics] was controversial enough to be made the subject of a Division on either Second or Third Reading in either House. Eighteen of the thirty-six were so extraordinarily uncontroversial that they were allowed to pass through their Second Reading, a most important stage in the House of Commons, without debate and without a word, even of explanation, being said on their behalf.'[15] Further, 'if we eliminate balloted Bills, Ten Minute Bills and Bills which pass unopposed, we find that the total of "other" Bills has fallen from over 100 a year before 1914 to almost nothing at all in the past few years or so'. Their decline, says *Bromhead*, 'is significant of a change in the general conception of the function of Parliament. . . . By now people have become accustomed to the notion that the Government is the normal initiator of legislation and they have come to recognise that the scope of Private Members' Bills had better be kept within certain bounds, recognised though not necessarily very well defined'.[16]

Nevertheless – and bearing in mind the recent increase in Private Members' time[17] – some aspects of procedure are worthy of inclusion here. We illustrate (1) the most frequent method of defeating a Bill – by the 'talk-out'; (2) the successful use of S.O. No. 35; (3) the successful use of the Ten Minute Rule; and (4) the successful use of the Ballot. The example chosen for the last category also provides further illustration, during its long and chequered history, of categories (1) and (3).

(b) *Unsuccessful Private Members' Bills*. Of 68 Private Members' Balloted Bills which failed to pass, 1948–49 to 1953–54, 5 were withdrawn, 18 not debated, 3 counted out, 21 talked out, 3 withdrawn at Second Reading, 2 defeated by failure to carry the Closure, 5 defeated at Second Reading, 2 passed at Second Reading but proceeding no further, 2 defeated in Standing Committee, 4 passed in Committee but proceeding no further, through lack of time, 2 defeated on Third Reading, and 1 passed through all stages in the Commons but not in the Lords. It is unnecessary to provide examples of each category; indeed, when Bills are withdrawn or not debated there is nothing to report save the nature of the Bills and the reasons for their fate – matters which cannot be discussed on the basis of *Hansard*. Bills which were debated, though not ultimately carried, in most cases illustrate no aspects of procedure differing

[15] *Ibid.*, Intro. pp. 1–2.   [16] *Ibid.*, p. 153.   [17] *See* below, p. 338.

from those illustrated by successful Bills. But the most frequent
single cause of defeat, being *'talked out'*, is worth illustrating.

A Bill may be talked out because Members object to it, or
because they object to one which is to come up after it, and aim
to prevent the latter's having a Second Reading.

On February 9, 1951, the *Common Informers Bill* was almost
talked out in order to prevent a Bill to allow increased use of
motor cars for elections in rural constituencies from coming up.
This second Bill was itself talked out on April 20, 1951.

The Second Reading Debate on the Common Informers Bill
opened at 11.10 a.m., Friday, February 9, 1951,[18] with a speech
by Mr. Lionel Heald.[19] We are not concerned with the subject-
matter of Mr. Heald's Bill, though his forty-minute speech
contained much interesting historical matter. The Bill, he
thought, showed 'that Private Members can make a useful
contribution to the function of legislation in Parliament' and
were also 'able notwithstanding acute political differences, to
work our free and democratic machinery'. Mr. Parker[20] congratulated Mr. Heald and hoped for a unanimous Second Reading.

The Attorney-General intervened at 12.22 p.m. He pointed
out that the Bill did not abolish the activity of the common
informer in relation to Parliamentary disqualifications, a matter
'of some constitutional importance in which it was right that
the Government should take the responsibility for legislation'
(though he could give no guarantee when this would be introduced). He commended the Bill to the House.[21] Much of the
subsequent debate was concerned with the omission to which
the Attorney-General had drawn attention.

By 1.9 p.m. Mr. Bing[22] was saying 'how difficult it is . . . for
any hon. Member of the House to say anything more about this
Bill',[23] though he spoke for nearly twenty minutes. Mr. James
Hudson[24] also thought that 'the speeches we have heard . . . do
not seem to have left very much room for further comment . . .'[25]
but he spoke for just over fifteen minutes. Mr. Hale,[26] although
he did 'not wish to delay the discussion on this matter',[27] spoke
for as long. Mr. Eric Fletcher[28] rose at 2.8 p.m. and did 'not

---

[18] *H.C. Debates*, Vol. 483, cols. 2079–2162.
[20] Lab., Dagenham.
[22] Lab., Hornchurch.
[24] Lab., Ealing North.
[26] Lab., Oldham.
[28] Lab., Islington East.

[19] Cons., Chertsey.
[21] *H.C. Debates*, Vol. 483, cols. 2101–2106.
[23] *H.C. Debates*, Vol. 483, col. 2115.
[25] *H.C. Debates*, Vol. 483, col. 2121.
[27] *H.C. Debates*, Vol. 483, col. 2129.

feel called upon in any way to apologise for venturing to take up the time of the House for a few minutes before [Mr. Heald] replies to the debate and asks the House to give this Bill a Second Reading'.[29] He went on for some twenty-five minutes with the assistance of some quotations from Sir William Holdsworth's *History of English Law*. He had reached the Stuarts when Sir Thomas Moore[30] interjected, 'Progress'.

Mr. Deputy-Speaker: The hon. Member does not appear to be keeping his remarks to common informers of today.[31]

Mr. Fletcher was still with the Stuarts a column later when Sir Thomas Moore again interjected, 'Progress'. A little later, Mr. Marlowe[32] inquired:

Has the hon. Gentleman reached the stage of his argument where he is able to indicate that he is for or against the Bill, or is he merely *against the next one on the Order Paper?* (Our italics).[33]

Mr. Fletcher had not proceeded much further when Sir Thomas Moore asked:

Is the hon. Member aware that everything he has said up to now was said earlier by [Mr. Heald] and also by the Attorney-General. . . .?[34]

But Mr. Fletcher continued his historical survey and was again interrupted by Mr. Remnant:[35]

Before the hon. Member finishes his speech, could he tell us in what relation he thinks the common informer stands to what the Americans call a filibuster?[36]

Mr. Fletcher preferred to 'pass it by'. But Mr. Pannell[37] saw fit to begin his speech, which lasted half an hour, with a disclaimer 'of any desire to filibuster'. At one point he was engaged in a virtually private debate with Mr. Remnant on the Lord's Day Observance Society. A little later, Mr. Speaker wished to know 'what all this has to do with the common informer, which is what we are debating'.[38]

Mr. William Ross,[39] who had 'not intended to speak or take part in this Debate other than adding my vote in support of

[29] *H.C. Debates*, Vol. 483, col. 2132.
[30] Cons., Ayrshire.
[31] *H.C. Debates*, Vol. 483, col. 2134.
[32] Cons., Hove.
[33] *H.C. Debates*, Vol. 483, col. 2136.
[34] *Ibid.*, col. 2136.
[35] Cons., Wokingham.
[36] *H.C. Debates*, Vol. 483, col. 2138.
[37] Leeds West.
[38] *Ibid.*, col. 2149.
[39] Lab., Kilmarnock.

what I consider a very necessary Measure', had discovered examples of the common informer in Scotland, which enabled him to speak of the circulation of Scottish bank notes for just under ten minutes.

To Mr. Douglas Houghton[40] it seemed 'imperative that we should get on with' abolishing the common informer. [Hon. Members: 'Hear, hear.'] He asked that the Government should 'ensure that facilities are given for the further stages of the Bill and that there will be no delay in getting it finally passed'. He, and Lieut.-Colonel Lipton[41] after him, commented on the fact that Mr. Heald had been supported by few Members on his side of the House.

One may perhaps venture to suggest that Mr. Heald might well have thought of his supporters on the Labour side of the House what the Duke of Wellington thought of his soldiers – 'I don't know what they'll do to the enemy, but, by God, they scare me!' Mr. MacColl,[42] indeed, spoke of the 'long and careful consideration' given to the Bill and added to it by some fifteen minutes.

The Bill was then read a Second time and committed to a Standing Committee. Its subsequent history may be briefly summarised. It passed through Committee at one Sitting (March 14) and through its Report and Third Reading stages in twelve minutes (compared with four and a half hours on Second Reading). The Lords spent twenty-four minutes on Second Reading and one minute in Committee and on Third Reading. Their Amendments occupied the Commons for four minutes. The Bill received the Royal Assent in June, 1951.

The Second Reading Debate, however, had served its purpose. Mr. Marples's[43] Representation of the People (Amendment) (No. 1) Bill was introduced by him at 3.45 p.m. after 'a most agreeable day of tranquil meanderings from hon. Gentlemen opposite'.[44] At this stage the Amendments tabled do not concern us. Mr. Marples spoke – with several interruptions – until 4 p.m., when 'further proceedings stood adjourned'. The Bill had thus been successfully talked out by the debate on the preceding Bill.

(c) *Successful Bills:* (i) *Under Standing Order No. 35.* In the

---

[40] Lab., Sowerby.
[42] Lab., Widnes.
[44] *H.C. Debates,* Vol. 483, col. 2162.

[41] Lab., Lambeth, Brixton.
[43] Cons., Wallasey.

nature of things, successful Bills under S.O. No. 35 provide no exciting passages in *Hansard*, for they are inevitably unopposed and often undebated. Promoters must 'have had full discussions with all Members and outside bodies who might conceivably be interested, and ensure that every interest, including the Government, has shown itself satisfied that the Bill should pass'. If these preliminaries are neglected, someone is sure to object. The Government itself normally sees to it that someone objects, unless it has been fully consulted and satisfied'.[45] Our examples, therefore, are brief, relatively uninformative, but typical.

On Friday, December 5, 1952,[46] after Private Members' Motions dealing with Home-Grown Timber (Policy), Nationalised Industries (Parliamentary Questions) and – very briefly – Industry (Application of Science), two Orders of the Day were taken. The first read, simply:

AGRICULTURAL LAND (REMOVAL OF SURFACE SOIL) BILL

Read a Second Time.
Committed to a Committee of the Whole House. – [Mr. Vaughan-Morgan.] Bill immediately considered in Committee; reported without Amendment; read the Third Time, and passed.

The House of Lords spent thirty-five minutes on the Bill, and on March 27, 1953, the House of Commons dealt with Lords' Amendments in eight minutes. The Bill then received the Royal Assent.

On Friday, February 12, 1954,[47] after the Protection of Animals (Anaesthetics) Bill, the Protection of Animals (Amendment) Bill and the Coroners Bill had been given a Second Reading, Mr. Arthur Skeffington[48] rose at 1.56 p.m. to move the Second Reading of the *Law Reform (Miscellaneous) Bill*. He outlined its purpose briefly, referring to 'two most important and authoritative legal committees' which had recommended the proposed changes in Clauses 1 and 2 (enforcement of contracts). Clause 3 was concerned with written notices of summary charges and Mr. Skeffington was 'prepared to give

45 P. A. Bromhead: *op. cit.*, p. 18   46 *H.C. Debates*, Vol. 508, col. 2010.
47 *H.C. Debates*, Vol. 523, cols. 1565–1578.   48 Lab., Hayes and Harlington.

an undertaking that if the Home Office has weighty objections, on the Committee stage, I shall be prepared to drop the Clause or to alter it. . . .' He spoke for less than fifteen minutes.

The non-party nature of the Bill was emphasised by Mr. Derek Walker-Smith.[49] Like Mr. Skeffington, who had spoken briefly because he understood 'that many hon. Members [were] interested in the Measure which is to come next', he also aimed to facilitate consideration of that Measure and also 'the Bill after that, which is to be moved by my hon. Friend, Mr. Ian Harvey'. (An interesting example of 'give and take' among Members.)

Mr. G. R. Mitchison,[50] one of the six lawyers of the nine Members supporting the Bill, commented on the inadequate 'machinery for putting into effect recommendations for law reform'.

The Joint Under-Secretary of State for the Home Department[51] stated that the Government had no objection in principle to the objects of the Bill. Although 'considerable redrafting' would be necessary, he did not wish to advise against giving a Second Reading.

The Bill was read a Second Time without a Division and committed to a *Standing Committee*. There, the Bill was disposed of at one Sitting on March 10, 1954.

Report and Third Reading were taken on Friday, April 9, 1954.[52] Mr. Arthur Skeffington moved to leave out Clause 3. He had wished to do this in Committee, because he 'was convinced that . . . as drafted it would not meet the purposes which I had in mind', but to his surprise and discomfort, had not been allowed to do so. After discussion, the Clause was deleted from the Bill.

Mr. Skeffington then moved to change the title of the Bill to *Law Reform (Enforcement of Contracts) Bill*. This was agreed to, as were two small Amendments, without debate.

At 3.52 p.m. Mr. Skeffington moved the Third Reading in a brief speech. Mr. Marlowe said he thought it was 'not such a good Bill as it was when originally drafted and when it went to Committee'. In his remarks it was just possible, perhaps, to discern an intention to talk the Bill out at that late stage. But just before 4.0 p.m. Mr. Skeffington successfully moved the *Closure*.

[49] Cons., Hertfordshire East.   [50] Lab., Kettering.
[51] Sir Hugh Lucas-Tooth.   [52] *H.C. Debates*, Vol. 526, cols. 745–759.

The Bill was read a Third time.

It was debated for just over half an hour on Second Reading in the Lords. No Amendments were made and the Bill eventually received the Royal Assent.

(ii) *Under the Ten Minute Rule*. On Wednesday, December 2, 1953,[53] after Questions, Mr. Fenner Brockway[54] successfully moved the Adjournment under S.O. No. 9 to discuss the deposition of the Kabaka of Buganda. The Motion stood over until 7.0 p.m.

At 3.39 p.m. Miss Irene Ward[55] moved, 'That leave be given to bring in a *Bill to regulate the exercise of Statutory rights of entry* by or on behalf of Gas Boards and Electricity Boards, and for purposes connected with the matter aforesaid'.

She stated that its purpose was to ensure that forcible entry should only be exercised after a warrant had been obtained from a justice of the peace, signed, after sworn information given in writing. This was the procedure under the Water Act, 1945. She referred to a case, in 1951, of forcible entry after authorisation by the Eastern Gas Board had been shown to a neighbour – 'not a very satisfactory way of proceeding'. The owner of the property, which was unoccupied, had failed in his claim of 'illegal entry'. The North Thames Gas Consultative Council had recommended the changes suggested in the Bill; the Minister of Fuel and Power and the Opposition had been consulted.

The Question was put, and agreed to without debate or Division, and six hon. Members were ordered to 'bring in the Bill'. It was presented accordingly and read the First time, ordered to be printed, and Second Reading fixed for 'Wednesday next'.

In fact, it came up on Friday, December 11, after a long debate on a Private Member's Motion (Denationalised Steel Undertakings (Sale of Shares)). It was given a Second Reading without debate and committed to a Committee of the Whole House. Its remaining stages, taken on the same day, were all unopposed. The House of Lords gave it a Second Reading on February 24, 1954, after less than half an hour's debate. Without further discussion the Bill passed through all its stages and received the Royal Assent.

[53] *H.C. Debates*, Vol. 521, col. 1163.   [54] Cons., Eton and Slough.
[55] Cons., Tynemouth.

The conditions required for success under the Ten Minute Rule are well illustrated by this example: a simple, non-controversial point, no opposition from Government, Opposition or individual Member, luck in getting time on a Friday or, exceptionally, on a Government day, and the continuance of all these conditions until the final stage.

(iii) *A Balloted Bill.* Although the primary reason for the choice of the *Bill dealing with Football Pools Accounts* is that it was successfully carried, the choice also further illustrates the technique of 'talking out' a Bill.

On Friday, January 29, 1954, Mr. Frederick Mulley,[56] who had been fortunate in the Ballot, moved the Second Reading of his *Pool Betting Bill* as the Second Order of the Day.[57] The first Bill, Slaughter of Animals (Amendment) Bill, had already been debated until 2.40 p.m. (not, it should be noted, for the purpose of delaying the debate on Mr. Mulley's Bill).

Mr. Mulley described his Bill as an attempt to implement the non-controversial parts of the Royal Commission's Report of 1949 – 51. It was primarily concerned to obtain publication of football pool promoters' accounts, which would be available at local authority offices.

Mr. Mulley stressed that he was 'only asking' the House 'to come to a decision about the principle of the regulation of pools betting and the publication of accounts'. He would do all he could 'to see that the Bill meets all objections from those concerned, so long as we safeguard the main general purposes'. Two Members supported.

Mr. Stephen McAdden[58] introduced the first critical note. He could not see why one particular kind of firm should be singled out for control. There was no evidence that there was anything wrong with the way the pools were being run. He wanted a comprehensive review of the whole question of gambling, not 'a fiddling piece of legislation which will only make the matter more complicated'.

Two further Members spoke briefly, expressing their readiness to let the Bill go to Committee. Major H. Legge-Bourke,[59] however, opposed the Bill, although he had received letters from his constituency urging him to vote for it.

[56] Lab., Sheffield, Park.
[58] Cons., Southend East.
[57] *H.C. Debates*, Vol. 522, cols. 2109–2134.
[59] Cons., Isle of Ely.

Captain M. Hewitson[60] rose at 3.48 p.m. to make a speech which, in a subsequent debate,[61] Mr. Beverley Baxter[62] described as 'an outrageous piece of obstruction'. He began with an analysis of where the punter's money went, emphasising the 30 per cent. Purchase Tax, Post Office charges, etc. At one point, Mr. Nally[63] asked Mr. Speaker to urge Captain Hewitson to observe the 'rules . . . which are laid down in the interest of decency and dignity' and give the Minister an opportunity to reply.[64]

Mr. Speaker: There is nothing I can do to assist in the matter. So far, the Minister has not shown any disposition to speak.

Captain Hewitson continued, with many interruptions, repeating – as one Member complained – arguments already put forward by Mr. McAdden.

Just before 4.0 p.m. Mr. Mulley was refused permission to move the Closure and the Bill was talked out, after a brief appeal from Mr. Geoffrey de Freitas[65] that the Government should find time on another occasion.

This, however, proved unnecessary, for on Friday, February 12, 1954, after the Protection of Animals (Anaesthetics) Bill, the Protection of Animals (Amendment) Bill, the Coroners Bill and the Law Reform (Miscellaneous Provisions) Bill[66] had all been given a Second Reading, Mr. Mulley's Bill came up again as the fourth Order of the Day. The Debate began at 2.36 p.m.[67]

The Joint Under-Secretary for the Home Department[68] referred to the 'considerable feeling . . . both inside and outside the House that that part of the Royal Commission's Report which is covered by the Bill should be dealt with apart from the other recommendations. . . .' This was 'not impracticable'. The Government would 'assist in seeing that [the Bill] received a Second Reading today.' It might need considerable amendment in Committee and he was not committed to finding time for later stages, though, 'owing to the events of a fortnight ago', four other Bills had now received priority and they should not long hold up Mr. Mulley's Bill. On the suggestion that the Bill

[60] Lab., Kingston-upon-Hull Central.
[61] *H.C. Debates,* Vol. 523, col. 1581
[62] Cons., Southgate.
[63] Lab., Bilston.
[64] *H.C. Debates,* Vol. 522, col. 2132.
[65] Lab., Lincoln.
[66] *See* above pp. 185–187.
[67] *H.C. Debates,* Vol. 523, cols. 1579–1607.
[68] Sir Hugh Lucas-Tooth.

be postponed until the results of a poll organised by the Pool Promoters' Association were known, he said that those results could be considered at a later stage.

Mr. Chuter Ede[69] hoped that when the Bill emerged from Committee it would be in such form that the Government could continue to assist its progress. Mr. Beverley Baxter[70] contrasted the 'outrageous piece of obstruction' in the previous debate with the endeavour by mutual agreement to secure a Second Reading – 'an example of the adaptability of the House and of the machinery with which we conduct our business'.

Mrs. Braddock began by saying she had no intention of opposing the Bill or talking it out. During the course of a much-interrupted, twenty-minute speech she fulfilled her 'duty' to put the promoters' point of view (not necessarily her own) by *reading their prepared document*. After four paragraphs, Mr. Shepherd[71] asked if it were in order to read a lengthy document prepared by outside sources. Mr. Speaker ruled it in order to read anything relevant. After nine more paragraphs, Mr. Nabarro asked whether Mrs. Braddock, while not intending to talk the Bill out, 'had in mind the purpose of reading [it] out'. Mr. Speaker, referring again to the reading of documents, thought that Mrs. Braddock.

is quite capable of putting, in her own eloquent and forceful way, the arguments from the document from which she is reading.

Sir Charles Taylor[72] asked whether it was not in order to read a document or quotation, long or short – making his point at some length. Mr. Julian Snow[73] asked how much there was of the document and was it not normal usage to circulate such material to the Committee? Mr. Bishop[74] wanted to know whether hon. Members should not take responsibility for views expressed by them. Mrs. Braddock continued by commenting at length on these points, and asked for the Speaker's ruling. Mr. Speaker was reluctant but, pressed by Mr. Baxter, he thought that if a Member believed a certain viewpoint was deserving of expression in the House, he was entitled to give it. Mr. Nabarro[75] persisted in inquiring whether it was in order

[69] Lab., South Shields.
[70] Cons., Southgate.
[71] Cons., Cheadle.
[72] Cons., Eastbourne.
[73] Cons., Lichfield and Tamworth.
[74] Cons., Harrow Central.
[75] Cons., Kidderminster.

'to try and read out a Bill'. One and a half pages had been read; there were twenty-one pages. In the end, after considerable discussion as to the actual number of pages the document contained, Mrs. Braddock declined to proceed further with her case.

My constituents will see how it has been obstructed in certain ways and they will probably come to their own conclusions.

Mr. William Teeling,[76] who had had 'the sorrow of seeing [his] Bill talked out', assured Mr. Mulley it was not his intention to reply in kind. He was, however, 'deeply suspicious of the Bill' and hoped that it would be 'thoroughly vetted' in Committee. He spoke critically for about twelve minutes.

Just before 4.0 p.m. the Bill was given a Second Reading and committed to a Standing Committee. Here it occupied three Sittings between March 17 and 31, having originally come up as the ninth Order of the Day. The Report stage was taken in the House on Friday, May 7, 1954.[77]

Some minor Amendments to Clauses 1 and 5 were briefly explained by Mr. Mulley and agreed to without a Division. Long debate, however, ensued on Clause 10 (ready-money betting by post) and Mr. Reader Harris[78] moved that the Clause be 'left out'. The Joint Under-Secretary supported the Clause as necessary to secure accurate accounts, but Mr. Ian Mikardo[79] argued lengthily against it. At several points there was argument about what had actually happened in Committee. The Debate also tended to range widely over the betting laws in general. Mr. Mulley, replying to the Debate, said that he would withdraw Clause 10 if there was.

a lot of opposition . . . for the obvious reason that a Private Member seeking to pilot a Bill through the House has no very strong powers. If there had been substantial opposition in Committee I should have been prepared for the Clause to be dropped.

He then argued the case for the Clause. The Amendment was defeated by 69 votes to 6.

Third Reading followed immediately at 3.40 p.m. Mr. Mulley briefly thanked hon. Members on both sides of the House who had helped him and those in charge of preceding

[75] Cons., Brighton, Pavilion.
[78] Cons., Heston and Isleworth.
[77] *H.C. Debates*, Vol. 527, cols. 760–806.
[79] Lab., Reading.

Bills for making it possible to go ahead. He also expressed gratitude to the Home Office, who had placed expert knowledge and the assistance of Parliamentary draftsmen at his disposal.

The Bill was read a Third Time without a Division.

2. PRIVATE BILLS: THE LEEDS PRIVATE BILL, 1956

It is not intended to deal in any considerable detail with Private Bill procedure, nor to make any but brief reference to those aspects which are not 'proceedings in Parliament'. We have selected as our example the Leeds Private Bill, 1956. One of the authors was personally concerned with this Bill and a full account of its origin and progress, from its beginning in the minds of the local authority responsible to its final administrative implementation by that authority is contained in 'The Leeds Private Bill, 1956'.[80]

The Bill was duly deposited in the Private Bill Office (there were no petitions claiming that due legal procedure had not been complied with), and considered by the two Examiners (one from each House) to ensure that Parliamentary Standing Orders governing Private Bills had been complied with. (There was no need to seek dispensation for non-compliance, as may be granted if both Houses agree.) The Bill was allocated to the House of Commons for its initial consideration and given a formal First Reading. On the usual return to the Private Bill Office, to make doubly certain that Standing Orders had been complied with, the Bill met no trouble.

Time had then to be provided for Second Reading in the House of Commons. This Bill was not unopposed and therefore, after Second Reading, there was no question of its going to the Committee on Unopposed Bills, where 'proceedings are more brief and less formal than those of a committee on an opposed private bill'.[81]

A brief indication of the purposes of the Bill – it consisted of the Preamble and seventeen Parts, 297 Clauses in all – may be given. An extension of the city boundaries was proposed and a large variety of powers in respect of street improvements, sanitation, nuisances and other health matters, food, caravans,

[80] *Journal of Public Administration*, Spring 1957, pp. 25–44. H. V. Wiseman.
[81] *Erskine May*, 16th ed., p. 976.

burial boards, weights and measures, and a number of special matters such as the building of an Exhibition Hall, the establishment of an Insurance Fund, an Art Fund, an Institute for Teachers, were included. The most 'political' Clauses concerned concessionary fares for various categories of persons, including Councillors when on Council business; transport facilities for the aged and handicapped; the sale of school clothing; and a cold air store. These created most interest on the occasion of the Second Reading.

Many Private Bills are not opposed on Second Reading. If, however, there is objection by only one M.P. and it is persisted in when the Bill is put down on the Order Paper – as happened three times in this case – a date must be fixed for Debate. The Leeds Private Bill was set down for March 8 but had to be postponed until March 21 owing to an 'emergency' debate on Cyprus. For such Debate it is necessary to 'brief' interested Members of Parliament who are prepared to put the case for the Local Authority. Before dealing with the Debate, however, certain interesting items of procedure may be mentioned.

The original Order Paper for March 8 showed that one group of six M.P.s had given notice of an 'Instruction' (to the Private Bill Committee which would eventually take the Committee stage) to delete four Clauses. Another group of M.P.s wished to delete the Boundary Extension Clauses, but this did not, in the end, arise since objections by the West Riding County Council and the Tadcaster Rural District Council were removed – while the M.P. for the Parliamentary Division[82] affected had to leave for the Far East. One M.P. sought, further, to delete another Clause.

The problem arose whether there could be one general debate on the first four Clauses in question, with separate votes on each 'instruction' at the end, or whether each must be debated separately. The Chairman of Ways and Means held that the former procedure was possible. Mr. Charles Pannell[83], whose researches into precedents took him some 200 years back in parliamentary history, claimed that each Clause must be debated separately – and convinced the Chairman of Ways and Means. There then arose the problem that by talking at length on the first Clause until 9.0 p.m. (when the Debate normally closes) all discussion on subsequent Clauses, and possibly even

[82] Barkston Ash.   [83] Leeds West.

the vote on the first 'instruction', might be prevented. The Bill would thus go to the Select Committee without instructions. This would have suited the Leeds Corporation and the Leeds M.P.s supporting them, but not the M.P.s opposed to the Clauses in question. These M.P.s might, therefore, decide to oppose the Second Reading itself, rather than permit the Bill to go further without instructions.

It must be explained that a Private Bill must be given a Second Reading before instructions are moved. Moreover, no new opposed business – and an instruction to delete would be opposed – may be introduced in the House after 9.0 p.m. If, therefore, the Second Reading itself were opposed and general debate ensued, this might continue until 9.0 p.m. without discussion on particular Clauses, and even without a vote being taken. This had, in fact, happened on a previous Private Bill. To counter the possibility that, if the Second Reading were approved without Debate, supporters of the disputed Clauses might talk out time to prevent a vote on the instructions, the opponents of the Clauses hinted that they might prevent a Second Reading being given at all.

A very unusual course, for a Private Bill, was therefore agreed to by the Chairman of Ways and Means – that Standing Orders (i.e., the 'ten o'clock rule' – in this case nine o'clock) should be suspended. All M.P.s could therefore agree to give the Bill a Second Reading without debate and then proceed to discuss the instructions to delete, knowing that none could be talked out. Proceedings, therefore, began at 7.0 p.m., but instead of terminating automatically at 9.0 p.m., continued until 11.20 p.m.

Mr. Geoffrey Hirst[84] moved an instruction to leave out Clause 256 (cold air store and sale of ice). He and his friends could not support this attempt at municipal trading.

Mr. John C. Bidgood,[85] formerly a Leeds City Councillor, seconded. There was, he said, already surplus low temperature capacity in Leeds and the three firms making ice in the city had already cut down their capacity.

Mr. Charles Pannell[86] spoke in favour of the Clause. There was need for a modern abattoir – which could be built without ministerial consent; such an abattoir needed cold-storage

[84] Cons., Shipley.   [85] Cons., Bury and Radcliffe.
[86] Lab., Leeds West.

facilities – why should ministerial consent be necessary for that?

The Joint Parliamentary Secretary to the Ministry of Agriculture, Fisheries and Food[87] supported what 'his hon. Friends' had said. His principal point was that the powers were unnecessary. Mr. Gaitskell repeated that it ought not to be necessary for the Corporation to 'run to the Minister'.

Mr. David Jones[88] pointed out that neither of the two Conservative Leeds M.P.s had opposed the Clause. Mr. Kenneth Thompson[89] wished to know if any approach had been made by the Corporation to find out whether private enterprise was willing to undertake the work.

The Motion to delete Clause 156 was carried by 136 votes to 132.

Mr. Donald Kaberry[90] then moved an instruction to leave out Clause 269 (concessionary fares). He began by referring to the Public Service Vehicles (Travel Concessions) Act which in 1955 had granted local authorities the power to retain whatever concessions they were giving on November 30, 1954. Leeds already had certain powers, therefore, which seemed to make parts of the Clause unnecessary. So far as retired persons were concerned, the Clause was too widely drawn. The main cleavage of opinion, however, was on concessionary fares to city councillors. Mr. Hirst seconded the Motion.

Mr. Pannell pointed out that the opponents of the Clause could have put down an Amendment to delete the section dealing with councillors. He pointed out that if Leeds were a county, instead of a county borough, fares would be refunded. On the other categories, he assured the House that what the Corporation had in mind was concessionary fares in 'off-peak' periods of travel. Mr. Hirst interjected that the Clause was drawn widely enough for further concessions to be made.

Mr. Edward Short[91] and Miss Alice Bacon[92] defended the proposed concessions to councillors, which were already operative in administrative counties, as distinct from county boroughs. Mr. Denis Howell[93] said that every one of the proposals in the Clause was enjoyed by citizens of Birmingham.

The Joint Parliamentary Secretary to the Ministry of Trans-

[87] Mr. Harmar Nicholls.
[88] Lab., The Hartlepools.
[89] Cons., Liverpool, Walton.
[90] Cons., Leeds North-West.
[91] Lab., Newcastle-upon-Tyne Central.
[92] Lab., Leeds South-East.
[93] Lab., Birmingham, All Saints.

port and Civil Aviation[94] pointed out that the difference between the two types of local authority in regard to councillors' travelling expenses was contained in the Local Government Act, 1948. On a previous occasion he had suggested that Parliament ought to consider whether such a distinction was justified; but he thought that any change ought to be effected by public, not by private legislation. Mr. Molson also emphasised the difference between permitting a local authority to continue what it was already doing and giving a new power.

Mr. R. J. Mellish[95] held that Mr. Molson could not reconcile general sympathy for the purpose of the Clause with support for an instruction to delete it. He ought at least to give some undertaking about future Government legislation. Mr. John Edwards[96] urged that the Clause go to Committee. The Motion was, however, pressed to a Division and carried by 153 votes to 130.

Wing-Commander Bullus[97] then moved the deletion of Clause 276 (power to sell articles of school clothing). This was a further 'unnecessary and undesirable element of municipal trading which was not possessed by any other local authorities for these articles'.[98] His speech was punctuated by some interruptions and points of Order. It was seconded by Mr. Arthur Tiley.[99]

Miss Bacon spoke on behalf of the Clause. She spoke of the near-monopoly enjoyed by the four or five shops supplying articles of school uniforms and quoted prices as well as comments on quality by the British Standards Institution. Mr. F. A. Burden[1] doubted whether prices could be reduced by the Corporation.

The Parliamentary Secretary to the Ministry of Education[2] pointed out that under Section 81 of the Education Act, 1944, authorities were permitted to assist with the cost of a school uniform upon an income basis. He undertook to look at the limitations imposed by the regulations under the Act, but the Clause went far beyond the intention of the Act. Mr. Michael Stewart[3] said that if Leeds could not sell in competition with the private traders it would not pay to use the power. But as a

---

[94] Mr. Hugh Molson.
[95] Lab., Bermondsey.
[96] Lab., Brighouse and Spenborough.
[97] Cons., Wembley North.
[98] H.C. Debates, Vol. 550, col. 1364.
[99] Cons., Bradford West.
[1] Cons., Gillingham.
[2] Mr. Dennis Vosper.
[3] Lab., Fulham East.

city with exceptional facilities in the clothing trade, and where uniforms appeared to be expensive, it was right 'to allow a certain amount of experiment in the degree of powers which local authorities can exercise'.[4]

The Debate then tended to range over the arguments for and against school uniforms in general. In the end, the Motion was carried by 150 votes to 124.

Colonel Malcolm Stoddart-Scott[5] then moved an instruction to delete Clause 153, which provided that no calf less than seven days old should be taken into any slaughterhouse in the city of Leeds to be slaughtered.

The farmers do not understand it, the butchers do not understand it, the veterinary surgeons . . . see no reason for it, nor do the doctors, and the R.S.P.C.A. does not support it.[6]

The clause would cost the farmers 12,000 gallons of milk. It was unenforceable because no one could accurately decide the age of a calf until it was three or four weeks old. Mr. Paul Bryan[7] seconded.

Mr. Gaitskell stated that during the last quarter of 1954, forty-three calves were dead or dying upon arrival at the abattoir. If they were sent when a little older they could better stand up to the journey.

Mr. Grant-Ferris[8] agreed that the position as described needed to be looked into, but this was not really the subject for a Private Bill. Mr. Clifford Kenyon[9] blamed the R.S.P.C.A. and was glad that one corporation was coming forward to try to deal with the matter.

The Joint Parliamentary Secretary to the Ministry of Agriculture, Fisheries and Food[10] said that the Government yielded to no one in their wish to stamp out the practices described. But the Clause was unnecessary, as legislation already covered the subject.

Despite an appeal to allow the Clause to go to Committee, the Motion was carried by 127 votes to 91.

Considerable work was done on the Bill locally, between this Debate and the Committee stage, but we turn to further

---

[4] *H.C. Debates*, Vol. 550, col. 1380.   [5] Cons., Ripon.
[6] *H.C. Debates*, Vol. 550, col. 1389.   [7] Cons., Howden.
[8] Cons., Nantwich.   [9] Lab., Chorley.
[10] Mr. Harmar Nicholls.

proceedings at Westminster. On a Private Bill the procedure in Committee is 'quasi-judicial' in character. The House of Commons Committee on the Leeds Bill consisted of two Conservative and two Labour M.P.s, one of the former being Chairman. In addition to the Leeds Parliamentary Agents, there were seven other agents. The Corporation briefed two Q.C.s and one Junior Counsel. Petitioners against the Bill briefed two Q.C.s and two Junior Counsel.

Of the fifteen petitions originally deposited against the Bill, eight had been withdrawn as a result of negotiations. Seven remained to be heard. They were from the British Transport Commission, the Central Committee on Camping Legislation, the North-Eastern Gas Board, the Public Transport Association Ltd., the Salvation Army, the West Yorkshire Road Car Co. Ltd., and the Parish of Barwick-in-Elmet.

It may be pointed out here that, contrary to the statement which still appears in all standard text-books, the Preamble is not proved before consideration of Clauses. It is read formally. Opposed Clauses are then considered in whatever order suits the convenience of counsel and witnesses, subject to the Committee's approval. The case for the Part or Clause in dispute is opened by counsel for the Promoters; evidence is called; counsel for the Petitioners cross-examines and then states his case (possibly calling witnesses); counsel for the Promoters then winds up if a right of reply exists. The Committee then deliberates in private and announces its decision. Petitions are read 'to get them on the minutes'. On the Leeds Bill, proceedings lasted for six days, just over one day being devoted to unopposed Clauses.

On the first day, Wednesday, April 18, 1956, the Preamble of the Bill was read and Mr. Thesiger, Q.C., opened for the Corporation on the Extension of the Boundary Clauses. He then read the petition from the Barwick-in-Elmet Parish Council. As 'policy witness', Alderman David Beevers, Leader of the City Council, was called. He was examined by Mr. Thesiger, asked questions by the Chairman, and by other Members of the Committee, briefly cross-examined on behalf of the Petitioners and re-examined by Mr. Thesiger. An expert witness was then called on behalf of the Corporation. He was followed by the Leeds City Architect. Finally, the Committee deliberated in private and subsequently announced that they found 'so much of the Preamble as relates to Part II ... proved'.[11]

Junior Counsel then opened for the Corporation on Clause 49, Exhibition Hall, which involved the compulsory purchase of certain areas of land. The outstanding petition against the Clause was on behalf of the Salvation Army, whose hostel and land were affected. The City Engineer was called as witness, examined, cross-examined on behalf of the Petitioners, re-examined and then questioned by Members of the Committee. After deliberation, the Committee excluded the site in question from any powers of compulsory acquisition.

On the second day, Junior Counsel opened for the Corporation on Clause 75, 'Welfare of aged and handicapped persons'. The main point at issue was the provision of assistance towards the cost of transport for such persons to enable them to use various recreational facilities. The British Transport Commission, one of their subsidiary bus companies, and the Public Transport Association opposed. Certain sections of the petitions were then read, and Alderman Beevers gave evidence.

The following is an extract from his cross-examination by Mr. Eric Blain, representing the Public Transport Association:

Mr. Blain: If 2,000 or 3,000 people are to benefit to the extent of £500 a year, this is a Clause to give them something between 3s. and 5s. each a year.
Ald. Beevers: Yes, put that way it probably would.
Mr. Blain: A Clause to add between 3s. and 5s. a year to what the taxpayers of the country pay in the form of national subsidies that apply over the whole year to these people?
Ald. Beevers: I suppose you could put it that way, yes.
Mr. Blain: Would you mind telling me what case there is in Leeds for such an aged person to get 5s. a year more than his opposite number in Leicester or Huddersfield?
Ald. Beevers: Well, as Deputy-Chairman of the Regional Hospital Board and a member of the Geriatric Committee, I should be very pleased if all the towns in this particular region were granted these facilities.
Mr. Richard Winterbottom (Committee Member): I would like to interrupt and say that the learned Gentleman has used a very inapt illustration because they are getting it in Leicester.
Mr. Swingler (Committee Member): Under the 1955 Act some are getting it and some are not.
Mr. Blain: Alderman, just let us see that. This particular Clause in

[11] *Public Administration*, Spring 1959, p. 29.

the form in which you introduced it into this Bill you have probably been told by the Town Clerk was in the Leicester Bill, was it not?
Ald. Beevers: I did not know it was in the Leicester Bill.
Mr. Blain: And was disallowed?
Ald. Beevers: I did not know it was in the Leicester Bill. If I had been told –
Mr. Blain: I have heard a whisper which was so gentle that it only just reached me that it was disallowed in the other House. But it failed to pass into law so that the residents of Leicester cannot have it; that is right, is it not?
Ald. Beevers: I do not know.
Mr. Richard Winterbottom: No.

Later Mr. Blain addressed the Committee at length on this question of national and local legislation, and a representative of the Ministry of Housing and Local Government warned that if the Clause were accepted it would have to be made clear that the expenditure would not have to be taken into account in calculating the Exchequer Grant.

The Committee finally approved the Clause subject to a minor amendment.

In the afternoon the Committee considered the Clauses relating to 'Moveable Dwellings'. The Central Committee on Camping Legislation had petitioned against this. The Medical Officer of Health was examined and cross-examined and many questions were asked by the Chairman and Members of the Committee. Consideration of the Clause was continued on April 24th, when Committee Members had further questions to ask. The Committee eventually approved the Clause subject to two minor Amendments, one of which was the insertion of a new sub-clause to meet certain points raised.

The fourth opposed Clause, that on District Heating, which was petitioned against by the North Eastern Gas Board, was then taken. Discussion was resumed at 2.15 p.m. The City Architect was examined and cross-examined at great length, and the Corporation also called an expert on district heating. The Committee continued the examination of the Clause the next day and continued into the afternoon. Eventually the Committee agreed to the Clause subject to amendments making it clear that the Corporation would supply heating only to 'premises owned or built on land owned by the Corporation or forming part of or ancillary to a housing scheme approved by the Minister'.

There remained to be considered the unopposed Clauses on which certain Government Departments had observations to make. Clause 59 (power to sell land without consent of Minister) may be cited as an example of a Clause which was unprecedented, which had already been thrown out three times and to which the Minister objected. The Committee ordered it to be struck out. Consideration of Clauses continued the next day, April 26. Clause 78 (forecourts injurious to amenities of street) is an example of a Clause amended by the Committee so that its powers 'should not go beyond those of the model clause' cited by the Home Office. Clause 115 is a simple example of the amendment of a general Act (Section 150 of the Public Health Act) by a local Act. In the course of this examination there were also many examples of Clauses amended to meet the wishes of particular Ministries, and for this reason accepted by the Committee.

Clause 168 (unauthorised games on school playing fields), on the other hand, is an example of the acceptance of a Clause against the objections of a Ministry. It provided for a penalty not exceeding £5 on summary conviction for trespass. The Home Office reported that there was no precedent for the Clause, which would make trespass a criminal offence. It had been deleted from three previous Private Bills. The Committee agreed to the Clause subject to an Amendment affecting voluntary schools.

The Committee met again briefly on May 3 to agree to accept certain amendments made as a result of earlier undertakings.

In the House of Lords, further petitions against the Bill were lodged by the Central Committee on Company Legislation, by Messrs. J. Marsland and Sons, Ltd. (owners of land on the Exhibition Hall site) and by the North Eastern Gas Board. The first petition was rejected, as in the Commons Committee. So also was the second, subject to a minor amendment. Messrs. Marsland, however, succeeded in obtaining the exemption of their site from compulsory purchase order. The Preamble was then 'proved', and the Clauses and Schedules were read and agreed to, with certain amendments.

The final stages of the Leeds Private Bill (Third Reading in each House, following upon the Reports of the respective Committees), went through without further debate.

Of the original 297 Clauses, four were deleted by instruction on Second Reading, seven were lost before the Select Committee and ten withdrawn by the Corporation, mainly due to supervening legislation. This left 276, but the addition of six Clauses agreed to after negotiations with certain Ministries and other bodies brought the number up to 282. The Bill, which received the Royal Assent on August 2, 1956, while not containing every power sought by the Corporation, was, in the words of the Town Clerk, 'one of the largest, in some respects the most controversial, and one of the most successful for many years'.

8

DELEGATED LEGISLATION

1. STATUTORY INSTRUMENTS

THE 'Statutory Instrument', a term coined by the Statutory Instruments Act of 1946, is the commonest form of delegated legislation. These Instruments are issued by Ministries under powers delegated to the appropriate Ministers by the so-called 'parent' Acts, and are subject, of course, to the rule of *ultra vires*. 'The conditions of the making of Statutory Instruments and the degree of parliamentary control over them', says *Erskine May*, 'will depend in each case upon the particular statute which authorises them.[1] From the standpoint of parliamentary control, they may be divided very broadly into two classes, viz. (1) those that require the affirmative approval of Parliament by way of Resolution, and (2) those that 'can be annulled, within a time-limit, if either House records its disapproval'.[2] To enable Parliament to deal with them, they have to be 'laid on the Table', the procedure for doing which is governed by the Statutory Instruments Act of 1946, which also prescribes a standardised period of forty days in respect of the second class of instruments.

The so-called 'negative' procedure, which applies to the great majority of Statutory Instruments, permits any Member of the House to move a 'Prayer' to Her Majesty that the Instrument be annulled. The effect of the acceptance of such a 'Prayer' by the House is that the Instrument is withdrawn, but this does not 'prejudice the making of a new instrument of similar effect'.[3] Parliament has no power, however, to secure the amendment of a Statutory Instrument, which means that if a Member has

[1] *Erskine May*, 16th ed., p. 849.   [2] *Ibid.*, p. 849.   [3] *Ibid.*, p. 853.

objection to any part of it, however small or incidental, he can attempt to secure rectification only by 'praying' against the whole Instrument. If such a Prayer is carried, or, on promise of concession by the Ministry concerned, not pushed to a Division, the usual effect is for the Instrument to be withdrawn and immediately remade with the objectionable part amended in the manner that has been suggested.

Prayers are exempted business, which means, in practice, that they are moved at the completion of the day's business, immediately before the moving of the half-hour adjournment motion. This rule, as we shall see, has enabled the right of 'praying', on certain occasions, to be used as a parliamentary tactic that can be variously described as 'delaying', 'harrying', or 'filibustering'.[4]

To advise the House of Commons as to the suitability of Statutory Instruments as expressions of the powers delegated, a Statutory Instruments Committee was established in 1944 and has subsequently been reappointed annually.[5] This Committee, however, has very limited powers to go into questions of 'merits', and consequently presents no advice on those instruments which, although unobjectionable from the standpoint of legality or regularity, are questionable as acts of policy or administration, which is the case with many. In respect of most Prayers, therefore, the advice of the Select Committee is not available to Members.

Debates on Prayers are usually 'political', and the whips ensure that, if the issue is put to the vote, the Government's automatic majority is mobilised to prevent the proposed annulment from being carried. Occasionally, however, objection is taken to a Statutory Instrument because it has been reported by the Statutory Instruments Committee for some kind of irregularity or for 'unusual or unexpected use' of the powers by virtue of which it has been made. As the Committee is an inter-party body, the debate is then of a less partisan character – although the vote, if any, may nevertheless be a party-controlled one. In the debates summarised below, 'unusual and unexpected use', to the detriment of civil liberties, was the substance of the charge against the Instruments, but for reasons which are explained the House was deprived of the advantage of a Com-

[4] But *see* below, p. 211.   [5] *See* below, pp. 302–309.

mittee Report, and the contributions of most Members were characterised by strong partisanship.

Seizure of Food Order, 1946. This Order, which was made under emergency powers granted to the Ministry of Food in wartime, substantially repeated a previous Order made in 1942. Its purpose was to enable the Ministry to seize and, if necessary, sell articles of food suspected of having been acquired on the 'black market', i.e., in violation of rationing and price-control legislation. The mover of the Prayer for its annulment, Sir John Mellor[6], objected, not to its basic purpose, but to what he considered to be its inadequate and inequitable provisions for financial restitution to those who, having had their food seized and sold, were subsequently acquitted of any offence under the Regulations or not prosecuted for any such offence.

It is properly provided [he said] that where no conviction of the owner takes place, or perhaps there is no prosecution, the proceeds of sale of the article of food shall be paid to the owner, but – and this is the critical point, and the object of my main objection – the proceeds of sale are defined as the proceeds, less the Minister's expenses of seizure and sale. I think that that leads to a rather curious and indeed astonishing result. It means that an innocent owner whose goods have been seized by an officer of the Ministry pays the Minister's expenses of seizure, although the seizure is proved totally unnecessary.[7]

The Parliamentary Secretary to the Ministry might reply, he continued, that since the original Order had been made, in 1942, there had been no complaints; but that was no reason why a mistake made in an Order of 1942 should be repeated in an Order of 1946, 'especially when we are now in a position to regard these Statutory Orders with a far greater degree of vigilance than was possible in the House in 1942'. He had previously questioned the Minister on the matter, and had received the reply that 'expenses in connection with seizure and sale' in practice meant 'expenses incurred in selling the goods'. No injustice was therefore involved, the Minister had alleged, as such expenses would have been incurred by the owner in any case. Did that mean that *no* expenses were incurred in respect of seizure? That could hardly be true, and in some cases it was clear that seizure could be a costly operation.

[6] Cons., Sutton Coldfield.
[7] *H.C. Debates*, Vol. 430, cols. 1542–1543, November 26, 1946.

The obvious thing for the Ministry to do was to cancel the present Order and to make a new one which omitted the objectionable words.

Sir John concluded by appealing to Members on the opposite side of the House to support his Prayer. It was an opportunity for them 'to show a spirit of independence without running the risk of bringing down the Government'. For once, they would be 'able to pride themselves on the fact that . . . they voted on the merits'.[8]

After Mr. Spence[9] had Seconded and Mr. Marlowe[10] spoken in support, a strongly political note was introduced by Sir Ian Fraser,[11] who said:

It is deplorable that hon. Members, who come to this House declaring their belief in freedom and their interest in the common people, should sit there ignobly and pusillanimously willing to allow to pass by, merely for the sake of convenience or for the *amour propre* of a Minister, a piece of legislation which, if it were in a Bill and had to go through all the stages of a Bill, would undoubtedly be thrown out.[12]

When he continued by attempting to enlarge on the rights of the House of Commons to 'prevent Governments from making tyrannical and objectionable proposals', he was pulled up by the Speaker, who said:

The hon. Gentleman is getting on to a very wide subject and is now speaking of all kinds of Orders. He must deal with the Order under discussion and must not continue in such general terms.[13]

Mr. Challen,[14] like Mr. Marlowe, thought it important that the 'authorised officer' should be required to have a 'reasonable belief' which could be subsequently challenged before the High Court, particularly in view of the fact people very low down in official hierarchy could be 'authorised'. Embroidering this theme, he said:

It is quite obvious that the person authorised can be a constable, can be any office boy or clerk, in fact any individual, male or female, delegated by some gentleman or lady in the Ministry of Food. This particular individual may hear some gossip in a local café or public house about some particular goods owned by a retailer and then go off and seize those goods or, as my hon. and learned Friend the

---

[8] *Ibid.*, col. 1544.   [9] Cons., Aberdeen and Kincardine.
[10] Cons., Brighton.   [11] Cons., Lonsdale.
[12] *H.C. Debates*, Vol. 430, col. 1549.   [13] *Ibid.*, col. 1549.
[14] Cons., Hampstead.

Member for Brighton said, take his chicken off his table and sell it merely upon his own belief.[15]

Mr. Janner,[16] the first speaker from the Government benches, complained that the supporters of the Prayer had not read the Order properly or appreciated its significance.

At this point, the Chairman of the 'scrutiny' Committee, Col. Sir Charles MacAndrew[17], rose to explain that his Committee had not considered 'reporting' this Order because it was in the same terms as the Order of 1942 and therefore could not be described as 'unexpected'. 'But I do feel', he continued,

that if the Order had come before us for the first time, if it had been new to us, it would have been unexpected, and it would have been one about which we would have called for evidence from the Department.[18]

Mr. Royle,[19] who spoke both as a former food trader and as a former Ministry of Food officer who had 'done some seizing', claimed that those who asked for the annulment of the Order were 'playing into the hands of the black marketeers'.

Sir Wavell Wakefield[20] took this opportunity to assert that the Conservative Party was showing itself as the 'champion of the rights of the common man', while another Opposition Member, Mr. Raikes[21], pointed out that the House was not discussing the question of the black market but the altering of the words of an Order so as to prevent possible injustice. Major Legge-Bourke[22] catalogued further examples of the Order's 'untidiness', and Mr. Manningham-Buller[23] claimed that it raised a 'matter of high principle'.[24]

At 11.8 p.m., after the debate had been in progress for about an hour and ten minutes, the Parliamentary Secretary to the Ministry of Food[25] rose to reply. After claiming that Mr. Marlowe had misinterpreted Regulation 55AB, under which the Order was made, pointing out that this was the first complaint against the prescribed procedure, and suggesting that the whole matter was of small importance in view of the fact that since 1942, 1,100 prosecutions had yielded only 10 acquittals, she said:

[15] *H.C. Debates*, Vol. 430, col. 1550.
[16] Lab., Leicester.
[17] Cons., Ayr and Bute, Northern.
[18] *H.C. Debates*, Vol. 430, col. 1553.
[19] Lab., Salford West.
[20] Cons., St. Marylebone.
[21] Cons., Liverpool, Wavertree.
[22] Cons., Isle of Ely.
[23] Cons., Northants South.
[24] *H.C. Debates*, Vol. 430, cols. 1561–1562
[25] Dr. Edith Summerskill.

In no circumstances do we charge what might be regarded as the Ministry's expenses. We charge only the expenses of transport and any expenses incurred in seizing and selling the article.[26]

As might have been expected, this statement was not received quietly, and Dr. Summerskill attempted to answer her critics by 'recalling a case':

We were trying to trace some cooking fats to an hotel on one occasion and the enforcement officers were making investigations near the hotel. They found 5,000 eggs in dustbins. What happened? First, the police van was called to take those eggs on the first little journey. Then transport of another kind, a car, lorry, or whatever it was, took the eggs to the nearest packing station. Expenses of that kind would be charged.

'Why?' asked Mr. Marlowe.

Dr. Summerskill: The hon. and learned Member must remember that even if the man is innocent, the Ministry of Food has incurred expenses in the selling of the innocent man's eggs which the innocent man would have incurred himself.

Lieut.-Commander Gurney Braithwaite:[27] But this is for seizure.

Sir J. Mellor: Would the hon. Lady tell us quite squarely why an innocent owner should bear any of the Ministry's expenses for seizure?

Dr. Summerskill: I have explained to the hon. Member. I find it very difficult to understand what he means by expenses of seizure.

Sir J. Mellor: It is in the Order.[28]

Dr. Summerskill then embarked on another – and rather confused – explanation, which ended with an assurance that the Order under discussion contained nothing 'that was not in the Seizure of Food Order, 1942, made at the time of the Coalition Government'.

This gave Sir Charles MacAndrew the opportunity to remind her that the original Order was made when no Scrutiny Committee existed, and that it was as a result of the 'outcry' from 'all sides of the House to check this sort of thing that the Committee was set up'. If 'anything like this had come up, the Committee would have drawn the attention of the House to it'. Mr. Silverman,[29] a Labour Member of the Scrutiny Committee, immediately dissented.

Continuing, Dr. Summerskill said, amid further interruptions, that she thought that 'an innocent man probably would have to incur expenses approximately the same as we incurred

---

[26] *H.C. Debates*, Vol. 430, col. 1564.
[28] *Ibid.*, col. 1565.

[27] Cons., Holderness.
[29] Lab., Nelson and Colne.

on his behalf', and reminded the House 'that if the Order were annulled the Minister would have no power of seizure at all'. She then indicated how necessary such powers of seizure were, a fact that had not been denied by the movers of the Prayer, and made the following concession to the Opposition's case:

I would not, for one moment, say that an acquitted man might not experience some injustice. But there is no need to annul this Order (*Hon. Members:* Remedy it.) Certainly, I am quite prepared to look at every case.[30]

This, as might have been expected, provoked fresh interruptions.

In a final speech for the Opposition, Mr. Boyd-Carpenter[31] said that Dr. Summerskill's announcement was 'of not inconsiderable importance', and reverted to the question of principle involved. Her admission, he held, was an 'overwhelming argument' in favour of taking back and recasting the Order. This was not a party matter, and he hoped that 'hon. Members opposite' would 'respond to the appeal made by the movers of this Prayer'.

A closure motion was carried by 232 to 78, and the Question was negatived by 227 to 77. Both divisions followed party lines.

Seizure of Food Order, 1948. The same matter came up again on April 22, 1948, when Sir John Mellor moved a Prayer for the annulment of the new Seizure of Food Order which had replaced that of 1946. Sir John expressed his astonishment that the words of the old Order had been repeated. Seconding, Mr. Boyd-Carpenter underlined this point by reminding the Parliamentary Secretary that, in reply to a Question on the previous day, she had admitted that the Ministry did not 'retain expenses in connection with the sale' when the owner was acquitted or not prosecuted. During his speech an attempt was made to have the House 'counted out' – a 'state of affairs' which he considered not to be 'wholly accidental'.

Without waiting for further contributions to the debate, Dr. Summerskill rose to reply. She began by defending her Department and showing that on no occasion had injustice been done by the application of the Orders. She then brought matters to a conclusion with the following statement:

Having said that, and having defended my Department and our

[30] *H.C. Debates*, Vol. 430, col. 1567.   [31] Cons., Kingston-upon-Thames.

action in this matter, I want to say I recognise that it is important not only to dispense justice, but to make it transparently clear that justice is being done. If hon. Members opposite think we can do that by amending this Order, then I am prepared to amend it so as to limit the power to deduct expenses to cases in which a conviction has been obtained.[32]

The argument about *vires* that followed this statement was of interest only to lawyers, and probably of very minor interest even to them. After it had finished, Sir John Mellor said:

The hon. Lady has met us in a very frank manner which gives us satisfaction.[33]

He then asked Dr. Summerskill to agree to the motion for annulment, but on being told that this would give rise to some technical difficulties, accepted her assurance that she would 'set the machine in motion and get a new Order as soon as possible'. The Motion was then, by leave, withdrawn, and at 10.45 p.m., after a debate lasting less than three-quarters of an hour, the House passed on to the Adjournment Motion.

It might be argued that these two Debates emphasise the importance of having a Report from the Select Committee on Statutory Instruments when matters of this kind are being discussed; for it may be that the absence of such a Report facilitated the dragging down into the party arena of a fairly straightforward matter of civil liberties. Certainly, the movers of the Prayer, who belonged to the 'socialism-equals-tyranny' school, used it as a stick to beat the Government with, and the Government benches responded in the manner that was doubtless expected of them. As a consequence, an almost unchallengeable case against the Order was spoiled, the issue was confused by all kinds of irrelevancies, the Government, confronted with a political challenge, found difficulty in making a quite harmless concession, and the righting of a minor but indisputable wrong was delayed by many months. On the other hand, it is possible that, in the circumstances of 1946–48, a Report from the Committee on this particular Order would itself have become the subject of a political battle.

Nevertheless, that the wrong *was* eventually righted is testimony to the value of the Prayer as a means of checking executive discretion.

[32] *H.C. Debates*, Vol. 449, col. 2141.   [33] *Ibid.*, col. 2145.

'*The Banstead Harriers.*' There remains to be illustrated the use of the 'Prayer' as an instrument of delay. The possibility of using it thus is now restricted, under a sessional order first adopted in 1953–54, which gives the Speaker 'power to put the question forthwith upon any Motion for the approval or anulment of a Statutory Instrument still under discussion at half-past eleven o'clock, or alternatively to adjourn the debate on such a Motion until a subsequent day'.[34] The need for such an Order arose from the attempts of a group of Conservative back-benchers to 'harry the life' out of the Labour Government of 1950–51, which had a very small majority in the House, by 'praying' into the small hours of the morning. The first occasion on which this was seriously attempted was on March 8, 1951.[35]

The ordinary business of that day was heavy. The business of Supply (Army Estimates) was exempted from Standing Order No. 1, and only began after fairly lengthy discussions on the Composition of Standing Committees[36] and on a Complaint of Privilege.[37] The Question, 'That Mr. Speaker now leave the Chair', was put at about 2.10 a.m., following which a Redistribution of Seats Order was approved, without debate, after a short statement by the Under-Secretary for the Home Office. At 2.13 a.m., the 'harrying' began.

Mr. Harmar Nicholls[38] opened the bowling by 'praying' against the Sewing Cottons and Threads (Maximum Prices) Order, 1951.[39] He talked about the importance of keeping down thread prices, gave copious details of alterations in such prices since 1945, sentimentalised over the woes of 'ordinary families', assigned some responsibility for a deplorable situation to the devaluation of the pound and some to the operations of the Raw Cotton Commission, quoted at length from the Cotton Trade Union Journal, and claimed that 'this Statutory Instrument is merely the last piece of evidence of the failure of the Government during the whole of the last five years'. At 2.35 he sat down, to allow Col. Crosthwaite-Eyre[40] formally to second the Motion. The Parliamentary Secretary to the Board of Trade, Mr. Hervey Rhodes, then gave a careful but brief

---

[34] *Erskine May*, 16th ed., pp. 386, 394.
[36] *Ibid.*, cols. 668–675.
[38] Cons., Peterborough.
[40] Cons., Hants., New Forest.

[35] *H.C. Debates*, Vol. 485, cols. 864–916.
[37] *Ibid.*, cols. 675–688.
[39] S.I. 1951, No. 166.

explanation of 'what this Order was about' and asked for the withdrawal of 'rather a foolish Prayer'.

Evidence that the Labour Party was, as yet, unfamiliar with the tactics of the 'harriers' was then provided by Mr. Lennox-Boyd,[41] who pointed out that the 'foolish prayer' had been supported by two Labour Members. Mr. Hynd,[42] who followed, appeared also to be unaware of the game that was being played, for although he protested against a procedure which allowed 'such a ridiculous proceeding to take place at such an unearthly hour', he went on to deal with the substance of the Prayer, while Members interrupted him with alleged Points of Order. Mr. Grimond,[43] although no 'harrier', found the occasion appropriate for singing a brief hymn in praise of free competition, after which Sir Herbert Williams[44] occupied another minute or so clearing up certain 'misconceptions'. Mr. Nally[45] expressed the opinion that 'these Prayers' were 'carefully timed by the Opposition so as to cause the maximum inconvenience to those of us who are without cars'. After Mr. Boyd-Carpenter had wound up for the Opposition, the Question was put, and negatived, without a Division, at one minute to three. Another two or three minutes were occupied by Mr. Lennox-Boyd in alleged points of Order about the voting. On a further 'Point of Order', Mr. O'Brien[46] asked the Deputy-Speaker whether it was 'for the good order of the conduct of this House, at this time in the morning, that the hon. Gentlemen opposite should move six or seven prayers and then not enforce them by a Division', to which the Deputy-Speaker replied that that was not a point of Order and that as many Prayers might be tabled as Members wished.

At 3.7 a.m. the most skilful and least inhibited of the 'harriers', Sir Herbert Williams, began his Prayer against the Furniture (Maximum Prices) (Amendment No. 3) Order, 1951.[47] In a speech persistently interrupted by noise and interjections he claimed that this Order had been improperly made because its 'related schedules' could not be located in the Vote Office. Hon. Members, therefore, were not in a position to discuss the Order, as 'the effective part of it had never been

---

[41] Cons., Mid-Bedfordshire.
[42] Lab., Accrington.
[43] Lib., Orkney and Shetland.
[44] Cons., Croydon East.
[45] Lab., Bilston.
[46] Lab., Nottingham North-West.
[47] S.I. 1951, No. 205.

made available to them'. Asked by Sir Herbert whether it was in Order to discuss an incomplete document, the Speaker replied:

Give you a Ruling at this time of the morning? I understand that the hon. Member has made several observations, but at this time of the morning I do not know what they were about. I rule that this is in order; that is all I can say.

After further 'points of Order' had been dealt with, Sir Herbert began to 'explain the extent of the related schedules' by reading them. After a few minutes of this the Speaker interrupted to say that it was 'pure obstruction' and to ask 'what the argument was'. Amid complaints from Members of the 'scandalous abuse' of the rules and privileges of the House, Sir Herbert continued his 'explanation'. To a further weary protest from the Speaker, he replied: 'I take punctilious care, Mr. Speaker, as you will agree, never to break the rules of Order.' He went on for several more minutes before being caught out, after a lengthy argument with the Speaker, for repetition.

After Sir John Mellor had formally seconded, one of the Government Whips, Mr. R. J. Taylor[48], rose to move the closure. This was accepted by the Speaker and the Question was put and negatived. Then followed some angry exchanges on 'points of Order,' during the course of which even the Speaker lost his usual equanimity.

The next Prayer, moved at 4.0 a.m. by Wing-Commander Bullus,[49] was against the Iron and Steel Scrap Order, 1951.[50] Sir John Mellor formally seconded, and after a short intervention from Mr. Jack Jones[51] the Parliamentary Secretary to the Ministry of Supply[52] satisfied Commander Bullus's nocturnal thirst for information in a one-minute speech. The Question was put and negatived, again without a Division.

At 4.5 a.m. the indefatigable Commander, now claiming to represent the 'harassed housewife', prayed against the Candles (Maximum Prices) Order, 1951.[53] He was seconded by Mr. Harold Roper,[54] and replied to briefly by Mr. Rhodes. The Question was put and negatived.

[48] Lab., Morpeth.
[49] Cons., Wembley North.
[50] S.I. 1951, No. 208.
[51] Lab., Rotherham.
[52] Mr. John Freeman.
[53] S.I. 1951, No. 206.
[54] Cons., Cornwall North.

At 4.10 a.m., Mr. Braine[55] asked for the annulment of the Utility Apparel (Waterproofs) (Amendment No. 2) Order, 1951.[56] Squadron-Leader Burden[57] seconded, and then, rather surprisingly, a Labour Member, Mr. Bing[58], took the floor, claiming that he had supported the Prayer for serious reasons. At 4.30 a.m. Mr. Rhodes briefly replied, and the Question was then put.

The House [reports *Hansard*] proceeded to a Division; but no Members being willing to act as Tellers for the Ayes, Mr. Deputy-Speaker declared that the Noes had it.

At 4.36 a.m. Squadron-Leader Burden opened fire against the Utility Apparel (Women's Domestic Overalls and Aprons) (Manufacture and Supply) Order, 1951,[59] drawing from Mr. William Ross[60] the comment: 'The Prayers of the wicked will be as nothing.' Mr. Remnant,[61] seconded, and Mr. Rhodes replied. At 4.48 Mr. Janner[62] said that unless a vote were taken the Opposition would be 'shown not to have been serious in these Prayers and to have been playing a game with a view to deceiving the electorate'. When the Question was put the House divided, Ayes, 0; Noes, 182, the two Labour Members who had – no doubt to their regret – supported the Prayer acting as Tellers for the Ayes.

After a few more points of Order, the House proceeded to a consideration of the Feeding Stuffs (Prices) (Amendment) Order, 1951,[63] on a Prayer moved by Mr. Crouch.[64] His seconder, Mr. Deedes,[65] by dint of establishing, at least to his own satisfaction, that the sacking problem was essentially one of 'relations between India and Pakistan', was able to keep the ball rolling for another fifteen minutes, in which task he was considerably assisted by frequent interruptions. These continued during the course of the Ministry of Food's reply, delivered by Mr. Fred Willey, the Parliamentary Secretary. At last the Question was put and negatived, and at 5.41 the House reached the half-hour adjournment debate, on which it considered the question of the Deportation of one Mr. Ignatius

---

[55] Cons., Billericay.
[57] Cons., Gillingham.
[59] S.I. 1951, No. 213.
[61] Cons., Wokingham.
[63] S.I. 1951, No. 236.
[65] Cons., Ashford.

[56] S.I. 1951, No. 167.
[58] Lab., Hornchurch.
[60] Lab., Kilmarnock.
[62] Lab., Leicester North-West.
[64] Cons., Dorset North.

Musazi. The Sitting came to an end at ten minutes to six.

Affirmative Resolutions. There is no very clear distinction between Instruments that may be 'prayed' against and those that require affirmative resolutions. It might be assumed that the latter would be more important than the former, but such is by no means invariably the case (although the Select Committee on Statutory Instruments, in its Special Report of 1944–45, expressed the opinion that it should be so). Many Instruments requiring affirmative resolutions are, in fact, so minor and non-contentious in character that they are passed 'on the nod'. Many others are agreed to, without a Division, after a ministerial representative, at the request of the Opposition, has briefly explained their purport.

The Draft Census of Distribution (1958) (Restriction on Disclosure) Order, 1956, for instance, was disposed of in less than one minute, during which the Parliamentary Secretary to the Board of Trade[66] answered Mr. Douglas Jay's[67] request for 'a word explaining this Order'.[68]

During the next few days, several other Orders requiring Affirmative Resolutions were disposed of almost equally expeditiously. It is by no means the rule, however, that Orders subject to Affirmative Resolutions get through easily. Some of them deal with matters of the highest social and political importance, and hence provoke lengthy debates, ending in Divisions along party lines. One such was the Draft Housing Subsidies Order, 1956, which came up for debate on December 13, 1956. This Order, made in accordance with the terms of the Housing Subsidies Act, 1956, had the effect of abolishing, with one exception, the 'general needs' subsidy for houses and flats. To the Opposition, therefore, it was totally unacceptable, and Labour Members expressed their dislike of it to the extent of continually interrupting the Minister of Housing and Local Government,[69] who moved it on behalf of the Government. Pressed to a Division, the Order was approved by 275 votes to 241, in a vote along strict party lines.[70]

This may serve as an example of many debates of a similar kind.

---

[66] Mr. F. J. Erroll.
[68] *H.C. Debates*, Vol. 560, col. 1460.
[70] *H.C. Debates*, Vol. 562, cols. 697–758.

[67] Lab., Battersea North.
[69] Mr. Duncan Sandys.

2. SPECIAL PROCEDURE ORDERS

We were in some doubt whether to treat the Special Procedure Order as a sub-species of Private Legislation or as an
example of Delegated Legislation. *Erskine May*, quite logically,
devotes to it part of a chapter in his Book III: Proceedings in
Parliament: Private Business. Jennings includes it in his chapter
on Delegated Legislation. As either course seemed equally
satisfactory, we decided to deal with the matter under Delegated Legislation for the sole reason that otherwise our section
on Legislation itself would have become unwieldy.

The Special Procedure Order is one of a group of instruments which includes also the Provisional Order and the
Special Order. Between the '70s of the last century and 1949,
Provisional Orders were widely used as an alternative to
Private Bill procedure. Under a statute specifying the use of
this procedure for a particular purpose, an Order would be
issued by a government department on the application of the
party (usually a local government authority) requesting the
additional powers. In some cases its issue would be preceded
by the holding of a local inquiry. The Order would then be
embodied in a Provisional Order Confirmation Bill, which, at
its Committee stage, became subject to the Standing Orders
regulating proceedings on Private Bills, so far as applicable. If
the Order were opposed, the equivalent of legal proceedings
were conducted before the Committee, which had the right
to confirm, reject, or amend. From the Report stage onwards,
the Confirmation Bill followed the normal course of any other
Public Bill, except that it was taken at the time of Private
Business. Most Confirmation Bills were unopposed, and parliamentary proceedings on them were entirely formal. Those that
were opposed, however, could easily give their Promoters almost
as much trouble and involve them in as much expense as an
opposed Private Bill.

It was for this reason that, after the Second World War,
Parliament sought to substitute a quicker and cheaper procedure. This was already provided, in respect of Gas and
Electricity undertakings, by the Special Order, which required
only an Affirmative Resolution; but this represented too severe
a self-denying ordinance for Parliament to wish to generalise,

and all statutory powers to make Special Orders of this kind were repealed in 1948. The solution adopted was embodied in the Statutory Orders (Special Procedure) Act, 1945. The immediate occasion was the need to expedite the passing into law of Orders promulgated under the new Water, Town and Country Planning and Local Government Boundary legislation; but it was contemplated that the special procedure should eventually replace procedure by Provisional Order almost entirely, and this was indeed effected (by an Order in Council authorised by the 1945 Act itself) in 1949, when, as Lord Campion said, 'all the hitherto most fruitful sources of Provisional Orders (except by Private Legislation Procedure (Scotland) Act, 1936) were diverted into the Special Procedure Order system'.[71] The general effect of the new procedure is described by *Campion* thus:

Broadly speaking, in so far as the Orders are challenged as a matter of national policy, the issue is decided on the floor of the House; in so far as private rights are affected, something like the present Private Bill procedure is available.

The Special Procedure Order, like the Provisional Order, is issued by the relevant Minister, sometimes after a local inquiry. If there are no petitions against it, it automatically becomes law at the end of a prescribed period. If there are Petitions, these are referred to the Chairman of Committees of the House of Lords and the Chairman of Ways and Means of the House of Commons, who check compliance with Standing Orders and divide them into Petitions of General Objection and Petitions for Amendment. Within fourteen days after the Chairmen have reported, either House can kill the Order by a resolution of annulment. Alternatively, on a Motion for annulment, it can remit a Petition of General Objection to a Joint Committee of the two Houses. If there is no Motion for annulment, or if such Motion fails, Petitions for Amendment are automatically referred to the Joint Committee, which hears evidence and reports to the two Houses. Where an Order is reported without amendment it comes into operation without any further proceedings. When reported with amendment, 'if the responsible Minister considers that it should take effect as so amended, the order, as amended, is brought into operation on such date as the

[71] For details, *see Erskine May*, 16th ed., pp. 1028–1030.

Minister may determine. . . .' But 'if the Minister considers that it is inexpedient to bring into effect an order which has been amended . . ., he may withdraw the order by giving notice in the manner prescribed by the standing orders'. When the Joint Committee Reports that an Order be not approved, it cannot take effect unless confirmed by Act.[72]

One of the advantages of the new special procedure [writes Campion] is the speed with which an unopposed order may become law.

This speed, which may easily be exaggerated, is illustrated by the first of our examples, the Leeds (Armley Heights) Compulsory Purchase Order, 1955, which was selected from a mass of similar Orders only because the necessary documentation to follow its progress was kindly made available to us by the Town Clerk of Leeds. The second example, the Mid-Northamptonshire Water Order, 1948, illustrates procedure on an Order opposed by Petitions of Amendment and shows how this differs from the normal Private Bill and the former Provisional Order procedure. Notes on two subsequent cases of opposed Orders are appended, principally to bring out certain procedural difficulties which arise when there is a Petition of General Objection.

The Leeds (Armley Heights) Compulsory Purchase Order, 1955, was made by 'the Lord Mayor, Aldermen and Citizens of the City of Leeds, acting by the Council of the said City' on February 2, 1955, in accordance with the terms of the Education Acts, 1944 to 1953, and the Acquisition of Land (Authorisation Procedure) Act, 1946. It authorised the Council 'to purchase compulsorily for the purpose of the erection thereon of a county secondary school and the provision of school playing fields the land and the leasehold interest in the land' described in a Schedule and delineated on an annexed map.

On February 18, the Town Clerk applied to the Minister of Education for confirmation of the Order, enclosing copies of the Council's resolution, of the map, of the issue of *Yorkshire Post and Leeds Mercury* containing the public notice of the making of the Order, and of the notice that had been served on the owners of the property involved, the Armley Common Right Trust. The District Valuer's Report on the value of the land, said the letter, would be forwarded as soon as received.

[72] *See Erskine May*, pp. 1041–1042.

As you are of course aware [it concluded] the land in the Order falls within the special categories referred to in Section 1 (2) of the Acquisition of Land (Authorisation Procedure) Act, 1946, and it is appreciated that this Order will be subject to special parliamentary procedure.

On March 10, the civil servant in charge of this matter at the Ministry replied to the effect that he would be obliged to hold the Order in abeyance until the necessity for the establishment of the school had been considered and the decision announced under Section 13 (4) of the Education Act, 1944. He requested that in the meantime the Town Clerk would submit to the Ministry certain forms specified in the Appendix to one of the Ministry's circulars. These forms were duly submitted on March 16.

On May 31st, the Ministry wrote to announce the confirmation of the Order by the Minister, which had been effected on May 18, and to point out that it would not become operative until notice of its confirmation had been published in accordance with the relevant Acts and until the requirements of the Statutory Orders (Special Procedure) Act, 1945, had been carried out.

A notice of confirmation, addressed to the Secretary of the Armley Common Right Trust, was given by the Town Clerk on June 14, and on the same day an identical notice was sent to the Press for publication. It drew attention to the legal rights of persons aggrieved by the Order, and to the fact that the Order had been deposited in the Town Clerk's Office, where it might be seen 'at all reasonable hours'. On July 9, copies of the *Yorkshire Post* containing the notice of confirmation, together with a certificate of due publication, were dispatched to the Ministry.

Thereafter, apart from a request from the Ministry for a 'true to scale map' on stout cartridge paper (to 'meet the durability requirements of the Clerk of the Records' of the House of Lords), which was duly complied with, correspondence about the Order ceased until October 25, when the Clerk wrote to the Ministry asking if the requirements of the Statutory Orders (Special Procedure) Act, 1945, had been complied with. The Ministry replied, on November 4, that the laying of the Order had been delayed owing to the summer recess, and that as soon as the requirements had been complied

with the Town Clerk would be informed to that effect. Notice
of confirmation by Parliament came on December 6, when the
Ministry announced that the Order had been laid before
Parliament on November 1 and had become operative on
November 29.

On January 10, 1956, the Town Clerk sent a 'Notice to
Treat' to the Secretary of the Armley Common Right Trust
and 'all persons having or claiming any estate or interest in the
lands specified' in the Order. On October 8, 1956, this was
followed by a Notice of Intention to Enter.

In this case, all the stages in the making of the Order were
entirely formal. There were no objections, no local inquiry,
and no petitions, either of amendment or of general objection.
Consequently, the machinery of the Joint Committee did not
come into operation, and Parliament approved the Order 'on
the nod'.

In contrast with this comparatively trivial and entirely
uncontroversial use of the Special Procedure Order, we take
the example of the Mid-Northamptonshire Water Board Order,
1948, which involved a local inquiry lasting eleven days (the
shorthand transcript of which costs £80 to buy) and a further
six days of argument before the Joint Committee of the House
of Lords and the House of Commons, the record of which runs
to 184 double-column pages.

These proceedings arose out of the exercise by the Minister
of his powers under the Water Act of 1945, which authorised
him, through the making of Special Procedure Orders, to
amalgamate local authority and private water undertakings
into Joint Water Boards. The vested interests of the existing
undertakings, the parochialism of local authorities, and the
changes in cost-benefit relationship inevitably involved in the
process of amalgamation, together ensured that Orders of this
type would be hotly contested by at least some of the parties
concerned.

The Mid-Northamptonshire Order is interesting from this
point of view, but for us it has an even more immediate interest;
for it was, as the Counsel for the Ministry pointed out before
the Joint Committee, 'the first Order of its kind under the
Statutory Orders (Special Procedure) Act', and hence provided
the occasion for giving the new procedure its trial run.

The record of the local inquiry at Northampton was not available to us (except in so far as extracts from it were quoted during the Joint Committee proceedings), nor, of course, did we have access to the doubtless lengthy correspondence which passed between the Ministry and the affected authorities. Our starting point, therefore, is the reference to the Joint Committee (which was automatic) of the various Petitions for Amendment. (There were no Petitions of General Objection.)

The petitioners were the Northampton Rural District Council; the Wellingborough Rural District Council; the Higham Ferrers and Rushden Water Board, the Higham Ferrers Corporation and the Rushden Urban District Council; the River Nene Catchment Board; the Wellingborough Urban District Council; and the 'Institute of Chartered Accountants in England and Wales and others'. Counter-petitions to the Petitions for Amendment came from the British Association of Accountants and Auditors Ltd. (to the Petition of the Institute of Chartered Accountants) and from the Corporations of Northampton, Daventry and Kettering, the Urban District Councils of Corby, Desborough and Rothwell, and the Rural District Councils of Brixworth and Kettering (which jointly counter-petitioned against the Petitions of the Northampton Rural District Council, of the Wellingborough Rural District Council, of the Higham Ferrers Water Board and others, of the River Nene Catchment Board, and of the Wellingborough Urban District Council.) There were thus six Petitions of Amendment and six Counter-Petitions. Each Petitioner and Counter-Petitioner employed counsel and parliamentary agents. In all, four Q.C.s, five junior counsel, and five parliamentary agents were involved in the proceedings, which took place before a joint Committee consisting of three Members of the House of Lords (Lord Rea, Lord Belstead and Lord Darwen) and three of the House of Commons (Mr. Thomas Brooks, Captain Marsden, and Mr. Rankin). Lord Belstead was in the Chair.

The proceedings opened with an argument about procedure. Mr. Capewell, K.C., representing the Minister, announced that he and his learned friends had failed to 'reach any agreement as to how we should proceed'. He was therefore compelled to ask the Committee for its guidance in this matter. By way of explanation, he quoted the Standing Orders of the two

Houses, which appeared to prescribe an order of procedure the opposite of that applying to a Private Bill; for the onus of proof was placed on the petitioners, not on the promoters.

. . . the Minister having made the Order, it is not for him to come before a Joint Committee and prove all over again, to the satisfaction of the Committee, that the Order is necessary.

But this gave rise to an obvious difficulty, viz. :

. . . before you can deal with any particular Petition you would want to know, of course, the nature and scope of the Order, and it does appear to me (and I think to my friends also) that it is impossible for a Petitioner fairly or fully to put before the Committee the true scope and intent of the Order, and that that alone can be done on behalf of the Minister.

Mr. Capewell therefore suggested (a) that he should make a 'short opening' on the general scope of the Order; (b) that thereafter each Petition should be taken separately and the Petitioners should tender their evidence; and (c) that he, on behalf of the Minister, should tender evidence against each Petition.

He insisted, however, that, although each Petition should be heard separately, the Committee should not give its decision at the conclusion of each hearing. His reason for this request is interesting, as it illustrates one of the difficulties that can arise on consideration of a contested Special Procedure Order:

. . . it was suggested by a Memorial,[73] provided for under the Standing Orders, that the total effect of some of these Petitions (four of them in number) was to defeat the general object of the Order, and that therefore they ought to be treated in combination as a Petition of General Objection; but the Lord Chairman and the Chairman of Ways and Means considered that Memorial and decided otherwise; they decided that each Petition was a Petition of Amendment and not of General Objection, and each is entitled to be heard. It follows from that that I must contend, on behalf of the Minister, that if they are all acceded to in the terms of their Petition, that does in fact defeat the general object of the Order, and therefore I would ask the Committee to reserve their decision upon each petition until the whole have been heard.

He concluded by asking the Joint Committee who should

[73] Within seven days of the presentation of a petition, the Minister concerned or the applicant may deposit a memorial objecting to the petition being certified as proper to be received, or alleging that the petition, presented as one of amendment, is really one of general objection. (*See Erskine May*, p. 1037.)

have the last word and how the Counter-petitions were to be treated.

Against this argument, Mr. Cope Morgan, K.C., representing the Wellingborough Rural District Council, the Higham Ferrers and Rushden Water Board, the Higham Ferrers Corporation and the Rushden Urban District Council, contended that, although the burden of proof 'at the end' was on the Petitioners, it was obviously right and convenient that the scheme which was being criticised should first be put before the Committee, so that they might understand it, and be supported by evidence. Whereas Mr. Capewell, while recognising that certain inconveniences would arise, took his stand on the letter of Standing Orders, Mr. Cope Morgan took his on what he conceived to be the spirit of the Special Procedure. A mere general opening statement by the promoters was objectionable, as it would be 'unsupported by evidence' and 'unchallengeable by any Petitioner at that stage'. The only 'fair and convenient' way was for the Promoters to call evidence and allow cross-examination. There was no reason to depart from this 'old and tried' method.

He was supported by the two counsel, Mr. E. J. C. Neep, K.C., and Mr. Harold Willis, appearing respectively for the Northampton Rural District Council and the River Nene Catchment Board. The latter strongly emphasised the inconvenience of the procedure proposed by Mr. Capewell, who nevertheless stood his ground.

The Committee then considered these procedural submissions and, through the Chairman, gave its ruling on them. Although it would have preferred to hear the whole of the Promoters' case first, it had had to come to the conclusion, 'after looking carefully at the Act and at Standing Orders', that that was not what was intended.

We feel [said the Chairman] that we are expected to hear the Petitions first and that it is right to do so. That is what we should wish to do, but we should be glad of a short explanatory statement confined to that by Mr. Capewell, if he would be good enough to give it.

Accordingly, Mr. Capewell embarked upon his 'short explanatory statement', which lasted an hour.

He began by giving an account of the events leading up to the making of the Order. In 1943 the Northampton Corporation had promoted a Bill to secure powers to construct an 'impounding reservoir' at Pitsford. This proposed reservoir had been opposed, as excessively large, by a number of other local authorities, who had argued that a Joint Board ought to be established. On the Northampton Corporation's promise to give the establishment of such a Board favourable consideration, their objections had been withdrawn and the Northampton Corporation's Bill had become an Act. The Minister then (1946) convened a conference of the authorities concerned to discuss the Joint Board proposal. Nine local authorities had supported it; some had been neutral; and some hostile. Subsequently, using the powers he had recently acquired under the Water Act of 1945, the Minister had made a Draft Order for the establishment of a Board, and had conducted the local inquiry statutorily required. At this inquiry eight of the local authorities wholly included within the scope of the proposed Board had supported the Order, and seven had opposed it. All of these authorities contended that they should be severally excluded from the Order's scope.

Mr. Capewell then embarked upon an explanation and justification of the Order, first taking it clause by clause. By way of general answer to the Petitioners, he drew attention to the lack of centralised administration and co-ordination of water supply in an area deficient in resources, to the administrative and financial weakness of the smaller authorities, to the awkwardness of the system whereby one authority undertook to supply another, either wholly or partly, and to the anomalies arising from disparities in methods of charging.

We want [he said] an area which will be efficient, which can confer benefits not at present existent on the authorities within the area, and yet will not be too small to achieve that object. . . . The amalgamation of a number of small undertakings, of which some are deficient in supplies or working on narrow margins, into a substantial undertaking will be to the ultimate advantage of the districts concerned.

In accordance with the decision of the Committee that it was for the Petitioners to prove their objections, not for the Minister to prove the need for the Order, Mr. Capewell called no evidence, and was immediately followed by the counsel for the first group of petitioners, Mr. Cope Morgan, K.C., who represented the Higham Ferrers and Rushden Water Board, the

Corporation of Higham Ferrers, the Rushden Urban District Council and the Wellingborough Rural District Council.

Using a map, he drew the Committee's attention to a 'blue' area within which was enclosed a 'brown area'. He asked (*a*) that the blue area should be excluded from the scope of the Order and (*b*) that, if this should be rejected, the brown area should 'quite certainly' come out. The Ministry had argued that there was no alternative to the new scheme. That might be true so far as a large part of Northamptonshire was concerned; but it was not true of his area. The water engineer, Mr. Hawksworth, had maintained at the Inquiry that its inclusion was 'geographically desirable'; but this was not so. So far as his area was concerned, in fact, the whole scheme was quite contrary to the principle of the Water Act, 1945.

He further objected to the proposed method of charging for the water supplied, which would be partly through a 'deficiency rate', levied on all rateable properties, to cover losses.

The new idea is this: whether or not people are taking water they shall all contribute to the deficiency rate which may arise on the supply of water.

This was 'most unfair', and had been introduced solely because 'it was nice and convenient for someone in an office'.

Of all the alleged justifications for bringing an area into the new scheme, that given in a Ministerial letter of August 6 was the only one that could possibly apply to his area – and it was a ridiculous one. The Minister had pointed out that the impounding reservoir at Sywell, the principal source of supply for the Joint Board, was within the 'brown' area.

Did you ever hear of a case like that – that merely because the impounding reservoir happens to be physically just inside a bit of our area which is in their supply area, therefore the whole bag of tricks is going to them?

Having concluded his speech, Mr. Cope Morgan proceeded to call his evidence. The first witness, Mr. Roger Le Geyt Hetherington, was called, sworn and examined by Mr. Cope Morgan's junior, Mr. Royston Askew. As is the usual form on these occasions, the first questions were intended to make manifest the qualifications and experience of the witness, viz.:

1. Mr. Roger Le Geyt Hetherington, you are a Member of the

Institution of Civil Engineers, of the Institution of Water Engineers and of the Society of Consulting Engineers? – *Yes*.

2. Are you a partner in the firm of Binnie, Deacon and Gourley, Chartered Civil Engineers, practising in Westminster? – *Yes*.

3. I think your firm specialises in the design and construction of works of water supply of various types? – *Yes*.

4. And they advise a number of public authorities, companies and water boards? – *Yes*.

5. And has your firm acted for the Higham Ferrers and Rushden Water Board for a number of years? – *Yes*.

6. I believe you are at the present time carrying out an improvement scheme for that Water Board? – *That is so*.

Most of the questions, like those addressed to subsequent witnesses, were highly technical in character and neither they nor the answers to them were fully intelligible without reference to the map and to the various tables of figures that had been handed to the Committee. Indeed, the Committee itself sometimes found them difficult to follow.

Most of Mr. Askew's detailed questions were aimed at leading up to the following key passage in the evidence:

84. Having looked at the position all round . . ., do you, speaking as an engineer advising this authority, see any engineering justification for the inclusion in the proposed Water Board of this area outlined in brown? – *No, I do not*.

85. Do you see any valid reason at all? – *No* . . .

87. You are familiar with a number of reservoir schemes up and down the country, are you not? Have you ever before heard it suggested that that [i.e. the Sywell reservoir's being within the limits of the new Joint Board's area of supply] was a reason for the extension of the water limits? – *Certainly not; it seems absurd to me*.

Mr. Arthur Capewell's cross-examination of Mr. Hetherington was mainly aimed at casting doubt on his cost estimates and on the financial viability of the Higham Ferrers Water Board, at proving that the 'brown' area was not so self-contained a unit as the Petitioners claimed it to be, at suggesting that Mr. Hetherington's knowledge of the water supply arrangements of the authorities other than those by whom he had been employed as a consultant was too limited to enable him to judge soundly of the scheme as a whole, and at gaining from him the admission that the Order, when put into operation, would yield considerable economies of scale.

When the witness was re-examined by Mr. Cope Morgan, all six Members of the Committee used the occasion to secure further clarification. Throughout the proceedings, in fact, it was at the 're-examination' stage that the Members intervened most frequently. At other stages, they were for the most part content to listen to the speeches, the examinations or the cross-examinations.

The next witness was Mr. Joseph Allen, a member of the Rushden Urban District Council and a former chairman of the Higham Ferrers Water Board. Examined by Mr. Cope Morgan, he expresssed opposition to absorption, pride in the achievements of his Board and confidence in its financial future. In cross-examining him, Mr. Capewell endeavoured to show that the Higham Ferrers Board was inadequately staffed and that the main reasons for his opposition to the new scheme were a desire not to lose an identity which had been separate since 1902 and a fear that water supplies might cost more.

Mr. Frank Edward Price, an expert with great experience of advising local authorities on the financial aspects of their public utility undertakings, was then called and examined by Mr. Royston Askew, on behalf of the Petitioners. Expressing opposition to the proposed deficiency payments from rates, he said that they were contrary to general practice and would lead 'to most extraordinary anomalies as between one type of person and another'. Mr. Askew's aim was to establish, on the basis of Mr. Price's expert knowledge, the following conclusions: (*a*) that the Minister had underestimated both the capital and the working costs of the new scheme; (*b*) that the Higham Ferrers Board could supply the water needs of its area more cheaply than they could be supplied by the proposed Joint Board; (*c*) that the Joint Board would not be 'weakened or stultified' financially by the exclusion of the 'brown area' from its jurisdiction; and (*d*) that by going into the Joint Board the Higham Ferrers Board, and its constituent local authorities, would be unable to reap the advantage of the impending extinction of a major part of its loan charges.

Mr. Price's professional caution, however, prevented him from giving Mr. Askew the unqualified support which the latter was trying to obtain.

In cross-examination, Mr. Capewell endeavoured to establish (*a*) that the burden of capital charges would not be unfairly heavy for Higham Ferrers in comparison with the other authorities involved; (*b*) that the charging of a water deficiency rate was quite usual, that such a rate was already charged by the Higham Ferrers Board, and that its future incidence was likely to be both higher and less stable than any corresponding charge that the new Board might be called upon to impose; (*c*) that other authorities, not opposing the Order, enjoyed comparative cost advantages even superior to those enjoyed by Higham Ferrers, but were 'prepared to sacrifice that benefit for the good of the area as a whole'.

After re-examination of his witness, Mr. Cope Morgan declared:

That is the case for the two areas that I represent, the Board and the Wellingborough Rural District.

This was followed by a short argument about procedure, the main issue in which was whether the Counter-Petitions should be heard severally in connection with the Petitions to which they were related, or all together after the hearing of these Petitions had been concluded. The Chairman ruled that, as far as the local authority Petitions and Counter-Petitions were concerned, it would be generally convenient to take the remainder of the Petitions and then to hear the Counter-Petitions to them, 'if required', before the final speeches. The Accountants' Petition, which differed in character from the others, would be heard 'afterwards'.

Accordingly, the Committee went on to hear the Petition of the Wellingborough Urban District Council, introduced by Mr. E. J. C. Neep, K.C.

His reasons for advocating the exclusion of 'his' area were very similar to those advanced by Mr. Cope Morgan in his submissions on behalf of the previous Petitioners. Evidence of a highly technical character was taken from Mr. Arnold Horace Santo Waters, a water engineer, consultant to two water companies, and Chairman of the South Staffordshire Water Company.

Mr. Price, the financial witness, was then called again and gave evidence as to the iniquity of the rate deficiency proposals, the financial harmlessness of leaving the Wellingborough Urban District Council out of the scheme, the increased financial burden on water consumers and ratepayers involved in bringing it in, and the extra burden they would have to suffer as a result of 'severance'.

The Petition of the Northampton Rural District Council, which had jurisdiction over another allegedly 'fringe' area, was taken next, with arguments on both sides differing only in detail from the previous ones. On Mr. Neep's announcement that his case was concluded, the Chairman again cleared the room. After the Committee had deliberated, he announced that it was of the opinion that neither the Wellingborough Urban District Council nor the Northampton Rural District Council had made out a case for exclusion from the Joint Board. Hence it would not be necessary to hear the relevant Counter-Petitions. The Committee could therefore proceed to deal with the Counter-Petitions still outstanding, viz., those against the undecided Petitions of the Wellingborough Rural District Council and of the Higham Ferrers and Rushden Water Board, the Higham Ferrers Corporation and the Rushden Urban District Council. After Mr. Capewell had established his right, as representing the Promoters, to be heard, he announced that he would call his evidence first and address the Committee afterwards.

His first witness was Mr. Sidney Robert Raffety, a water engineer with '45 years' experience devoted almost entirely to waterworks and water supply in all branches', and recently concerned with the setting up of Water Boards under Private Bill legislation. Mr. Raffety justified the scheme on the grounds that it would improve co-ordination, eliminate a number of small and inefficient authorities, enable part-time to be replaced by full-time officers, and permit the abandonment of uncertain underground water supplies in favour of a large central reservoir. Mr. Capewell's second witness was Mr. Stanley William Hill, a financial adviser to local authorities in respect of their public utility undertakings. His firm had been connected with the promotion of the scheme under consideration. During the course of his evidence two Members of the Committee engaged in discussion both with him and between themselves as to what might be described as the ethics of water-charging.

Mr. Rankin

1572. Everybody will pay for water under the deficiency rate? – Yes, everybody.

1573. Even though they may not actually be getting a water supply? – That is quite true, Sir. It is rather comparable in a way to the other Public Health and sanitary services; in the same way that every rated property contributes to a sewerage system of a district and to the sewage disposal arrangements as well as to every other local government service, it puts the water supply on exactly the same basis. It so happens that in this case the facts are such, that it almost gets to that stage in any case because the number of those unsupplied is very small.

1574. But they are reaping the benefits that come from the exist-ing water supply even though they may not be getting it directly? – That is a view to which I subscribe.

Captain Marsden

1575. Would you kindly say what benefits they are reaping? – The benefit of their being an adequate water supply and its effect on health generally throughout the district.

Mr. Rankin

1576. In much the same way as people who pay an education rate but yet do not derive benefit from children attending school and so on. They are partaking of a general benefit to the community that accrues from education. I assume the analogy is quite good? – Yes, I think that is a parallel.

Captain Marsden

1577. Might I just ask this question? In the case of education any-body can make use of the educational facilities provided, but surely that is very different from this water system where this water is not laid on and they cannot make use of it? – Well, Sir, unless water can be laid on to practically all premises the whole justification for the Water Board does go, but the whole object is to get water ideally to every house.

Mr. Capewell, in his address, contended that the area chosen was of good size from the administrative point of view, that it could be administered economically and that through the Joint Board the water in the area could be made available to every part of the area 'quite readily and economically'.

After clearing the room for consultation, the Chairman made the following announcement:

The Committee is of the opinion that this Petition should be granted as to what Mr. Cope Morgan described in his opening as the brown area, but not as to the parishes outside.

He was not clear, however, whether there were five parishes outside or six. Mr. Cope Morgan explained that the sixth parish was Sywell, which was outside the distribution system of the other five, which were the ones with which he was concerned. The Chairman thereupon said:

We have considered that at great length, but we have not been able to decide in favour of excluding those five parishes.

There followed a slight procedural muddle.

And your Lordship does not wish to hear me on that? [asked Mr. Cope Morgan]. It is only to safeguard one's own position. I should have submitted that you could not have taken an adverse view on part of my case on which you had not heard me. Of course, your Lordships could have granted my position without hearing me, but your Lordships would not surely deprive me of my right without hearing me on the matter?

The Chairman admitted that there was substance in these submissions, and after further interchange of views between Committee and counsel, it was eventually decided to hear the Counter-Petition in respect of the remainder of the 'blue' area (i.e. the five parishes) and Mr. Cope Morgan's arguments for its exclusion from the scheme. The announced decision of the Committee in respect of this area was therefore once more open to argument. Not, however, for very long. After Mr. Ashworth had spoken shortly for the Counter-Petitioners, Mr. Cope Morgan held out a bait to the Committee. He was instructed, he said, during the course of his address, to give the following undertaking:

. . . if we are allowed to have my whole blue area, including the five parishes, out, both the rural district and the Higham Ferrers Board will immediately take steps to apply to the Minister for the making of a joint Board to cover the whole of the area.

The Committee, however, was not thus to be won. After a further clearing of the room, the Chairman thus announced its decision:

Gentlemen, we have paid very careful attention to the submissions of Mr. Cope Morgan, but we feel that it is right that these five parishes should go into the new Joint Board.

That matter having been finally decided, the Committee proceeded to give its attention to the Petition of the River Nene Catchment Board, presented to it by Mr. Harold Willis.

The Catchment Board's complaint was of alleged excessive extraction of water from the River Nene under the new scheme.

Mr. Willis specified 'five major points' on which it required protection. He was particularly critical of certain discretionary powers over water abstraction which the Minister, by the Order, had conferred upon himself. The regulation of this matter, which involved arbitration between different river interests, ought, he said, to be reserved for Parliament.

Evidence was called from Mr. Harold William Clark, the Chief Engineer of the River Nene Catchment Board, and from Mr. William John Penn, the Chairman of the Northampton-shire Branch of the National Farmers' Union. The examination of the latter contained the only overt example of humour to be found in the entire proceedings. Questions dealing with the location of Mr. Penn's farm ran as follows:

1837. Is that very close to the point where the Corporation's sewage discharges into the river? – Within 2½ miles.
1838. So that you have some personal experience of what happens? – Yes.
Chairman: It must be below it, then.

After the cross-examination of this witness by Mr. Capewell, counsel for the Petitioners announced that his case was con-cluded. Mr. Capewell himself then called Mr. Thomas Edwin Hawksley, a water engineer, who had advised the Northampton Corporation and had been engaged on the promotion of the Bill which authorised the construction of the Pitsford Reservoir. After his cross-examination and re-examination, Mr. Capewell briefly recalled Mr. Raffety 'on two points'. Messrs. Capewell and Willis then successively addressed the Committee, and after it had consulted, the Chairman thus announced its decision:

The Committee have decided that the intake at Duston is to remain at 20 million gallons per day and may be reduced below that, but not in any case below 16 million gallons, as and when and for as long as the Catchment Board notify that there is a necessity. The Petitioners' application to alter the period of abstraction to exclude October is not granted. The Minister's application for power to extend the period of abstraction or to reduce the minimum flow cannot be acceded to. The Petitioners' application to put a pro-hibition on the taking of water from Merry Tom when the flow is below 2.5 million gallons cannot be brought into operation at once.

It will be noted that the Committee, while not accepting all the submissions made on behalf of the Catchment Board, did agree with Mr. Willis's contention that the discretionary powers of the Minister embodied in the Order were improper.

The next, and final, business was the hearing of the Auditors' Petition. Before this commenced, Mr. Michael Rowe, K.C., who appeared on their behalf, announced, to the Chairman's great content, that the Counter-Petition, 'threatening an internecine battle between the Accountants', had been disposed of between Mr. Neep and himself.

Mr. Rowe, in his opening speech for the Accountants, was at pains to prove that his clients were 'the cream of the accountancy world'. Their objection was simply to the provision, embodied in the Order, making District Audit of the Joint Board's accounts compulsory. He asked the Committee to say that to limit the Board to District Audit was wrong and that it should be given the alternative between District Audit and professional audit. In support of this request he quoted copious examples and precedents, with particular reference to other Water Boards, and contended that professional audit was the best form for trading concerns, as had been recognised by Parliament. His witness, who was cross-examined by Mr. Capewell, was Mr. Frank Edward Price, who had already testified before the Committee on several occasions. To give evidence against the Petition, Mr. Capewell called Mr. Frederick Laurence Edwards, an Assistant Secretary in charge of the Finance Division at the Ministry of Health. Mr. Edwards was cross-examined by Mr. Rowe but not re-examined. In his speech, which followed the hearing of this evidence, Mr. Capewell advanced many reasons for refusing the right of professional audit. His contentions, however, did not apparently impress the Committee. After consultation, the Chairman announced its decision as follows:

The Committee have considered this at some length and with very great care, and they have come to the conclusion that the amendment should be allowed.

There followed a discussion between Committee and counsel, amicably concluded, about the precise form that the amendment should take.

Concluding the proceedings, the Chairman said:

It has been a very pleasant occasion and apparently is going to be a precedent. I think we shall have our own views as to the advantage of this procedure.

To this, Mr. Capewell replied:

I have no doubt your Lordship will make a report on the procedure, and how it has worked in this particular case; whether it has been shorter or longer than the other procedure.

Both the Clauses, and the Schedules, with Amendments, were then read and agreed to, and it was Ordered:

That the Lord in the Chair do report the Order with amendments to the House of Lords and that Captain Marsden do report the Order with amendments to the House of Commons.

The procedure employed in Joint Committee on the Mid-Northamptonshire Water Board Order did indeed constitute a precedent. It cannot, however, be said to have given entire satisfaction, as was indicated by the remarks of Mr. Capewell at the beginning of the proceedings on the Essex River Board Order, 1951. Opening for the Promoters, he referred to the 1948 case and quoted Lord Belstead's procedural ruling.

From then onwards [he continued] in these various orders that has been the position, and I have endeavoured to make what has been falsely described as a short and non-contentious opening speech. The latter adjective has not always been approved by my opponents, but I have always done my best, as I will on this occasion.

As there were only two Petitions for Amendment, proceedings on the latter Order were comparatively brief.

A further procedural point arose in connection with the Great Ouse River Board (Old West Internal Drainage District) Order, 1952. The Cambridgeshire County Council's Petition of General Objection was the first petition of this type to be referred to a Joint Committee. This gave the counsel for the Petitioners, Mr. Gerald A. Thesiger, Q.C., the opportunity of arguing that the procedure used for Petitions for Amendment was inappropriate, and ought to be reversed, the onus of proof being placed on 'those supporting the Order'.

After an exchange between Mr. Thesiger and the Chairman about the implications or Standing Orders, the Committee conferred. The Chairman then asked Mr. Thesiger why he thought there was no onus of proof on the Petitioner in this case, to which Mr. Thesiger replied: 'Because the Order and the Petition are both referred to this Committee'. After further consultation, the Chairman announced that it would not be necessary to hear Mr. Capewell on the point, and gave the Committee's ruling thus:

Mr. Thesiger, we are against you on this point. You raised the question of the burden of proof, so let me say that we think that the burden of proof is on you in this matter. In that connection, the best procedure would be – I think we appreciate that there is no exact precedent for this – that you should open the case without any factual statement from the Promoters. We think that S.O. 209 of the House of Lords and S.O. 243 of the House of Commons govern this point and that the order in which the procedure is set out there should be followed by us. So we decide now that the burden of proof is on the Petitioners and that consequently the Petitioners should open the case, followed of course by the Promoters of the Order, and in the final speeches the usual consequences would follow.

So the upshot was that the procedure followed the pattern established by previous cases, with the sole difference that the Promoter's 'short opening statement' was eliminated. How logical this is a moot point.

The scrupulousness of the Committees in following the letter of Standing Orders has certainly caused some inconveniences, and we are informed that, at the time of writing, the whole question of procedure in Joint Committee for the consideration of Special Procedure Orders is again under discussion.

9

FINANCIAL PROCEDURE

I. INTRODUCTION

EACH session, the House of Commons spends a large proportion of its time on finance. Twenty-six days are devoted to Supply, four to the Budget proposals, and an indefinite – but usually considerable – number to the various stages of the Finance Bill. However, it is mainly on the Committee and Report stages of the Finance Bill, when taxation proposals are given detailed discussion, that finance is the genuine as well as the ostensible subject of debate. When dealing with the Budget proposals, the House ranges widely over the whole field of economic policy. When dealing with Supply, it rarely attempts to 'vet' the Estimates that have been presented to it, but uses the occasion for discussing the Government *policies* with which those Estimates are associated. Yet the procedure of the House is designed to maintain the fiction that Supply Days are concerned with the amount and distribution of the money to be granted to the Crown for the maintenance of the various public services. Ancient forms of debate, going back to the period when the Commons granted money with great reluctance and attempted to ensure that it should be spent on the services for which it had been demanded, have gradually been adapted to new purposes. The result is a procedure of peculiar complexity and tortuousness, which even experienced Members do not always fully understand.

It would not be true to say, however, that the House has ever entirely reconciled itself to the uselessness of attempting, in a 'committee' of 630 members, to exercise effective control of the Estimates. From time to time back-benchers, on both sides of the House, become uneasy about the apparent readiness of the front benches to allow sums running into thousands of millions of pounds to be granted 'on the nod'; and recently this unease has been greatly reinforced by the growing habit of giving no more than formal consideration to the Votes set down for debate and then devoting the House's time to the discussion of a Government or Opposition resolution. In February 1960, there was a veritable revolt on this issue, which received considerable publicity. Consultations followed, and on July 26 Mr. Butler announced the Government's decision to make certain modifications in the procedure for dealing with Estimates. These events have not been included in our general account of the House's financial procedure, which deals with the Session 1958–59, but are described in the Appendix to this chapter.[1]

Financial procedure, as we have indicated, is extremely complex, and our difficulty was to find the best way of illustrating it through appropriate 'case-studies'. The solution we have adopted is to treat the whole of the financial business of one Session, in so far as it was transacted on the floor of the House, as a single case. This has the disadvantages of length and tortuousness; but we think, on balance, that it makes the procedure more intelligible than would the alternative solution of splitting it up into bits and pieces. Explanations of what the House is doing and why it is doing it are offered where apparent oddities seem to make this necessary; but full intelligibility, for readers not already familiar with the general outlines, will demand that the 'case' should be read in conjunction with a text-book. Perhaps the clearest outline account is that provided by the financial chapter of Dr. Eric Taylor's *The House of Commons at Work*. Sir Herbert Brittain's book on *The British Budgetary System* may also be strongly recommended. Details may be filled in, and the puzzles that *Hansard* so frequently presents solved, by reference to the latest edition of *Erskine May* and to Lord Campion's *An Introduction to the Procedure of the House of Commons*.

The two Select Committees on Finance, the Public Accounts Committee and the Estimates Committee, are dealt with separately, as we considered it desirable, in our arrangement of this book, to give Select Committees of all kinds a section to themselves.

[1] *See* p. 271.

2. THE SESSION, 1958–59

(a) *From the Beginning of the Session to the end of the 1958-59 Financial Year (March 31, 1959)*

The financial business of the 1958–59 Session of the House of Commons began, in the usual way, with the following statement in the Queen's Speech:[2]

Members of the House of Commons. Estimates for the Public Services will be laid before you in due course.

Again as usual, the passing of the 'Humble Address', at the end of the six days' debate on the Queen's Speech, was followed by the setting up of the Committees of Supply and of Ways and Means through the usual standard resolutions.

Up to the Christmas recess, there was no business to cause the House to go into Committee of Supply, but the Committee of Ways and Means met on one occasion, as a preliminary to the introduction of a certain type of Bill, and on another the House went into a specifically convened 'money' committee for the same purpose. In both cases it was about to consider Bills which, being exclusively concerned with the imposition of charges on the revenue, had to be preceded by, and founded on, a money resolution.

Apart from the normal financial resolutions accompanying the Second Readings of other Bills, this was the total extent of the House's financial business before the Christmas recess.

The business of Supply began on February 10, 1959, the first 'allotted day', when a Supplementary Estimate for 1958–59[3] in respect of National Insurance and Family Allowances was the subject of a day's debate.[4] The amount in question was £26,496,000. The debate revealed that this Vote had been chosen by the Opposition – perhaps not very appropriately – as providing an occasion for a discussion of employment policy. However, the Government spokesman, Miss Edith Pitt[5], confined her short opening speech almost entirely to an explanation of the reasons for the Supplementary Estimate, which were the higher birth rate and the higher incidence of unemployment.

---

[2] October 28, 1958.   [3] Class X, Vote 4.
[4] 3.31 p.m. – 10.0 p.m.
[5] Joint Parliamentary Secretary to the Ministry of Pensions and National Insurance.

'It is not for me', she said, 'to deal with the vigorous measures which the Government have taken and are taking to deal with this matter (i.e. unemployment) (Hon. Members: Why not?). They are not the responsibility of my Department'.[6] After allegations that the Government was trying to evade the issue, the first Opposition spokesman, Mr. Frederick Lee,[7] launched an attack on the Government's employment policy, during the course of which he criticised the Minister of Labour for an alleged time-lag in making unemployment figures available. In response to a demand for the latest ones, the Minister[8] intervened thus:

As the Committee knows, I have never been reluctant to give figures, but the Opposition did not put either my Vote down for debate – although I have a Supplementary Estimate – nor that of the President of the Board of Trade. That is why we thought the Opposition wished the debate to be confined to National Insurance.[9]

He nevertheless gave the figures.

Subsequent speakers, both Labour and Conservative, talked almost exclusively about unemployment in the context of general economic policy, most of them being careful to bring in numerous 'constituency' references. Consequently, at 7.33, the Parliamentary Secretary to the Board of Trade[10] decided to enter the fray, saying:

Although this debate takes place on the Supplementary Estimate of the Ministry of Pensions and National Insurance, the Committee has shown that it wished to debate the wider problem of . . . unemployment. Therefore, I think it might be for the convenience of the Committee if I now intervene.[11]

After further back bench contributions, none of them notable, the Minister of Pensions and National Insurance[12] replied to what he described as 'an extremely wide and interesting debate'.

We have touched on economic policy, the trade cycle, policy in the Middle East, and what Sir Hartley Shawcross, as he was then, did or did not do in connection with Far Eastern trade.[13]

Such a wide debate on a 'narrow foundation', he very reason-

[6] H.C. Debates, Vol. 599, col. 1004.
[7] Lab., Lancashire, Newton.
[8] Mr. Iain Macleod.
[9] H.C. Debates, Vol. 599, col. 1008.
[10] Mr. John Rogers.
[11] H.C. Debates, Vol. 599, col. 1082.
[12] Mr. John Boyd-Carpenter.
[13] H.C. Debates, Vol. 599, col. 1120.

ably claimed, made it 'extraordinarily difficult to reply at the end of the day'. However, he made no complaint, except of certain Members' lack of generosity in criticising Miss Pitt for 'confining herself to the Estimate'; and, in introducing his remarks about the unemployment problem, asserted that the Government had done its best.

to meet the point of view and wishes expressed on both sides of the Committee that the Supplementary Estimate should be used as a vehicle for the discussion of this immensely important problem.[14]

Sir Winston Churchill's attack on debates on Supplementary Estimates as 'the most worthless of any I have known in my career' is familiar. This was said as long ago as 1931, but Sir Ivor Jennings finds the criticism to be still, on the whole, valid. Although such debates, he considers, offer an 'effective sanction' against extravagance, they are either 'a series of disjointed speeches punctuated by calls to order' or 'repetitions of stale arguments'.[15] This view surely now requires modification. When a Supplementary is for a large sum, the expenditure of which has wide policy implications, the debate on it can provide a vehicle for the criticism of the government's record just as useful as that provided by a Main Estimate. The discussion on the Pensions and National Insurance Supplementary, reported above, was neither 'disjointed' nor 'punctuated by calls to order'; and the arguments used in it by Members were not noticeably 'staler' than those heard in any other debate on unemployment, which is a subject to which Parliament, in a period of economic recession, quite rightly wishes to give frequent attention. Indeed, this debate, although its *point d'appui* may be criticisable, was a much more useful parliamentary exercise than one of the subsequent debates on the Army, Navy and Air Force Main Estimates,[16] which was indeed disjointed and bedevilled by points of Order.

The second Alloted Supply Day (Wednesday, February 18) was devoted to the Vote on Account for the Civil Estimates and Estimates for the Revenue Departments, together with the Estimate for the Ministry of Defence. This Vote, as is well known, provides the basis of that part of the Consolidated Fund (No. 1) Bill which authorises expenditure by the departments concerned from the beginning of the new financial year on

---

[14] *Ibid.*   [15] *Parliament*, 2nd ed., 1957, p. 302.   [16] *See* below, p. 243.

April 1 to the passing of the annual Appropriation Act in the summer. The Motion made and Question proposed ran thus:

That a sum, not exceeding £1,272,018,000 be granted to Her Majesty on account, towards defraying the charges for the following Civil and Revenue Departments and for the Ministry of Defence for the year ending on the 31st day of March, 1960, viz. . . .[17]

As the Prime Minister and Foreign Secretary had already announced their intention to visit Moscow, the Vote was used as an occasion for a debate on Foreign Affairs, opened by the Leader of the Opposition, Mr. Gaitskell.[18] At 10 p.m. it was concluded with the usual formalities, viz.:

Question put and agreed to. Resolved. . . . Resolution to be reported. Report to be received Tomorrow. Committee to sit again Tomorrow.[19]

On the third Allotted Supply Day, Tuesday, February 24, the business of Supply was reduced to the formality of agreeing to the above Resolution, on Report. Then, as already arranged 'behind the Speaker's Chair' and announced to the House by Mr. Butler on February 19,[20] debates took place on two Opposition motions, the first relating to Legal Aid, the second to Prison Camp Conditions in Kenya. To enable the day to count as a Supply Day, in spite of the fact that Supply was not being debated, a resolution had to be formally passed to permit the discussion of business other than Supply to be taken before 10 o'clock, thus, in effect, suspending the operation of Standing Order 16, which specifies that on an allotted day 'no business other than the business of supply shall be taken before ten of the clock'.

On the fourth Allotted Day, March 3, the Committee of Supply turned its attention to the Army Estimates, Vote A, Number of Land Forces. To understand this selection of topic it is necessary to bear several things in mind. The first is that the method of providing for the 'interim' financial needs of the Services has always been different from that of providing for those of the civil departments. The latter receive Votes on Account. The former are given Votes in respect of the pay of officers and other ranks (always a large item) and certain other kinds of expenditure, the moneys granted being available, by the process of 'virement', for the meeting of commitments

[17] H.C. Debates, Vol. 600, col. 552.   [18] Leeds South.
[19] H.C. Debates, Vol. 600, col. 676.   [20] Ibid., col. 546.

arising under Votes not debated in Committee of Supply before the end of the current financial year and therefore not incorporated in the Consolidated Fund (No. 1) Act. Before considering the March Service Votes in detail, however, the House requires (or thinks it requires) an opportunity for *general* debates on Service matters. These were formerly provided by the device of 'moving the Speaker out of the Chair' when first going into Committee on each of the Service Estimates; but, since the Session of 1955–56, this procedure has been allowed to lapse (as is permitted by a 1948 Amendment to Standing Order 17), the Speaker having ruled that the general debate, in respect of each of the three Services, can take place on Vote A, which does not grant money but authorises total establishments. The effect of this is that back-benchers no longer have the opportunity to move amendments, which they previously had – by ballot – when the motion 'That the Speaker do now leave the Chair' was used.

Vote A for the Army, on this occasion, ran:

That a number of Land Forces, not exceeding 351,000, all ranks, be maintained for the safety of the United Kingdom and the defence of the possessions of Her Majesty's Crown, during the year ending on the 31st day of March, 1960.[21]

The debate, mainly about manpower and equipment, was interrupted at 7.0 p.m., as the Labour Party had previously secured the acceptance of an 'emergency' adjournment resolution on the affairs of Nyasaland.[22] The Chairman accordingly left the Chair and the Speaker resumed it, to preside over a 'Nyasaland' debate which lasted until 10 p.m. The House then went into Committee of Supply again, and continued to discuss the affairs of the Army until 1.53 a.m.[23]

On the fifth Allotted Day, Thursday, March 5, Vote A of the Air Estimates was taken, another two hours' extension of

---

[21] *H.C. Debates*, Vol. 601, col. 228.

[22] This did not involve the postponement of the Allotted Supply Day, as Standing Order 16 specifies a Motion of Adjournment 'on a definite matter of urgent public importance' as the *only* other business that can be taken before 10 o'clock on such a day.

[23] As time lost to an emergency adjournment debate can be made up automatically, the House, which had already passed a resolution suspending Standing Orders to permit Supply discussion to continue 'for two hours after 10 o'clock', could have sat for as long after midnight as the time occupied by the Nyasaland debate supplemented by the half-hour normally occupied by the ordinary adjournment motion, i.e., 3½ hours.

debating time having been previously provided for by resolution. Much of the discussion was again about manpower and equipment, but some Members, as might be expected on such a Vote, chose to express their views on defence strategy.

The debate illustrated, in a small way, the fact that questions of Order can often be inhibiting when a Supply Resolution is taken 'straight', instead of being tailored to fit the real needs of debate. Where the relevance of a Member's remarks to a particular vote is concerned, the House seems on these occasions to strain at gnats while swallowing camels. The Temporary Chairman pulled up Mr. Rankin[24] for saying that the Royal Air Force 'made a mess at Suez', and got into argument with him when he attempted to deal with the R.A.F. staging posts at Gan. The latter, said the Temporary Chairman, were the responsibility of the Commonwealth Relations Office, so far as negotiations with the Maldivian Government were concerned, although the Air Ministry was paying for all the constructional work. Mr. Rankin would therefore be in order only if he confined himself 'to discussing the amount spent under this Vote on that matter.'[25] The same Member was also called to Order for talking about a television programme which he considered to have some relevance to defence policy.[26] On the other hand, several Members were allowed quite freely to talk about nuclear disarmament – a subject which, although technically in order (in so far as the R.A.F. is equipped with nuclear weapons), had implications which went far beyond Vote A.

The only other feature of interest in this debate is that although it could have continued until midnight, it came to an end at 9.41. This suggests either that Members were very little interested in the Air Force or that they had already said, in the Defence Debate, all the general things about it that they wanted to say. The latter was probably the case. If so, it supports the contention, made by a witness before the Select Committee on Procedure of 1958–59, that too many discussions on defence are concentrated in the early part of the calendar year.[27]

The Debate on Vote A for the Navy (sixth Allotted Day, March 9) not only failed to reach its time limit, but was so dull and so poorly attended that Commander J. W. Maitland[28]

[24] Lab., Glasgow, Govan.   [25] *H.C. Debates*, Vol. 601, col. 666.
[26] *Ibid.*, col. 668.   [27] *See* H.C. 92–91 of 1958–59, p. 167, Question 1046.
[28] Cons., Horncastle.

found himself moved to deny that it was 'at all representative of the country's feelings about the position of the Royal Navy today'.[29] It consisted mainly of a few long, often highly technical but hardly very authoritative speeches about manpower, equipment, economies, production policy, deployment, and the role of the Navy in modern war.

On the following day (Tuesday, March 10: seventh Allotted Supply Day) the 1959–60 Estimates for the three Services (pay, etc.) were taken, together with their Supplementary Estimates for 1958–59. As the discussion of all these Estimates had to be concluded before 10 p.m., Mr. R. J. Mellish,[30] opening for Opposition, said that his Party was willing to co-operate in ensuring that the Navy and Air Force got their share of the time by confining the debate on the Army Esti-mates to three hours. This, he suggested, 'might be convenient' to Members. He was immediately challenged by Mr. Wigg,[31] who protested at the 'carving up' of the Votes in the interests of the two front benches. His claim that opportunities for 'redress of grievances' ought not to be thus restricted had – as such points of 'principle' often have – a strongly personal note; for on his main interest, the organisation of the Army and the welfare of soldiers, he subsequently intervened to raise a variety of questions which, as he himself said, he had been prevented by illness from raising in previous debates. Another type of procedural objection came from Mr. F. J. Bellenger,[32] who disliked the current method of debating Service Estimates.

Hon. Members [he said] may get answers to some of the points which they raise, but these seem to me to be taken out of their context. The proper context should be the Minister presenting his Service Estimates.[33]

Vote 1 (Pay, etc., of the Army) was agreed to by 4.40 p.m., after a reply by the Under-Secretary of State for War[34] to the miscellaneous points raised in debate. Vote 2 (Reserve Forces, Territorial Army and Cadet Forces) took only another hour, some of which was occupied with further procedural complaints. 'Our Estimates debates', said Mr. James Simmons[35] 'are becoming a farce'. Alleging that it was 'scandalous' to expect

---

[29] H.C. Debates, Vol. 601, col. 1006.
[31] Lab., Dudley.
[33] H.C. Debates, Vol. 601, cols. 1099–1100.
[35] Lab., Brierley Hill.

[30] Lab., Bermondsey.
[32] Lab., Bassetlaw.
[34] Mr. Hugh Fraser.

the House 'to take nine, ten, or eleven Votes in three hours', he demanded that action be taken 'to restore some of the rights of back-benchers to discuss the Estimates in greater detail than has been possible during the last two years'.[36] By way of reply to this complaint, Mr. Roy Mason[37] pointed out that, in its previous (Vote A) Service debates, the House had failed to exhaust the time available to it. A little later, Mr. Wigg returned once more to procedure, suggesting the appointment of 'a committee of secrecy . . . every year to which the separate Estimates would be remitted so that they could be gone through with a toothcomb behind the scenes'.[38] He was denied such opportunity as he may have wished to develop this proposal, for the Chairman found that his remarks were reaching the verge of Order.

Vote 6 (Supplies, etc.) was disposed of in less than twenty minutes, Mr. Wigg and Dr. R. Bennett[39] using the occasion to deal respectively with diet and the R.A.S.C. fleet (the existence of which was probably as much news to most Members as it was to the authors of this book).

Vote 7 (Stores) took 35 minutes, during which time ammunition, technical stores, guided missiles, clothing, and haircuts for Gurkhas all received mention, and Mr. Wigg succeeded in making a number of technical criticisms of the manner in which the Estimates were presented.

Vote 8 (Works, Buildings and Lands) took only five minutes, which were occupied by a speech from Dr. Bennett about the 'closing by the War Office of a road called Wallington Hill'.[40]

Vote 9 (Miscellaneous Effective Services), which occupied the House from 6.35 to 6.54, enabled Mr. Wigg to raise 'two very important and serious matters', viz., the loss, by the Sandhurst Museum, of a V.C. Medal (won in 1857) which had been on loan to it, and the alleged shabby treatment by the Government of 700 contract workers formerly employed in maintaining the Suez Canal Base and imprisoned by President Nasser. Mr. Fraser, in replying, agreed to 'look into' both of them.

Vote 10 (Non-Effective Services) provided six minutes in which Mr. Mellish[41] talked about pensions for V.C.s and Mr.

[36] *H.C. Debates*, Vol. 601, cols. 1112–1113.   [37] Lab., Barnsley.
[38] *H.C. Debates*, Vol. 601, col. 1118.   [39] Cons., Gosport and Fareham.
[40] *H.C. Debates*, Vol. 601, col. 1144.   [41] Lab., Bermondsey.

Wigg gave his views on Long Service and Good Conduct Medals.

Vote 11 (Additional Married Quarters) provided seven minutes in which Mr. Fernyhough[42] asked whether the War Office could make funds available to Local Authorities for the housing of time-expired men.

The Supplementary Estimates were agreed to without debate.

Discussion on the Navy and Air Force Estimates followed much the same pattern, occupying the House until 9.58 p.m.

One can sympathise with those Members who found this Estimates Debate little to their taste. Detailed consideration of the Estimates, an exercise in which the House used to engage frequently but which is now almost entirely confined to this occasion, is nearly always a waste of time; and when the debate is as restricted by time-table considerations as this one was, it becomes entirely futile. All Members can do is to raise a series of isolated points which happen to have come to their attention, and receive promises from the relevant ministerial spokesman that their representations will be 'looked into'. This can be done equally well at Question Time or through private communication with the Ministers concerned.

Although the House is currently in one of its periodical moods of misgiving about the ease with which Estimates are accepted, and plans have been announced to make available days on which the Reports of the Select Committee on Estimates may be specifically debated,[43] there is still wide agreement that Supply Days can best be used for the discussion of fairly broad fields of government policy, and that the Votes are no more than a convenient 'peg' on which such discussions may be hung. All the subsequent Supply Debates of 1958–59 that we shall be mentioning are of this character.

On the eighth Allotted Day, March 12, the House began by formally agreeing to the Roads Estimate, on which a debate had been arranged, on Report, for the next Allotted Day. It then proceeded to discuss the health services, on the occasion of the presentation of a Supplementary Estimate[44] of £16,589,706 for the National Health Service. Winding it up for the Government, the Parliamentary Secretary to the Ministry

[44] Class V, Vote 5.
[42] Lab., Durham, Jarrow.   [43] *See* below, p. 277.

of Health[45] summarised it as 'fairly discursive' and 'useful'.[46] After the putting of the Question at 7.30 p.m., it was followed by one and three-quarter hours' discussion of health in Scotland, occasioned by a Scottish Supplementary N.H.S. Estimate of £2,376,501, and by fifteen minutes of 'question and answer' on four Supplementary Estimates relating to agriculture.

At 9.30 this business was cut short, in accordance with Standing Order 16, the relevant part of which runs:

On a day not earlier than the seventh allotted day, being a day before the 31st March, the chairman shall, at half-past nine of the clock, put every question necessary to dispose of the vote then under consideration.

Accordingly, the Question on the agricultural Supplementaries was put and agreed to. Then, also following the procedure laid down by S.O. No. 16, the Chairman

proceeded to put severally the Questions. That the total amounts of all outstanding Estimates supplementary to those of the current financial year as have been presented seven clear days, and of all outstanding Excess Votes, be granted for the Services defined in those Supplementary Estimates and Statements of Excess.[47]

It may be noted, in passing, that the total 'civil excesses' thus agreed to by the Committee amounted to £94,262 18s. 1d., distributed between the Fire Service, National Insurance and Family Allowances.

These resolutions[48] were followed by the repetitive but technically necessary resolutions in Committee of Ways and Means.

The ninth Allotted Day, March 17, was occupied, up to 7.0 p.m., with the debate on Report on Roads in England and Wales.[49] Explaining the Opposition's selection of this topic, Mr. Ernest Davies[50] said:

It seemed to us desirable to assess whether the [road] programme is adequate to meet the traffic needs of today and whether the Government are proceeding on the right lines.[51]

At 7 p.m., Standing Order 16 (as modified for this occasion by a previous resolution) came into operation again. The

---

[45] Mr. Richard Thompson.   [46] H.C. Debates, Vol. 601, col. 1523.
[47] Ibid., col. 1573.
[48] Particulars are set out in cols. 1573–1576 of Hansard, Vol. 601.
[49] Class IX, Vote 2.   [50] Lab., Enfield East.
[51] H.C. Debates, Vol. 602, col. 215.

'roads' Resolution was 'disposed of', and each of the remaining resolutions reported from the Committee of Supply but not yet agreed to by the House was put and passed. When the corresponding Ways and Means Resolutions had also been passed, the way was procedurally clear for bringing in the Consolidated Fund Bill, designed to authorise departmental expenditure for the first part of the forthcoming financial year. Accordingly, the Bill was 'ordered to be brought in' and formally presented. Normally, this purely formal procedure would have been taken at 9.30 p.m., as specified in Standing Orders. By the resolution already mentioned, however, the House had decided to take it, on this occasion, at 7.0 p.m., in order to allow time on that day for debates on Opposed Private Business, viz., the Torquay and Buckinghamshire Water Bills.

On Wednesday, March 18, the Consolidated Fund Bill was given its formal Second Reading and committed to a Committee of the whole House. Members then occupied the rest of the day with a debate on unemployment which covered much the same ground as had already been covered by the previous debate on that subject in Committee of Supply.[52]

On the following day, March 19, the formalities connected with the Consolidated Fund Bill were concluded. It was 'considered in Committee', 'reported, without amendment', and 'Read a Third Time and Passed', all 'on the nod'. Then, as on the previous day, the House proceeded to a general debate, this time on the subject of Cyprus, introduced by a Government motion expressing approval of the recently concluded 'Cyprus Agreement'.

(b) *From the Beginning of the 1959–60 Financial Year (April 1, 1959)*
to the Passing of the Finance and Appropriation Acts

The next financial business of the House was the most important of the Session; the hearing of the Chancellor's Budget Statement on April 7. With the House in Committee of Ways and Means, Mr. Derick Heathcoat Amory began his Statement at 3.20 p.m. and continued without interruption (as is normal) for two hours. Like all modern Budget Statements, it included a broad survey of the country's economic health during the financial year 1958–59 and an assessment of its future prospects.

[52] *See* above, pp. 238–240.

The keynote of the Statement was contained in the following sentence:

I can ... now contemplate with safety some tax reductions that will lead to a fuller use of our resources without creating dangerous pressures on the economy.[53]

As is the invariable rule (the reasons for which are obvious), the Committee proceeded, immediately the Chancellor had resumed his seat, to agree, without debate, to a series of resolutions (in this case seventeen out of a total of eighteen) authorising the changes in taxation that had been proposed. The remaining resolution, not immediately passed, was the one to which the subsequent Budget debate was to be 'pegged'. Couched in standard form, it read:

That it is expedient to amend the law with respect to the national debt and the public revenue and to make further provision in connection with finance. ...[54]

The remainder of the day was devoted to the opening stages of the Budget Debate. This first part of the debate, by tradition opened by the Leader of the Opposition with a short speech beginning with congratulations to the Chancellor, is inevitably of a rather 'impromptu' kind, as obviously Members have not had advance notice of the Chancellor's proposals. The Budget *Day* debate, therefore, is treated mainly as an occasion when back-benchers can produce their 'off-the-cuff' reactions.

After Mr. Gaitskell had foreshadowed the main lines of the Opposition's attack, Mr. A. W. Cooper[55] opened the batting for the Government with a defence of a 'first-class' Budget.[56] Mr. Frank Allaun,[57] however, found it 'unfair, mean, and harsh,' describing it as 'the shareholders' delight, but the poor man's disappointment'.[58] Other Labour Members attacked it in general and in detail. Most of the Conservative contributors gave it their general approval but expressed misgivings about specific proposals touching their constituents or interests for which they regarded themselves as spokesmen. Mr. Reader Harris,[59] for instance, regretted that it made no reduction in the petrol tax, gave no encouragement to house-ownership, and

---

[53] *H.C. Debates*, Vol. 603, col. 49.
[55] Cons., Ilford South.
[57] Lab., Salford East.
[59] Cons. Heston and Isleworth.

[54] *Ibid.*, col. 74.
[56] *H.C. Debates*, Vol. 602, col. 79.
[58] *H.C. Debates*, Vol. 602, col. 90.

did nothing to 'stimulate investment by the purchase of stocks and shares'.

Only one Member chose to criticise the procedure for debating the Budget Statement. He was Mr. Ellis Smith,[60] who renewed a complaint – which he said he had been making 'for years' – that a debate on the Economic Survey was included as part of the debate on the Budget. This, he considered, placed too much of a strain on both Chancellor and Members.

On the following day, April 8, Labour's big guns opened fire, with speeches by Mr. Harold Wilson[61] and Dr. Hugh Dalton.[62] The former Member, Labour's 'shadow' Chancellor, made the opening statement, which drew a reply from the Paymaster-General, Mr. Maudling. In this day's debate, which concluded at 10 p.m. without further front bench intervention, most of the speeches were long and carefully prepared. Some dealt with the whole economic and budgetary situation, while others concentrated, by way of commendation or criticism, on specific aspects of the Chancellor's proposals.

On Thursday, April 9, after a Bill to give effect to one of the Budget proposals, the Income Tax (Payment of Post-War Credits) Bill, had been 'read' a first time, the debate was resumed with a speech for the Government from Mr. David Eccles, the President of the Board of Trade. He was followed by Mr. Douglas Jay,[63] a former Economic Secretary to the Treasury. Among other contributors was Mr. Peter Thorneycroft,[64] who had been Chancellor in Mr. Macmillan's Cabinet until, after his resignation arising from disagreements with his colleagues over economic policy, Mr. Heathcoat Amory had taken over the office.

At 10 p.m., two financial resolutions were formally passed, viz., in respect of Exchequer Advances and Import Duty Reliefs. Resolutions of this technical and formal kind, tucked away at the end of the day, often cause the casual reader of *Hansard* to conclude that our Parliamentary procedure is unintelligible. In this case, the explanation is simply that these were resolutions authorising certain *expenditures* consequential to the provisions of the Budget. According to the procedure of the House, such resolutions cannot be agreed to in commit-

---

[60] Lab., Stoke-on-Trent.
[62] Durham, Bishop Auckland.
[64] Cons., Monmouth.

[61] Lancashire, Huyton.
[63] Lab., Battersea North.

tee on the day on which the Chancellor opens his Budget.

Unlike Ways and Means Resolutions, notice must be given of them before they are moved, and they are consequently considered in Committee of the whole House on a subsequent day.[65]

The fourth day's debate on the Budget Proposals took place on Monday, April 13. Mr. Alfred Robens opened for the Labour front bench and was followed by Mr. J. E. S. Simon, the Financial Secretary to the Treasury. The debate was concluded, as is normal, with a reply from the Chancellor, and the Question on the 'amendment of the law' resolution put and passed, also as normal, without division.

On the following day the Ways and Means Resolutions, together with the Finance (Exchequer Advances) and the Finance (Import Duty Reliefs) Resolutions, were reported to the House and formally agreed to. The Finance Bill was then 'brought in', 'read' a first time, and ordered to be read a second time on Monday next. The House occupied the remainder of the day with a debate on the Second Reading of the Income Tax (Repayment of Post-War Credits) Bill.

Between these budgetary proceedings and the Second Reading of the Finance Bill, which actually took place on Tuesday, April 28, the House returned to Supply, the tenth Allotted Day being taken on April 20. This was another occasion when Supply Business[66] was dealt with formally, in this case to enable the House to discuss a resolution, proposed for the Opposition by Mr. H. A. Marquand,[67] on retirement pensions. Consequently, to enable the day to count as a Supply Day, the House had to resolve that 'Business other than Supply' might be taken before 10 o'clock.

The Second Reading of the Finance Bill (April 28) provided, as usual, the occasion for a full-scale debate. The Financial Secretary to the Treasury, Mr. J. E. S. Simon, opened with an exposition and justification of its proposals.

Again this year [he said] these provisions fall into five main groups. First, there are measures for reduction of taxation, which are particularly striking and widespread in the Bill: Income Tax, beer duty, Purchase Tax, bus licences and Stamp Duty all reduced, and Corporation Duty abolished. Secondly, there are the measures to

---

[65] *Erskine May*, 16 ed., p. 795.
[66] Class X, Vote 2, Ministry of Pensions and National Insurance.
[67] Lab., Middlesbrough East.

encourage investment. Last year, there were initial allowances, and this year, there are the investment allowances. Thirdly, there is a major project of fiscal reform.[68]

The reader may comment that all these things had already been debated, in general terms, on the Budget Resolutions – and so they had. The debate that followed was therefore in many respects simply repetitive, but it did have the advantage of enabling Members to concentrate on the financial proposals themselves, whereas previously they had been equally – and, in some cases, much more – concerned with general issues of economic policy.

In leading off for the Opposition, Mr. Gordon Walker[69] indicated that there was an important political factor which would affect the attitude adopted by the Opposition during the Bill's various stages.

This is a long and complex Bill and it has been said that it is an obstacle to an early General Election, but if the Finance Bill stands in any way in the light of an early General Election that must not be attributed to the Opposition. We certainly want to study it very closely and to improve it, but we should be ready to expedite the passage of the Bill if, thereby, we could have an early General Election. In that case, one good – the need to scrutinise and improve the Bill – would give way to a greater good, that of getting rid of the Government. . . . If this offer is not accepted, and if this Session takes its normal course, then normal considerations must apply and we shall have to give very close, careful and detailed consideration to this long and involved Bill.[70]

The back-bench speeches that followed were variously patterned. Some Members covered many subjects. For instance, Mr. Nabarro,[71] who is never more at home than when a Finance Bill is being debated, spoke competently and vigorously on Income Tax, Purchase Tax, the beer duty and methods of financing nationalised industries. At the other extreme was Mr. Bryant Godman Irvine,[72] who both expressed and kept to the intention of 'confining his remarks to cider.'[73] No one chose to challenge his authority on that subject.

On Thursday, April 30, the House returned to Supply. At this point *Hansard* once again reveals something that immediately strikes the layman as a procedural anomaly. Before the Supply Debate, which was devoted to Youth Employment

---

[68] *H.C. Debates*, Vol. 604, col. 1106.
[70] *Ibid.*, cols. 1125–1126.
[72] Cons., Rye.

[69] Lab., Smethwick.
[71] Cons., Kidderminster.
[73] *H.C. Debates*, Vol. 604, col. 1168.

Problems, the results were announced of the 'Ballot for Notices of Motion on Going into Committee of Supply'. The Rev. Ll. Williams,[74] Mr. Frank Allaun,[75] and Mr. Leavey,[76] the successful Members, proclaimed their intention to deal respectively with Development Area Policy, the Need for Increased Aid to the Aged, and the Civil Service. But had not the House already gone into Committee of Supply on numerous occasions? And was it not about to go into Committee of Supply again on a subject which had no relation whatever to any of the matters on which the three Members were to move Motions? The answer is that the House had not gone, and was not yet about to go, into Committee of Supply on Civil Estimates considered as one of the five main branches of Estimates. This is done by the traditional method of 'moving the Speaker out of the Chair' – a procedure which was once employed for each of the main branches (four as they were then) but, as we have seen, was discontinued in respect of the Navy, Army and Air Force Estimates in 1956–57. The Motions announced by the Members successful in the Ballot would be – as we shall see – moved as amendments to *this* Resolution, and not in connection with any Committee of Supply resolution on a specific Vote.[77] This is another obscure corner of financial procedure which even fairly experienced Members might find difficulty in explaining.

Another peculiarity of the proceedings on Thursday, April 30, was that the Supply debate was 'pegged' to two 'token' sums.[78] The Question read as follows:

That a further sum, not exceeding £20, be granted to Her Majesty, towards defraying the charges for the year ending on the 31st day of March, 1960, for the following services connected with the Youth Employment Problems with particular reference to Apprenticeship and Industrial Training Schemes, namely:

Civil Estimates, 1959–60

Class VI, Vote 9 (Ministry of Labour and National Service) .	£10
Class IV, Vote 1 (Ministry of Education)	£10
TOTAL . .	£20

---

[74] Lab., Abertillery.   [75] Lab., Salford East.
[76] Cons., Lancashire, Heywood and Royton.
[77] This opportunity for Private Members has now been withdrawn, but they have received 'compensation' (*see* below, p. 338).
[78] These should be distinguished from Token *Votes*, which serve a different purpose. *See Erskine May*, 16th ed., pp. 711 and 737.

The reason for the adoption of this procedure was as follows. Youth Employment, which the Opposition wanted to discuss, was not the subject of any particular Vote, but financed (partly) by appropriations made available to both the Ministries mentioned in the resolution. It *could* have been discussed on the *whole* of Vote 9 (Class VI) and the *whole* of Vote 1 (Class IV), or by passing these votes formally and then moving a resolution on this specific problem (having first provided that business other than Supply might be taken before 10 o'clock). Either of these alternative methods, however, would have precluded the Opposition from discussing the Ministry of Labour's and the Ministry of Education's Votes on some future Supply Day, so as to deal with other aspects of the activities of these two departments. A form of Question tailor-made to the Opposition's requirements was therefore devised. Much ingenuity is used (some might say misused) to enable the House, without transgressing the rules of Order, to discuss precisely what it wants to discuss (or what the Opposition wants it to discuss) when it is pretending to be concerned with finance.

The debate on the above Resolution produced plenty of interesting and well-informed speeches and very little political heat. It was also noticeable, in contrast with the Budget and Finance Bill debates, that Members had no difficulty in taking up the points made by those who had preceded them. This is one of the advantages of a debate on a limited and clearly defined subject.

However, despite the fact that the political temperature was low, the Opposition decided to divide the House. The division was taken on a Motion by Mr. Robens to the effect that Item Class VI, Vote 9 (Ministry of Labour and National Service), should be reduced by £5. Ayes, 146; Noes, 195.[79]

On the thirteenth Allotted Supply Day (Thursday, May 7) the House used two token sums[80] to debate Traffic Congestion in Large Cities. This again was largely non-political, and it attracted so little interest that an attempt was made to count out the House during the course of Mr. Nugent's winding-up speech. It concluded at 7.0 p.m., when the House proceeded to the Second Readings of the Lancaster Corporation Bill and the

[79] *Ibid.*, col. 1598.
[80] Class IX, Vote 1, Ministry of Transport and Civil Aviation; Class IX, Vote 2, Roads, etc., England and Wales.

Halifax Corporation Bill, having already safeguarded itself for this purpose by passing two resolutions: (1) enabling business other than Supply to be taken before 10 p.m.; (2) exempting 'any Private Business set down for consideration at seven o'clock this evening' from the provisions of S.O. No. 1 (Sittings of the House) and from those of S.O. No. 7 (Time for Taking Private Business) to the extent of enabling the debate on the two Bills to go on after 9 o'clock.

On Monday, May 11, the House began what can now be regarded as the Session's only 'financial' business that is seriously and genuinely concerned with finance, viz., the Committee Stage of the Finance Bill. The debate opened with the moving by Mr. John Hall[81] of an amendment to Clause 4 (Excise Licences required for Registered Clubs; Abolition of Duty on Statements) designed to secure 'that small clubs, whose members number many thousands throughout the country, do not pay more in Excise duty or in licence fee than they are doing under the existing rates.[82] After a fairly lengthy discussion of this subject and a promise by the Government spokesman of 'further consideration', the mover of the amendment asked leave to withdraw it. This being objected to, it was pressed to a Division, which (although the mover was a Conservative) took place along straight party lines, the Ayes mustering 174 votes and the Noes, 210.

The second amendment, which was to Clause 5 (Abolition of Requirements as to Monopoly Value) gave rise to a procedural discussion in which Mr. Harold Wilson explained the Opposition's purpose in the choice of its amendments.

In choosing Amendments [he said] we have attempted, as far as possible, to ensure that time spent on the Bill in Committee will be purposefully directed to three or four of the key issues raised by the Bill. I am sure that it is the feeling of the Committee generally that we do not need to spend an excessive time on the Finance Bill this year and on going into minutiae on some of the Clauses. We have chosen Amendments in such a way as to influence, as far as lies in our power, the course of debate in the way that my hon. Friend [Mr. Ellis Smith] wants, namely, so that there will be an adequate discussion at reasonable times of the day on some of the general issues, rather than getting the Committee bogged down in too much detail.[83]

---

[81] Cons., Wycombe.   [82] *H.C. Debates*, Vol. 605, col. 861.
[83] *H.C. Debates*, Vol. 604, col. 878.

This is not, of course, an invariable Opposition attitude. The various stages of the Finance Bill not being subject to the 10 o'clock rule, the Opposition will sometimes endeavour to keep the House up to all hours of the night and morning. In view of the character of the 1958–59 Finance Bill and the imminence of a General Election, however, such behaviour was not seen as politically advantageous.

After the Division on Clause 5 (which, although obscure, had the effect, according to the Opposition, of presenting an annual £750,000 to those pillars of the Establishment, the brewers), the Chancellor apologised for and rectified a procedural fault. He had failed to table a Motion, as agreed with the Opposition, for debating Schedules 1 and 2 before Clauses 6–28. He therefore presented such a Motion on the spot and promised to introduce similar Motions, when needed, at subsequent stages of the Committee's proceedings. Mr. Wilson, while accepting this Motion on behalf of the Opposition, pointed out that this was not the first time that the Chancellor had been guilty of such carelessness, and used the occasion to expatiate on the Opposition's 'helpfulness'.

The two schedules were, in fact, quickly agreed to, and so were Clauses 6 (Rebate on Heavy Oils) and 7 (Increased Quota for Certificated Colonial Sugar), after certain explanations had been given. Clause 8 (Extension of Import Duties Act, 1958), however, caused more controversy. For the Opposition, Mr. Hector Hughes[84] said: 'We oppose this Clause for six reasons, which I shall summarise' (Laughter).[85] His essential objection, coming appropriately from a Member for a fishing constituency, was that its result would be the flooding of the processing factories in British ports with imported herrings – 'relieved herrings which come in free of duty'. In the discussion that followed, Labour spokesmen championed the herring fishermen – who did not appear, however, to have been very vocal in their objections – and one Conservative[86] expressed misgivings. With humorous intent, Mr. G. R. Mitchison[87] dealt with the difficulties he had encountered in discovering the facts relating to this rather esoteric matter.

I have had some difficulty in finding what the present position is. I got hold of the Customs Tariff and discovered quite soon that herring meal attracted no duty. I then began to look for herring. That is not as easy as one would think. Herring are not in the list; fish are. I turned to fish and then discovered that I got into the wrong part. These were fish fit for human consumption, while for fish unfit for human consumption – which I think are the kind of fish we are discussing now – I had to look somewhere else, to a mysterious chapter called: 'Products of animal origin not elsewhere specified or included.' I must say I was distracted at this point because I read the notes. That is how I find my way about. I found this: 'Throughout this Schedule, elephant, mammoth, mastodon, walrus, narwhal and wild boar tusks, rhinoceros tusks and the teeth of all animals are regarded as ivory.' It would be too much to expect the Minister of State, Board of Trade, to give us information about the import of mammoth and mastodon tusks into this country in any given year. However, herring meal was to be found there somewhere and it attracted, as far as I could see, a 10 per cent. duty. That, I believe, is what we are discussing now.[88]

Eventually, after explanations by the Minister of State, Board of Trade,[89] the Clause was agreed to without a division.

Under Clause 9 (Excise Duties on Mechanically-Propelled Vehicles kept, but not used, on Roads) there was a rather lengthy discussion of cars left unlicensed on highways. As this seemed as remote as it could possibly be from herrings, Mr. Ernest Davies[90] was moved to protest at the manner of doing business on the Committee Stage of the Finance Bill.

I do not know who arranges the order of the Clauses of the Finance Bill [he said]. Three Clauses ago we were discussing the relief of certain vehicles from oil duty. We jumped to sugar and then to herring and now we are back again to vehicles. I should think that it would be for the convenience of the Committee as a whole, let alone for the Ministers who specialise in attending to certain of the Clauses, if Clauses dealing with the same subject-matter could be close together.[91]

The discussion of Clause 10 (Vehicles (Excise) Hackney Carriages) was notable for critical speeches by several Conservatives, particularly those who had already expressed concern, in the Budget Debate, about rural transport.

Clause 11 (Agricultural Tractors. Carriage of Produce, etc., at Agricultural Rate of Duty) produced a minor amendment from Col. Richard H. Glyn,[92] which, after support from another

---

[88] *H.C. Debates*, Vol. 605, col. 934.
[90] Lab., Enfield East.
[92] Cons., Dorset North.

[89] Mr. Vaughan-Morgan.
[91] *H.C. Debates*, Vol. 605, col. 945.

Conservative and a Labour Member, was accepted by the Government.

Another minor Amendment to the same Clause, moved by Mr. Geoffrey Stevens,[93] was accepted in principle, but in view of the fact that it did not, as phrased, 'fit well' into Clause 11, the Government persuaded Mr. Stevens to withdraw it, on the understanding that a similar and more appropriately phrased amendment would be introduced by the Government at a later stage.

The Committee then turned to Clause 12, which dealt with changes in the rate of Purchase Tax, a subject which had caused procedural difficulties on many previous occasions, and did not fail to do so again. Mr. Harold Wilson opened what proved to be a lengthy and at times rather acrimonious discussion about the method of debating Clause 12, by moving 'That the Chairman do Report Progress and ask leave to sit again'.

I move this Motion not merely because we have . . . made remarkable progress on the first day of the Finance Bill Committee Stage. . . . There is another, and rather more serious reason. If we were to continue tonight we should be proceeding with Clause 12 . . . and it has become clear that, because of the Financial Resolution tabled by the Government during the Budget debate, the Committee is being denied its usual facilities for debating Purchase Tax. We have given notice of this point to the Chancellor of the Exchequer and the Leader of the House. An extremely serious situation has arisen on which we shall in a few moments wish to hear a statement from the Chancellor.[94]

Mr. Wilson went on to explain that the Opposition accepted the undesirability of having a debate on the individual items in the Purchase Tax schedule, which tended to degenerate into a kind of 'Dutch auction', but was strongly of the view that what he alleged to be the usual practice should be observed, i.e., that there should be opportunity to debate each of the main rates, viz., 50 per cent., 25 per cent., $12\frac{1}{2}$ per cent. and 5 per cent. The Opposition had sought to table amendments along these lines, but had been informed by the Public Bill Office that it would be out of Order, because the Chancellor, without consultation and in defiance of established practice, had altered the basis of the Financial Resolution. As a result 'this year, almost for the first time in ten years, we find that we cannot debate the four rates

[93] Cons., Portsmouth, Langstone.   [94] H.C. Debates, Vol. 605, col. 983.

of Purchase Tax'. An Amendment to reduce (but not to abolish) could be moved only for the 5 per cent. rate. As for the other – and more important – rates, it was only possible to move that they be raised back to the level from which the Budget had reduced them – which, obviously, no one wanted. Mr. Wilson could not believe that this was what the Chancellor really meant. There must have been a drafting error which had escaped the Chancellor's notice, as it has escaped the Opposition's notice until they came to study the Financial Resolution closely. He hoped that the Chancellor would give a 'satisfactory explanation' and say what he intended to do to put the matter right.

The Chancellor, however, turned a deaf ear to this appeal. He admitted that the Resolutions had been 'drawn in restrictive form', but this was to avoid the protracted debates of the previous year 'when we spent several days in discussing at some length what were really very minor changes'. Such debates might have been reasonable then, because he had proposed 'what amounted to recasting almost the whole tax', but the situation was different this year. He thought that the restrictions were 'what the Committee would have wished', and challenged the applicability of Mr. Wilson's alleged precedents. Moreover, the Resolutions had been before the Committee throughout the four days' Budget debate, when the Opposition had raised no objection to them. Why had it chosen to bring them up only at so late a stage?

Mr. Wilson thereupon expressed his 'amazement', to no avail, while Mr. Jay[95] complained that the procedure was being reduced to a 'farce'. For Mr. Cronin,[96] it was 'a matter of the utmost gravity and concern to all back-benchers'.

After Mrs. Eirene White[97] and Mr. Donald Wade[98] had added their protests, the Chancellor admitted that he himself had discovered the 'unusual restrictiveness' of the Resolution only after it had been passed, but thought that it did not matter, as adequate debate could take place on the Motion that 'the Clause stand part of the Bill'. However, he was prepared to consider 'agreed arrangements' on 'future occasions'.[99] This did not satisfy Mr. Wilson, who nevertheless announced that

[95] Lab., Battersea North.   [96] Lab., Leicestershire, Loughborough.
[97] Lab., Flint East.   [98] Lib., Huddersfield West.
[99] H.C. Debates, Vol. 605, col. 1003.

he did not propose to 'press' the Chancellor any further that night and suggested that the latter should 'look at this matter again' before the resumption of the debate on the following day. The Question was put and agreed to at 11.02 p.m.

Mr. Wilson opened the next day's proceedings by again moving that 'the Chairman do Report Progress and ask leave to sit again'. For about half an hour Labour Members pressed the Chancellor with arguments not substantially different from those of the previous night, without, however, extracting any concession from him. On a Division, the 'Progress' Motion was defeated by 203 votes to 249. Mr. Douglas Jay then moved one of the few Amendments now open to the Opposition. Introducing it, he said:

This Amendment, and some of the consequential Amendments, illustrate the extraordinary position in which the Chancellor placed the Committee by his remarkable blunder . . . over the Financial Resolution. The effect of the Amendments would be to reduce the 5 per cent. rate of Purchase Tax to 1 per cent. That is what we are compelled by this Financial Resolution to move. What we would wish to move and wish to argue is that the 5 per cent. rate should be reduced to nil. . . . I agree with the spokesman of the Liberal Party, who intervened just now, that it exposes our debates to derision if we are compelled, in our Amendments, to move something quite different from what we wish to lay before the Committee.[1]

However, in the rather lengthy debate that followed, which covered 'clothing in the widest sense, including gloves, hats, all footwear and all furniture', the Members who participated did not seem to suffer from many inhibitions. As Mr. Jay had moved 'in page 12, line 33, to leave out "and" ', the Division was on the Motion 'That "and" stand part of the Clause'. It was carried, on a strict party vote, by 247 to 203. The Chairman then announced that 'other Amendments to this Clause are either out of Order or fall', and the House proceeded to a general discussion of Purchase Tax, opened by Mrs. Eirene White,[2] on the Motion 'That the Clause stand part of the Bill'. This, which was punctuated by further sporadic protests about procedure, enabled Conservative as well as Labour Members to express their dislike of taxation on purchases, with particular reference to 'cultural' items, such as gramophone records, musical instruments and sports equipment. The Chancellor, replying, said:

[1] *Ibid.*, col. 1067.   [2] Lab., Flint East.

I kept a list during the debate of the articles which I was advised to exempt from Purchase Tax entirely. It is not a complete list, but it includes musical instruments, records, pottery, hollow-ware, textiles, jewellery, bicycles, sports requisites, furniture and fishing gear. Every one of these items, of course, was described as vitally important and quite exceptional. If I were prepared to accept the advice offered me, I should reduce the tax to utter and complete chaos.[3]

One can see why the Government, in framing its Financial Resolution, was determined to avoid the 'Dutch auction'.

A further speech from an Opposition Member was followed by cries of 'Divide'. The Question was then put and agreed to but without a Division; and Mr. Wilson, in moving that 'the Chairman to Report Progress and ask leave to sit again', thus chided the Government benches:

Their suggestion that we should divide against the Question that Clause 12 stand part of the Bill (i.e., a clause making tax reductions of which the Opposition could not fail to approve) only shows how little they know of the whole procedural situation in which the Committee has been placed by the Chancellor's action.[4]

He concluded by warning the Chancellor that progress with the Committee Stage of the Finance Bill on the following day would depend 'on how accommodating he is to the excellent and constructive Amendments which we have put on the Notice Paper'. The Chancellor, however, did not choose to take up this point, contenting himself with the hope that, if tomorrow's progress was as good as today's, Members would 'all go away for their Whitsun holiday feeling that that holiday had been well earned'.[5]

Mr. Wilson evidently did not intend his threat to be taken too seriously, for on the following day (May 13), the Committee succeeded in disposing of Clause 16 (Alterations in Reliefs), and Clause 17 (Restoration of Investment Allowances, and Additional Grant of Initial Allowances in Certain Cases) in spite of the fact that the Government resisted and defeated all proposed Amendments, apart from one moved by Mr. Geoffrey Stevens for the purpose of correcting a drafting error.

On the last day before the Whitsuntide Adjournment, the House returned to Supply (fourteenth Allotted Day). On this occasion, the time-honoured Motion 'That Mr. Speaker do now leave the Chair' was proposed, to allow the Rev. Ll. Williams,

[3] *H.C. Debates*, Vol. 605, col. 1192.   [4] *Ibid.*, col. 1201.   [5] *Ibid.*, col. 1203.

the first of the successful 'balloters', to move his resolution about the Development Areas.

After Whitsun, Supply business was resumed on June 3 (fifteenth Allotted Day), when Class VI, Vote 5 of the Civil Estimates (Financial Assistance in Development and Other Areas) was put down for discussion. The Opposition, however, wished to use the day for a debate on Industry, Employment and Roads in Scotland, i.e., to provide the House with one of its periodical opportunities to debate (in the words of Mr. Thomas Fraser) 'the success or failure of the Government's efforts to promote the economic well-being of Scotland.[6] This was achieved, procedurally (a) by moving 'that this day Business other than the Business of Supply may be taken before ten o'clock'; (b) by moving 'progress' immediately after the Supply Question had been proposed (thereby leaving the latter open to further debate on some future occasion, if desired); and (c) by hinging the Scottish debate on a Government Motion 'That this House takes note of the Report on Industry and Employment in Scotland and Scottish Roads, 1958'.[7] As usual on these occasions, all contributors to the debate were representatives of Scottish constituencies.

On June 10, the House once again went into Committee on the Finance Bill. Before the debate on Clause 18 (Purchase and Sale of Securities) opened, the Chairman, in whom is vested the power of selecting Amendments and new Clauses, revealed that out of 80 new Clauses tabled, only 20 would be called. ('So I suppose', he added wryly, 'that 60 hon. Members will be seeing me'.)

Purchase and Sale of Securities, which was the subject of Clauses 19 and 21 as well as that of Clause 18, provoked considerable debate on Labour Amendments designed to stop up tax-avoidance loopholes and Conservative Amendments to prevent the penalisation of 'persons engaged in legitimate activities'. None were accepted by the Government, which described them, through Mr. J. E. S. Simon, the Financial Secretary to the Treasury, as 'of very doubtful efficacy'.[8]

After brief discussion of Clause 25 (Profits Tax; increase of limits on deductions for Directors' Remunerations), on the basis of a Labour Amendment suggesting that the government had 'gone too far, as usual, in looking after directors',[9] the House turned to Estate Duty (Clause 26), on which there were a number of highly technical Amendments, some resisted by the Government, others withdrawn on promise of 'consideration' or of incorporation in the Bill at a later stage.

Clause 27, dealing with Exchequer Advances to Nationalised Industries and Undertakings, was the subject of an Amendment by Mr. Wilson

to make permanent, and not merely confine to one year, the provision introduced into the Finance Act, 1956, that borrowing by a nationalised industry should become a Treasury responsibility rather than be done by the boards themselves in the open market.[10]

This Amendment drew a conciliatory reply from the Chancellor who nevertheless rejected it.

Two new Clauses were then moved by the Government, one to deal with a technical matter relating to Estate Duty, the other to fulfil the 'assurances' given to Mr. Stevens when he had withdrawn his Amendment[11] about the exemption from Excise Duty of vehicles for clearing snow, etc.

The rest of the day was occupied with discussion on a new Clause, moved on behalf of the Labour Party by Mrs. Eirene White, for the repeal of the Entertainments Duty. By the Chairman's ruling, this was taken together with another new Clause, in the name of Sir Toby Low[12], for the *reduction* of the Entertainments Duty. All contributors favoured either the abolition or reduction of the tax. The Chancellor advised against the acceptance of Mrs. White's Clause, but found Sir Toby Low's more acceptable, although not phrased in the best possible way.

I am ... sympathetic to the principle of this Clause [he said] and I want to make some response to the appeals which have been made by hon. Members in all quarters of the Committee. I shall be willing on Report to move a Government new Clause which would embody the principle and general effect of the Clause tabled.[13]

At about 10.50, Mr. Wilson asked the Chancellor if 'he would agree to Report Progress' so that the debate might continue the next day, his reason being that the Opposition did not

[9] Mr. Diamond.
[11] *See* above, p. 249
[13] *H.C. Debates*, Vol. 606, col. 1133.
[10] *H.C. Debates*, Vol. 606, col. 1083.
[12] Cons., Blackpool North.

regard the Chancellor's concession as adequate and believed that the problem could be solved only by the acceptance of Mrs. White's Clause. With a little reluctance, the Chancellor agreed.

On the next day (June 11), after discussion of several complicated points of Order, not untypical of those that bedevil Finance debates, the Committee discussed the Entertainments Duty until 7.15 p.m. Although most speakers on both sides were favourable to the Opposition's Amendment (which was in a popular cause), it was defeated on a straight party vote by 196 to 162. The remainder of the day was occupied in discussion of new 'relief' Clauses. All those proposed by the Opposition were resisted and defeated, but one moved by a Conservative,[14] relating to Invalid Vehicles, was accepted in principle by the Government, which promised to move its own new Clause to give effect to Mr. Ridsdale's suggestions. When the Chancellor rose to bring the debate to an end, he expressed pleasure on the 'substantial progress' that had been made in an 'agreeable atmosphere'. Mr. Wilson agreed, but hoped that when the debate was resumed on Monday the Chancellor would show 'a spirit of greater accommodation' than he had shown 'in the earlier stages of this debate'.

Monday, June 15, was entirely devoted to new Clauses, none of major importance. Most of them, whether proposed by Conservative or by Labour Members, were resisted by the Government and either defeated or withdrawn, but one, moved by Mr. Douglas Houghton[15] for the Opposition, was accepted in principle, the Government undertaking to introduce its own new Clause to the same effect. When the last of the new Clauses had been withdrawn, the Committee Stage of the Finance Bill came to an end with the usual exchange of congratulations between Government and Opposition. The Bill, as amended, was then reported.

Between Thursday, June 18, and the Summer Recess, the House had to occupy nine more days with Supply, to bring the total up to twenty-six. As usual, the Votes debated were tailor-made to suit the subjects that the Opposition wished to debate. In some cases, a series of related token sums of £10 each was taken, the Opposition dividing the House on a Motion to reduce one of them by £5. The device of dealing with Supply

---

[14] Mr. Julian Ridsdale, Harwich.   [15] Lab., Yorkshire, West Riding, Sowerby.

formally and then passing on to debate a Resolution was also employed. By such means, the House gave its attention to Local Authority Housing, Housing in London, the Government's 'policy towards the firm of Messrs. S. G. Brown Ltd., of Watford', the Condition of Private Industry, the Dispute in the Printing Industry, Foreign Affairs, the National Health Service, Aircraft Production, Aid to Underdeveloped Areas, Civil Aviation, Pig Production and the Bacon Industry, and the Employment of Disabled Persons. In addition, it gave another day's debate to the economic affairs of Scotland, once more on a Motion 'taking note' of Command Paper No. 760.[16]

The penultimate stages of the Finance Bill were taken on Tuesday, July 7, when it was first recommitted for consideration of certain Government Amendments and new Clauses, which were quickly disposed of. It then passed to the Report Stage, where further Government Amendments and new Clauses were incorporated. Both Labour and Conservative Amendments were also moved, and there were several Divisions. The longest discussion was on the Government's new Clause giving effect to the promised relief from Entertainments Duty.[17] On the conclusion of the debate, the Bill was ordered to be read a Third Time. There followed a rather unusual episode in which a front bench Labour Member, Mr. George Brown,[18] challenged the 'virement' Resolutions which had been tabled in respect of Navy, Army and Air Force Expenditure for 1957–58. As this episode has a certain procedural interest, it deserves brief description and analysis.

As is well known, 'virement', or transfer of funds, can take place as between different Service Votes, so that surpluses on some Votes can be used to meet deficiencies on others. For this Treasury approval is necessary, and in theory such approval is only provisional, as it needs confirmation by a Committee of the Whole House known as the Navy, Army and Air Expenditure Committee – a Committee which is set up only in those sessions when this particular need arises.

Erskine May[19] notes that there are certain 'anomalies' connected with the work of this Committee. It has been ruled, for instance, that the debate (if any) on the Question 'That the application of such sums be sanctioned' must deal neither with

---

[16] *See* above, p. 262.   [17] *See* above, p. 263.
[18] Derbyshire, Belper.   [19] p. 748.

'the details of . . . surpluses or deficits' nor with 'virement' in general. It is limited, in fact, 'to the desirability of proceeding by the proposed transfer of surpluses to meet deficiencies in the particular case'.

These were the rules supposed to govern the procedure of the House when it turned its attention to this matter on July 7 (or, more correctly, July 8), at 12.15 a.m., by going into Navy, Army and Air Expenditure Committee. An additional complication, however, was provided by the fact that the Motions, and their attached Schedules, showed net unspent surpluses as well as surpluses on certain votes and deficiencies on others. This, it would appear from a reading of the debate, had the effect of somewhat loosening the strict rules of order that would otherwise have applied. At any rate, Mr. Brown was not pulled up when he demanded to know 'why we have not spent money on armaments for Her Majesty's ships and have turned it to some quite different purpose', and proceeded to confuse both himself and the House by comments such as the following:

If I switch from the thing labelled 'Deficits' to the thing labelled 'Surpluses', I . . . find myself . . . in a complete fog. Under 'Surpluses' we have a column headed 'Surpluses of Estimated over Actual Gross Expenditure'. I want to know how we can have such a thing. It is not a surplus at all. It really means that Her Majesty's Government did not manage to do the job for which the Minister of Defence took credit. I should have thought it a deficit if the job was not done.[20]

The Financial Secretary to the Treasury[21] responded with a careful explanation of what the House was doing and of the rules of Order applicable to it.

All we are concerned with [he said] is . . . a pure question of accountancy: namely, was the Treasury correct in exercising virement in the way it did within the discretion given to it by the Appropriation Act.[22]

Such discretion was exercised within the ambit of rules which had, for decades, been approved by the Public Accounts Committee. Moreover, the deficits involved were 'not out of scale with the amounts for which Parliament had given the authority requested in previous years'; nor were they 'of an unusual nature'. Hence it was not necessary, as Mr. Brown had alleged,

[20] *H.C. Debates*, Vol. 608, cols. 1299–1300.   [21] Mr. J. E. S. Simon.
[22] *Ibid.*, col. 1301.

for Service Ministers to be present to deal with Members' queries, 'for any matter that called for a reply from them would be out of order'.

Mr. Brown, however, was not satisfied, saying that he 'had never heard more words used to less purpose in his life'. The Question on Navy Expenditure, which was what had been under discussion, was then put and agreed to. This was followed by a similar wrangle over the Army and Air Force Expenditure resolutions, punctuated by a question on a point of Order to which the Chairman replied after a slight delay and somewhat uncertainly – as is fully understandable, Mr. Brown, no doubt, was really attempting to improve a very unshining hour by exposing the Government's alleged incompetency to organise the Defence Services, and obviously cared very little for the rules governing the discussion of 'virement'. Mr. Simon, however, stuck strictly to these rules, on which he, at least, appeared to have been adequately briefed.

Although Mr. Brown invited the Committee 'not to approve this proposal unless the hon. and learned Gentleman can explain why £1$\frac{3}{4}$ million voted for the business end of the Air Force has been transferred to a non-business end', the Air Force Expenditure resolution was put and agreed to, after which the House proceeded to discuss, on the Adjournment Motion, the politically more contentious but procedurally less complex subject of 'Uganda (Disturbances)'.

The final stage of the Finance Bill took place on Friday, July 10, when it was given a mercifully short Third Reading (11.5 a.m. – 2.50 p.m.), ending with a speech from the Financial Secretary to the Treasury which contained the following *requiescat*:

The Third Reading of a Finance Bill is habitually conducted in a peaceful atmosphere, and that has been so today. It is, of course, the peace of the graveyard. We may, out of habit, rattle our bones at each other and gibber at each other, but we know that in fact we are only the pale ghosts of our former selves.[23]

On the penultimate (twenty-fifth) Supply Day, when, after debate on the subject or subjects chosen by the Opposition (in this case, the Pig Industry and the Employment of Disabled Persons), it is normal to put all the outstanding votes without

[23] *Ibid.*, col. 1822.

debate, the day's proceedings began with a Resolution, which was immediately passed, providing sums of money for the Commonwealth Relations Office and Colonial Office under Class II, Votes 4 and 7. This surprised Mr. Ellis Smith,[24] and perhaps even more surprised Members less familiar than he with the complexities of financial procedure, if they happened to be paying any attention. The following dialogue then took place, illustrating the difficulties that even experienced Members sometimes encounter.

Mr. Ellis Smith: Can we have an explanation of what we are doing now, Sir Charles?

The Chairman: That Vote has been agreed to by the Committee. This one was taken formally so that it will be the one to be discussed first on Report.

Mr. Ellis Smith: Does it mean that it is automatically going through?

The Chairman: It has gone through.

Mr. Ellis Smith: Does it mean that this Vote, covering an expenditure of millions of pounds, which has not been examined in detail, has automatically gone through?

The Chairman: Nobody challenged it when I put the Question.

Mr. Ellis Smith: I am challenging it now, Sir Charles.

The Chairman: I have collected the voices.

Mr. Ellis Smith: Yes, Sir Charles, but you did it very quickly. I am not being critical, because I have a great respect for the Chair, which works very efficiently, but we must be on our guard as well. I admit that I was a little bit slow, but I should now like to know what is the position.

The Chairman: I am sorry if I went quickly, but I always do. The point is quite simple. This Vote can be discussed on Report on Wednesday. It has been put down as the first one on the Order Paper so as to get it to the top of the list.

Mr. Ellis Smith: Thank you, Sir Charles. That has brought that out.[25]

What was really happening was that the Chairman was procedurally paving the way for the debate on Central Africa, which the Opposition had chosen as its subject for the Report Stage. The connection between this and an undebated vote of money for the Colonial and Commonwealth Relations Offices was, however, by no means obviously apparent.

After the Disabled Persons debate had concluded, at about 9.30 p.m., with its appropriate Supply Resolution,

The Chairman then proceeded, pursuant to the Order of the House this day, forthwith to put severally the Questions. That the total

[24] Lab., Stoke-on-Trent South.   [25] *H.C. Debates,* Vol. 609, cols. 1085–1086.

amounts of the Votes outstanding in the several Classes of the Civil Estimates, including a Supplementary Estimate, and the total amounts of the Votes outstanding in the Estimates for Revenue Departments, and in the Ministry of Defence Estimate, and in the Navy, the Army, and the Air Estimates, including a Supplementary Estimates for Air Services, be granted for the Services defined in those Classes and Estimates. . . .[26]

The 'Votes outstanding' were thereupon put and agreed to, without any Division. Thus the way was clear for the Report Stage on the following day. The House then went into Committee of Ways and Means to resolve, formally,

That towards making good the Supply granted to Her Majesty for the service of the year ending on the 31st day of March, 1960, the sum of £2,814,085,357 be granted out of the Consolidated Fund of the United Kingdom.[27]

On the following day, July 22, the Supply Resolutions were reported, and a Motion made 'That this House doth agree with the Committee in the said Resolution' (the 'said Resolution' being the Colonial Office and Commonwealth Relations Office one that had puzzled Mr. Ellis Smith). On this basis, the House had its debate, opened by Mr. Gaitskell, on Central Africa. When it had finished, with a Division,

It being after half past Nine o'clock, Mr. Speaker proceeded, pursuant to Standing Order No. 16 (Business of Supply) to put forthwith the Questions, That this House doth agree with the Committee in the outstanding Resolutions reported in respect of Classes I to X of the Civil Estimates and of the Revenue Departments' Estimates, the Ministry of Defence Estimate, the Navy Estimates, the Army Estimates and the Air Estimates.[28]

The necessary Questions were accordingly put and formally agreed to. The Ways and Means resolution was then also reported, and, after formal agreement had been registered, the Consolidated Fund (Appropriation) Bill was

ordered to be brought in upon the said Resolutions by the Chairman of Ways and Means, the Chancellor of the Exchequer, and Mr. Simon.[29]

The Bill was given a formal Second Reading on July 23, when the House devoted its time to debating the coal industry.

[26] *Ibid.*, col. 1188.
[28] *Ibid.*, col. 1411.
[27] *Ibid.*, col. 1195.
[29] *Ibid.*, col. 1415.

It went through its Committee and Report Stages, with equal formality, on the 27th, and immediately proceeded to its Third Reading, which provided the occasion for the usual marathon debate, in which (by arrangement) Opposition back-benchers opened a series of discussions on Consumer Protection, Defence, Industrial Health, the Hola Report and the Casement Diaries. This concluded at 3.30 a.m.

Two days later, the Finance Act, 1959, and the Appropriation Act, 1959,[30] together with 33 other Bills, received the Royal Assent.

One or two comments on the 1958–59 financial business may perhaps be useful. It is not presented as a 'typical year', for there are no typical years, except in so far as the general framework of financial business is concerned – and even this continues to display a process of slow evolution. In some respects, it was an unusually quiet and unexciting year. The Finance Bill, for instance, went through exceptionally smoothly, without many late sittings or procedural arguments. Another feature was the rarity with which points of Order were raised in the Supply debates, for which some credit must also be given to the skill displayed in framing Supply resolutions in such a way as to enable the House to discuss clearly-defined subjects, and to the growing habit of taking Supply resolutions formally, in order to provide time for debate on Government or Opposition Motions. The tenuousness of the connection between Supply and the so-called Supply Days is well illustrated.

The Session's debates also emphasise the contrast between Committee of Supply and Committee of Ways and Means. In the latter, the Commons is actually doing what it is supposed to be doing, i.e., discussing taxation. Furthermore, both Government and Opposition Members can occasionally exercise real influence over policy, through persuading the Government to accept Amendments or to incorporate their substance in new Clauses. This raises the question of whether it might not be better to reduce the Business of Supply – except on the occasions foreshadowed by Mr. Butler on July 26, 1960[31] – to complete formality, and to use the days now allotted to it entirely to the discussion of Opposition resolutions and Government resolutions tabled with Opposition agreement.

[30] i.e., the Act based upon the Consolidated Fund (Appropriation) Bill.
[31] *See* below, p. 277.

3. APPENDIX

(a) *Granting Supply 'on the Nod': the Back-Bench Revolt of*
February–March 1960[32]

On February 23, 1960, after Questions had been disposed of,
the House formally passed a resolution 'That this day Business
other than Business of Supply may be taken before Ten o'clock'.
This was to enable the day to be entirely devoted to the discussion of a resolution, to be proposed for the Opposition by
Mr. Alfred Robens,[33]

That this House regrets that the list of Development Districts issued
by Her Majesty's Government fails to include many places for which
the special powers under the Local Employment Bill are needed.[34]

The Business of Supply, which it was intended to deal with
formally, consisted of the Vote on Account for the Civil
Estimates, and Estimates for Revenue Departments, together
with Estimate for the Ministry of Defence, 1960–61. The total
sum involved was £1,370,537,000.

Before the necessary resolution could be put and agreed to,
Viscount Hinchingbrooke[35] rose.

It may seem very strange indeed to the Committee [he began] that
any back-bencher should intervene, even for only four or five minutes,
before the Committee automatically nods its acceptance to
£1,370,537,000. I venture to make a very short speech of protest
before allowing the Committee to pass to the Motion which the
Leader of the Opposition has upon the Order Paper.

Recalling that 'it used to be the constitutional function of the
House of Commons to debate policy before granting Supply',
he protested against the abandonment of 'that ancient and
honourable practice', for which he blamed the Opposition.

The Opposition [he continued] are eager to spend. Therefore, they
pass these vast sums on the nod and they relish the ensuing debate
in which the right hon. and hon. Gentlemen will open their mouths
wider than ever before in asking that more State money should be
put into their various constituencies.

Unfortunately, the Government had been 'all too eager to fall

---

[32] *H.C. Debates*, Vol. 618, cols. 196–206; *ibid.*, Vol. 619, cols. 1302–1375.
[33] Lab., Blyth.   [34] *H.C. Debates*, Vol. 618, col. 207.
[35] Cons., Dorset South.

in with this idea', as was evidenced by the tabling of a Government Amendment to the Motion shortly to be discussed. Very large sums were involved – 'a total rise of £252 million over the original Estimate of twelve months ago'. The Committee should not pass this vast increase without examining, as far as it could, 'the procedure under which these things are conducted'. A more rational and constitutional way of handling the matter would be for the Opposition to agree to surrender 10 days out of their 26 for the financial investigation of the Votes under discussion. This could be arranged through the 'usual channels'. If it were not done, the back-benchers had sanctions which they could use.

We have only to rise in our places [he concluded] on every one of the 26 Supply Days when this procedure is adopted and we should frustrate the debate subsequently to take place on those days and, in the end, oblige the Government and the Opposition to come together and agree upon a more rational procedure.

Mr. Sydney Silverman[36] then briefly intervened to rebut Lord Hinchingbrooke's allegations that the procedure under discussion had been devised 'for the benefit of Socialism'. Mr. Silverman nevertheless expressed his preference for the 'old method', whereby 'one discussed grievances before voting Supply, and not afterwards, when it is too late'.

Moderate support for Lord Hinchingbrooke's protest came from a former Conservative Chancellor of the Exchequer, Mr. Peter Thorneycroft.[37] Although he did not think it right to interfere with the debate that had been planned – for 'we have all to live together here' – he thought it right for Lord Hinchingbrooke to have taken his stand.

Further support came from Mr. J. Grimond,[38] who spoke as 'an impartial observer', and from Major H. Legge-Bourke.[39]

The Leader of the House, Mr. R. A. Butler, then rose to say that, although the objectors had a 'valid point', the House was only following 'an absolutely definite tradition' which had been 'used and taken advantage of' by the Conservatives themselves when in opposition.

That does not mean [he continued] that it was not right for my noble Friend to rise in his place and make this protest, or observa-

---

[36] Lab., Nelson and Colne.
[37] Cons., Monmouth.
[38] Lib., Orkney and Shetland.
[39] Cons., Isle of Ely.

tion, or that it was wrong for my right hon. Friend and other hon. Members to have taken part in this discussion, but it does mean that if we are to change the situation it could not be done without proper discussion between the usual channels [sic].

He offered to discuss the whole matter with any Members who wished to do so.

Mr. Hugh Gaitskell then assured the House that the Opposition was quite conscious of its responsibilities. He doubted the value of a 'wide-ranging debate on the Civil Vote on Account', and held that the Opposition did in fact use part of its time for 'doing the kind of thing' that Lord Hinchingbrooke wanted. But if there was to be 'any far-reaching change', whereby the House spent far more time discussing detailed expenditure, the Opposition was not prepared to give up its own time for the purpose.

If the Government want to make time available so that we can investigate in detail the Estimates of the Ministry of Housing and Local Government, the Ministry of Health, or whatever it may be, we should not oppose that in any way at all. It rests with the Government.

Nor would the Opposition object to 'some further study of the Committee system'.

After further support for Lord Hinchingbrooke from Mr. Nabarro[40] the Question was put and agreed to, and the House proceeded to its debate on Mr. Robens's Motion. The whole episode occupied twenty-eight minutes.

(b) *The Revolt Continues: The Second Reading of the Consolidated Fund Bill, March 16, 1960*

Lord Hinchingbrooke is nothing if not persistent. On March 16 the Consolidated Fund Bill was due to be formally 'read' a second time, the 'usual channels' having arranged that the day should be devoted to the discussion of an Opposition Motion, again moved by Mr. Robens, on National Insurance Benefits. On this occasion Lord Hinchingbrooke tabled an Amendment: to leave out from 'That' to the end of the Question and to add instead thereof:

this House, before consenting to the Second Reading of this Bill, desires to be satisfied that no improvement can be made in the

[40] Cons., Kidderminster.

machinery for the control and limitation of expenditure, as well by the supervision of the Treasury as by the informed and effective exercise of the authority of this House.

Mr. B. T. Parkin,[41] however, had evidently decided that there was no reason why Conservative back-benchers should have a monopoly of the 'grievances before Supply' slogan, and immediately rose, on the Motion 'That the Bill be now read a Second Time', to avail himself 'of the traditional right of a back-bencher, when Supply is being discussed, to raise any grievance related to the administration and connected with the affairs of the area which he represents'.

I do so on this occasion [he said] for two reasons, first, that for some time now my experience has been that in the area that I represent there have been a number of cases of breakdown of the administrative work of the Welfare State which call for greater co-ordination, which call for an improved system of welfare work to eliminate overlapping and to eliminate the waste which arises when a citizen's problem is dealt with by one Department and could have been solved only in collaboration between several Departments.

The second reason I raise today is that last week I put a Question to the Home Secretary to which the Answer was unsatisfactory and I would have been justified in seeking leave to raise it at the earliest opportunity.

It was not until Mr. Parkin had occupied the attention of the House for forty-two minutes that Viscount Hinchingbrooke got the opportunity to move his Amendment. Far from objecting to the delay, however, he congratulated Mr. Parkin on his initiative.

The hon. Member for Paddington North [he said] has used an individual key to open the door of historical access to these debates, and in doing so has put to shame the desire of the leaders of his party to suppress our ancient constitutional usages and to overformalise our proceedings.

Viscount Hinchingbrooke devoted his speech to an elaboration of the points that he had made on February 23. In support of his demand for more careful parliamentary scrutiny of expenditure he attempted to enlist 'three great authorities', viz., (1) Dr. Paul Einzig, whose book on 'The Control of the Purse' he commended; (2) Lord Campion, the former Clerk of the House, whose proposal for a united public expenditure

[41] Lab., Paddington North.

committee, made to the 1946 Select Committee on Procedure, he quoted with approval; and (3) Sir Edward Fellowes, one of Lord Campion's successors, whose suggestion for an additional Vote on Account in the Autumn he thought worthy of consideration. Lord Hinchingbrooke reiterated his hope that the Opposition would agree to devoting 10 out of the 26 Supply Days to an examination of the Estimates. He also suggested (a) that there was 'need for an up-to-date statement on financial control within the spending Departments'; (b) that the 'spending agencies of the Treasury' (e.g., the University Grants Committee and the Arts Council) should be 'hived off'; and (c) that there should be a 'pound per man' statistic, 'so that the sheer administrative cost for each £ of expenditure voted to a spending Department could be compared with previous years'.

He concluded with an appeal for economy of a kind that suggested that he was perhaps even more exercised about the total volume of government expenditure than about the 'value for money' question.

Mr. Grimond, who followed, also expressed alarm at the increase in government spending, which he attributed to the pressure exerted on Members of the House by their constituents. His main suggestion was that the House should delegate detailed consideration of expenditure to 'specialised committees'.

Further support for Lord Hinchingbrooke came from Mr. John Eden.[42]

Mr. Sydney Silverman, after deploring that Viscount Hinchingbrooke's speech had been 'complicated . . . by all sorts of party points', went on to make two 'practical suggestions'. First, he pointed out that there was nothing to stop anyone from doing what Mr. Parkin had done that afternoon.

Anybody can do that. The fact that the official channels have agreed to take the Measure formally is not binding on the House. It has never been binding on the House.

Secondly, he suggested that the objection to the present procedure was not that the official Opposition chose the subject for debate, but that, when this debate was concluded, there was no possibility of raising other grievances, because Supply had already been formally granted.

The suggestion I make is that, in any reconsideration of the matter,

42 Cons., Bournemouth West.

all that is necessary is to dispense with this procedure and restore the rights of the back-benchers on what is essentially a back-benchers' occasion.

Among the other speakers to the Amendment, one of the more interesting was Mr. Emrys Hughes,[43] whose solution to the problem was no less than a revival of the so-called 'Jowett' plan for the 'municipalising' of House of Commons procedure.

Lieut.-Col. Bromley-Davenport[44] devoted the greater part of his speech to the alleged extravagant spending of the nationalised industries, with special reference to a Gas Board training establishment within his constituency.

Major Legge-Bourke,[45] like Mr. Emrys Hughes, revived a proposal of which nothing had been heard for a long time. He believed that real financial control could be achieved only by fundamental constitutional reform, and suggested the establishment of 'something in the nature of a third House of Parliament': an Industrial House.

In his reply, Mr. Butler first dealt briefly with the specific grievances' aired by Mr. Parkin and others. Turning to Lord Hinchingbrooke's amendment, he admitted that 'there was something not quite right in the manner in which the House of Commons examines Supply'. On Treasury control, he asked the House to wait for the report of the Plowden Committee, which was examining it. On the main question raised by the Amendment, he said:

the first problem to which we must apply ourselves . . . is the extent to which the House as a whole should undertake this task of Supply and the extent to which we should delegate it to one of our existing committees, either enlarged or amalgamated, or the extent to which we should create a new committee which should report to the House.

After critically going over some of the suggestions that had been made during the course of the debate, he expressed the view that they ought to be the subject of discussion. On the general character of Supply debates, Mr. Butler, while admitting that Members preferred 'discussing policy and politics', felt that if expenditure was to be examined in more detail by a Committee, 'as a *pendant* or balance', their should also be an opportunity of considering the recommendation of that body on the floor of the

---

[43] Lab., South Ayrshire.   [44] Cons., Knutsford.   [45] Cons., Isle of Ely.

House. This statement provided Viscount Hinchingbrooke with a suitable occasion for withdrawing his Amendment, and at 7.12 p.m. the House proceeded to its discussion of Mr. Robens's much delayed Motion.

(c) The Government's Response: Mr. Butler's Statement of July 26, 1960

The discussions promised by Mr. Butler took place, both through the usual channels and with members of all three parties. On July 26 he made a statement, immediately after Question Time, advancing 'certain proposals which should be put into effect next Session'.

The Select Committee on Estimates was to be reorganised so as to be able to present Reports, in good time, on the Spring Supplementaries, and was to be 'asked to examine the principal variations between the Estimates before the House and those of the preceding year', thus providing the House 'with a basis upon which to debate Government expenditure in the autumn.[46]

New opportunities during the Session for debate on Reports from the Estimates Committee and from the Public Accounts Committee will be provided on three days on the floor of the House. One of these days will be in Government time; two will be allotted Supply days – one which the Opposition have agreed to allocate, the other to take the place of the day upon which you, Mr. Speaker, are moved out of the Chair on Civil Estimates.

On the third of these days, Private Members would therefore lose their existing opportunity to move resolutions. Mr. Butler hoped, however, that they would agree that

this day has been successfully superseded by the additional four half-days for Private Members which were allotted this Session as an experiment,[47] and which I will now say, we propose to continue next Session.

To enable the House to debate Estimates Committee Reports more regularly it was important that they 'should be made as early as possible in the Session and be somewhat shorter than at present'.

In the autumn, there would be a White Paper 'on the investment programmes in the public sector including, of course, the nationalised industries'.

[46] See below, p. 294.   [47] See below, p. 338.

In the Government's view, this White Paper and any Reports which may have been received from the Select Committee on the national-ised industries would provide suitable subjects for debate on the three days which are customarily allocated out of Government time for debates on the Reports from the various boards themselves.

The uneven distribution of Supply Days, criticised by the Select Committee on Procedure,[48] would be rectified, with the agreement of the Opposition, by making 'the necessary arrange-ments to take two or more allotted Supply Days before Christmas'.

Mr. Butler concluded by suggesting that debate on this statement should be deferred until the autumn, so that Members should have adequate opportunity to study it.

It was well received, and only Mr. Nabarro saw fit to look the gift horse in the mouth. For the Opposition, both Mr. Gaitskell and Mr. Wilson expressed their general satisfaction with it.[49]

[48] *See* below, p. 337.   [49] *H.C. Debates,* Vol. 627, cols. 1292–1302.

10

SELECT COMMITTEES

IT would have been possible, and some might think more appropriate, to deal with the four Select Committees treated in this chapter by placing each under a suitable subject heading. Thus the Public Accounts and Estimates Committees would have come under 'Finance' and the Statutory Instruments Committee under 'Delegated Legislation', while the Select Committee on Nationalised Industries might have been appended to our example of the debate on the Report and Accounts of a nationalised industry. Our decision to bring them together in one chapter was influenced by two considerations, viz: (1) that the four Committees employ similar procedures and have similar relationships to the House of Commons as a whole; (2) that, in view of the fact that the more extensive use of Select Committees to advise the House on matters of administration is a subject of current procedural interest, it seemed to us useful to describe successively the work of the existing Committees which are largely concerned with precisely this function.

It should be noted, therefore, that this chapter has a specific focus of interest, and does not attempt to cover all the Select Committees of which the House makes, or has made, use. There is no mention, for instance, of the Committee of Privileges, which is dealt with elsewhere;[1] nor are we concerned here with the *ad hoc* Select Committees, such as those on Procedure[2] which the House establishes from time to time.

1. THE PUBLIC ACCOUNTS COMMITTEE

First established in 1861, the Public Accounts Committee is certainly the most powerful, and probably the most useful, of

[1] *See* Chap. 1.　　　　　[2] *See* Chap. 11.

the select committees appointed by the House of Commons. Annually nominated by the House under Standing Order No. 90, for the examination of the Appropriation Accounts and such other Accounts as it thinks fit, it consists of fifteen members, meeting under the chairmanship of a member of the Opposition who is usually a former Financial or Economic Secretary to the Treasury. Its basic duties are (a) to report on cases where moneys granted by Parliament appear to have been expended on purposes other than those for which they were appropriated, or to be in excess of the relevant appropriations; (b) to report on any Excess Vote that may have been presented; (c) to report on the Treasury's exercise of its powers of 'virement', i.e., of provisionally authorising a surplus on a Defence Department's Vote to be transferred to another Vote of the same department, in order to cover a deficiency on that Vote; (d) to make recommendations, as the occasion may require, for improving the method of presentation of the national accounts.

In practice, its duties are wider than these. A former Chairman of the Committee, Mr. Osbert Peake, has said that it not only ensures that money is spent as Parliament intended, but considers whether due economy in the expenditure of it has been observed, and attempts to maintain high standards of morality in matters of public finance.[3] These unofficial terms of reference enable it to investigate a wide range of questions which come under the headings of 'economy' or 'financial probity', and even, as we shall see, to make recommendations with implications for government policy. Although it is supposed to be investigating past expenditure, while the Estimates Committee considers proposed expenditure, the work of the two Committees overlaps to a considerable extent, and the suggestion has been made that they should be amalgamated.[4]

The great authority enjoyed by the P.A.C. is largely due to its possession of an expert adviser, the Comptroller and Auditor-General, whose staff of about 540 is continuously at work investigating departmental accounts. As Dr. Chubb says,

The control it effects is unintelligible unless the work of checking

---

[3] See Public Administration, Vol. xxvi (1948), p. 80, and Basil Chubb: The Control of Public Expenditure (Oxford, 1952). The major part of the latter work is occupied with a comprehensive historical and analytical account of the Committee.
[4] See below, p. 322.

and audit is first understood, for the points which come before the Committee are those which remain after a complicated sifting process has been carried out.[5]

The results of that sifting process are embodied in the Comptroller and Auditor-General's Reports on the Appropriation Accounts, on which the bulk of the Committee's examination of witnesses is founded. Both the Comptroller and Auditor-General and a representative of the Treasury are regularly present, as witnesses, at the Committee's meetings, and the former maintains a close advisory relationship with its Chairman at other times.

The Committee's Reports are not only laid on the Table of the House, but sent to the Treasury, which, after consultation with the Departments concerned, produces replies to the recommendations which they contain. These replies (termed 'Minutes' and issued under the authority of 'My Lords of the Treasury') are published by the Committee of the following Session as Special Reports. (It should be noted that the Committee, although one of the best-established of parliamentary bodies, does not continue in being from one Session to another, but, like the other Select Committees dealt with in this section, is specifically appointed for each Session.)

The Committee's work is here illustrated in two ways: (1) by the Reports that it produced during the Session 1951–52; (2) by a dialogue that took place, over three Sessions, between the Committee and the Treasury about a disputed matter of finance. An account is also given of a series of Parliamentary Questions based upon recommendations contained in one of its 1950–51 Reports.

(1) *The Reports for the Session 1951–52.* The Public Accounts Committee of Session 1951–52 held thirty-four meetings, on Tuesdays and Thursdays at 4.0 p.m. At the first meeting, on November 29, 1951, the late Mr. John Edwards, a former Labour Financial Secretary to the Treasury, was 'called to the Chair'. He presided over every meeting but two, at which he was replaced by Mr. Hoy. All meetings at which evidence was taken were attended by the late Sir Frank Tribe, the Comptroller and Auditor-General, and by Mr. P. S. Milner-Barry,

---

[5] *Ibid.*, p. 169.

then a Treasury Officer of Accounts. Other Treasury representatives were called in to give evidence as the occasion required.
The heads (or deputy-heads) of the departments whose accounts
were under examination sometimes gave evidence alone, and
sometimes were accompanied by other departmental representatives.

Three Reports were issued, on February 5,[6] on May 22,[7] and
on July 24.[8] These, as usual, were later gathered together as a
consolidated volume,[9] which also included the Proceedings of
the Committee, Minutes of Evidence, Appendices and an
Index. On only one occasion, in connection with the draft of a
proposed paragraph of the 3rd Report, did the Committee
divide.

The first two Reports, as is normal, were short ones. In the
First Report, the Committee explained its reasons for continuing the practice, initiated the previous year, of 'early
presentation and publication of the Treasury Minute' (i.e., of
the replies by My Lords of the Treasury to the Reports of the
Committee of the previous Session). These were accordingly
included as an Appendix to the First Report.[10] They were
followed by Tables setting forth the Comparison of Audited
Expenditure with Exchequer Issues and by the General Abstract
of the Appropriation Accounts for 1949–50. The publication of
these with the First Report was also an innovation, as the normal
practice had been to publish them in the Summer with the
Final Report. As they had been handed in by the Treasury on
December 4, 1951, however, the Committee decided that 'no
useful purpose would be served by this delay'.

The Second Report contained the Committee's formal approval of the Treasury's exercise of its powers of 'virement' in
respect of the Service Votes.

If it had followed the previous practice, it would also have
contained the Committee's comments on the Service Accounts
themselves. On this occasion, however, the Committee stated
that although it had completed its examination of these
Accounts, it proposed to defer reporting on them until it had
received additional information which it was seeking from all
three Service Departments. As a consequence of this decision,

[6] H.C. 85.   [7] H.C. 199.
[8] H.C. 253.   [9] H.C. 85-I, 199-I, 253-I.
[10] Under present practice the Treasury Minute is published as a Special Report.

all the recommendations of the Public Accounts Committee for the Session 1951–52 were concentrated in its Third and final Report. This practice is now standard.

The Third Report began with certain 'general' animadversions, i.e., critical remarks not specifically tied to any set of Accounts. In respect of *Housing for Armed Forces and Civilian Employees*, the Committee expressed its alarm at what appeared to be excessive expenditure, saying that it was not satisfied by the evidence it had taken that the methods of control adopted by the Treasury had been fully effective in securing the degree of economy that existing economic circumstances demanded. At the same time it expressed satisfaction at the Treasury's statement to the effect that discussions were in progress concerning the 'cutting down' of 'some of the more expensive schemes', and hoped that the Treasury would have the full co-operation of the Departments in this matter. It also asked for an investigation of the rents charged by the Service Departments, to discover whether the degree of subsidisation of tenants in which they were engaging was justifiable.

In respect of *Accounting Treatment of Blocked Currency*, a highly technical matter, the Committee expressed its concern 'lest under existing arrangements funds of considerable size belonging to Her Majesty's Government might lie, as departmental assets, without the knowledge of Parliament, in the possession of foreign banks over a long period', and made recommendations designed to prevent this from happening. Determination to ensure that neither by accident nor by design should the Departments have access to funds for which they are not fully accountable to Parliament is typical of the Public Accounts Committee. This was also their concern under the third 'general' heading of the Report, viz. *Expenditure not brought to charge in Appropriation Acts*. Certain financial transactions of the Ministry of Transport and the Ministry of Agriculture and Fisheries were here subjected to criticism.

The section of the Report dealing with *Civil Appropriation Accounts* began with a criticism of the Treasury under *Class I, Vote 9. Exchequer and Audit Department. Standard of Audit*. In view of the fact that 'an efficient audit' was 'a vital factor in securing economies', the Committee was alarmed to find the Treasury 'economising' at the expense of the audit staff itself.

Under *Class IV. Vote 1. Ministry of Education*, it broached a subject later to cause a much-publicised national controversy: the actuarial position of the *Teachers' Superannuation Scheme*. A report from the Government Actuary had revealed that, although Departmental accounts of revenue and expenditure under this heading showed a surplus of £167 million at March 31, 1948, there was an actuarial deficiency of £102 million as at that date, rising to an estimated £146 million by March 31, 1952.

It therefore appears [reported the Committee] that, while the Exchequer has been and is still receiving substantial sums annually from the current excess of contributions over benefits paid, heavy burdens have been accumulating for future years. Your Committee regard this as a highly unsatisfactory situation, and they are glad to learn that means of preventing further deterioration are at present under consideration. They hope that action will not long be delayed.

It was important, not only that the actuarial position should be rectified, but that Parliament should have more frequent information about it than that provided by the septennial reports of the Government Actuary. To this end, the Appropriation and Finance Acts should include notes of estimated actuarial deficiencies and of accumulated balances.

The Report then referred to a subject that was in the course of becoming a hardy annual; *Grants to Universities*.[11] The problem here arose from the efforts of Parliament, the Public Accounts Committee, the Comptroller and Auditor-General and the Estimates Committee to exercise some supervision over the expenditure of moneys granted to the universities through the University Grants Committee. How much control could reasonably be enforced without dangerously encroaching on university independence was the question on which differences of opinion had developed. It was already clear that, whatever arrangements were finally agreed on, current (i.e., quinquennial) grants and non-recurrent (i.e., capital) grants would have to be treated differently.

In its Report, the Committee expressed its agreement with the Estimates Committee[12] that arrangements in respect of recurrent grants

are a reasonable compromise between the general desire to maintain the independence of the universities and the need for the exercise

---

[11] Class IV, Vote 11.   [12] 5th Report, Session 1951–52.

of proper financial control both by the University Grants Committee and by Parliament.

If, however, large additional grants were made during the course of the quinquennium (as had been the case during the quinquennium 1948–49 to 1951–52), further safeguards were needed

to satisfy Parliament that they are used solely for the purposes for which they are granted and to ensure that any accumulated balances of unspent special grants are not applied by the universities to the general purposes for which the quinquennial grants were made.

As for non-recurrent grants, the Committee noted with pleasure that, as from 1952–53, details of major works to which these were being devoted would be 'appended to the Estimates, for the information of Parliament', but were of the opinion that

the present system of controlling these grants, which stops short at an examination of plan and estimates, is less than Parliament is entitled and accustomed to expect when such appreciable amounts of voted money are involved.

It did not think that such an examination would involve 'any objectionable infringement of university autonomy', and accordingly recommended that this expenditure should be 'more closely controlled by the University Grants Committee and that the records of it should be open to examination by the Comptroller and Auditor-General'.[13]

The next subject, *Festival of Britain, 1951: Gifts of Public Property*,[14] again illustrates the Committee's solicitude for the maintenance of full parliamentary financial control, in matters small as well as great. The Treasury had given the Festival Office authority to offer gifts of 'scientific and artistic material' to public bodies in advance of parliamentary authorisation, provided that the Office informed the 'proposed recipients that such authority would have to be obtained'.

It may well be [commented the Committee] that the public interest called for action in advance of Parliamentary sanction in this particular case, but Your Committee would deprecate any tendency to depart from the recognised rule which requires a prior sanction. They were therefore glad to hear the Treasury say that they would

[13] The reader may find a fully documented account of the 'Grants Committee' controversy in H. V. Wiseman: *The University Grants Committee* (*Public Administration*, Spring 1956 and Summer 1957).
[14] Class IV, Vote 13.

not anticipate Parliamentary authority lightly in a minute of this kind, and they are confident that they can rely on that Department to scrutinise very closely any similar proposals they may receive from other Departments in future.

The Report then gave its attention to the major question of *National Health Services: Levels of Remuneration and Profits*.[15] In its Fourth Report of the previous Session, it had complained about the 'gaps' in Departmental knowledge of the facts relative to the 'assessment both of proper remuneration of those employed in the Services and of fair and reasonable prices for goods supplied'. Unfortunately, in its view, little progress had been made towards filling these gaps. In particular, it criticised the lack of any investigation into drug manufacturers' costs. None of the reasons advanced by the Departments concerned to justify their inaction impressed the Committee, which was particularly sceptical about the allegedly beneficent workings of competition.

To obtain information as to actual costs of production [said the Report] appears to them to be the most effective method of testing the reasonableness of any prices whose fairness is not clearly established by competition; and they would expect that in this way it might often be possible to ensure fair and reasonable prices without recourse to price control.

Emergency Housing[16] was another subject carried over from the Fourth Report of the Committee of the previous Session, which the Committee quoted to the effect that financial arrangements between the Ministry and the local authorities deprived the latter of 'incentives to economy'. It trusted that the discussions which it had recommended and which were then taking place would lead 'to at least a substantial part of the cost being borne by those local authorities'. It also found that the Ministry's authority, under the relevant Vote, to provide food at rest centres was 'challengeable'. Nevertheless, after consideration of all the circumstances, it did not feel that it would be justified in recommending disallowance of the expenditure made on this service. This passage in its report was the only one to provoke a Division in the Committee. Four members at the meeting of July 24, 1952, voted for disallowance, and four against. The Division was along Party lines, and the Chairman resolved the issue by giving his casting vote against disallowance.

[15] Class V, Votes 2 and 15.   [16] Class V, Vote 3.

The next subject was the *Exchequer Equalisation Grant* to local authorities.[17] As is well known, the distribution of this grant depended on the relative rateable values per head of (weighted) population of the various County and County Borough Councils. Consequently, to avoid the unfairness which would result from different local methods of valuation, the Inland Revenue had been given the task of conducting a uniform revaluation of rateable property throughout the country. For various reasons, however, completion of this valuation had been postponed, with the result that the grants were still being made on the basis of the old, locally-determined valuations. This worried the Committee, as it involved a probable misapplication of funds voted by the House of Commons. It therefore recommended that 'the Departments, as part of their investigations of the operation of the grants, should ascertain whether the revaluations so far made reveal serious differences in standards of assessment'. If so, they 'should consider at once whether interim adjustments for equalisation grant purposes are desirable to avoid continuing unfairness beyond the date at which Parliament expected revaluation to be completed'. It also asked the Departments to look into the problem of 'double compensation' arising from the inclusion of a 'rating resources' element in grants other than the Equalisation Grant itself.

As sufficient illustration has now been given of the Committee's general approach to its task, it is hardly necessary to summarise the remainder of the Report.

(2) *Dialogue between Committee and Treasury.* One subject, hitherto unmentioned, will now be used to provide an example of the continuity of succeeding committees' proceedings, from year to year. The Report dealt with it under the heading *Class IX, Vote 1, Ministry of Supply: Prices of Government Purchases of Iron and Steel Products.* This matter had first been raised in the Fourth Report of the Committee of the previous Session (1950–51), where it was complained that the Comptroller and Auditor-General had not been able to obtain information about the process of fixing controlled prices of iron and steel products and consequently could not advise the Committee as to the reasonableness of the prices actually paid by the Ministry for its own purchases. The Ministry had justified its refusal on the grounds that it was 'not satisfied' that the Comptroller and

17 Class V, Votes 4 and 17.

Auditor-General had the authority to examine the basis upon which it discharged its statutory responsibility for fixing the prices 'for the community generally, when the Government was no longer the predominant purchaser, subsidies, apart from those on imports, had ceased, and competitive tenders could be obtained'. The Committee of 1950–51, however, had not been satisfied with the validity of these arguments. It denied that there was effective competition, and doubted whether Government purchases represented a smaller proportion of total production than in 1937, when the Committee's predecessor had 'first asked for fuller information on costs'. Accordingly, it had asked that the Comptroller and Auditor-General should be given all the information that the Ministry possessed 'relating to the reasonableness of the prices for iron and steel products'.

In its reply, published in the Committee's First Report of 1951–52, the Treasury admitted that competition was imperfect (being, as the Ministry had already admitted, in respect of dates of delivery and not of prices), and that the Comptroller and Auditor-General had the duty to seek data on behalf of the Committee. It 'doubted', however, whether that official needed the information demanded 'in order to satisfy himself that . . . prices were fair and reasonable'. Under statute, the Ministry was obliged to fix maximum controlled prices for consumers *generally*. These were also the prices which it actually paid for its own purchases. If the Committee were permitted to investigate the fairness of these prices and the 'precise methods' by which they were arrived at, the result might be to give Government departments an unfair advantage as against ordinary consumers. As the Minister was acting under statutory authority, a *presumption* that the prices were reasonable must hold. In evidence before the Committee, the representative of the Ministry of Supply, after repeating this somewhat over-subtle line of argument, stated that the Ministry

was not prepared, unless directed by Parliament, to make available to the Comptroller and Auditor-General data which had been obtained for a purpose other than judging of the fairness of prices for government purchases.

However, the Ministry did undertake

to discuss with the Comptroller and Auditor-General to what extent their [i.e., the Committee's] purpose might be secured without trespassing on any special responsibility the Ministry might have to consumers as a whole.

In the Report under consideration, the Committee welcomed this concession, while reaffirming its disagreement with the arguments that the Treasury and the Ministry had advanced. To this, the Treasury replied as follows:[18]

My Lords regret that the Committee has not found these arguments, which were further developed in evidence and set down in the Committee's Report, convincing. Nevertheless, they appreciate the anxiety of the Committee lest they should appear to be hampered in the exercise of their normal functions by any unreasonable withholding of information which is available to the Ministry and is relevant to the prices which the Government, in common with other consumers, has to pay for iron and steel products. My Lords welcome, as do the Committee, the Ministry's undertaking to discuss this matter further with the Comptroller and Auditor-General. They for their part are anxious to co-operate in seeking a solution which will go as far as possible towards meeting the Committee's legitimate wishes.

What would have been the outcome of the discussions referred to we shall never know, for in the meantime the whole situation was altered by the passage of the 1953 Iron and Steel Act, which gave price-determining functions to the newly-established Iron and Steel Board. In its Third Report, the Committee of 1952–53 noted that as a result of this, although the Ministry's powers of price-control remained (under the Defence Regulations), it was 'quite likely that they would cease to be exercised before long'. The right of the Comptroller and Auditor-General to have access to the Ministry's price-fixing records might 'therefore become somewhat academic', and there was no point in pursuing the matter further. Nevertheless, the Committee still expected to be satisfied 'that the prices paid for Government purchases were fair and reasonable', and hoped that the purchasing Departments would provide the Comptroller and Auditor-General 'with all the information available to enable him to assist future Committees in their consideration of this matter'.

The Treasury's final word appears in the Special Report of the Committee of 1953–54,[20] which contains the following Minute:

[18] 1st Report, Session 1952–53, H.C. 48.   [19] H.C. 67.

My Lords agree that in view of the passage of the Iron and Steel Act, 1953, the proposed discussions between the Minister of Supply and the Comptroller and Auditor-General would serve no useful purpose. As they have previously emphasised, they fully accept the right of the Committee to seek to satisfy themselves that the prices paid by Government Departments for iron and steel products, as for any other goods, are fair and reasonable.

The Committee of 1953–54, for its part, was by no means slow to avail itself of this admitted right, for in its Third Report it turned its attention to the subject of the Ministry of Supply's non-competitive contracts.

Thus ended a controversy that was spread over three Sessions. It illustrates both the determination of succeeding Committees to have access to the information that they think they need for the maintenance of proper Parliamentary control, and the resistance of the Treasury and the Departments to any suspected illegitimate extension of the Committee's prerogatives in this respect. One should not, however, be led by this isolated example of disagreement to imagine that the relations between Committee and Treasury are normally unco-operative or hostile. Quite on the contrary, the two bodies are engaged in the common struggle against extravagance.

3. *The Committee and the House.* While it would be quite untrue to suggest that Members take no notice of the Reports of the Public Accounts Committee, it is a fact that they are comparatively rarely referred to in debate.[20] Apart from the record of its appointment and of changes in its membership, there are few references to the Committee in *Hansard* for the Sessions 1951–52 and 1952–53. There are, we think, three main reasons for this apparent lack of parliamentary interest, viz., (1) that much of the Committee's work is of a highly technical kind, without much obvious political significance; (2) that the Committee's most important Report of the Session is usually the last one, which is tabled at a time when the House is winding up its sessional business; (3) that, although in constitutional theory the Committee reports to the House, in fact its recommendations are aimed directly at the Treasury and the other Departments. Of these three reasons, the last is probably the most important.

[20] Changes in financial procedure which would enable Reports from the P.A.C. to be debated were announced by Mr. Butler on July 26, 1960 (*see* above, p. 277).

Nevertheless, if a Member wants a stick to beat the Government with, he can often find one in one of the Committee's Reports. An example of this is provided by the series of Questions asked by Sir Waldron Smithers[21] in June, 1951.

On June 5 he asked the Secretary of State for War[22]

if his attention had been called to the criticisms of the financial control and misappropriation of his Department's funds in Sections 9–15 of the 2nd Report of the Committee of Public Accounts, Command Paper [sic] No. 183, and what action had been taken to prevent a repetition of these and similar practices.

The Minister replied that his attention had been so called and briefly explained the steps he had taken. Three further Questions, two of them about stores accounting and one about the finances of the Territorial Army, similarly based on H.C. No. 183, also received replies from Mr. Strachey.[23]

On the following day it was the turn of the Admiralty and the Air Ministry, both of whom were asked what action they intended to take about misappropriations revealed in the Public Accounts Committee's Report. Mr. Callaghan and Mr. Henderson gave explanations.[24] Two further Questions asked by Sir Waldron Smithers of Service Ministries on June 7 were also based on information contained in the Report.[25]

All these Questions had received written answers, but later in the month Sir Waldron had the opportunity to fire a much heavier gun, on the floor of the House. His subject was the expenditure of £400,000 on Changi Airfield, which had been criticised in Sections 33–37 of the same Report; and he wanted to know whether the Air Minister, Mr. Henderson, would 'take steps to reorganise the branch of his Department which was concerned with the making of contracts such as that concerned in this case'. Mr. Henderson replied that he shared the Committee's regret at the waste involved, that he had already, in an answer of April 11, explained the circumstances of the case, that the responsible organisation was the Air Ministry Directorate of Works and not the Air Ministry Contracts Branch, and that the trouble was due to defects of judgment and not defects of organisation. This answer gave rise to a number of Supplementaries, at the end of which Mr. W. Fletcher[26] announced that in

[21] Cons., Kent, Orpington.
[22] Mr. John Strachey.
[23] H.C. Debates, Vol. 488, Written Answers, col. 90.
[24] Ibid., Written Answers, cols. 118–119, 128–129.
[25] Ibid., Written Answers, cols. 139–140.
[26] Cons., Bury and Radcliffe.

view of the unsatisfactory nature of the Minister's replies he intended to raise the matter on the Adjournment.[27] There is no record of his having had the opportunity to do so.

2. The Select Committee on Estimates

By comparison with the Public Accounts Committee, the Select Committee on Estimates has had a brief and chequered history. First established in 1912, it was discontinued during the First World War (although eventually replaced by a National Expenditure Committee), revived in 1921, discontinued again (and again replaced by a National Expenditure Committee) during the Second World War, and re-established in 1946.

Originally, the idea was that it should look at and report on the Estimates from the 'economy' angle, thereby doing what the House was notoriously failing to do on its Supply Days. Even the hope was expressed that the Committee might have reports ready for the various Supply debates, so that Members, being provided with expert guidance through the mass of semi-intelligible figures, could really talk about expenditure on those occasions. These ideas and expectations bore no fruit, and, indeed, so long as the Committee continued to think of its functions in the light of them, it achieved very little and had so low a reputation that Members were reluctant to serve on it. For there was no point in having a Committee to duplicate, inexpertly, the functions that the Supply Division of the Treasury was already performing; and the desire to make Members, with appropriate assistance, economy-minded rather than politically-minded on Supply Days has never been realised more than sporadically, although recently-announced changes in Estimates procedure, described above[28], represent one of the most determined attempts, so far, to induce them to get their noses down to the financial grindstone.

It was not until the Estimates Committee decided to adopt the outlook and methods of the two war-time National Expenditure Committees (which had not been tied to Estimates, because there were none) that it began to acquire both utility and status. This was in 1946, since when the reputation of the Committee has been steadily climbing. The outstanding fea-

[27] *H.C. Debates*, Vol. 489, cols. 1357-1359.   [28] pl. 277-278.

tures of the post-war Estimates Committee, in contrast with
those of the pre-war one, are: (1) that it largely disregards the
Estimates *qua* Estimates, using them mainly as a starting point
for investigations of administrative efficiency, designed to discover whether the taxpayer is getting his full 20s. worth of value
for every pound spent; (2) that to do this more effectively it
divides itself into sub-committees, each of which has the
assistance of House of Commons clerks. Its formal terms of
reference, however, have not changed since 1921. They are:

To examine such of the Estimates presented to this House as may
seem fit to the Committee, and to suggest the form in which the
Estimates shall be presented for examination, and to report what,
if any, economies consistent with the policy implied in those
Estimates may be effected therein.

The more important Reports of this Committee now receive
very adequate notice in the more serious newspapers, and
occasionally get into the columns of the popular press –
particularly, of course, if some major sin of commission or
omission has been discovered. Sometimes they are specifically
debated, and nearly always provide material for Questions and
for speeches. But even if the House appears to take no notice
whatever of an Estimates Committee Report, it by no means
represents wasted effort; for it is sent to the Department or
Departments with which it is concerned, and these always consider and express opinions on the proposals and suggestions that
it contains.

The work of an Estimates Committee is very closely related
to that of the Public Accounts Committee, and contact between
them is ensured by appointing the Chairman of the former a
member of the latter. In 1946, Lord Campion, in evidence to
the Select Committee on Procedure, proposed that the two
Committees should amalgamate to form one 'comprehensive
Committee on Public Expenditure'. The Government, however,
resisted this proposal and little has been heard of it since.

On July 26, 1960, important modifications in the work of the
Estimates Committee were announced by Mr. Butler.[29] The
membership of the Committee would be increased, in the
following Session, from 36 to 43, in order to allow it to set up an
additional sub-Committee, which, Mr. Butler hoped, would be

[29] *H.C. Debates*, Vol. 627, cols. 1292–1294.

able to 'examine and report briefly upon the Spring Supplementary Estimates'. The production of such a Report would 'become an early and urgent task for the Committee each Session'.

It is also proposed [the Leader of the House continued] that the Committee, in addition to its detailed examination of selected Estimates, should be asked to examine the principal variations between Estimates before the House and those of the preceding year. Its Report would provide the House with a basis upon which to debate Government expenditure in the autumn.

Additionally, new opportunities would be provided during the Session for debating Reports from the Estimates Committee (and also from the Public Accounts Committee) on the floor of the House. Three days would be allotted for this purpose, one in Government time, and two from the allotted Supply days – 'one which the Opposition have agreed to allocate, and the other to take the place of the day upon which you, Mr. Speaker, are moved out of the Chair on Civil Estimates'.

If the House was thus to debate Estimates Committee's Reports more regularly, some change in their character and timing would be required. They 'should be made as early as possible in the Session and be somewhat shorter than at present'.[30]

The Select Committee on Estimates, 1953–54: The Civil Defence Report. Eight Reports were issued by the Select Committee on Estimates for the Session 1953–54. The first of these, on Civil Defence,[31] was the work of the previous Session's Committee.

Of the other seven, five[32] received departmental replies during the course of the Session. Replies were also received to two of the previous Session's Reports – on Rearmament and the Post Office.

The Session's work was planned by the Committee at its first meeting on December 2, 1953, when it also issued the completed Civil Defence Report. As usual, six sub-committees were set up; five to examine Estimates and one, generally known as the

[30] The best information on the Estimates Committee is to be found in Basil Chubb: *The Control of Public Expenditure* (Oxford, 1952). *See* also A. H. Hanson: *The Select Committee on Estimates, 1945–50,* in *Yorkshire Bulletin of Economic and Social Research,* Vol. 3, No. 2, July, 1951,

[31] H.C. 19, December 2, 1953.

[32] Civil Defence, Grants in Aid, British Field Products, Fire Services and Regional Organisations.

co-ordinating sub-committee, to 'consider matters relating to the Estimates which are of general interest to the Committee, and the allocation of Estimates to sub-Committees for examination'. This was to consist of the Chairman of the Committee, the Chairmen of the five investigating sub-committees, and three additional members. To each of the investigating sub-committees eight members were appointed. The Committee then allocated to each sub-committee a group of Estimates, specifically indicating the subject that it was expected to examine. Thus, for instance, sub-committee D was given a long list of Classes and Votes 'so far as these Estimates relate to expenditure on Regional Organisations'; while sub-committee E's shorter list contained the proviso 'so far as these Estimates relate to expenditure on the staff of and buildings for, the Foreign Office'.[33]

In this 'case' we shall be concerned with the Civil Defence Report, which was the work of sub-committee C of the previous Session's Estimates Committee. The Report of this sub-committee, of course, came before the full Committee for consideration, and was approved by it.

The Report began by specifying the Estimates relevant to Civil Defence which the Committee had examined, and the Departments and other bodies from which it had taken evidence.

The scope of the inquiry was explained in the following words:

They have limited their inquiry to the progress and administration of Civil Defence mainly in England and Wales, and have not extended it to cover arrangements made by the Service Departments for passive defence. Your Committee's task has been to examine how it is proposed to spend the sum of over £40 million during the current year, and in doing so, it has been necessary to examine how money voted in the previous four years has been spent. The policy behind this Civil Defence programme is not the concern of Your Committee, even if they were competent to judge it, but it has been found impossible to consider expenditure except in the context of the political decisions reached by this or previous Governments.[34]

To make precise sense of the last sentence of this statement is neither possible nor necessary. It was clearly intended to show that the Committee, having found real difficulty in separating

[33] *First Special Report, 1953–54*, H.C. 20.
[34] Civil Defence Report, 1953, pp. x–xi.

'policy' from 'administration', had virtually abandoned the attempt to do so. An unusually 'political' and controversial Report might therefore be expected.

The first main section dealt with the 'Machinery of Planning and Control'. Largely descriptive, this was intended 'to establish clearly how the activities of the various Departments are co-ordinated, how policy decisions are taken and enforced and with whom the final responsibility for the size and efficiency of the Civil Defence programme really lies'.[35] It contained no specific recommendation, but contrived to indicate a certain uneasiness.

The following section, on the 'Planning and Progress of the Civil Defence Programme', was more overtly critical. The Committee pointed to the considerable short-fall on estimated expenditure for the two years 1951–52 and 1952–53, and found the fact that Departments had over-estimated their expenditure during those two years by 75 per cent. a 'disquieting one'. 'These figures', they said, 'show that little attention has been paid to the Civil Defence plan'.[36]

The Departments concerned with Civil Defence, the Committee considered, had had 'no plans which were . . . precise in content or in the time by which they should be completed'.[37] The policy seemed to be that of 'a little progress on all fronts', rather than one of 'giving priority to certain projects'. In respect neither of capital works nor of equipment had any clear sense of priorities been displayed.

Coming to the Civil Defence Services themselves (i.e., the Civil Defence Corps, the Auxiliary Fire Service and the National Hospital Service Reserve), the Committee again found cause for disquiet. Of the Civil Defence Corps, they wrote:

The question really is whether to continue the façade of a Civil Defence Corps on a national scale or whether the duties which it was set up to perform would not be carried out more economically if they were to revert to being purely local authority functions.[38]

The A.F.S. was 'rather better', because there was a 'country-wide peace-time organisation on which to build'; but delays in reaching decisions about water-storage facilities and the stock-

[35] *Ibid.*, p. xiv.   [36] *Ibid.*, p. xvii.
[37] *Ibid.*, p. xvii.   [38] *Ibid.*, p. xxxiv.

piling of piping caused anxiety, and there was 'some doubt' about the adequacy of liaison in respect of this service between the counties and the boroughs. Liaison was also weak – indeed, almost non-existent – between the local authorities and the Hospital Boards, which were responsible for the National Hospital Service Reserve. This was serious, as it meant that there was an unfilled gap in the casualty services. The trouble appeared to arise from the difficulty of reconciling different departmental views on the subject.

Civil Defence Training Establishments seemed to the Committee to be in reasonable shape, but they saw no excuse for the schools not being filled to capacity (recommending that Commanders should be given authority to fill vacancies at short notice), and criticised the conditions of service for the instructional staff. What impressed them most was the Experimental Mobile Column at Epsom. Indeed, their admiration for it gave them a 'line' for the next, and in some respects most important, part of their Report, entitled 'Comparison between Expenditure on Various Civil Defence Services and Organisations'.

Here they emphasised both the value and the cheapness of mobile columns, and suggested that it would be

a far more satisfactory peace-time foundation for Civil Defence if a number of skeleton mobile columns were created side by side with a much smaller Civil Defence organisation on a local basis.[39]

While not suggesting that mobile columns were an unique answer to Civil Defence problems, they recommended that urgent consideration should be given to the balance of expenditure between the Civil Defence Services and mobile columns.

Under 'Financial Procedure', they criticised the variations in grant rates for different services, having been 'informed that these . . . were based on nothing more substantial than the history of what happened in the last war'; and expressed their amazement

that nearly five years after the passing of the Civil Defence Act which made it obligatory for the designated Ministers to lay regulations before Parliament for approval, not one of these statutory instruments authorising grants had been so laid.[40]

[39] *Ibid.*, p. xi.   [40] *Ibid.*, p. xliii.

This omission had been criticised by the Public Accounts Committee in the Session 1950–51, but apparently without effect.

On accounting procedure, they expressed the view that it was both

inefficient and wasteful that the division of responsibility for the welfare section of the Civil Defence Corps should result in the local authorities having to make separate claims on the Home Office, the Ministry of Housing and Local Government, the Ministry of Health and the Ministry of Food for the expenses they incur on the training and administration of this one section of the Corps.[41]

They suggested that this could be avoided if the Home Office were used as paying agent. They also sympathised with the local authorities' complaints at having to seek specific permission for the expenditure of small sums, and recommended that a 'system of annual estimates', as for the fire services and the police, should 'receive urgent consideration'.[42]

In their conclusions, they emphasised lack of planning, imprecision in allocating priorities, over-estimating, delays in taking decisions, poor co-ordination, and wasteful expenditure as the main vices of the Civil Defence set-up. That they took a very unfavourable view of the whole organisation was obvious, but they evidently felt that they had to engage in a certain amount of circumlocution in order to avoid the charge of going beyond their terms of reference.

As might be expected, the House paid far more attention to this controversial document than it does to most of the Estimates Committee's Reports.

On January 21 the Home Secretary, Sir David Maxwell-Fyfe, was asked if he had 'taken note' of the Select Committee's Report 'dealing with the inadequacies of Civil Defence' and, what action he proposed to take. Sir David replied that he was considering the Report together with his colleagues and that he hoped soon 'to be in a position to deal with the criticisms made by the Select Committee on the *policy* (our emphasis – A.H.H. and H.V.W.) and administration of Her Majesty's Government'.[43]

On January 26 Brigadier Clarke[44] asked the Prime Minister if he would consider transferring responsibility for Civil Defence from the Home Office to the Ministry of Defence for

[41] *Ibid.*, p. xliv.   [42] *Ibid.*, p. xlv.
[43] *H.C. Debates*, Vol. 522 Written Answers, cols. 185-186   [44] Cons., Portsmouth West.

better co-ordination; and Mr. Emrys Hughes[45] asked him whether, in view of the Select Committee's disclosures, he would appoint a 'new Minister of Cabinet rank with the sole duty of dealing with problems of Civil Defence'. The Prime Minister[46] rejected both suggestions, and, on being pressed by Supplementaries, said that the existing arrangements had been carefully considered between the military and civil authorities and worked satisfactorily. The exchange concluded with an announcement by Mr. Emrys Hughes to the effect that he intended to raise the matter on the adjournment.[47]

Two days later, in reply to a Question from Mr. Ian Harvey,[48] the Home Secretary took the rather unusual step of circulating a rather lengthy Written Answer dealing with the Select Committee's criticisms.[49] This gave expression, in measured terms, to the Government's annoyance with the Committee for going beyond its terms of reference and attempted to repair the damage done to the ministerial reputation by its incursion into 'policy' matters. The distinction between what were, in the Home Secretary's view, the legitimate and the illegitimate activities of the Committee was firmly made in the first two paragraphs, which ran thus:

After consultation with, and on behalf of, all the Ministers concerned with Civil Defence, I have sent to the Select Committee a memorandum dealing with the recommendations which come within their specific terms of reference and are consistent with the policy implied in the Estimates relating to Civil Defence.

Apart from such matters, the Select Committee in their Report have made certain criticisms of the policy of Her Majesty's Government. These criticisms are largely based on a misapprehension of the policy governing Civil Defence preparations which has been pursued both by Her Majesty's Government and by the previous administration, and it is therefore necessary for me to restate that policy, even though it has frequently been explained in the annual statements on Defence and in speeches by Ministers.

The Home Secretary went on to state that 'deterrence' was the main object of defence policy, and that the priorities given to the various aspects of Civil Defence had been 'carefully selected' in the light of this general principle. Over-estimating was inevitable in a new and experimental field, and its extent

---

[45] Lab., South Ayrshire.   [46] Mr. Winston Churchill.
[47] H.C. Debates, Vol. 522, cols. 1604–1606.   [48] Cons., Harrow East.
[49] H.C. Debates, January 28, Vol. 522 Written Answers, cols. 272–278.

was being reduced. As for the allegations of 'extravagance and inefficiency', Her Majesty's Government regretted the implication that the 'progress made' did not reflect 'great credit' on all concerned. Delay in making Regulations, which could not be avoided when such complicated matters were under consideration, had not meant 'the slightest hold-up'. In any case, complete agreement had now been reached between the Government and the local authorities, and the Regulations had in fact been made on December 3, 1953, and were now in force. Certain other delays criticised by the Select Committee were equally explicable. As for the alleged lack of balance in equipment-purchasing policy, the Government of course recognised that uniforms and sandbags were not all that was needed, but the substantial stocks of sandbags accumulated had proved very useful during the East Coast floods.

Finally, Her Majesty's Government do not accept the Committee's conclusion about the absence of leadership, direction and guidance, and they regret that the Select Committee should have seen fit to criticise officials for matters for which Her Majesty's Government are solely responsible. As regards the machinery of Government, Her Majesty's Government are satisfied that the policy of assigning Civil Defence responsibilities to the departments with whose normal functions they are most closely related is right and that the existing organisation for the co-ordination of departmental measures of Civil Defence which follows an accepted and well-tried patttern is appropriate for dealing with the position at any rate in the present stage of development.

This statement was subsequently printed together with the Departmental Reply, dealing with the Committee's 'legitimate' criticisms, to which Sir David Maxwell-Fyfe had referred.[50] This Reply, couched in that rather remarkable civil service language that contrives to be simultaneously clipped and circumlocutory, was almost equally unyielding. A proposal that continued membership of the Civil Defence Corps should be conditional upon each volunteer 'achieving and maintaining certain standards of training within certain specified periods' was 'not accepted'. The suggestion that commandants of colleges should be given authority to fill vacancies on courses was not considered to be of 'any advantage'. Ideas for the more efficient running of the Staff College were said to be already in

[50] February 3, 1954, H.C. 74.

'practice'. The view that the Civil Defence Corps was extravagant and inefficient was rejected. Although it was proposed to introduce a system of annual estimating by local government authorities, it was not 'thought practicable to treat these estimates as the basis of approval of global expenditure'. 'All possible steps' were being taken to ensure greater accuracy of estimating. 'As at present advised', the Government considered nothing further need be done to provide a 'more compact and economical direction of the Civil Defence effort'. There were, however, certain concessions made to the Select Committee's point of view. Its proposals for a clearer and more intelligible presentation of the Civil Defence Estimates (the details of which hardly concern us in this context) were promised 'consideration'. A suggestion that the personnel of future mobile columns should be drawn either from the Army or the Air Force, but not from both, would also be 'considered'; and 'consideration' was being given to the possibility of expanding the mobile column organisation. Lastly, a proposal that 'a nucleus of first-class personnel should be established on a permanent basis in the various training schools and in mobile columns' was accepted 'in principle'.

During February, further Questions, clearly inspired by the Select Committee's Report, were put to the Home Secretary, several of them by Mr. Albu, the Chairman of the investigating sub-committee.

In the Defence Debate, held on March 2, after Mr. Strachey had referred to 'the most scarifying picture of the actual state of Civil Defence preparations under the present Government' presented by the Select Committee's Report, the Parliamentary Secretary to the Ministry of Defence[51] announced what amounted to the acceptance of one of the Committee's major recommendations, when he revealed that details were being worked out for the use of men trained in the forces as a Civil Defence reserve. In the Air Estimates Debate two days later, Mr. de Freitas,[52] while deploring the 'weakness' of this scheme, said that it represented a 'tremendous concession' made by the Service Departments and expressed the hope that the Air Ministry would 'make this work'.[53]

Another *de facto* acceptance of one of the Select Committee's

[51] Mr. Birch.   [52] Lab., Lincoln.
[53] *H.C. Debates*, Vol. 524, col. 1559.

proposals had already been made, on February 25, when the Home Secretary announced that it had been decided that the Civil Defence Staff College 'should have an established cadre'.[54]

A new and ominous note was introduced into the House's discussions on Civil Defence on April 1, when Mr. Emrys Hughes and Mr. George Thomas[55] asked the Home Secretary about the H-Bomb, the first explosion of which had just taken place.[56] It might have been considered that this dreadful development had made both the Government's plans and the Select Committee's criticisms of them virtually obsolete. Nevertheless, Mr. Albu continued to ask the Home Secretary Questions on the Report, and this document was again used by Members in their speeches in a full-scale Supply Debate on Civil Defence, held on July 5, 1954.[57]

Only Mr. Henry Brooke[58] ventured to suggest that the Committee had been wrong in any essentials, or that it had erred in going beyond its terms of reference, and a spirited defence of its attitudes and recommendations was undertaken by Mr. Albu himself. He considered that the Estimates Committee was 'perfectly entitled to say so if it thought that the administration of a Department was inefficient and lacked leadership and direction'.[59]

The Report on Civil Defence, therefore, after weathering a few storms, appeared to be winning acceptance for what it was – a document which, although controversial, was serious and non-partisan, and which raised issues far too grave to be the mere sport of party rivalry. One must beware, however, of over-estimating the excitement that it caused – as can easily be done when the discussion on it is isolated, for purposes of analysis, from the other proceedings of Parliament. Not a large number of Questions were inspired by it, and the Civil Defence debate from which we have just quoted was by no means a great parliamentary occasion.

3. THE SELECT COMMITTEE ON STATUTORY INSTRUMENTS

That the House should establish a Committee to scrutinise delegated legislation was first suggested by the Report of the

[54] *H.C. Debates*, Vol. 524, cols. 566–567.   [55] Lab., Cardiff West.
[56] *H.C. Debates*, Vol. 525 Written Answers, col. 227.
[57] *H.C. Debates*, Vol. 529, cols. 1794–1831; 1832–1914.
[58] Cons., Hampstead.   [59] *Ibid.*, col. 1880.

Committee on Ministers' Powers, published in 1931. Not until 1944, however, was such a Committee set up, and then with terms of reference considerably different from those that the Report had suggested. In origin, the Select Committee on Statutory Rules and Orders (as it was then) represented the war-time Coalition Government's response to the complaints of back-benchers, on both sides of the House, that Parliament was quite unable to exercise any effective control over the spate of subordinate legislation issued under the authority of the 'emergency' Acts. Although conceded with some reluctance, it has been appointed annually ever since, and now constitutes a minor but useful part of the parliamentary machine with which the House is not likely to wish to dispense. A Select Committee on Delegated Legislation, which sat and reported during the Session 1952–53, spoke favourably of its work.

The Committee's terms of reference, as summarised by *Erskine May*, are as follows:

to draw the attention of the House to provisions which (i) impose a charge on the public revenues, (ii) are made under an enactment which excludes challenge in the law courts, (iii) appear to make some unusual or unexpected use of the powers conferred by the statute, (iv) purport to have retrospective effect where the parent statute does not so provide, (v) have been withheld from publication or from being laid before Parliament by unjustifiable delay, (vi) have not been notified in proper time to the Speaker in cases where they come into operation before being presented to Parliament . . ., or (vii) call for elucidation of their form or purport.[60]

It will be noted that, according to a strict interpretation of these terms of reference, the Committee is concerned solely with what might be summarised as the constitutionality, regularity and intelligibility of Statutory Instruments, and not with their 'merits' (i.e., with the policy that is embodied in them). The fact that the day-to-day task of scrutinising Statutory Instruments is undertaken, on its behalf, by the Counsel to Mr. Speaker (who at each meeting presents the Committee with a memorandum on the Instruments before it), tends to ensure that those Instruments that are brought to its notice are the ones to which objection might be taken on 'technical' rather than on 'policy' grounds. Many of them, in fact, are politically of minimal importance, as can be seen from the examples that follow.

[60] *Erskine May*, 16th ed., p. 857.

The Committee, therefore, occupies a modest corner, where it lives a comparatively unexciting life. But its existence may be said to have a salutory effect upon those responsible for framing delegated legislation, who appear to approach their task with greater care than they did when there was no Committee.[61]

The account that follows is of the work of the Committee during the Session 1955–56.

During this Session – an unusually long one, lasting from June, 1955, to November, 1956 – the Select Committee on Statutory Instruments held twenty meetings, at each of which Statutory Instruments were considered and resolutions passed. At one meeting oral evidence was taken. Six Reports were made, to draw the House's attention to six Statutory Instruments which appeared to display objectionable features. Twelve Instruments to which there were *prima facie* objections were considered by the Committee, but not reported to the House. By resolution, the Committee decided that, in the light of its terms of reference, 76 Instruments requiring an affirmative resolution from the House and 498 Instruments subject to 'prayers'[62] were unobjectionable.

At its first meeting, on June 23, 1955, Mr. Eric Fletcher was 'called to the Chair'. A Resolution was passed, in standard form, to the effect that:

it is unnecessary to draw the special attention of the House to the following Statutory Instruments and drafts requiring affirmative resolutions . . . or to the following Statutory Instruments. . . .

The Committee then ordered

That the Secretary of State for Foreign Affairs be requested to submit a memorandum in explanation of the Draft International Organisations (Immunities and Privileges of Western European Union) Order, 1955.[63]

From its second meeting, on July 5, 1955, emerged the following Report on the above Instrument:

Your Committee have considered the Draft International Organisa-

---

[61] A good general account of the Committee's work is contained in B. Schwartz: *Law and the Executive in Britain* (Cambridge, 1949). *See* also: *Public Administration*, A. H. Hanson: 'The Select Committee on Statutory Instruments, 1944–49' (Winter, 1949); H. Stacey: 'The Select Committee on Statutory Instruments' (Winter, 1950); A. H. Hanson: 'The Select Committee on Statutory Instruments, a Further Note' (Autumn, 1951); and E. H. Beet: 'Parliament and Delegated Legislation, 1945–53' (Autumn, 1955).
[62] *See* above, pp. 203–205.   [63] H.C. 16.

tions (Immunities and Privileges of Western European Union) Order, 1955, a copy of which was presented to the House on 14th June, 1955, and are of the opinion that the special attention of the House should be drawn to it on the ground that it purports to have retrospective effect when the parent Statute confers no express authority so to provide.

Appended to this Report, for information, were (*a*) the letter sent, on behalf of the Committee, by its Clerk, Mr. F. G. Allen, to Sir Gerald Fitzmaurice, of the Foreign Office, explaining the grounds of the Committee's *prima facie* objection to the Order and asking for 15 copies of an explanatory memorandum by Friday, July 1; (*b*) the memorandum, thus requested, issued in the name of the Secretary of State for Foreign Affairs.

This Memorandum admitted that the Order, the purpose of which was to grant exemption from income tax to certain international officials, was retrospective in its effect, but denied that this was in any way improper. It was based upon what was believed 'to be the intention and proper interpretation' of the International Organisations (Immunities and Privileges) Act, 1950, which contained 'no express provision either authorising or prohibiting Orders in Council made under it to be given retrospective effect'. Furthermore, it followed the precedents set by Orders previously made under the Act in respect of the International Wheat Council, the Customs Co-operation Council and North Atlantic Treaty Organisation. The Memorandum continued by explaining why it was administratively necessary and reasonable, as well as constitutionally proper, that the Order should have been given this form. The Act under which the Order was made enabled certain 'immunities, privileges and capacities' to be granted by Order to International Organisations and 'persons connected therewith'. Section 1 (1), together with the Schedule, provided that that Section, which was the 'main source of authority for the present Order', should apply to any organisation declared by Order in Council to be an organisation of which the United Kingdom and one or more foreign sovereign powers were members. By implication, therefore, it was contemplated that the Government should have become a member of the organisation concerned before the date on which an Order was made conferring immunities, privileges or capacities, on the organisation. Indeed, in some cases the Government could not become a member without accepting the provisions of the organisation's constitution providing for the conferment of the immunities, privileges or capacities. In any case, the practice was to ratify the agreement with the relevant foreign powers before provision had been made to give effect to the consequent obligations, where such obligations were subsidiary to the main purpose of the agreement. If this were not so, there might be 'intolerable delay in the ratification and entry into force of important agreements'. Moreover, as all international agreements were laid before Parliament prior to ratification, it was always open to Parliament to object to their provisions. Turning from the general to the particular, the Memorandum stated that this particular Order was required to give effect to an agreement on the status of the Western European Union, its national representatives, and its international staff. This agreement had been signed in Paris on May 11, 1955. It was not yet in force, but Article 28 (2) provided that it should enter into force when the Protocols to the Brussels Treaty, signed in Paris on October 23, 1954, themselves entered into force. These Protocols were in effect as from May 6, 1955. Her Majesty's Government were therefore under an obligation to provide the necessary exemption from income tax with effect from that date.

It is submitted [the Memorandum concluded] that this Agreement is a particularly good illustration of the need to interpret the Act as authorising Orders in Council made under it to be given retrospective effect. On any other interpretation it would be impossible for Her Majesty's Government to accept all the obligations under an agreement in the terms of the present one.[64]

This Memorandum has been summarised at some length because it is in many ways typical. It provides a detailed reply to the Committee's criticisms. It justifies the Instrument on three grounds, viz., (1) that it is based upon a proper interpretation of the powers conferred by the parent Act; (2) that it is similar to other Instruments considered unobjectionable by the Committee; and (3) that it could have been made in no other way without involving administrative inconveniences. Most of the Departmental replies tend to follow this pattern.

The Committee 'reported' this Order, despite the explanation given by the Foreign Office, and did not attempt to

[64] H.C. 16-II.

justify its action by 'explaining away' the explanation. It never does enter into printed argument, as a Committee, but contents itself with reporting an Order under the appropriate heading of its terms of reference, and leaves Parliament to judge from the annexed evidence – which usually consists of no more than the Committee's letter to the Department concerned and the Departmental reply – whether 'special attention' to the Order is required.

At the same meeting that produced this Report, the Committee ordered that the Ministry of Agriculture, Fisheries and Food and the Secretary of State for Scotland should be asked to provide memoranda on the Food Standards (Table Jellies) (Amendment) Order, 1955, No. 828, and the corresponding Order for Scotland. Presumably these Memoranda satisfied the Committee, for at its next meeting it included these two Orders in this list of those to which no objection need be made.[65]

At its next five meetings[66] it found *prima facie* objection to only four Instruments, on which it called for Memoranda, but issued no Reports. Its Second Report, dated February 14, 1956,[67] dealt with the Police (Overseas Service) (Cyprus) Regulations, 1955, No. 1852, which the Committee had found *prima facie* unacceptable at its previous meeting on January 31. This Instrument was now reported as 'unusual and unexpected', after the Committee had taken the comparatively rare step of hearing evidence from the relevant Department (the Colonial Office) as well as considering its Memorandum. The Committee's objections to the Regulations, as expressed in its letter addressed to Mr. Lemberger, of the Colonial Office, were (1) that they 'involved legislation by reference' of a particularly objectionable kind, in so far as the reference was 'not to the law even of this country but to that of Cyprus, with such unspecified modifications as may be necessary'; (2) that they provided for matters that were outside the scope of the parent Act, in so far as they implied that, to come within their ambit, a man must be a member of the Cyprus Police Force.

The Committee's Third Report[68] was also concerned with 'unusual and unexpected use', the reported Instrument being the Prevention of Damage by Pests (Application to Shipping) (Amendment) Order, 1956. In this case, alleged sub-delegation

[65] *Proceedings* of July 29, 1955, H.C. 16-III.   [66] H.C. 16-IV to VIII.
[67] H.C. 16-IX-I.   [68] H.C. 16-X, February 28, 1956.

constituted the only objection. The Secretary's letter to Sir A. A. Weston, of the Ministry of Agriculture, said:

In allowing the appropriate Minister to prescribe the charges, whose making and recovering it authorises, the Order in Council constitutes a sub-delegation not authorised by the principal Act.

As such, moreover, it enabled a 'charge to be imposed which would not be subject to Parliamentary control'.

The Fourth Report[69] addressed itself to the Derbyshire (New Streets) Order, 1956,[70] the form of which, it considered, called for elucidation. What the Committee complained about was that, although the application of the parent Act, by Order, to a Rural District Council was conditional upon a request by the appropriate County Council that it should be so applied and upon previous consultation with the Rural District Council itself, there was no specific reference to such proceedings in the Derbyshire Order. The Committee, therefore, had no means of knowing whether the prescribed application and consultation had actually taken place. Such doubts might be dispelled if subsequent Orders of this kind declared that the necessary conditions had been fulfilled.

In its Fifth Report, the Committee returned to one of its favourite subjects: sub-delegation. The Teachers' Superannuation (Approved External Service) Amendment Rules, 1956,[71] displayed, in its opinion, 'unexpected use' of the powers conferred 'inasmuch as paragraph (ib) of Rule 2 appears to add, as a category of service to be treated as approved external service, . . . any employment approved by the Minister of Education'.

The Sixth and last Report,[72] employed the 'unexpected use' clause, rather oddly, to object to the inadequacies of an Explanatory Note accompanying the Provision of Clothing (Amendment) Regulations, 1956.[73]

To the best of our knowledge, none of these Reports received any mention on the floor of the House during the Session 1955–56. Of the twenty 'prayers' moved during the course of that Session, none dealt with an Instrument to which the

[69] H.C. 16-IX, March 13, 1956.
[70] No. 153.
[71] No. 262.
[72] H.C. 16-XV, June 5, 1956.
[73] No. 559.

'special attention' of the House had been drawn by the Committee. In this respect, as in respect of the kind of work that the Committee undertook, the Session was a typical one.

4. THE SELECT COMMITTEE ON NATIONALISED INDUSTRIES (REPORTS AND ACCOUNTS)

The proposal to establish a Select Committee to inform and advise the House of Commons on the affairs of the nationalised industries was originally advanced by Mr. Hugh Molson in an article in *The Times*.[74] It was approved of by the second Report of a Select Committee established in 1951 to 'consider the methods by which the House . . . is informed of the affairs of the Nationalised Industries' and to report 'what changes . . . may be desirable'.[75] The first Committee of the suggested type was set up in 1955. Instructed to 'examine the Reports and Accounts of the Nationalised Industries' and to 'obtain further information' about their 'current policy and practices', it was simultaneously debarred from considering matters which '(*a*) have been decided by or clearly engage the responsibility of any Ministers; (*b*) concern wages and conditions of employment and other questions normally decided by collective bargaining arrangements; (*c*) fall to be considered through formal machinery established by the relevant Statutes; or (*d*) are matters of day-to-day administration'. These terms of reference proved so restrictive that on November 14, 1955, the Committee reported that it had 'insufficient scope to make inquiries or to obtain further information which would be of any real use to the House'. A year later, on a government motion, a new Select Committee was constituted, with terms of reference as wide as those of its predecessor had been narrow. It was given the duty of examining 'the Reports and Accounts of the Nationalised Industries established by Statute whose controlling Boards are appointed by Ministers of the Crown and whose annual receipts are not wholly or mainly derived from moneys provided by Parliament or advanced from the Exchequer'.

Appointed on Thursday, December 20, 1956, the Committee consisted of thirteen members. It elected Sir Patrick Spens Chairman and, after seventeen meetings, produced a Report[76]

---

[74] September 8, 1949. [75] *See* H.C. 235 of 1953.
[76] H. of C. Paper 304 of 1956–57.

dealing generally with Ministerial control of the Nationalised Industries and specifically with the affairs of the North of Scotland Hydro-Electric Board. Reappointed on Wednesday, November 27, 1957, with two changes of membership, it held fifteen meetings, under the Chairmanship of Sir Toby Low, before producing another Report on the National Coal Board. Some of the evidence on which this Report was based had been taken by the previous Session's Select Committee.

It is with the latter Report, dated April 29, 1958, that we are principally concerned. Largely factual in character, it provided the student of the coal industry with much valuable information difficult or impossible to obtain from other sources. From consideration of the evidence received it drew seven conclusions, of which one of the most important was as follows:

Your Committee approve the purpose of the 'Gentlemen's Agreement', under which the Minister of Power exercises control over coal prices, but they do not like its informality. The Board, when proposing alterations in coal prices, should consult the Minister as to the public interest and, having done so, should then take full responsibility for their price determinations. The Minister should have power to give the Board specific directions in relation to prices in the national interest, but this power should be statutory and its use disclosed to Parliament.[77]

This recommendation, the object of which was to enable Parliament and the public to 'be fully informed about the respective responsibilities of the Minister and the Board in a particular case',[78] followed a searching examination of the *modus operandi* of the 'Gentlemen's Agreement', during the course of which witnesses from the Ministry of Power were closely questioned. This was part of a wider inquiry into the relationships between the Ministry and the Board.

The House's 'coal' debate on July 14, 1958,[79] was the second occasion on which it had a Report from this Select Committee for its information and guidance (the first being the Debate on the North of Scotland Hydro-Electric Board). The Parlia-

---

[77] H.C. 187-I of 1957–58, p. 26.   [78] *Ibid.*, p. xviii.
[79] *H.C. Debates*, Vol. 591, cols. 825–946. The terms of the Motion were 'That this House takes note of the Report from the Select Committee on Nationalised Industries . . . and of the Annual Report and Statement of Accounts of the National Coal Board for 1957'.

mentary Secretary to the Minister of Power,[80] in his opening speech, congratulated the Select Committee on 'a fair and objective Report',[81] but disagreed with some of its recommendations. He said that the suggestion that the Coal Board should lay before the House its reply to the Report of the Select Committee was 'a mistake', as 'after all, the Ministry of Power is responsible to Parliament for the industry and it is felt that the proper thing to do is for the Government to inform the House of their views and of the views of the Board'.[82] He also rejected the Committee's proposals on the 'Gentlemen's Agreement', saying that the Government felt that it was 'inescapable in this matter that responsibility should be shared, and . . . that to introduce a formal direction would be a very grave step and would hinder the proper relations between the two'.[83] Of the recommendation that 'the price of coal should be increased to cover the full cost of depreciation on a replacement basis', he said that 'it certainly should not be given high priority', at which point Sir Toby Low intervened to say that the Committee 'did not make any such clear recommendation that the price of coal should be increased at once'. The Board, said Sir Ian, had 'doubts' about the recommendation that 'the limit given to divisional authorities for capital expenditure should be increased', but was 'considering the point'. Two recommendations, however, were accepted, viz., (1) that the Board's annual reports 'should include comparisons of results achieved from its investments with the estimates made' (This recommendation, said Sir Ian, was 'acceptable to the Board'.); (2) that 'the Ministry of Power should make a greater financial check upon the Board's investment schemes, particularly the marginal ones'. The Parliamentary Secretary made it rather obvious that acceptance of the latter recommendation was in the nature of a sop thrown to the Committee. 'The Government', he said, 'feel that the information furnished by the Board is a sufficient check, but they accept the Committee's recommendation and are making arrangements with the Board for action along these lines'.[84]

When, in 1956, the motion for the establishment of the Select Committee had been before the House, the Opposition had been highly critical, and had actually divided the House on

---

[80] Sir Ian Horobin.
[81] *H.C. Debates*, Vol. 591, col. 842.
[82] *Ibid.*, col. 843.
[83] *Ibid.*, col. 843.
[84] *Ibid.*, cols. 843–845.

an amendment, proposed by Mr. Callaghan,[85] to the effect that

this House, while recognising the need for improving arrangements for Parliamentary discussion of the affairs of the Nationalised Industries, does not consider that the appointment of the proposed Select Committee is the appropriate way of dealing with this problem.[86]

It is therefore of interest to note that, on the occasion with which we are now dealing, Mr. Alfred Robens,[87] the front-bencher who opened for the Labour Party, announced his conversion to the Select Committee idea. He went on the criticise the Government's rejection of the Select Committee's recommendation on the 'Gentlemen's Agreement'.

We in this House and the public outside [he said] do not know exactly what fight is going on between the Government and the National Coal Board. We do not know whom to blame for what takes place. When, as a consequence, we examine the accounts and are critical about the losses made – the Parliamentary Secretary referred to the £30 million deficit – whom are we to blame? Should we blame the Government for preventing the Board obtaining proper prices or should we blame the Board for its inefficiency in not having its prices properly attuned?[88]

In general, the Select Committee had an excellent reception from all parts of the House. The only speaker in the debate who voiced doubts about its value was Mr. Shinwell,[89] who had not, like Mr. Robens, undergone a 'conversion'. On the 'Gentlemen's Agreement', he announced that he accepted the Government's view and rejected the Committee's.[90]

Of the eleven back-benchers contributing to the debate, four were members of the Select Committee. Among them was the Committee's Chairman, Sir Toby Low,[91] who presented a reasoned justification of its recommendations. On the nature of the Committee and the kind of work which it was fitted to perform, he made the following judgment:

I do think that it is an extremely good thing that a Committee carrying out an inquiry like this is a Committee of laymen, because the worst thing we could do in this House would be to set up from among ourselves a body of men who thought that they were experts in the matter and who might try to blur the responsibility of the

---

[85] Lab., Cardiff South-East.
[87] Lab., Blyth.
[89] Lab., Durham, Easington.
[91] Cons., Blackpool North.

[86] *H.C. Debates*, Vol. 591, col. 604.
[88] *Ibid.*, cols. 852–853.
[90] *Ibid.*, col. 901.

Coal Board, the House of Commons, the Minister and the Parliamentary Secretary.[92]

He also tried to lay to rest the fears, expressed in 'Government and Parliament' by Mr. Herbert Morrison and evidently still retained by certain members of the Opposition, that 'the Committee might develop into a body of anti-nationalisers and pro-nationalisers, who might use the Committee for the purpose of discrediting public ownership, on the one hand, or, on the other, for the purpose of seeking to say that the work of the Board was perfect'. That, he said, with complete justification, 'was not done; there was an objective analysis'.[93]

In his concluding speech for the Government, the Paymaster-General[94], on congratulating the Select Committee on its work, said:

It is a remarkable thing that such a Report could receive so wide a measure of agreement in this House. On some previous occasions it would have been almost unthinkable to have such a report from a Select Committee on the coal industry which would meet with such general approval. This reflects credit not only on the members of the Select Committee but on those who gave evidence before it. It must be a fairly frightening thing for the most seasoned people to give evidence for the first time before a Select Committee of this House, and we are indebted to them for the clear and helpful way in which their evidence was laid before it.[95]

Since then, and up to the time of writing, the Select Committee has produced three further Reports. Its very substantial examination of the Air Corporations appeared on May 14, 1959;[96] on July 28, 1959, it published a Special Report recommending that it should be provided with expert assistance;[97] and July 11, 1960, saw the publication of its *chef d'oeuvre*, the Report on British Railways.[98]

One cannot say, as yet, whether the Committee will become a permanent part of the machinery of the House of Commons. Its immediate future, however, seems to be assured. Few Members now doubt the value of the work it is doing, and the question currently under discussion is not whether it shall be continued but how it can improve its methods of investigation.

[92] *H.C. Debates*, Vol. 591, col. 883.
[94] Mr. Reginald Maudling.
[96] H.C. 213 of 1958–59.
[98] H.C. 254 of 1959–60.

[93] *Ibid.*, col. 884.
[95] *H.C. Debates*, Vol. 591, col. 935.
[97] H.C. 276 of 1958–59.

There seems to be general agreement that it needs more than the services of House of Commons Clerks; but even the Committee itself is not prepared to demand that it should be equipped with an official of the status of the Comptroller and Auditor-General.[99]

[99] As had been originally suggested in H.C. 235 of 1952–53.

11

THE HOUSE CONSIDERS ITS PROCEDURE

1. THE SELECT COMMITTEE ON PROCEDURE, 1945–46

WHATEVER government might have been in power, it was inevitable that parliamentary procedure should receive an overhaul at the end of the Second World War. With a Labour Government in power, the need was all the greater, because the large-scale programme of social and economic change to which Labour was committed could not but impose new strains on an already overstrained parliamentary machine. The new government, therefore, lost no time in appointing a Select Committee[1] 'to consider the Procedure in the Public Business of this House and to report what alterations, if any, are desirable for the more efficient despatch of such business'. It was instructed, in particular, to 'report as soon as possible upon any scheme for the acceleration of proceedings on Public Bills which may be submitted to them on behalf of Her Majesty's Government', and, to this end, was permitted to meet during the Parliamentary recess. This permission it employed to such good effect that it was able to produce its First Report[2] by October 16, 1945.

The 'scheme' on which it was asked to report had originally been drafted by a committee of Ministers of the Coalition Government, but had never received Cabinet approval. Its most important part consisted of 'Proposals for Expediting the Committee Stage of Bills'.

On most of these proposals the Committee reported favourably. It agreed, for instance, that substantially all Bills should be referred to a Standing Committee, the main exceptions being (a) Bills of first-class constitutional importance, and (b) small,

---

[1] August 24, 1945. [2] H.C. 9-I.

non-contentious Bills. This would involve only making fuller use of a procedure for which existing Standing Orders already provided. It also agreed that as many Standing Committees should be appointed as were 'necessary expeditiously to dispose of the Bills coming up from the House', and saw 'no procedural reason' for continuing the limitations on number imposed by Standing Order 47 (1), i.e., five, including the Scottish Standing Committee. To enable more Committees to be appointed, it proposed that the size of each Committee, apart from the Scottish Committee, should be reduced to a maximum of 50 (instead of 85). There should be a permanent nucleus of 20, and not more than 30 Members appointed in respect of each particular Bill. The Quorum should be 15. The constitution and quorum of the Scottish Committee should not be changed.

To enable these Committees to cope more expeditiously with their assignments, the Government Memorandum proposed that the number of sitting hours per week should be increased substantially over the pre-war minimum of four. The Select Committee agreed with the suggestion that morning sittings should be extended from 2 to $2\frac{1}{2}$ hours (10.30 a.m.–1 p.m.), but felt doubtful about the expediency of prescribing three (instead of two) sitting days, considering that this should be 'regarded as an expedient to relieve congestion, rather than as a normal practice'. With the proviso that 'there should be no further inroad into the already severely curtailed time available to Private Members', it supported the proposal that an adjournment of the House might be moved at the commencement of Public Business so as to permit Committees to sit concurrently during the afternoon. This would involve a re-enactment of Standing Order No. 49A, which had been repealed in 1933.

Its main disagreement with the Memorandum related to the machinery proposed for prescribing and enforcing a time limit on the proceedings in Standing Committee. The Memorandum favoured a 'special type of guillotine resolution', specifying the time to be occupied by each of a Bill's stages, and a Special Emergency Business Committee to subdivide the Committee stage. The Select Committee considered that the guillotine resolution should do no more than name the date by which the Bill should be reported, and that the subdivision of the Committee stage should be the responsibility of a 'business sub-committee' of the Standing Committee, consisting of its

Chairman and seven other members nominated by the Speaker.

Of the two remaining proposals on Committee procedure contained in the Memorandum, the Select Committee agreed with one and rejected the other. It agreed 'that fuller use should be made of the practice by which the Minister in charge of the Bill circulates to the Committee notes on any clauses which are not readily understood without explanation'. It rejected, as neither desirable nor necessary, the suggestion that, if a Clause had been amended, debate should not be permitted on the motion 'That the Clause stands part of the Bill' unless the Chairman was of the opinion 'that the principle of the clause, or any substantial point arising thereon' had not been adequately discussed.

The remainder of the Committee's First Report dealt with 'Minor Changes in Financial Procedure on Bills'. It rejected the suggestion that, when the Financial Resolution on a Bill was reported to the House, the Question should be put without amendment or debate; for it considered that the saving of time thereby would be 'negligible' and that debate might be important if the Government had amended the Resolution. It 'saw no objection', however, to the suggestion that the rule which prevented two stages of a Financial Resolution being taken on the same day should be abandoned, provided that the right of any Member to object to this procedure was preserved. Two other suggestions on financial procedure it relegated as more appropriate to a later stage of its inquiries.

Action on the Committee's First Report was swift. No immediate amendments to Standing Orders were made, but the Government, on November 15, secured the agreement of the House to a number of sessional orders which modified Standing Orders (i.e., for the duration of the Session) in such a way as to give effect to certain of the Committee's recommendations which required formal procedural changes for their operation. (It should be noted that the House had previously agreed, in 1939, to this method of temporarily modifying Standing Orders 'to meet varying conditions of emergency'.[3]) The number of Standing Committees was raised to as many as necessary, the membership of each reduced to a maximum of 50 (20 'nucleus' *plus* not more than 30 appointed for a particular Bill), and the morning sittings extended to two and a half hours. Business

[3] *See Erskine May*, 16th ed., p. 321.

Sub-Committees were provided for Standing Committees, the adjournment of the House was permitted to facilitate concurrent Committee sittings, and the Law Officers of the Crown given *ex officio* membership of Standing Committees, without vote. Resolutions of Money Committees were to be 'reported forthwith', if the House agreed.

The Second Report, entirely devoted to Questions and Divisions, appeared on January 24, 1946. It rejected suggestions made to it by witnesses that the number of permitted oral Questions per Member per day should be reduced from three to two, and that there should be certain procedural changes designed to restrict opportunities to ask Supplementaries. It agreed that the period of notice for oral Questions should be extended from twenty-four hours to two days (with an 'extension' for week-ends), and that Departments should be expected to provide written answers within seven days and to reply to letters from Members within a fortnight. It rejected a variety of proposals, including mechanical voting systems, designed to reduce the amount of time spent on Divisions, and on this subject did not go beyond expressing the hope that some saving of time would be effected when the new Chamber was built.[4]

This Report called for little action by Parliament, but the main recommendation that required a modification of Standing Orders was put into effect within two months. On March 22, after a brief debate, the House passed a sessional order modifying paragraph 4 of Standing Order No. 7 in such a way as to extend the period of notice for oral Questions to two days.

In the meantime, the Committee had begun to take the evidence on which it was eventually to base its third, most substantial and most controversial Report, which appeared on October 31, 1946. The pattern and inspiration of this document was provided by a 'comprehensive scheme for the reform of Parliamentary procedure' prepared by Sir Gilbert Campion, the Clerk of the House. Sir Gilbert's Memorandum, printed as an Appendix to the Committee's Third Report,[5] is one of the most important and thought-provoking criticisms of parliamentary procedure ever produced.

The Report began by comparing the tasks facing the Select

---

[4] The old Chamber had been destroyed by enemy action in the Second World War.

[5] H.C. 189-I.

Committee with those that had faced its immediate predecessor of 1931-32.

The problem facing that Committee was how to adapt procedure to the growing pressure of business, a problem which, as they recognised, was by no means new and presents itself 'in almost every elective assembly in countries where modern views as to the powers and duties of the State are finding expression'. The problem facing your Committee is fundamentally the same – in the course of the intervening fifteen years it has only become more acute. But the atmosphere in which Your Committee approach their task is entirely different from that in which the former Committee found themselves. The country was then undergoing a time of severe economic stress, of industrial depression and widespread unemployment, and there was a tendency to criticise all the institutions of government, including Parliament itself. Correspondingly, many of the remedies proposed to that Committee were of a kind which would have fundamentally changed the whole character and function of Parliament. Your Committee have been appointed at a time when the country has recently emerged from a war in which parliamentary activity was maintained and contributed in large measure to its successful prosecution. Consequently there is not at the present time any strong or widespread desire for changes in the essential character of the institution. Indeed, the prestige of Parliament has probably never been higher.[6]

Consequently, it did not feel called upon to 'consider or recommend any proposal to alter the essential character of the House of Commons'. But it recognised that the 'overwhelming burden' which the 'growth of Government activity' had placed on Parliament made certain procedural adaptations necessary, for, as Sir Gilbert Campion had remarked, parliamentary procedure always tended 'to be a little out of date'.

Following Sir Gilbert's Memorandum, it grouped its major recommendations under the headings of (a) Legislation, (b) Control of Policy and Administration, and (c) Control of Finance. To these it added two further sections, respectively entitled 'Private Members' Business' and 'Miscellaneous Proposals'.

Under 'Legislation' it first considered Sir Gilbert's scheme for the reorganisation of Standing Committees, designed to speed up and 'streamline' the legislative process. Sir Gilbert had proposed that a Standing Committee should become responsible for the Report stage as well as the Committee stage

[6] Report, p. v.

of its Bill. This rather radical proposal did not commend itself to the Select Committee, which agreed with the Speaker's view that it would involve a 'drastic interference with the rights of private Members'. The Committee also considered that it would have an adverse effect on the opportunities for smaller parties to contribute to the legislative process, and stressed the danger that 'bottlenecks' in Standing Committee might appear.

Rejection was also the fate of an alternative proposal, made by representatives of the Government, that at the Report stage of a Bill debate should be restricted to the consideration of (a) Government amendments, (b) points left over for consideration from the Committee stage, and (c) any new points arising after the completion of the Committee stage. Also rejected was Sir Gilbert Campion's proposal that the Second Reading of Scottish Bills might be undertaken by the Scottish Standing Committee.

On Control of Policy and Administration, the Committee gave attention to four major criticisms of the existing procedure by Sir Gilbert Campion, viz., (1) that a disproportionate amount of time was spent on the discussion of Supplementary Estimates; (2) that, whereas Supply Days were needed throughout the session, in fact they were confined to the period from February to July; (3) that debate on Supply Votes afforded 'at best a very rough-and-ready peg on which to hang a criticism of administrative policy'; and (4) that the rules excluding reference to legislation in Committee of Supply were restrictive and anomalous.

To rectify the first and second of these defects, Sir Gilbert proposed that the time spent on Supplementary Estimates and in 'moving the Speaker out of the Chair' should be included in Supply Days, the number of which should be increased to twenty-eight, spread out evenly over the whole Session. The Committee agreed with this, provided that it would involve no curtailment of the time normally made available to the Opposition. A further suggestion from Sir Gilbert, to the effect that there should be a fixed day for the taking of Supply each week, it considered impracticable, but nevertheless expressed the opinion that in so far as this could be arranged it would be of 'convenience' to the House.

For the rectification of the third and fourth defects, Sir Gilbert proposed (a) that debate on amendments to the question 'That Mr. Speaker do now leave the Chair' might be introduced as an alternative to the 'normal' Supply Debate, and (b) that when this alternative was used the rule about references to matters requiring legislation should be waived. The Committee rather cautiously recommended 'that as an experiment the new procedure should be permitted on four other allotted days – the choice of the four days to be settled by agreement between the Government and the Opposition through the usual channels'.

There could thus be not more than eight allotted days on which debate would be on an amendment to the question 'That Mr. Speaker do now leave the Chair', and there would seem to be no longer any advantage in specifically allocatting one each to the Army, Navy, Air and Civil Estimates.

On parliamentary control of administration, the Committee agreed with Sir Gilbert that 'the amount of time devoted to really administrative points, so far from tending to increase with the growth of administrative activity', had 'greatly diminished'. In considering how to rectify this anomaly, however, it confined its attention entirely to the field of delegated legislation (i.e., to the most formal and generalised kind of exercise of administrative authority). Considering that opportunities for parliamentary supervision of delegated legislation were 'extremely limited and not altogether satisfactory' (an average of 1.6 days per session), it viewed with some sympathy Sir Gilbert Campion's suggestion that the terms of reference of the Select Committee on Statutory Rules and Orders (the predecessor of the present Select Committee on Statutory Instruments) should be extended to enable it to examine a Rule or Order, not merely from the standpoint of its legality and constitutional propriety, but also 'from the point of view of its efficiency as a means of carrying out the purposes named by the governing Act'. The final decision of the Committee, however, was that the 'delegation of legislative power' raised issues which went beyond its terms of reference. Accordingly it recommended that in the coming Session a Select Committee or Joint Committee should be appointed to inquire into the whole matter.

Under the general heading 'Control of Finance', taxation and expenditure were separately considered. On taxation, the Committee had before it a Government-sponsored proposal to 'formalise' the Report stage of the Budget Resolutions. The purpose of this was to avoid what the Government representatives considered to be a wasteful duplication of debate. The Committee, however, rejected it, mainly because it 'would still further curtail the opportunities of Members for taking part in one of the most important debates of the year'.

On control of expenditure, the Committee gave its blessing to Sir Gilbert Campion's controversial proposal for the merging of the Public Accounts Committee and the Estimates Committee in a Public Expenditure Committee. It recognised that there were objections to this course of action, but considered them outweighed by the advantages that would accrue. It also considered that the Reports of such a Committee might be given precedence on not more than two Supply Days.

On Private Members' Business, it recommended an early restoration of Private Members' time (in abeyance since the beginning of the war), and, in particular, the reintroduction of facilities for the bringing in of Bills under the 'Ten Minute Rule'.[7] It also recommended that Private Members' time should be distributed more evenly throughout the session.

However, it rejected Sir Gilbert's suggestion that balloting for the right to introduce Bills and Motions should be replaced by precedence according to volume of support, recommending instead that

there should be a single ballot for Bills and Motions. Members successful in the ballot would have the choice of either introducing a Bill or moving a Motion and according to their place in the List would have precedence in choosing a Friday.

It deplored the 'progressive decline in availability' of Emergency Adjournment Motions under Standing Order No. 8, and recommended that the rules about the acceptance of such Motions should be given a 'less narrow interpretation', and that 'the time spent on the motion should automatically be made up by exempting the superseded business for the corresponding amount of time'.

Having already provided, by sessional orders, for the widening of those procedural bottlenecks most likely to cause immediate embarrassment, the Government was in no great hurry to express its views on the Committee's Third Report.

[7] S.O. No. 10.

Although the Report was presented to the House on October 31, 1946, it was not until March 17, 1947, that the Lord Privy Seal, Mr. Arthur Greenwood, presented the Government's attitude towards its recommendations.[8] The Government, he said, were in general agreement with the proposed reorganisation of Supply procedure, but wished to have twenty-six instead of twenty-eight Supply days and to remove all limitations on the introduction on Supply days of the Motion, 'That Mr. Speaker do now leave the chair'. It opposed the suggested inquiry into parliamentary supervision of delegated legislation, on the ground that more experience was needed of the working of the Statutory Instruments Act of 1946. It also opposed the suggested creation of a united Public Expenditure Committee from the existing Select Committees on Public Accounts and Estimates. As for Private Members' time, it agreed that the Select Committee's proposals should be put into effect *when* Private Members' time was restored. Of Government suggestions rejected by the Committee, three were to be persisted with: (1) The Report stage of the Budget Resolutions should be taken without amendment or debate, i.e., 'formalised'. (2) There should be a Committee of the House (consisting of the members of the Chairman's Panel together with five others) 'with the function of sub-dividing the time allocated, by guillotine resolution or voluntary agreement, to the Committee stage of any Bill taken on the Floor of the House, and to the Report stage of all Bills'. (3) In Committee proceedings, the Chairman should have the power to disallow debate on the Motion, 'That the Clause stand part of the Bill'.

As these intentions were announced by a formal statement in reply to a Question, there was no debate on them. The House had to wait until November 4, 1947, before the Government made debating time available. By that date it had the necessary amendments to Standing Orders ready to present to the House for its approval.[9]

The Question to which the Debate was 'pegged' was, 'That the Third Report of the Select Committee on Procedure be now considered'. The first speaker, Mr. Herbert Morrison, immediately moved, 'That this House approves the proposals contained in the statement made by the Lord Privy Seal on

[8] *H.C. Debates*, Vol. 435, cols. 29–32.
[9] *H.C. Debates*, Vol. 443, cols. 1547–1790.

17th March, 1947, arising out of the recommendations of the Select Committee on Procedure'. Mr. Morrison's speech consisted of a general review of the Committee's work and a reasoned defence of the Government's proposals. No summary of his arguments is necessary, but his explanation of the Government's attitude towards the 'sub-dividing committee' deserves noting. The original proposal had been for a special 'Emergency Business Committee'. This had been rejected by the Select Committee in favour of a 'business sub-committee' for each Standing Committee. The Government had accepted this proposal and given effect to it in sessional orders, but now also wished to make provision for the allocation of time in respect of Bills whose committee stages were taken on the Floor of the House and in respect of the Report stages of all Bills. This was the purpose of the Lord Privy Seal's proposal. The Committee it was proposed to establish had the advantage that it 'would be able to deal not only with allocations of time fixed by allocation of time orders but also with allocations made by voluntary agreement between the various parties in the House'.[10]

The Debate that followed was not an outstanding one. Few Members paid consistent or sustained attention to the general principles governing the procedure of the House; most preferred to talk about the easier and more popular topics of increased time for private Members, time limits to speeches, etc.

This general debate was followed by the introduction of new Standing Orders and amendments to existing ones, so as to give effect to the proposed procedural changes. Some of these, of course, involved no more than the permanent incorporation in Standing Orders of procedures already operating, on a temporary basis, by authority of the sessional orders first introduced by the Government on November 15, 1945.[11] All of the new and amended Orders attracted debate, and most were divided against.

As these Orders embodied the major procedural changes made by the Government after its consideration of the Select Committee's Reports, it will be useful to summarise their effect, and to indicate where the relevant Orders may now be found in the revised Standing Orders book:

[10] *H.C. Debates*, Vol. 443, col. 1560.   [11] *See* above, p. 317.

Changes Made	*Relevant Order (1958)*
New procedures in Committee of Supply (i.e., number of Supply days, March guillotines, etc.) . . .	16
Wider use of the motion, in Committee of Supply, 'That Mr. Speaker do now leave the Chair', and exemption of debates on Amendments to this Motion from the Rule forbidding references to matters requiring legislation	17
Power of a Money Committee to report its Resolution to the House 'forthwith'	84
'Formalising' of the Report Stage of the Budget Resolutions	86 (2)
Appointment of a 'business committee' to allot time for the various stages of a Bill considered in Committee of the whole House and on Report	41
Chairman of a Committee of the whole House given discretionary power to disallow debate on the Motion 'That the Clause stand part of the Bill' . . .	45
Changes in numerical membership of Standing Committees and in number required for a quorum . .	57 and 58
Changes in the times of meeting of Standing Committees	63
Appointment and duties of 'business sub-committees' of Standing Committees	64
Attendance of the Law Officers at the meetings of Standing Committees	65
The 'making up' of time on business postponed through having been interrupted by a debate on an 'emergency adjournment' motion	9 (2)
Possible adjournment of the House, at the commencement of public business, to facilitate the concurrent meeting of Standing Committees.	10
Longer period of notice for Questions requiring oral answers	8

Further amendments to Standing Orders to cover matters considered by the Select Committee were few and of minor importance, with one exception. On April 28, 1948, new Standing Orders for Scottish Business were adopted. These were quite out of line with the Select Committee's recommendations on this subject. By S.O.s 60 and 61 it became possible to refer Scottish Bills to the Scottish Standing Committee for what amounted to a second reading, and in the same Committee to hold the discussion of Scottish Estimates.[12]

---

[12] Further amendments relating to Scottish business (affecting S.O.s 57, 59, 60 and 61) were made on December 18, 1957: *see H.C. Debates*, Vol. 450, cols. 400–458, and Vol. 580, cols. 514–568.

In sum, the above changes were so extensive that the Government came to the conclusion that revision of the Standing Orders book was needed. Accordingly, the House appointed a Select Committee on Standing Orders (Revision). It presented its Report in the summer of 1948, and on July 28 of that year the House resolved that the existing Standing Orders should be replaced by those recommended by the Committee in the Appendix to its Report.[13]

Of changes in practice recommended by the Select Committee on Procedure but not requiring any amendment to Standing Orders, the most important were the increase in the number of Standing Committees to six and the restoration of private Members' time (rearranged in accordance with the Committee's recommendations) in 1949.

One of the new procedures has never yet been brought into operation. At no time has an adjournment of the House been moved at the commencement of public business to enable Standing Committees to meet simultaneously in the afternoon.[14] Another new procedure, enabling debate on an amendment to the motion 'That Mr. Speaker do now leave the chair' on *any* Supply day (provided that the motion is moved by a Minister) has been used rarely.

The best secondary source on most of the post-war changes in parliamentary procedure described above is Chapter X of Lord Morrison's *Government and Parliament*.[15] This may be supplemented by reference to the Hansard Society's mimeographed volume entitled *Parliamentary Reform, 1933–1958*.[16]

2. THE SELECT COMMITTEE ON PROCEDURE, 1958

The reasons for establishing another Select Committee on Procedure in 1958 were very different from those responsible for the establishment of the 1945 Select Committee. The immediate cause was a Private Member's Motion moved by Mr. A. E. Oram[17] on January 31, 1958.[18] The Debate which followed indicated some of the considerations which Members

---

[13] *H.C. Debates*, Vol. 454, cols. 1344–1352.
[14] *See Parliamentary Reform, 1833–58* (Hansard Society), p. 102, and *Parliamentary Affairs*, Vol. IX, No. 3.
[15] Oxford, 1954.   [16] Chap. III.
[17] Lab., East Ham South.   [18] *H.C. Debates*, Vol. 581, cols. 669–771.

had in mind when agreeing that a Select Committee on Procedure should be set up.

Mr. Oram began by referring to the major difficulty of time. The long string of supplementaries after the Business Question on Thursdays, asking for additional debates, suggested that something was wrong. Were the hours of sitting the most sensible? Were powers of judgment at their highest in the late evening? Would not morning sittings more often than on Fridays be feasible and wise?

As to the use of time, too often the Chamber was occupied by groups of specialists examining with meticulous care the details of complex legislation; that might be done better by an extension of the use of committees. Further, too many important reports went undiscussed in the House because of the lack of time for general debates.

There was also the vexed question of the length of speeches. Should there be a time limit? And what of the custom that Privy Councillors enjoyed precedence in being called whenever they wished to speak?

Mr. Wedgwood Benn[19] began by rebutting the current charges about the declining standards of M.P.s themselves, and went on to suggest that neither the frequent attacks on the party system nor the cry for more free votes went to the root of the problem.

What is wrong is that, faced with a complexity of public business and a huge volume of complicated Government legislation it is impossible for us to keep abreast of all the important issues which confront us.[20]

Mr. Benn was in favour of greater Committee work, though he did not want to see every Department surrounded by a group of 'expert' M.P.s. The two main functions of M.P.s were, first, to shape policy, secondly, to act as watchdogs. Neither was satisfactorily performed.

Sir Robert Boothby[21] thought that there was grave danger that the House would gradually cease to exercise any effective control over the Executive in the fields of public expenditure and administration. Standing Committees, he thought, were the answer. All Bills, except possibly the Finance Bill, should

[19] Lab., Bristol South-East.
[21] Cons., Aberdeenshire East.
[20] *H.C. Debates*, Vol. 581, col. 679.

go upstairs, and when Committees were fully at work the House should not sit at all.

Mr. Geoffrey de Freitas[22] said that many Government back-benchers felt frustrated because there was so little they could do. He would even take the Finance Bill upstairs, as well as many detailed aspects of departmental administration. On the Floor of the House they should restrict themselves to 'a Second Reading atmosphere'.

Sir Spencer Summers[23] added that a minor defeat in the Committee stage of a Bill, wherever it was taken, should not be regarded as a world-shaking event justifying the Government's resignation. He also wanted better facilities for 'pairing' to avoid unnecessary waiting about in the expectation of a Division.

Sir Robert Cary[24] wanted a more orderly and expeditious way of dealing with Questions. Mr. Glenvil Hall[25] saw merit in the limiting of speeches. He would also reduce the number of Questions which a Member could put for Oral Answers to two per day and restrict the number of supplementaries.

Mr. Peter Kirk[26] wanted more time to debate important topics like the Wolfenden Report, and more regular consideration of the Reports of the Select Committees on Estimates and Public Accounts. It might be possible further to save time if all but the most important Bills were considered on the lines of Private Bills, with experts giving their testimony to four Members. Certainly there should be permanent committees for special subjects and such committees ought to meet when the House was not sitting and even during Recesses.

Mr. Ellis Smith[27] spoke mainly of modernising Supply procedure. Mr. Anthony Kershaw[28] wanted more time for general debates but feared that if more work were taken upstairs proceedings might, in fact, be prolonged.

Mr. Shinwell[29] was almost alone in suggesting that procedure was not a topic of burning interest, but he agreed that all Bills should go upstairs for the Committee stage, and possibly even for the Report Stage. There were occasions when the House need not meet at all and five or six Committees might be in operation.

[22] Lab., Lincoln.
[24] Cons., Manchester, Withington.
[26] Cons., Gravesend.
[28] Cons., Stroud.

[23] Cons., Aylesbury.
[25] Lab., Colne Valley.
[27] Lab., Stoke-on-Trent South.
[29] Lab., Easington.

Mr. R. Gresham Cooke[30] had returned to England impressed by the way the United States Congress managed to get in as many as fifty or sixty speakers in a six-hour debate. Mr. Martin Lindsay[31] thought that there were too many all-night sittings, and also that it was most inconvenient to have a Division at 3.30 p.m. on a Motion to suspend the Ten o'clock Rule.

The Leader of the House, Mr. Butler, then rose to present the Government's view. It was clear to him as Leader of the House that the time was ripe for a further examination. The basic problem was 'to find a way between the leisure to decide major issues here and . . . the frustration which hon. Members experience through being here for hours on end . . . and then ending up the day with a Division which . . . is always a fore-gone conclusion. . . .'[32] He was not, however, enamoured of the suggestion that the Government need not regard themselves as being defeated on every occasion when they were 'overstepped in a Division by the other side'. That raised the fundamental issue of Parliament today – that they were there in a 'struggle for power'.

The real problem was that of devolution. More matters might be referred to Select Committees or Standing Committees. The suggestion that the Finance Bill should go upstairs was a possibility, though that was 'not in accordance with our traditional or our constitutional development'.[33] In regard to the nationalised industries, the immense complications of social legislation, and our modern mercantile State, 'there should be methods ancillary to this Chamber that feed this Chamber with the major issues and do a great deal of the detailed work'.[34]

But Mr. Butler was firm on the question of specialised com-mittees on finance, economics, defence, foreign affairs, etc. Such committees would create 'something absolutely opposite to British constitutional development, because the fact that there is a certain degree of power and authority delegated to those Standing Committees in America, and in a different way in France, is largely due to our friend Montesquieu. Their Constitution is different from ours. The Executive does not sit, and is not perpetually badgered and bullied, in the legislature itself. The Executive is not part, as Ministers are here, of the

[30] Cons., Twickenham.
[31] Cons., Solihull.
[32] H.C. Debates, Vol. 581, col. 759.
[33] Ibid., col. 761.
[34] Ibid., col. 762.

legislature itself. . . . It is almost impossible to reconcile a system of Standing Committees *à l'Américain* with the British Constitution, and the Executive being present in Parliament as occurs here.'[35]

After further contributions, Mr. Oram rose just before four o'clock and claimed to move 'That the Question be now put'. His purpose, of course, was to allow the House to come to a decision before the automatic adjournment. The Motion was carried and the original Motion agreed to.

It will appear from the foregoing Debate that, as in 1945, one of the basic problems was the congestion of the parliamentary time-table. But whereas at the earlier date it was primarily a question of enabling the Government to get through its legislation, at the later date emphasis was on opportunities for backbenchers. This was partly a problem of party discipline, but primarily a problem of the ever-increasing demands of the Government in terms both of time and of authority. Thus the need to get more time on the Floor of the House was related to the broader demand for more effective control and criticism of the Executive. But 'devolution' to satisfy the one might imply methods which, in satisfying the other also, might not appeal to the Government: witness Mr. Butler's remarks about specialised Committees.

The Select Committee, therefore, would obviously be faced with the danger that the more radical suggestions might be be opposed on 'constitutional' grounds – or, in the case of morning sittings, on the ground that too many M.P.s should not be 'full-time professionals'. Yet in recommending relatively minor changes – in Question Time, in the length of speeches, in Privy Councillors' privileges, for example – the Committee might fail to solve any of the more serious problems. We have now to examine the work of the Select Committee itself and the fate of its recommendations.

As in 1945 the Committee was presented with a 'working paper' by the Clerk of the House, Sir Edward Fellowes.[36] He began by saying that sooner or later the House of Commons would have to approach legislation from the angle that Parliament laid down very general principles and that it was the business of the Executive to administer the law inside

[35] *Ibid.*, col. 763.
[36] H.C. 92-I, Minutes of Evidence, pp. 1–19.

those principles. But the House was not yet ready for such a delegation of its legislative powers, so that further efforts must continue in the more orthodox forms of delegation. It would be worth while to reduce still further the number of Members who had to attend a Standing Committee merely to make up numbers, but to give greater opportunities to those interested in particular Bills.

He referred also to the lack of time for discussion of matters of public interest and concern, but warned that procedural reforms designed to ease the burden on the legislative function of the House had only encouraged Governments to expand their legislative output. On these, and other general points, he based his concrete proposals which are summarised below:

1. *Committees on Public Bills:* The House should delegate all Committee stages of Bills and most Report stages. There should be Committees on: (*a*) Unopposed Public Bills, (*b*) Opposed Public Bills, (*c*) the Finance Bill.[37]
2. *Sittings of the House:* There should be three morning sessions, on Mondays, Wednesdays and Fridays. On Tuesdays and Thursdays in the mornings and on Wednesdays in the afternoons and evenings, Committees on Public Bills would sit. On Wednesday afternoons the House, as such, would not sit.
3. *Business of the House: Questions.* On two days a week these would be taken before three Grand Committees, with the House not sitting at the same time. On Tuesdays and Thursdays they would be taken in the House.[38]

    Private Members' Time: Various suggestions for an increase and rearrangement of time under this heading; they are dealt with later.[39]

    Private Members' Motions: Suggestions as to the selection of subjects.[40]

    Motions for the Adjournment: Suggestions to make less restrictive the conditions under which Emergency Adjournments[41] might be obtained. These are also discussed later.[42]
4. *Financial:* To make procedure more intelligible, the Committee of Ways and Means should be limited to 'putting

---

[37] paras. 1–14.
[38] paras. 38–43.
[39] paras. 44–49.
[40] paras. 49–51.
[41] S.O. No. 9.
[42] paras. 52–56.

money into the Exchequer' and the Committee of Supply
'would cover all facets of the business of getting money out
of the Exchequer'. Arrangement of 'Finance Days' would
provide, instead of the present twenty-six allotted Supply
days and four Consolidated Fund or Appropriation Bill
days, seventeen allotted days, six Consolidated Fund or
Appropriation Bill days and nine days for Government
Supply Business – thirty-two instead of thirty days.[43] A
simplified procedure for 'virement' should be introduced.[44]
Money Resolutions should be considered by the Committees
on the Bills, not in Committee of the Whole House.[45]

5. *Miscellaneous*: Various suggestions for dealing with Divisions
and 'pairings',[46] Public Petitions[47] and Specialist Com-
mittees. Under the latter heading the Clerk suggested a
Joint Standing Committee on Colonial Affairs and a Defence
Committee to consider Estimates.[48] Other suggestions on
Guillotine procedure, dilatory Motions and a review of
Standing Orders.

In the Debate on July 13, Mr. Herbert Morrison remarked
of this Memorandum, based on an instruction that means of
saving time should be found, that the Clerk to the House and
the Committee itself knew it would be unacceptable. As for
saving time, 'the true answer is that it cannot be done'.[49] The
following account of the ultimate results of the Select Committee's labour appears to support this gloomy conclusion.

The House of Commons debated the Report of the Select
Committee on Procedure on July 13, 1959, and on February 8,
1960, on the second occasion considering the Government
statement of December 16, 1959.

Some relatively minor changes recommended by the Committee were accepted virtually without discussion. As a result,
Public Business Standing Orders are now printed separately;
a drafting Committee on Standing Orders has been established;
the Order Paper will 'give a clear indication in consecutive
order of the items of business to be taken for the day ...';
the Business statement on Thursday will announce business for

---

[43] paras. 57–69.
[45] paras. 72–73.
[47] para. 77.
[49] *H.C. Debates*, Vol. 609, col. 97.

[44] paras. 70–71.
[46] paras. 74–76.
[48] paras. 78–80.

the week beginning with the next Tuesday and ending with the following Monday, thereby giving slightly longer notice to Members; the time allowed for a count is increased from two to four minutes; and seconders will not be required for Motions or Amendments save on certain ceremonial occasions.

A recommendation concerned with the relaxation of the rules governing 'urgency motions' under S.O. No. 9 was fully discussed and virtually rejected. The Select Committee thought that these had become increasingly rigid. They suggested attention to three points: (i) the rule against 'anticipation' of other debates, (ii) the issue of 'public importance' (which might be left to the House), and (iii) the need for 'government responsibility' to be involved (a wider definition to cover 'matters which come within the scope of possible government action in foreign affairs' might be considered). Mr. Butler insisted upon avoiding 'anticipation' of debates already arranged. He agreed with Mr. Herbert Morrison that the issue of 'public importance' should not be left to forty Members. He also thought that 'some government responsibility must be involved'. He was, however, ready to discuss with Mr. Speaker the possibility of delaying his Ruling, though the recent delay of a whole week-end seemed too long. The Ruling should be given on the same day – in an hour or two. Further pressed during the Debate, he also said that he was willing to discuss with Mr. Speaker the restrictive effect of past rulings. 'Within reason, we do not want to restrict a matter that is both urgent and of public importance.' On these assurances Mr. Mitchison withdrew his Amendment to implement the Select Committee's recommendations.

We turn now to the proposals to reduce the amount of business taken on the Floor of the House in the expectation that 'preference would be given to general debates in the use of time saved by the more expeditious transaction of business'.

Two concerned (1) the reservation of an hour during major debates for five-minute speeches, and (2) an alteration in the practice relating to Privy Councillors' rights in speaking. In July, 1959, Mr. Butler welcomed the former. But Mr. Bowles, among others, thought the suggestion would divide the House into two classes or gradings and Mr. Herbert Morrison described five-minute speeches as 'something like a speakers' class in a junior Conservative association'. Mr. Iremonger[50] thought that the value of a five-minute speech was nugatory as compared with that of the ten-minute speech and Mr. Richard Marsh[51] put the case for ten minutes. Mr. John Hall considered that speeches in general might be limited to fifteen minutes. Generally, however, Members wished to leave the matter to the good sense and discretion of the House.

On Privy Councillors' speeches both Mr. Butler and Mr. Morrison thought that the House should take no action but leave the matter to the Chair.

'I would only say', Mr. Butler added, 'that in implementing the recommendation of the Select Committee you would certainly have me on your side, Mr. Speaker, if you occasionally adopted the Nelson blind eye in regard to Privy Councillors, especially in the course of debates.' In general, their right of precedence should be continued but Mr. Speaker should use his discretion 'when, for example, there is a string of Privy Councillors waiting to intervene and it is impossible for a Private Member to get in'. This should be the practice also with supplementary questions. Mr. Blackburn,[52] however, urged that in such a matter the onus should not be placed upon Mr. Speaker. Mr. Pannell[53] quoted Mr. Speaker Morrison as having 'generally agreed with the recommendation that Privy Councillors should have no special rights'. An Amendment to implement the Select Committee's recommendation that Privy Councillors should have special rights only in regard to supplementary questions and that Mr. Speaker should not be bound to call them in debate in preference to other Members was negatived without a Division.

Time-tabling is of the essence of expeditious despatch of business, particularly for legislation. The Select Committee wanted a business committee to consider all bills committed to a standing committee after second reading. It should report to the House the date by which each Bill should be reported back and, if thought appropriate, the number of sittings required, subject to the right of amendment. The Government (or Private Member in charge of his Bill) might then move a motion instructing the standing committee in the sense of the report. Such motion would be debatable, though not necessarily

[50] Cons., Ilford North.   [51] Lab., Greenwich.
[52] Lab., Stalybridge and Hyde.   [53] Lab., Leeds West.

so if the business committee were unanimous. There should, however, be no obligation on the Government 'to move' if they thought the most expeditious handling of the Bill could be achieved by other methods. The actual details of clauses and amendments to be considered at each sitting should be settled by the Chairman of the standing committee in consultation with the Minister in charge and Opposition representatives.

These suggestions were debated at some length on July 13, but almost entirely ignored on February 8. No changes were introduced.

Nevertheless there was some disposition to accept parts of the Select Committee's recommendations relating to the greater use of Standing Committees. The Committee itself had rejected the idea of specialist committees and, despite some support in both debates for the idea, an Amendment moved by Mr. Hale[54] to establish one for Colonial Affairs was defeated by 220 votes to 89. But the recommendation that parts, at least, of the Finance Bill might be taken 'upstairs' was not so cavalierly dismissed. The idea was guardedly welcomed by Mr. Butler (July, 1959), who thought that 'an experimental approach to the Finance Bill would be the best'. Mr. Bellenger[55] saw no reason why the whole of the Finance Bill, after its second reading, should not go to a Standing Committee. Mr. Morrison agreed, but Sir Hendrie Oakshott[56] thought it entirely wrong. Mr. Philips Price[57] thought that certain clauses might be selected and dealt with upstairs by the 'experts', while those 'likely to arouse emotions and dealing with first principles' were kept on the Floor. Mr. Mitchison, who in the Select Committee voted against sending the Bill upstairs, had now come round to the view that parts might be so treated.

In the same Debate, Mr. Blackburn tabled an Amendment to S.O. No. 38 so as automatically to commit the Finance Bill to a Standing Committee unless the House otherwise ordered. Mr. Oram regretted that this proposal, so important to the basic purpose of providing more time for general debates, had not been accepted. Mr. Douglas Houghton,[58] however, thought that it 'would lead to many inconveniences and disappoint-

---

[54] Lab., Oldham.   [55] Lab., Bassetlaw.   [56] Cons., Bebington.
[57] Lab., Gloucestershire West.   [58] Lab., Sowerby.

ments', and suggested, as an alternative, a Taxes Management Act to separate administrative questions from the Finance Bill. All was not completely lost. Mr. Butler, replying, pointed out that the Bill could be taken upstairs either by means of a Sessional Order or an Order amending S.O. No. 38. He would not exclude the possibility of taking part of the Bill upstairs but preferred to deal with it *ab initio* and not by amending Standing Orders. Mr. Blackburn, feeling that Mr. Butler was in full agreement with the object he had in mind, withdrew his Amendment.

As for the proposed Welsh Grand Committee, in July, 1959 Mr. Butler felt that the case had not been made out; but in February, 1960 he announced that he had discussed the matter with the Minister for Welsh Affairs, who thought it a good idea. With reservations about such questions as powers, sittings and the existing 'Welsh Day', he suggested consultation with Mr. Ness Edwards[59] (who had given evidence to the Select Committee) and his friends. Mr. Ness Edwards accordingly withdrew his Amendment on the subject.

The Select Committee also made recommendations about the composition and procedure of standing committees. In February, 1960, Mr. Butler announced the proposed Government alterations to S.O. Nos. 57 and 58. The quorum of a standing committee was to be reduced to one-third of the number of its members, excluding the Chairman, and each standing committee (except the Scottish Standing Committee) was to consist of a Chairman and not less than twenty nor more than fifty members. In nominating such members the Committee of Selection should have regard to their qualifications and to the composition of the House. The distinction between the 'nucleus' and the 'added members' was thus removed.

There were no objections to these proposals. But Mr. Mitchison complained that none of the Select Committee's major suggestions for taking matters off the Floor of the House and for making better and bigger use of committees had been accepted. Mr. Blackburn also regretted this, and doubted whether even as regards individual Bills there would be greater specialisation in the Standing Committees.

Two related matters may be mentioned here. Opinion was

[59] Lab., Caerphilly.

firmly against taking Report stages of Bills upstairs, a suggestion made by the Clerk of the House in 1945 and 1958. But to organise the Committee and Report stages more effectively the House accepted the recommendation that the Chair should announce, at the beginning of each sitting, the Amendments which had been selected for debate.

We turn now to some aspects of financial procedure. A new form of approval, to make clear the significance of the authorisation of 'virement', was embodied in Amendments to S.O. No. 16 (paras. 3 and 16). But Mr. Butler refused to agree to a recommendation which would have abolished the recommittal of a Bill where amendment of the financial resolution was necessary. Mr. Douglas Houghton urged that the procedure was antiquated, was related to the fact that Mr. Speaker used to be a partisan of the Crown, and was little comprehended by Members. But his Amendment, to make recommittal unnecessary when the charge, etc., was within the terms of the original financial resolution, was defeated without a Division. Money resolutions, in fact, were made 'exempted business' automatically for three-quarters of an hour.

Scant attention was paid to the recommendation that the scope of debate on Supplementary Estimates should be widened, perhaps because in practice there was little restriction. But better use of Supply days was envisaged in the recommendation that allotted days should be spread more evenly throughout the session. The difficulty arose from the fact that the Estimates were not presented until late February. Admittedly, the Opposition were able to use what the Chief Whip called 'spoof' Supply days earlier in the session if they gave up the equivalent number later. But, as Mr. Heath[60] explained, this could be done only by moving Mr. Speaker out of the Chair, following which the Opposition moved an Amendment which could not itself be amended – 'and Governments do not like to have a situation in which they cannot safeguard their own position'. The Select Committee had recommended that the Opposition be given a right to a fixed number of 'Supply' days before the Estimates were presented. In July, 1959, Mr. Butler suggested consultations with the Opposition on this matter, but in February, 1960, these had still not led to any concrete proposals.

[60] Cons., Bexley.

Problems connected with Question Time were discussed at length. Mr. Butler, and the House in general, were clearly anxious that every support should be given to Mr. Speaker in checking the number and length of supplementary questions. Mr. Shinwell suggested that many Answers were far too long. He was also concerned with the 'parochial' nature of many Questions; the Scottish Members, for example, might well have their own session on Fridays in Edinburgh! Mr. Butler also announced the acceptance of the proposal to reduce the number of oral questions from three to two on any one day. He further told the House that to encourage more requests for Written Answers, instructions would be issued to the Departments that, provided three working days' notice of an unstarred Question were given, they should answer in three days.

On the proposal to take Prime Minister's Questions at 3.15 p.m. on Tuesdays and Thursdays, Mr. Butler reserved his opinion until he had heard the Debate. Later, he announced that the Prime Minister's Questions would begin at No. 40 instead of No. 45 on each of the two days – which would have the same effect as the Select Committee's recommendation and be less of a break with tradition. The experiment would be tried until Easter. Mr. Blackburn accordingly withdrew his Amendment on the subject.

Various changes were made in the procedure affecting the traditional opportunities for Private Members. On December 16, 1959, Mr. Butler announced that two Mondays and two Wednesdays would be provided for Private Members' Motions, in addition to the twenty Fridays for Motions and Bills. He also indicated that in accordance with the Select Committee's recommendations the Chairman's Panel had passed a Resolution that if at any two meetings of a Committee on a Bill the Committee were adjourned for lack of a quorum before twelve noon the Bill should go to the bottom of the list of Bills and remain there until all others were disposed of. This would prevent obstruction in the form of delaying a non-contentious Bill in order to delay a later contentious one. Further consideration was also being given to certain other features of the arrangements for Private Members' Bills.

On Bills under the Ten-minute Rule, the Select Committee had recommended that not more than one should be introduced on any one day. This was accepted by Mr. Butler. The recommendations that one week's notice be required for any such Bill was implemented by an addition to S.O. No. 12.

The Select Committee was very keen that drafting assistance should be provided for back-benchers. Mr. Butler refused to accept a proposal for drafting assistance in connection with Amendments, but agreed to look further into the matter so far as Private Members' Bills were concerned.

On December 16 Mr. Butler announced that Mr. Speaker was in favour of a suggested change in the method of balloting for Half-hour Adjournment Motions: the ballot would be held a fortnight ahead; eight ballot days would be allotted to the first eight successful Members; Mr. Speaker would select the subject for debate on one day a week. In the course of the Debate on February 8, Mr. Butler accepted an Amendment moved by Mr. Mitchison which permitted incidental reference to be made to legislation on Motions for the Adjournment. But the House paid little attention to the recommendation that a Member's right to change the subject of a balloted Adjournment Motion should be restricted.

Two recommendations concerned Private Bills. The first, to provide for their earlier presentation so as to advance the date for second readings, was accepted on December 16. A proposal to simplify procedure for 'blocking' the second and third readings, the subject-matter of an Amendment on February 8, was accepted by Mr. Butler subject to an examination of the drafting.

Finally, a new Sessional Order to replace S.O. No. 1 was accepted. It was a lengthy Order covering four columns of *Hansard*, but its principal effect was that Government Motions to 'suspend the ten o'clock rule' should stand over until the interruption of business at 10.0 p.m. The Order was detailed to cover every possible contingency – 'a fine piece of work of parliamentary counsel and comparatively comprehensible', said Mr. Butler. There was some argument as to whether it was merely 'for the convenience of lawyers' but Members generally welcomed relief from the necessity of attending for a possible Division at 3.30 p.m. each day. One realist suggested that since no Government would be defeated, a Division was unnecessary anyway!

Those who hoped for more radical amendment of procedure were disappointed. The Select Committee had itself turned down Specialist Committees and morning sittings, and only about one-half of its own very moderate recommendations had been accepted by the Government.

The question of specialised committees was raised again on February 23, 1960, when Lord Hinchingbrooke referred to Sir Gilbert (Lord) Campion's Memorandum which had suggested combining the Select Committee on Estimates and the Public Accounts Committee into a public expenditure committee.[61] Mr. Grimond[62] thought that the House should consider legislation in its wider aspects only and should delegate other matters to 'more specialised Standing Committees'.[63] Mr. John Eden[64] added that they 'must bring the special Committees of the House into closer association with the House itself'.[65] Mr. Sydney Silverman[66] also wanted Lord Campion's Memorandum to be reconsidered. Mr. Nigel Birch,[67] on the other hand, did not think Select Committees provided the answer 'for the simple reason that under our system Select Committees can deal only with administration and not with policy'.[68] Mr. Emrys Hughes[69] thought that there was a great need for hon. Members who were specialists; he not only argued for a Standing Committee dealing with the Navy, the Army and the Air Force, but revived the late Fred Jowett's proposal for a 'municipal system'. 'Until we get the committee system of government as against the Cabinet system,' he said, 'we shall never get real democracy.'[70] Major Legge-Bourke[71] reverted to the Campion Memorandum and reminded the House of the Select Committee on National Expenditure during the war. He also revived the idea of a 'third House of Parliament', an 'Industrial House'.

Mr. Butler replied for the Government. On the Campion Memorandum, he said, he would 'rather examine the possibility of either some enlargement of the Committee on Estimates or ... a Committee on Expenditure [with] an opportunity of considering administrative policy earlier in the year'.[72] There should then be greater opportunity for the House to consider

---

[61] *H.C. Debates*, Vol. 619, cols. 1302–1375.
[63] *Ibid.*, col. 1329.
[65] *Ibid.*, col. 1336.
[67] Cons., Flint West.
[69] Lab., South Ayrshire.
[71] Cons., Isle of Ely.

[62] Lib., Orkney and Shetland.
[64] Cons., Bournemouth West.
[66] Lab., Nelson and Colne.
[68] *Ibid.*, col. 1341.
[70] *Ibid.*, col. 1345-1346.
[72] *Ibid.*, col. 1371.

its reports. In reply to a question, he also mentioned the beginning which was to be made with a Welsh Grand Committee. (Details were announced on March 14, 1960.)

There appeared to be considerable agreement that effective reform of procedure must involve extended use of Committees, but still no real evidence that such fundamental changes were likely to meet with general approval.

[73] cf. H. V. Wiseman, 'Reform of House of Commons Procedure', in *Parliamentary Affairs*, Summer 1959; 'The House of Commons and the Select Committee on Procedure' in *ibid.*, Spring, 1960; A. H. Hanson and H. V. Wiseman, 'The Use of Committees by the House of Commons', in *Public Law*, Autumn, 1959; Bernard Crick, *Reform of the Commons* (Fabian Trust 319, 1959).

INDEX

ADAMS, MR. H. R.,
order, 34
ADDRESS,
Debate on:
Mr. Silverman's amendment, 51
Opposition amendment, 50
selection of amendments, 50–51
Humble, 45
ADJOURNMENT MOTIONS, 89
'half-hour', 51, 56, 68, 92–93, 95, 95–99, 106, 115, 214–215, 267, 339
'holiday', 95
notice of raising matter on, 72, 73
refusal of 'urgency' motion, motion regretting 104–107
'urgency', 64, 68, 74–76, 76–79, 99–104, 187, 322, 331, 333
validity of notice, 72, 73
AFFIRMATIVE RESOLUTIONS, 215, 216
AGRICULTURAL LAND (REMOVAL OF SURFACE SOIL) BILL, 185
AINSLEY, MR. J. W.,
point of order, 70
AIRWAYS CORPORATIONS,
debate on Reports and Accounts, 110–115
ALBU, MR. AUSTEN,
debate on refusal of 'urgency' motion, 107
Estimates Committee Report, 301–302
ALLAUN, MR. FRANK,
Budget debate, 249
debate on Address, 48
Supply, 253
ALLEN, MR. JOSEPH,
evidence before Special Procedure Joint Committee, 227
ALLOCATION OF TIME ORDER (see Guillotine Motion) 137, 142
AMENDMENTS,
to Allocation of Time Order, 138
to Consolidated Fund (No. 1) Bill, Second Reading, 273–274
to Finance Bill, choice of, 255
by House of Lords, 171–180
to Money Resolution, 134
to Motions, 108–110, 116–117, 119
on Report, 156–169
to Second Reading of Bill, 127

selection of, by Chairman of Standing Committee, 145, 147
to Special Procedure Orders, 217–218
in Standing Committee, 143–156
on Third Reading, 170
ANDERSON, SIR JOHN (LORD WAVERLEY),
Iron and Steel Bill, Second Reading, 130
ANNULMENT,
Motion for (Special Procedure Orders), 217
ANTICIPATION,
rule against, 124, 333
'ANY QUESTIONS' (B.B.C. Programme),
and Privilege, 6
APPROPRIATION ACCOUNTS, 280
Civil, 283–290
APPROPRIATION ACT, 241, 284, 332
'brought in', 269
Second Reading, 269
Committee, Report, Third Reading, 270
expenditure not brought to charge in, 283
ARTS COUNCIL, 275
ASKEW, MR. ROYSTON,
before Special Procedure Joint Committee, 225 passim
ATTEWELL, MR. H. C.,
Iron and Steel Bill, Committee, 151,
Lords' Amendments, 173
ATTLEE, MR. CLEMENT (Lord Attlee),
business arrangements, 29
election of Speaker, 15, 16–17
interruption of business, 27
on iron and steel nationalisation, 123
moves censure motion, 32
AWBERY, MR. S.,
Iron and Steel Bill, Third Reading, 171

BACK-BENCHERS,
in civil airways debate, 114–115
in debate on Address, 48–49, 52–53
rights of, 107, 338–339
BACON, MISS ALICE,
Leeds Private Bill, 195, 196
BALLOT,
for Private Members' Bills, 58–59, 322
for Notices of Motion on Going into

BALLOT—*continued*
    Committee of Supply, 283
    for Private Members' Notices of Motion, 57, 322, 339
BALNIEL, LORD,
    civil airways debate, 112
'BANSTEAD HARRIERS', 211–215
BARLOW, SIR JOHN,
    debate on Address, 55
    Iron and Steel Bill, Committee, 154
BAXTER, SIR BEVERLEY,
    Pool Betting Bill, 189, 190
    privilege, 9
BEAMISH, MAJOR TUFTON,
    Iron and Steel Bill, Lords' amendments, 175
    'Suez Crisis', 37–38
BEEVERS, ALD. D.,
    Leeds Private Bill, 199–200
BELLENGER, MR. F. J.,
    business, notice of, 63
    procedure, 335
    'Scarcroft' case, 85
    Supply, 244
BELSTEAD, LORD,
    Joint Committee, 221
BENN, MR. WEDGWOOD (Lord Stansgate),
    adjournment debate, 98–99
    motion regretting Speaker's ruling, 76, 104–107
    point of order, 65
    procedure, 327
    'urgency' adjournment, attempt to move, 74, 75
BENNETT, SIR PETER,
    Iron and Steel Bill, Third Reading, 171
BENNETT, DR. R.,
    Supply, 245
BESWICK, MR. FRANK,
    'urgency' adjournment debate (Perez-Selles), 102
BEVAN, MR. ANEURIN,
    business arrangements, 30–31, 67
    debate on Address, 51
    order, 21, 26, 39–40
    Perez-Selles case, 76, 78
    privilege, 7
BIDGOOD, MR. JOHN C.,
    Leeds Private Bill, 194
BILLS,
    hybrid, 124–125
    government, 121–180
    private, 53, 121
    private Members', 57–61, 115, 121
    public, 121
BING, MR. GEOFFREY,
    business arrangements, 30
    Common Informers Bill, 183

'prayer', 214
BIRCH, MR. NIGEL,
    Estimates Committee Report, 301
    Iron and Steel Bill, Report, 157
    procedure, 340
BISHOP, MR. F. P.,
    reading from documents, 190
BLACK ROD, 44
BLACKBURN, MR. F.
    procedure, 334, 335, 336, 338
BLAIN, MR. ERIC,
    Leeds Private Bill, 199–200
BOARDMAN, MR. H.,
    debate on Address, 54
BOOTHBY, SIR ROBERT (Lord Boothby),
    procedure, 327–328
BOSSOM, MR. A. C. (Sir Alfred),
    'Scarcroft' case, 83
BOWLES, MR. FRANK,
    business, 83
    procedure, 333
    suggested as Deputy-Chairman, 15
BOYD-CARPENTER, MR. JOHN,
    debate on Address, 49
    'prayer', 212
    Seizure of Food Order, 1946, 209; 1948, 209
    Supply, 239
BRADDOCK, MRS. ELIZABETH,
    'named', 19
    order, 49
    Pool Betting Bill, 190, 191
    'Suez Crisis', 43
BRADY, R., 122
BRAINE, MR. B. R.,
    'prayer', 214
BRAITHWAITE, LIEUT.-COM. GURNEY,
    Iron and Steel Bill, Report, 164, 166,
    Third Reading, 171
    Seizure of Food Order, 1946, 208
BRITTAIN, SIR HERBERT,
    on financial procedure, 237
BROCKWAY, MR. FENNER,
    'urgency' adjournment (Perez-Selles), 76–79, 100–102 (Kabaka of Uganda), 187
BROMHEAD, P., 180–181
BROMLEY-DAVENPORT, LT.-COL. W. H.,
    Supply, 276
BROOKE, MR. HENRY,
    Estimates Committee Report, 302
BROOKS, MR. THOMAS,
    joint committee, 221
BROWN, MR. GEORGE,
    challenges virement, 265–267
BRYAN, MR. PAUL,
    Leeds Private Bill, 197
BUCHAN-HEPBURN, MR. A.,
    election of Speaker, 15

BUDGET,
  debate, 249–251
  proposals, 236
  Resolutions, 249, 251, 252, 323
  Statement, 248–249
BULLUS, WING-COMMANDER E. E.,
  adjournment, 81
  Leeds Private Bill, 196
  'prayers', 213
  'Scarcroft' case, 81, 84, 85, 86
BURDEN, MR. F. A.,
  Leeds Private Bill, 196
  'prayer', 214
  privilege, 5
BUSINESS COMMITTEE,
  proposed, 334–335
BUSINESS, FINANCIAL, 236–278
  general characteristics, 236–237
BUSINESS, GOVERNMENT,
  arrangements for, 67
BUSINESS OF A SESSION, 57–61
BUSINESS OF THE HOUSE, 76
  Motion, 49, 57
BUSINESS OF THE WEEK, 50, 61–67, 83,
  333
  Announcement, 61, 64, 66, 82
BUSINESS SUB-COMMITTEE, 141, 142, 324
BUTLER, MR. R. A.,
  business of the House, 49, 50, 57–61,
    61–67, 76–79
  debate on Address, 52, 54, 55
  financial procedure, changes, 237,
    270, 276–278, 290n, 293–294
  nationalised industries, Questions, 89
  Perez-Selles case, 76–79, 99–104
  private Members' time, 115n
  privilege, 5, 7, 8, 9, 10
  procedure 329–330, 333 passim
  Supply, 272–273, 276–278

CALLAGHAN, MR. JAMES, 291
  Nationalised Industries Committee,
    312
  Perez-Selles case, 76
  'Suez Crisis', 43
CAMPION, SIR GILBERT (Lord Cam-
    pion),
  on financial procedure, 237
  memorandum to Select Committee
    on Procedure, 121, 318 passim, 340
  on order, 18
  on Questions, 69
  on privilege, 1
  on Special Procedure Orders, 217
  on Public Expenditure Committee,
    274, 293
CAPEWELL, MR. ARTHUR, Q.C.,
  before Special Procedure Joint Com-
    mittee, 221 passim

CARY, SIR ROBERT,
  procedure, 328
CENSURE,
  Motion of, 30, 32, 39, 43, 108
CHALLEN, MR. CHARLES,
  Seizure of Food Order, 1946, 206
CHAPMAN, MR. DONALD,
  debate on refusal of 'urgency'
    motion, 107
CHESTER, D. N.,
  on Questions, 69
CHETWYND, MR. G. R.,
  Iron and Steel Bill, Committee, 151
CHUBB, DR. BASIL,
  on Estimates Committee, 294n
  on Public Accounts Committee, 280–
    281
CHURCHILL, SIR WINSTON,
  election of Speaker, 15–16
  Estimates Committee Report, 299
  Iron and Steel Bill, Second Reading,
    127, 129–30, 131; Lords' Amend-
    ments, 178–179
  order, 20
  'Scarcroft' case, 86
  speeches made outside House, 24–25
  on supplementary estimates debates,
    240
CLANDESTINE OUTLAWRIES,
  Bill for the more effective preventing
    of, 44
CLARK, MR. H. W.,
  evidence before Special Procedure
    Joint Committee, 232
CLARKE, BRIGADIER, T. H.,
  Estimates Committee Report, 298–299
CLERK OF THE HOUSE,
  and election of Speaker, 13
CLIFTON BROWN, MR SPEAKER,
  rulings quoted, 96, 106
CLOSURE, 32, 33–36, 115, 117–118, 159,
  173, 174, 175, 176, 186
COMMON INFORMERS BILL, 182–184
COMPTROLLER AND AUDITOR-GENERAL,
  280–281, 285, 287–290, 314
  Sir Frank Tribe as, 281
CONSOLIDATED FUND (No. 1) BILL, 240–
  241, 242, 248, 273
  Amendment to Second Reading, 273
COOKE, MR. R. GRESHAM,
  procedure, 329
COOPER, MR. A. W.,
  Budget debate, 249
COOPER, MR. GEOFFREY,
  Iron and Steel Bill, Committee, 143,
    144, 147
COPE MORGAN, MR. S., Q.C.,
  before Special Procedure Joint Com-
    mittee, 223 passim
'COUNTING OUT' THE HOUSE, 27

CRICK, BERNARD,
  procedure, 340n
CRIPPS, SIR STAFFORD,
  Iron and Steel Bill, Second Reading,
    131
CRONIN, MR. J. D.,
  Finance Bill, 259
CROOKSHANK, MR. H.,
  business arrangements, 29–30
  interruption of business, 28
  suspension of Member, 34
CROSSMAN, MR. RICHARD,
  privilege, 9
CROSTHWAITE-EYRE, COL. O. E.,
  'prayer', 211
CROUCH, MR. R. F.,
  'prayer', 214

Daily Herald, 1
DAINES, MR. PERCY,
  business, 66
  Iron and Steel Bill, Lords' Amend-
    ments, 173
DALTON, DR. HUGH,
  Budget debate, 250
  on iron and steel nationalisation,
    124
DARWEN, LORD,
  joint committee, 221
DAVIES, MR. CLEMENT,
  election of Speaker, 17
  Iron and Steel Bill, Second Reading,
    130
DAVIES, MR. ERNEST,
  Supply, 247
DAVIES, MR. H.,
  order, 22, 71
DEATH PENALTY ABOLITION BILL, 58–
    61
DEEDES, MR. W. F.,
  'prayer', 214
  'urgency' adjournment debate (Perez-
    Selles), 101–102
DE FREITAS, MR. GEOFFREY,
  Estimates Committee Report, 301
  Pool Betting Bill, 189
  procedure, 328
DELARGY, MR. H. J.,
  point of order, 96
DELEGATED LEGISLATION, 203–235, 302–
    309
  Select Committee on, 303
  Special Procedure Order, 216–235
  Statutory Instruments, 203–216
DEPUTY-CHAIRMAN,
  order, 34–35
  orders withdrawal of Member, 169
DEPUTY SPEAKER (Chairman of Ways
    and Means),

anticipation, ruling against, 124
duties, 160
election of, 17
Finance Bill, 263–264; selection of
  Amendments and New Clauses, 262
Leeds Private Bill, procedure, 139,
  194
motion of no confidence in, 32
points of order, 20–21
procedure in Committee of Supply,
  268, 323
relevance, 183
'Reporting Progress', 258, 260, 261,
  262
Special Procedure Order, duties, 217
DISORDER,
  adjournment for, 28
DISTRICT AUDIT, 233
DONNELLY, MR. DESMOND,
  point of order, 96
  privilege, 7
DOWER, COL. A. V. G.,
  Iron and Steel Bill, Report, 169
DRIBERG, MR. T.,
  order, 35
DUGDALE, MR. JOHN,
  point of order, 77
  'urgency' motion (Perez-Selles), 99,
    100
DUNCAN, SIR ANDREW,
  Iron and Steel Bill, Second Reading,
    131

ECCLES, SIR DAVID,
  Debate on Address, 54, 55
  Income Tax (Payment of Post-War
    Credits) Bill, 250
  Iron and Steel Bill, 'guillotine'
    motion, 139
ECONOMIC SURVEY, 250
EDE, MR. CHUTER,
  business arrangements, 29, 82
  Iron and Steel Bill 'guillotine' mo-
    tion, 140
  moves 'no confidence' in Chairman
    of Ways and Means, 32
  order, 24
  Pool Betting Bill, 190
EDEN, MR. ANTHONY (Lord Avon),
  election of Speaker, 15, 17
  Iron and Steel Bill, 'guillotine'
    motion, 138–139
    Second Reading, 132
  on iron and steel nationalisation,
    124
  'Suez Crisis', 37–43
EDEN, MR. JOHN,
  procedure, 340
  Supply, 275

EDWARDS, MR. ALFRED,
Iron and Steel Bill, Third Reading, 171
EDWARDS, MR. F. L.,
evidence before Special Procedure Joint Committee, 233
EDWARDS, MR. JOHN,
Chairman, Public Accounts Committee, 281
Leeds Private Bill, 196
EDWARDS, MR. NESS,
procedure, 336
Supplementary Question, 73
EINZIG, DR. PAUL, 274
EMERGENCY BUSINESS COMMITTEE,
proposed, 315, 324
ERROLL, MR. F. J.,
affirmative resolution, 215
Iron and Steel Bill, Committee, 150, 153
Third Reading, 171
Lords' amendments, 173
ERSKINE MAY,
on Hybrid Bills, 125
on interruptions of business, 27
on maintenance of quorum, 28
on Motions, 94
on Order, 18
on Private Bills, 192
on privilege, 1
on Questions, 68
on Special Procedure Orders, 216
on Statutory Instruments, 203, 303
on token Votes, 253n
on virement, 265–266
ESSEX RIVER BOARD ORDER, 234
ESTIMATES, 236
Air, Vote A, 242–243
Army, Vote A, 241–242
Navy, Vote A, 243–244
Scottish, 325
Service, 241–246, 253
Supplementary, 238, 240, 244, 246, 247, 320, 337
'Token Sums', 253–254, 264–265
Token Votes, 253n
'Votes Outstanding', 268–269
ESTIMATES COMMITTEE (Select Committee on Estimates), 237, 246, 277, 279, 280, 292–302, 322, 323, 328, 340
Civil Defence Report, 294–302
features, 292–293
proposed changes, 293–294
terms of reference, 293
EVANS, MR. S. N.,
Iron and Steel Bill, Second Reading, 129
Committee, 146, 151, 154
Third Reading, 171

Lords' Amendments, 179
Evening News,
and Privilege, 6
EXCESS VOTES, 247, 280
EXEMPTED BUSINESS, 22, 31, 204

FAIRHURST, MR. FRANK,
Iron and Steel Bill, Second Reading, 130
FAREY-JONES, MR. F. W.,
civil airways debate, 113
FELLOWES, SIR EDWARD,
procedural proposals, 275, 330–332
FERNYHOUGH, Mr. E.,
order, 22, 23
Supply, 246
FINANCE ACT, 267, 284
FINANCE BILL, 236
Second Reading, 251–252
Committee Stage, 255–261, 262–264, 265
Reported, 264
Report Stage, 265
Third Reading, 265, 267
sending 'upstairs', 329, 335
FINANCIAL PROCEDURE,
proposed changes, 237, 270, 276–278, 290n, 293–294, 317, 331–332
FINANCIAL RESOLUTIONS, 133–135, 250, 258–261, 317, 318, 332, 337
FITZROY, MR. SPEAKER,
rulings quoted, 106
FLETCHER, MR. ERIC,
Chairman, 'Scrutiny' Committee, 304
FLETCHER, MR. W.,
adjournment notice, 291–292
FORT, MR. RICHARD,
debate on address, 54
FOSTER, MR. JOHN,
'urgency' adjournment debate (Perez-Selles), 101
FRASER, MR. HUGH,
Iron and Steel Bill, Second Reading, 129
Committee, 151
Report, 161
Supply, 244, 245
FRASER, SIR IAN,
Seizure of Food Order, 1946, 206
FRASER, MR. THOMAS,
business, 62, 65
debate on Address, 55
FREE VOTES, 58, 60, 66
FYFE, SIR DAVID MAXWELL, (Lord Kilmuir)
Estimates Committee Report, 298–300
on hybrid bills, 124–125

GAITSKELL, MR. HUGH,
Budget Debate, 249
business, 50, 64–65, 66
Debate on Address, 46–47, 54, 55
Leeds Private Bill, 195, 197
Perez-Selles case, 76
privilege, 8, 10
on respect for Chair, 107
'Suez Crisis', 37–43
Supply, 241
Supply Days, Opposition attitude,
273, 278
Supply Resolutions, 269
'urgency' adjournment motion, 75
GALBRAITH, COMMANDER T. G.,
order, 20–22
GALLACHER, MR. WILLIAM,
attempts to move Amendment to
Money Resolution of Iron and Steel
Bill, 134
GAS BILL,
Committee stage, 137–138, 142
Opposition attitude to, 121–122
GENERAL DIRECTIONS, 90, 91, 92–93
'GENTLEMEN'S AGREEMENT', 310, 311,
312
GLOVER, MR. DOUGLAS,
Debate on Address, 55
GLYN, SIR RALPH,
election of Speaker, 14
GLYN, COL. RICHARD H.,
Debate on Address, 53
Finance Bill, 257
GORDON, MR. D. J. (Second Clerk
Assistant),
evidence to Select Committee on
Nationalised Industries, 88
GORDON-WALKER, MR. PATRICK,
Debate on the Address, 52
Finance Bill, 252
'urgency' adjournment (Perez-Selles),
77, 101, 103–104
GOWER, MR. H. R.,
business, 65
Supplementary Question, 91
GRANT-FERRIS, MR. R. G.,
Leeds Private Bill, 197
GRANVILLE, MR. E.,
Iron and Steel Bill, Lords' Amend-
ments, 175
GREAT OUSE RIVER BOARD (OLD WEST
INTERNAL DRAINAGE DISTRICT)
ORDER, 1952, 234–235
GREENWOOD, MR. ANTHONY,
Debate on the Address, 53
GREENWOOD, MR. ARTHUR,
Select Committee on Procedure,
1945–46, recommendations, 323
GRIEVANCES,
opportunities for raising, 19

GRIFFITHS, MR. JAMES,
business, 62
Debate on Address, 49
moves censure motion, 43
GRIMOND, MR. JOSEPH,
Debate on Address, 49–50
'prayer', 212
private notice Question, 73
Supply, 272, 275
GUILLOTINE,
operation of, 142, 149, 150, 155, 156,
159, 162, 165, 166, 167, 169, 170,
171, 176
GUILLOTINE MOTION, 138, 316
Iron and Steel Bill, 135–137

HALE, MR. LESLIE,
on back-benchers' rights, 107
Common Informers Bill, 182
criticism of Speaker, 75
point of order, 97
privilege, 7
procedure, 335
'urgency' adjournment debate (Perez-
Selles), 102
HALL, MR. GLENVIL,
Iron and Steel Bill, Committee, 154
Report, 167, 169
procedure, 328
HALL, MR. JOHN,
Finance Bill, 255
procedure, 334
HAMILTON, MR. WILLIAM,
point of order, 64
HARDIE, MR. S. J. L,, (Chairman, Iron
and Steel Corporation),
status of correspondence with, 22–24
HARRIS, MR. F.,
order, 21
HARRIS, MR. READER,
Budget Debate, 249–250
Pool Betting Bill, 191
HARVEY, SIR ARTHUR VERE,
civil airways debate, 112
HARVEY, MR. IAN,
Estimates Committee Report, 299
HAUGHTON, MAJOR S. G.,
Iron and Steel Bill, 'guillotine' mo-
tion, 140
HAWKSLEY, MR. T. E.,
evidence before Special Procedure
Joint Committee, 232
HAY, MR. JOHN,
adjournment debate, 92–93
HEAD, MR. ANTONY, 33
HEADLAM, LIEUT.-COL. SIR CUTHBERT,
Iron and Steel Bill, Second Reading,
132

HEALD, MR. LIONEL,
  introduces Common Informers Bill,
  182
HEALEY, MR. DENIS,
  'Suez Crisis', 37, 38–39
HEATH, MR. E.,
  procedure, 337
HEATHCOAT AMORY, MR. DERICK,
  (Lord Amory),
  Budget Statement, 248–249
  Debate on Address, 54
  Finance Bill, 256 passim
HENDERSON, MR. A., 291
HERBISON, MISS MARGARET,
  Debate on Address, 54
HETHERINGTON, MR. ROGER LE GEYT,
  evidence before Special Procedure
  Joint Committee, 225–226
HEWITSON, CAPTAIN MARK,
  Pool Betting Bill, 189
HILL, MR. S. W.,
  evidence before Special Procedure
  Joint Committee, 229–230
HINCHINGBROOKE, VISCOUNT,
  Iron and Steel Bill, Second Reading,
  129
  'guillotine' motion, 140, 142
  Committee, 143, 145, 146, 148,
  151, 156
  Report, 161, 163–164
  procedure, 340
  Supply, 'back-bench revolt', 271
  passim
HIRST, MR. GEOFFREY,
  Leeds Private Bill, 194
HOGG, MR. QUINTIN (Lord Hailsham),
  Iron and Steel Bill, 'guillotine'
  motion, 139–140
HOMICIDE BILL, 58, 60, 66, 67
HOMOSEXUALITY AND PROSTITUTION,
  publication of B.M.A., 3
HORABIN, MR. T. L.,
  Iron and Steel Bill, Second Reading,
  130
HOROBIN, SIR IAN,
  on Nationalised Industries Commit-
  tee Report, 311
HOUGHTON, MR. DOUGLAS,
  Common Informers Bill, 184
  Finance Bill, 264
  procedure, 335–336, 337
HOWARD, MR. G. R.,
  Debate on Address, 55
HOWELL, MR. DENIS,
  business, 60
  Leeds Private Bill, 195
HUDSON, MR. JAMES,
  Common Informers Bill, 182
  Iron and Steel Bill, 'guillotine'
  motion, 139

HUDSON, MR. R. S.,
  on iron and steel nationalisation, 124
HUGHES, MR. CLEDWYN,
  civil airways debate, 112–113
HUGHES, MR. EMRYS,
  business, 60
  Estimates Committee Report, 299
  Iron and Steel Bill, Money Resolu-
  tion, 134
  'Jowett Plan', 276, 340
  procedure, 340
  'Suez Crisis', 37
HUGHES, MR. HECTOR,
  Finance Bill, 256
HUNTER, MR. A. E.,
  civil airways debate, 112
HUTCHINSON, SIR I. CLARK,
  adjournment debate, 98
  notice of raising matter on adjourn-
  ment, 73, 97
  Questions, 72–73
HUTCHISON, COL. J. R. H.,
  Iron and Steel Bill, Committee, 144,
  147
HYLTON-FOSTER, SIR HARRY,
  elected Speaker, 17
HYND, MR. H.,
  'prayer', 212

INCOME TAX (PAYMENT OF POST-WAR
  CREDITS) BILL, 250, 251
'INSTRUCTION',
  moving of, 194
  notice of, 193
INTERRUPTION OF BUSINESS,
  unexpected, 27–32
IREMONGER, MR. T. L.,
  procedure, 334
IRON AND STEEL BILL, 121–180
  introduction, 121–124
  a hybrid bill?, 124–125
  Second Reading, 125–133
  Money Resolution, 133–135
  Guillotine Motion, 135–141
  Committee Stage, 141–156
  Report Stage, 156–170
  Recommittal, 168
  Third Reading, 170–171
  Consideration of Lords' Amend-
  ments, 171–180
  Opposition attitude to, 121–122
  origins outside Parliament, 122
  Schedules, 168
IRVINE, MR. BRYANT GODMAN,
  Finance Bill, 252

JANNER, MR. BARNETT,
  'prayer', 214
  Seizure of Food Order, 1946, 207

JAY, MR. DOUGLAS,
  affirmative resolution, 215
  Finance Bill, 259, 260
  Income Tax (Payment of Post-War
    Credits) Bill, 250
  point of order, 71
  'Suez Crisis', 43
JENKINS, MR. ROY,
  Iron and Steel Bill, Committee, 154
    Report, 164
JENNINGS, SIR IVOR,
  on Questions, 69
  on Special Procedure Orders, 216
  on supplementary estimates debates,
    240
JENNINGS, MR. ROLAND,
  Iron and Steel Bill, Committee, 156
    Report, 159
JOINT COMMITTEE,
  on Consolidation Bills, 53
  on Special Procedure Orders, 217–
    218, 220–235
JONES, MR. DAVID,
  Leeds Private Bill, 195
JONES, MR. JACK,
  Iron and Steel Bill, Second Reading,
    130
    Committee, 150
    Report, 159
  'prayer', 213
JOURNAL OF THE HOUSE, 44
'JOWETT PLAN', 276
JUNOR, MR. JOHN,
  case of, 4–5, 8–11

KABERRY, MR. DONALD (Sir Donald),
  Adjournment, 81–82
  Leeds Private Bill, 195
  'Scarcroft' case, 79–82, 84
KENYON, MR. CLIFFORD,
  Leeds Private Bill, 197
KERSHAW, MR. ANTHONY,
  amendment to Private Member's
    motion, 119
  debate on refusal of 'urgency'
    motion, 107
  procedure, 328
KIRK, MR. PETER,
  procedure, 328
'KITCHEN' COMMITTEE, 56

LAGDEN, MR. GODFREY,
  Debate on Address, 53
  privilege, 6
LAW OFFICERS OF THE CROWN, 318
LAW REFORM (ENFORCEMENT OF CON-
  TRACTS) BILL, 186: and see Law Re-
  form (Miscellaneous) Bill

LAW REFORM (MISCELLANEOUS) BILL,
  185–187
LEATHER, MR. E. H. C.,
  Private Member's motion, 116
LEAVEY, MR. J. A.,
  Supply, 253
LEDGER, MR. RON,
  privilege, 6
LEE, MR. FREDERICK,
  Debate on Address, 54
  Iron and Steel Bill, 'guillotine'
    motion, 140
  Supply, 239
LEEDS (ARMLEY HEIGHTS) COMPULSORY
  PURCHASE ORDER, 1955, 218–220
LEGGE-BOURKE, MAJOR H.,
  Iron and Steel Bill, Lords' Amend-
    ments, 172
  Pool Betting Bill, 188
  procedure, 340
  Seizure of Food Order, 1946, 207
  Supply, 272, 276
LENNOX-BOYD, MR. A. T.,
  'prayer', 212
LEWIS, MR. ARTHUR,
  business, 65
  point of order, 63–64
LINDSAY, MR. MARTIN,
  Iron and Steel Bill, Second Reading,
    130
    Third Reading, 171
  procedure, 329
LINSTEAD, SIR H.,
  Supplementary Question, 73
LIPTON, MR. MARCUS,
  Common Informers Bill, 184
  Debate on Address, 48
  privilege, 3–4
LLOYD, MR. GEOFFREY,
  'Scarcroft' case, 85, 86–87
LLOYD, MR. SELWYN,
  Debate on Address, 51
  Iron and Steel Bill, Second Reading,
    131
  statement, 73–74
  'Suez Crisis', 38
LOGAN, MR. DAVID,
  election of Speaker, 14
LORDS, HOUSE OF,
  Amendments to Agricultural Land
    (Removal of Surface Soil) Bill, 185
  Amendments to Transport and Town
    and Country Planning Bills, 138
  Chairman of Committees, 217
  and Common Informers Bill, 184
  and Iron and Steel Bill, 122, 132–133,
    150, 154, 162, 164, 171–180
  Leeds Private Bill, 201
  Statutory Rights of Entry Bill,
    Second Reading, 187

Low, Sir Toby,
Chairman, Nationalised Industries
Committee, 310, 311, 312
Finance Bill, 263
Lowther, Mr. Speaker, 28
Lucas-Tooth, Sir Hugh,
Law Reform (Miscellaneous) Bill,
186
Pool Betting Bill, 189
'urgency' adjournment debate(Perez-
Selles), 102
Lyttelton, Mr. Oliver, (Lord Chan-
dos),
Iron and Steel Bill, Second Reading,
127–129
Committee, 143–156
Report, 157–160, 162–167
Third Reading, 170
Lords' Amendments, 174, 176, 179
on iron and steel nationalisation,
123

Mabon, Dr. J. Dickson,
Debate on Address, 55
McAdden, Mr. Stephen,
Pool Betting Bill, 188
MacAndrew, Sir Charles,
appointed Chairman of Ways and
Means, 17
as Chairman of Standing Committee,
Iron and Steel Bill, 142–156
on order, 20–21
Seizure of Food Order, 1946, 207, 208
suggested as Speaker, 16, 17
MacColl, Mr. J. E.,
Common Informers Bill, 184
Mackay, Mr. Ronald,
Iron and Steel Bill, Second Reading,
132
Lords' Amendments, 172–173
Maclay, Mr. J. S.,
Iron and Steel Bill, 'guillotine'
motion, 140
Macleod, Mr. Iain,
Debate on Address, 54, 55
Supply, 239
MacLeod, Mr. John,
Finance Bill, 256
Macmillan, Mr. Harold,
Debate on Address, 74–48
Iron and Steel Bill, Committee, 147,
149, 154
Report, 160, 161, 164, 168
Macmillan, Mr. Maurice,
'urgency'adjournment debate (Perez-
Selles), 102–103
Maitland, Commander J. W.,
Supply, 243–244
Maitland, Mr. Patrick,
privilege, 2–3

Mallalieu, Mr. E. L.,
Iron and Steel Bill, Third Reading,
170–171
Mandate,
doctrine of, 122, 124, 132–133, 150
Manningham-Buller, Sir R. E.,
Iron and Steel Bill, Committee, 142–
143, 145, 152, 153, 155
Report, 165, 168
Seizure of Food Order, 1946, 207
Manuel, Mr. A. C.,
order, 20–21
Marlowe, Mr. Anthony,
Law Reform (Enforcement of Con-
tracts) Bill, 186
'Scarcroft' case, 86
Seizure of Food Order, 1946, 206
Marples, Mr. A. E.
answers to Questions, 72–73, 90–91
Iron and Steel Bill, Second Reading,
132
Private Member's Bill, 184
Marquand, Mr. H. A.,
Supply, 251
Marsden, Capt. Arthur,
Joint Committee, 221, 230
Marsh, Mr. Richard,
procedure, 334
Marshall, Mr. Douglas,
Debate on Address, 54
Mason, Mr. Roy,
point of order, 70
Supply, 245
Maudling, Mr. Reginald,
Budget debate, 250
Nationalised Industries Committee,
313
Mellish, Mr. R. J.,
Leeds Private Bill, 196
Supply, 244, 245–246
Mellor, Sir John,
Iron and Steel Bill, Money Resolu-
tion 134, 135
'prayers', 213
Seizure of Food Order, 1946, 205–
206, 208
1948, 209–210
'Memorials',
under Special Procedure, 222
Mid-Northamptonshire Water
Order, 1948, 218, 220–234
Mikardo, Mr. Ian,
civil airways debate, 112, 113
Iron and Steel Bill, Committee, 145
Pool Betting Bill, 191
Milner, Major James (Lord Milner),
candidative as Speaker, 14–17
Milner-Barry, Mr. P. S., 281–282
Ministers' Powers, Committee on,
303

MITCHISON, MR. G. R.,
business, 62
Finance Bill, 256–257
Iron and Steel Bill, Committee, 154
186
Law Reform (Miscellaneous) Bill,
Report, 163
order, 23–24
procedure, 333, 335, 336, 339
MOLSON, MR. HUGH, (Sir Hugh),
Leeds Private Bill, 195–196
MONEY RESOLUTIONS: *see* Financial
Resolutions
MONSLOW, MR. W.,
Iron and Steel Bill, Second Reading,
129
MOORE, SIR THOMAS,
adjournment motion, notice, 72
Common Informers Bill, 183
MORRIS, MR. HOPKIN,
appointed Deputy-Chairman, 17
suggested as Speaker, 15
MORRISON, MR. HERBERT (Lord Mor-
rison),
election of Speaker, 15
'Government and Parliament', 326
Iron and Steel Bill, Second Reading,
132–133
Lords' Amendments, 179
on the mandate, 132–133
moves Guillotine Motion, 135–138
procedure, 323–324, 333, 335
supplementary Question, 73
unexpected interruption of business,
28
MORRISON, MR. W. S. (Lord Morrison),
election as Speaker, 12–17
quoted, 334
MORT, MR. D. L.,
Iron and Steel Bill, Third Reading,
170
MOTION,
Censure, 30, 32, 39, 43, 108
definition and classification, 94–95
examples, 95–120
Government and Opposition, 108–
115
notice of, 95
Private Member's, 115–120
'take notice', 109–111, 114
MULLEY, MR. FREDERICK,
Private Member's Bill, 188–192

NABARRO, MR. G. D. N.,
amendment to Private Member's
motion, 116–117
business, 62
Finance Bill, 252
Pool Betting Bill, 190–191
Supply, 273, 278

NALLY, MR. WILL,
Pool Betting Bill, 189
'prayer', 212
NATIONAL EXPENDITURE COMMITTEE,
292
NATIONALISED INDUSTRIES, 309–314, 329
debate, 110–115
Exchequer advances to, 263
NATIONALISED INDUSTRIES, SELECT COM-
MITTEE ON, 51, 88, 89, 278, 279,
309–314
debate on Report, 310–313
terms of reference, 309
NAVY, ARMY AND AIR EXPENDITURE
COMMITTEE, 266–267
NEAVE, MR. AIREY,
civil airways debate, 113–114
NEEP, MR. E. J. C., K.C.,
before Special Procedure Joint Com-
mittee, 223 *passim*
NICHOLLS, MR. HARMAR,
Leeds Private Bill, 195, 197
'prays', 211
NICHOLSON, SIR GODFREY, 70
on criticising the Chair, 106
privilege, 7
NOEL-BAKER, MR. FRANCIS,
Adjournment Motion, 92–93
notice of raising matter on adjourn-
ment, 91–92
Question and supplementary, 90
NOEL-BAKER, MR. PHILIP, 24
'Scarcroft' case, 80, 85
NUGENT, MR. G. R. H.,
Supply, 254

OAKSHOTT, SIR HENDRIE,
procedure, 335
O'BRIEN, MR. T.,
'prayer', 212
O'NEILL, SIR HUGH,
election of Speaker, 13–14
ONSLOW, MR. SPEAKER,
quoted, 15
OPENING CEREMONY, 44, 46
OPENING OF SESSION, 44–45
ORAM, MR. A. E.,
procedure, 326–327, 330, 335
ORDER, 12–43,
Campion on, 18
Erskine May on, 18
point of, 17–43
fraudulent, 63
genuine and fraudulent, 18 *passim*

PAGET, MR. R. T.,
point of order, 74, 77
privilege, 5
refusal of 'urgency' adjournment, 104
'urgency' adjournment, 74, 75, 77

'PAIRING', 328, 332
PANNELL, MR. CHARLES,
   Leeds Private Bill, 193, 194–195
   privilege, 6, 9
   procedure, 334
PANNELL, MR. N.,
   business, 63
PARKER, MR. J.,
   Common Informers Bill, 182
PARKIN, MR. B. T.,
   'grievances' before Supply, 274
PARLIAMENT ACT, 122, 123, 176, 179
PARLIAMENTARY AGENTS, 198
PATON, MR. JOHN,
   order, 25
PEAKE, MR. OSBERT, (Lord Ingleby)
   Iron and Steel Bill, Second Reading,
      129
      Committee, 144–145, 147, 148,
         150, 152, 153, 154, 155
      Report, 157, 161, 167, 168–169
      Third Reading, 171
   on Public Accounts Committee, 280
PENN, MR. J. W.,
   evidence before Special Procedure
      Joint Committee, 232
People,
   and privilege, 3
PEREZ-SELLES, JOAQUIM,
   case of, 76–79, 99–104
PETITIONS,
   against Special Procedure Orders, 217
   of General Objection, 217, 218, 220
   for Amendment, 217, 220, 221,
      222, 223–234
   Counter-Petitions, 221, 228, 229,
      233
PITMAN, MR. I. J.,
   business, 66
   Iron and Steel Bill, 'guillotine' mo-
      tion, 139
PITT, MISS EDITH,
   Supply, 238–239
'PLOWDEN' COMMITTEE, 276
POOL BETTING BILL, 188–192
POPPLEWELL, MR. ERNEST,
   supplementary Question, 91
'PRAYERS', 22, 50, 62, 203–204, 205,
   209, 211–215
PREAMBLE,
   of Private Bill, 198
PRENTICE, MR. R. E.,
   moves 'prayer', 50
PRICE, MR. DAVID,
   seconds Humble Address, 46
PRICE, MR. FRANK EDWARD,
   evidence before Special Procedure
      Joint Committee, 227–228, 233
PRICE, MR. J. T.,
   supplementary Question, 90–91

PRICE, MR. PHILLIPS,
   procedure, 335
PRIVATE BILL OFFICE, 192
PRIVATE BILLS, 192–202, 222, 339
   Halifax Corporation Bill, 255
   Lancaster Corporation Bill, 254
   Leeds Private Bill, 192–202
   Manchester Corporation Bill, 53
   procedure in Committee, 198–201
   'proving the Preamble', 198, 201
PRIVATE BUSINESS, 125, 192–202, 254–
   255
   exemption from S.O. Nos. 1 and 7,
      255
PRIVATE LEGISLATION PROCEDURE
   (SCOTLAND) ACT, 1936, 217
PRIVATE MEMBERS' BILLS, 57–61, 115,
   180–192, 338–339
   ballotted, 180, 188–192
   under S.O. 35, 180, 184–187
   successful, 184–192
   under Ten Minute Rule, 180, 187–
      188, 338–339
   talked out, 184
   unsuccessful, 181–182
PRIVATE MEMBERS' BUSINESS, 30, 47, 49,
   57–61, 115–120, 180–192, 316, 322,
   323, 326, 331, 338–339
PRIVATE MEMBERS' MOTIONS, 115–120,
   185, 187, 331, 338
PRIVILEGE, 1–11
PRIVILEGES,
   Committee of, 1, 4–11, 44, 51, 279
PRIVY COUNCILLORS,
   precedence, 327, 330, 333–334
PROCEDURE,
   Select Committees on, 53, 57, 77,
      243, 275, 279, 315–341
   Committee of 1945–46: appoint-
      ment, 315
      First Report, 315
      draft scheme, 315
      standing committees, 315–316
      financial procedure, 317
      Second Report, 318
      Questions, 318
      Third Report, 318
      Legislation, 319–320
      Policy and Administration, 320–
         321
      Control of Finance, 321–322
      Private Member's Business, 322
      Government response, 317–318,
         323 *passim*
      debate, 323
   Committee of 1958: origins, 326–327
      'working paper', 330–332
      recommendations and debate, 332–
         341
   Committee of 1931–32, 319

PROCTOR, MR. W. T.,
Iron and Steel Bill, 'guillotine' motion, 139
PROVISIONAL ORDERS, 216, 217
Confirmation Bills, 216
PUBLIC ACCOUNTS COMMITTEE, 237, 277, 279–292, 298, 322, 323, 328, 340
relations with House, 290–292
relations with Treasury, 287–290
Report for Session 1951–52, 281–287
Third Report 1951–52, 283–290
PUBLIC BILLS,
opposed and unopposed, committees on, 331
PUBLIC EXPENDITURE COMMITTEE,
proposed, 322, 323, 340
PURCHASE TAX,
controversy about method of debating, 258–261

QUEEN'S SPEECH, 44–45, 123–124
debate on, 45–46
selection of amendments, 50–51
'QUESTION' BEFORE THE HOUSE, 68
QUESTION TIME, 68–69, 246, 318, 338
QUESTIONS, 68–93, 318, 328, 330, 331
Erskine May on, 68, 87
inadmissible, 68
leading to notice of adjournment motion, 69–79
leading to judicial proceedings, 79–87
on nationalised industries, 68, 80, 87–93
Prime Minister's, 338
private notice, 43, 57, 73
supplementary, 68, 70, 71, 74, 75–76
QUORUM,
maintenance of, 27 passim
QUOTATION FROM DOCUMENTS, 22–24

RAFFERTY, MR. S. R.,
evidence before Special Procedure Joint Committee, 229
RAIKES, MR. H. V. M. A.,
Seizure of Food Order, 1946, 207
RANKIN, MR. JOHN,
Debate on Address, 48
Joint Committee, 221, 229–230
point of order, 112
Supply, 243
REA, LORD,
Joint Committee, 221
READING OF SPEECHES, 21–22
REMNANT, MR. P. F.,
Common Informers Bill, 183
'prayer', 214
RENTON, MR. DAVID,
Debate on Address, 51
Iron and Steel Bill, Money Resolution, 134

REPRESENTATION OF THE PEOPLE (AMENDMENT) (NO. 1) BILL, 184
RHODES, MR. HERVEY,
'prayers', 211–212, 213, 214
ROBENS, MR. ALFRED,
business, 62
Debate on Address, 54, 55
Nationalised Industries Committee, 312
'Scarcroft' case, 82, 83, 84
Supply, 254, 271, 273, 277
ROBERTS, MR. PETER,
Iron and Steel Bill, Committee, 152
Report, 157, 158, 164
ROGERS, MR. G. H. R.,
order, 21
Supply, 239
Romford Recorder,
and Privilege, 6, 8
ROPER, MR. HAROLD,
'prayer', 213
ROSS, MR. WILLIAM,
Common Informers Bill, 183–184
'prayer', 214
ROWE, MR. MICHAEL, Q.C.,
before Special Procedure Joint Committee, 233
ROYLE, MR. C.,
Seizure of Food Order, 1946, 207
RULES COMMITTEE, 106

SALISBURY, LORD,
on Iron and Steel Bill, 171–172, 177, 180
SANDYS, MR. DUNCAN, 22
affirmative resolution, 215
'SCARCROFT' CASE, 68, 79–87
SCOLLAN, MR. THOMAS,
Iron and Steel Bill, Money Resolution, 134
'SCOTTISH' DAYS, 262, 265
SCOTTISH GRAND COMMITTEE, 62, 65, 67
SCOTTISH STANDING COMMITTEE, 325
'SCRUTINY' COMMITTEE, 208: and see Statutory Instruments, Select Committee on
SELECT COMMITTEES,
extension of use proposed, 329, 340
SELECTION, COMMITTEE OF, 336
nomination of, 50
SESSIONAL ORDERS, 17, 44, 317, 318, 336, 339
SHAWCROSS, SIR HARTLEY,
as Attorney-General, intervenes in 'Scarcroft' case, 82–83
SHEPHERD, MR. W.,
Iron and Steel Bill, Committee, 150
Pool Betting Bill, 190
SHINWELL, MR. EMANUEL,
moves 'progress', 33

Nationalised Industries Committee, 312
point of order, 72
privilege, 7, 9
procedure, 328
'Suez Crisis', 39
suspension of Member, 35–36
SHORT, MR. EDWARD,
Leeds Private Bill, 195
point of order, 96
SILVERMAN, MR. SYDNEY,
amendment to Humble Address, 50–51, 54
business arrangements, 31, 66, 67
Death Penalty Abolition Bill, 58–61
Debate on Address, 54, 55, 56
points of order, 19, 25–27, 33–34, 69, 72
privilege, 4, 5, 7
procedure, 58–61, 340
Seizure of Food Order, 1946, 208
'Suez Crisis', 39
Supply, 272, 275–276
suspension of, 33–36
'urgency' motion debate (Perez-Selles), 99–100
SIMMONS, MR. JAMES,
Supply, 244–245
SIMON, MR. J. E. S.,
answers to Questions, 69–70
Budget debate, 251
Finance Bill, 251–252, 262, 267
virement, 266–267
SITTING OF THE HOUSE, 331
SKEFFINGTON, MR. ARTHUR,
Private Member's Bill, 185–187
SMITH, MR. ELLIS,
Budget debate, 250
procedure, 268, 328
SMITHERS, SIR WALDRON,
Iron and Steel Bill, Third Reading, 170
Public Accounts Committee, Questions, 291
'Scarcroft' case, 82, 85
SNOW, MR. JULIAN,
reading from documents, 190
SOSKICE, SIR FRANK,
Iron and Steel Bill Report, 158, 160, 164, 165, 166, 168
suggested as Speaker, 17
SPEAKER,
adjournment motions, selection of, 95, 96–97
adjournment,
validity of motion to raise matter on, 72
'urgency', granting of, 74–76, 77–79

answers from ministers, inability to compel, 43
anticipation, warning against, 124
'behind his chair', 49, 241
business arrangements, 30–31, 49, 60, 65
'catching eye' of, 49, 112, 115
Counsel to, 303
criticised, 75
duties of, general, 104
election of, 12–17
Hybrid Bills, 125
interruption of business, 27–28, 29, 30–31
Motion regretting refusal of 'urgency' motion, 104–107
regretting ruling, 76
'that Mr. Speaker do now leave the Chair', 94, 242, 253, 261, 294, 320, 321, 323, 326, 337
'naming' of Member, 34–36
order, duties of, 18
points of order, definition of, 19, 20
powers re 'prayers', 211
privilege, 1, 2, 3–4, 5, 6, 7–8, 10
qualities required of, 13–14
Questions, method of answering, 69–72
on nationalised industries, 88–89
supplementary, right to ask, 71–72
reading from prepared document, 190
reads Queen's Speech, 45
rules of order, responsibility for maintaining, 40, 64
selection of amendments to Humble Address, 50–51
of speakers, 55
suspends sitting, 42
SPECIAL ORDERS, 216
SPECIAL PROCEDURE ORDERS, 216–235
SPEECHES OUTSIDE HOUSE, references to, 24–27
SPEIR, MR. RUPERT,
adjournment motion, 95–97
SPENCE, MR. H. R.,
Seizure of Food Order, 1946, 206
SPENS, SIR PATRICK,
Chairman, Nationalised Industries Committee, 309
STANDING COMMITTEE,
analysis of discussions in, 145–146
changes, 317–318, 326, 336
extension of use proposed, 329, 335–336
proposals of 1945–46, 315–316, 319–320
Scottish, 316, 320, 336
suspension of sitting, 152
work of, 137–141, 141–156

STANDING ORDERS,
Commons, 30–31, 221–223, 248, 317,
  318, 323, 324, 332
No. 1, 29, 255, 339
No. 7, 255, 318
No. 8, 89, 322, 325
No. 9, 4, 68, 74, 94, 99, 104, 106, 136,
  187, 325, 333
No. 10, 322n, 325
No. 12, 180, 339
No. 16, 241, 247, 325, 337
No. 17, 325
No. 21, 35
No. 22, 33, 35, 36
Nos. 22–24, 36
No. 24, 42
No. 30, 118
No. 31, 145
No. 35, 180, 181, 184–185
No. 36, 125
No. 38, 335, 336
No. 41, 137, 325
No. 45, 325
No. 49A, 142, 316
No. 57, 145, 325
No. 58, 325
No. 60, 325
No. 61, 325
No. 63, 142, 325
No. 64, 137, 325
No. 65, 325
No. 84, 325
No. 86, 325
No. 90, 280
No. 224 (Private Business), 125
No. 243 (Private Business), 235
Lords, No. 209, 235
STANDING ORDERS,
Drafting Committee, 332
STANDING ORDERS (REVISION) SELECT
  COMMITTEE, 326
STANLEY, MR. OLIVER,
Iron and Steel Bill, 'guillotine'
  motion, 140
STATEMENTS,
Ministerial, 57, 64
STATUTORY INSTRUMENTS, 203–215
Act, 1946, 203
Candles (Maximum Prices) Order,
  1951, 213
Census of Distribution (1958) (Re-
  striction on Disclosure) Order,
  1956, 215
Feeding Stuffs Order, 1951, 214
Furniture (Maximum Prices) Order,
  1951, 213
Housing Subsidies Order, 1956, 215
Iron and Steel Scrap Order, 1951,
  213
'prayers' against, 203–204

Seizure of Food Order, 1946, 205–209;
  1948, 209–210
Utility Apparel Order, 1951, 214
STATUTORY INSTRUMENTS, SELECT COM-
  MITTEE ON, 51, 204–205, 210, 215,
  279, 302–319, 321
Session 1955–56, 304–309
terms of reference, 303
STATUTORY ORDERS (SPECIAL PRO-
  CEDURE) ACT, 1945, 217, 219
STATUTORY RIGHTS OF ENTRY,
Bill to Regulate, 187–188
STATUTORY RULES AND ORDERS,
Select Committee on: see Statutory
  Instruments
STEVENS, MR. GEOFFREY,
Finance Bill, 258, 261, 263
STEWART, MR. MICHAEL,
business, 63
Leeds Private Bill, 196–197
STODDART-SCOTT, COL. MALCOLM,
Leeds Private Bill, 197
STRACHEY, MR. JOHN,
'Suez Crisis', 43
STRAUSS, MR. G. R.,
civil airways debate, 111
Iron and Steel Bill,
  moves Second Reading, 125–127
  Money Resolution, 134–135
  Committee, 143, 146–156
  Report, 156–159, 163–165
  Third Reading, 171
  Lords' Amendments, 171–178
on iron and steel nationalisation,
  123
supplementary Questions, 91
'STRAUSS CASE' (Privilege), 10–11
'SUBDIVIDING COMMITTEE', 323
'SUEZ CRISIS', 36–43, 62, 64
SUMMERS, SIR SPENCER,
procedure, 328
SUMMERSKILL, DR. EDITH,
adjournment motion, 97–99
interrupts, 22
Seizure of Food Order, 1946, 207–209;
  1948, 209–210
Sunday Express,
and Privilege, 4–5, 8, 9
SUPPLY, COMMITTEE OF,
Ballot for Notices of Motion, 253
character of debates in, 246
contrast with Committee of Ways
  and Means, 270
establishment, 56, 238
order in, 243, 245
procedure in, 236–237, 253, 332
resolutions in, 247, 269
SUPPLY DAYS, 236–237, 238–248, 251,
  252–255, 262, 264–265, 267–270,
  275, 292, 320, 322, 323, 332, 337

as alternative to 'emergency' adjournment, 105
'spoof', 337
suspension of S.O. No. 16, 241, 251, 255, 262, 271
SUSPENSIONS,
of a Member, 33–36
of a sitting, 36–43
SWEARING-IN, 17
SWINGLER, MR. S.,
Leeds Private Bill, 199

'TALKING OUT', 115, 116, 117, 119, 181, 182–184, 188–189, 190
TAXES MANAGEMENT ACT,
proposed, 336
TAYLOR, SIR CHARLES,
privilege, 10
reading from document, 190
TAYLOR, DR. ERIC,
on financial procedure, 237
TAYLOR, MR. R. J.,
'prayer', 213
TEELING, MR. WILLIAM,
Pool Betting Bill, 191
TEN O'CLOCK RULE, 33, 329
exemption of Finance Bill from, 256
suspension of, 176, 194, 339
THESIGER, MR. GERALD A., Q.C.,
before Special Procedure Joint Committee, 234–235
THESIGER, MR. W., Q.C.,
Leeds Private Bill, 198
THOMAS, MR. G., 302
Iron and Steel Bill, Committee, 153
Third Reading, 171
THOMAS, MR. IVOR,
disregards 'anticipation' rule, 124
Iron and Steel Bill, Committee, 147, 148
Report, 167
THOMAS, MR. IVOR OWEN,
order, 23
THOMAS, MR. PETER,
moves Humble Address, 45–46
THOMPSON, MR. KENNETH,
adjournment debate, 98
Leeds Private Bill, 195
THOMPSON, MR. RICHARD,
Supply, 247
THORNEYCROFT, MR. PETER,
Income Tax (Payment of Post-War Credits) Bill, 250
Supply, 272
TIFFANY, MR. STANLEY,
Iron and Steel Bill, Committee, 151
TILEY, MR. ARTHUR,
Leeds Private Bill, 196
TOWN AND COUNTRY PLANNING BILL, 1947,

Committee Stage, 138, 142
TRANSPORT BILL, 1948,
Committee Stage, 137, 138, 142
TRANSPORT COMMISSION, 90–93

UNGOED-THOMAS, SIR LYNN,
order, 24
UNIVERSITY GRANTS COMMITTEE, 275, 284–285
UNOPPOSED BILLS,
Committee on, 192
'URGENCY' MOTIONS, 27

VAUGHAN-MORGAN, MR. J. K.,
Finance Bill, 257
'VESTING DAY' CLAUSE,
Iron and Steel Bill, 162–164, 170, 177–178
VIANT, MR. S. P.,
election of Speaker, 14
VICK, SIR G. RUSSELL, Q.C.,
'Scarcroft' case, investigation and report, 86–87
VICKERS, MISS JOAN,
Debate on Address, 53
VIREMENT, 241–242, 265–267, 280, 337
VOSPER, MR. DENNIS,
Leeds Private Bill, 196
VOTE ON ACCOUNT, 241

WAKEFIELD, SIR WAVELL,
Seizure of Food Order, 1946, 207
WALKER-SMITH, MR. DEREK, (Sir Derek),
Law Reform (Miscellaneous) Bill, 186
WARBEY, MR. WILLIAM,
'Suez Crisis', 37
WARD, MR. GEORGE,
Iron and Steel Bill, Money Resolution, 143
Committee, 152
WARD, MISS IRENE,
Private Member's Bill, 187–188
WATER ACT, 1945, 220, 224
WATERS, MR. A. H. S.,
evidence before Special Procedure Joint Committee, 228
WATKINSON, MR. HAROLD,
civil airways debate, 111
WAYS AND MEANS, COMMITTEE OF,
contrast with Committee of Supply, 270
establishment of, 56, 238
resolutions in, 247, 248, 251, 269
'WELSH DAY', 336
WELSH GRAND COMMITTEE, 65, 336, 340
WHEATLEY, MR. JOHN,
suspension of Member, 36

WHIPS, 1–3, 49
WHITE, MRS. EIRENE,
  Finance Bill, 259, 260, 263
WHITE PAPERS,
  on investment programmes, 277
  on iron and steel, 122
WHITELEY, MR. WILLIAM,
  election of Speaker, 15
  Iron and Steel Bill, Lords' Amendments, 173
WHITLEY, MR. SPEAKER,
  ruling quoted, 125
WIGG, MR. GEORGE,
  arranges 'counting out', 27
  point of order, 95–96
  on privilege, 1–3, 6
  Supply, 244, 245, 246
WILKES, JOHN, 9
WILLEY, MR. FRED,
  'prayer', 214
WILLIAMS, MR. C.,
  Iron and Steel Bill, Money Resolution, 134
WILLIAMS, SIR HERBERT,
  'prayers', 212–213
WILLIAMS, REV. LL.,
  Supply, 253, 261–262

WILLIAMS, MR. PAUL,
  Debate on Address, 55
WILLIS, MR. HAROLD,
  before Special Procedure Joint Committee, 223 passim
WILMOT, MR. JOHN,
  on nationalisation of iron and steel, 122–123
WILSON, MR. HAROLD,
  Budget debate, 250
  business, 62
  Finance Bill, 256 passim
  moves amendment to Address, 54
  point of order, 71
  Supply, 278
WINTERBOTTOM, MR. RICHARD,
  Leeds Private Bill, 199–200
WOODBURN, MR. ARTHUR,
  point of order, 70
WRIT,
  new, 49

YORKSHIRE ELECTRICITY BOARD,
  'Scarcroft' case, 79–87
'YOUR LIFE IN THEIR HANDS' (B.B.C. Programme), 72–73